ARMY, INDUSTRY, AND LABOR IN GERMANY, 1914-1918

ARMY INDUSTRY AND LABOR IN GERMANY 1914-1918

BY GERALD D. FELDMAN

PRINCETON UNIVERSITY PRESS
PRINCETON, NEW JERSEY
1966

Library of Congress Catalog Card Number: 66-10553

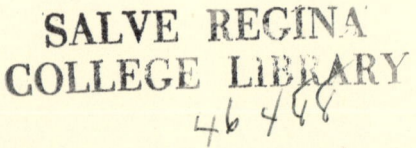

Printed in the United States of America
by Princeton University Press, Princeton, New Jersey

TO MY PARENTS

Isadore and Lillian Feldman

Preface

STUDENTS of Germany's recent history have always been concerned with the influence of her army, but they have only recently become interested in the details of her social and economic history. This partially helps to explain why historians have neglected the confrontation of army, industry, and labor in Germany during the First World War. In this book I have sought to combine military and socioeconomic history by giving a detailed account of this confrontation, for neither the role of the army in wartime Germany nor the very significant social and economic changes of this period, and particularly the development of collective bargaining, can be understood without it. Needless to say, this book is indirectly concerned with the much discussed phenomenon of "total war." I should make clear, however, that I have not attempted to deal with the theoretical debates concerning the nature of modern war, and I have not sought to study the techniques of total mobilization for their own sake. What I have tried to do is to examine Germany's wartime mobilization in the context of the broader problems of her socioeconomic development and as a function of interest-group politics.

When seen in such a context, the problems of food, raw materials, and labor supply, alternative weapons and munitions programs, organizational measures, and social policy and labor unrest assume a new importance alongside the traditionally discussed problems of war aims and political reform. At the same time it becomes necessary to avoid a narrow concentration upon the General Staff, the leading personalities of the Imperial government, and the political parties and to devote detailed attention to the long ignored Prussian War Ministry and other military agencies on the homefront, to the little known advisers who devised the programs and policies pursued by the men in high places, and to the frequently overlooked economic pressure groups.

At a time when historians are engaged in serious debate

concerning German war aims and internal politics during the First World War, the perspective provided by this study and its conclusions will, I hope, prove useful in clarifying some of the confusion. I have found, for example, that it is very difficult to treat the army as a monolithic unit because of the deep divisions within that institution. Similarly, I have found that the usual emphasis upon the differences between the military and civilian authorities is in need of modification. Although it is certainly correct to speak of an alliance between certain elements of the army and the leaders of heavy industry during the war, the bitter and continuous conflict between other segments of the army and the industrialists must be considered as well. Furthermore, I believe that it is important to recognize that there was an alliance between important elements of the army and the leaders of organized labor throughout the war. Historians have always placed great emphasis on the dictatorial power of General Ludendorff during the last two years of the war. Yet I would suggest that it is more fruitful to analyze his weakness, vacillation, and almost complete incapacity to control Germany's internal affairs. Finally, I would plead that historians pay greater heed to the social and economic development of wartime Germany and attempt to understand the very complex relationship between that development and those issues which have previously attracted so much scholarly attention.

In writing this book I have found it necessary to make extensive use of previously unexamined archival materials. With the notable exception of Albrecht Mendelssohn-Bartholdy's impressionistic, undocumented, somewhat inaccurate but very brilliant *War and German Society*,[1] there are no significant social and economic histories of the war. The available published documentary materials, memoirs, and secondary studies are inadequate. On the one hand, they are polemical in character and must be checked against more reliable sources

[1] Albrecht Mendelssohn-Bartholdy, *The War and German Society. The Testament of a Liberal*, New Haven, 1927.

of information. On the other hand, they seldom do justice to the complexity of wartime social history. If one is to bring the concrete problems of the wartime social conflict to life, it is necessary to penetrate beneath official directives, official pronouncements, and parliamentary debates to the confused mental gyrations which lie at their base. Herein lies the chief reason for the extensive use of and quotation from protocols in this book. For similar reasons I have made a deliberate effort to use the greatest possible variety of documentary materials. The wartime social history of Germany was a giant mosaic, and the selective use of every available type of evidence provides the only viable means of reconstructing the whole.

My debts to scholars and institutions at home and abroad are many. Dean Franklin L. Ford gave me constant encouragement and invaluable guidance when he directed this study as a dissertation. I have also received advice concerning research problems or substantive matters from Professors William L. Langer, Fritz T. Epstein, Klaus Epstein, Fritz R. Stern, and Thomas E. Skidmore. Professors Arno J. Mayer, Hans Rosenberg, Harold J. Gordon, Jr., and Wolfgang Sauer have read this manuscript at various stages, and their suggestions have done much to improve both its style and content. I wish to add an additional note of appreciation to Professor Sauer for having permitted me to utilize his forthcoming study of the German army in the Revolution. Lastly, my book has also benefited greatly from my many discussions with Professors Ira Lapidus and Irwin Scheiner and from the editorial advice of Mr. David C. Harrop and Mr. Edward Surovell of the Princeton University Press. Needless to say, the responsibility for all errors of fact and interpretation and for all infelicities of style rests solely upon myself.

The generosity of the Social Science Research Council made it financially possible for me to spend a year doing research abroad and to spend another year preparing the first version of this study. A Summer Faculty Fellowship awarded by the

President of the University of California and a grant from the Institute of Social Sciences of the University of California assisted greatly in the revision and final preparation of the manuscript.

I am extremely grateful to the archives and libraries in the United States and Europe that supplied the materials used in this study. I particularly wish to thank Dr. Harald Jaeger of the *Kriegsarchiv* in Munich and Dr. Wilhelm Arenz of the *Militärgeschichtliches Forschungsamt* for their exceptional helpfulness and kindness. I also wish to thank the archivists of the *Bundesarchiv* in Koblenz for having made my stay there so pleasant and so fruitful.

Professor Erich Matthias and Dr. Eberhard Pikart of the *Kommission für Geschichte des Parlamentarismus und der politischen Parteien* provided important documentary materials and valuable information. Professor Gerhard Ritter was extremely generous in giving me indispensable help in locating a number of very important documents.

I wish to thank Mrs. Wendy Bremner for her industry and devotion in the typing of the manuscript and Mr. and Mrs. James Diehl for their invaluable assistance in the preparation of the index.

Finally, I wish to express my gratitude to my wife, Philippa, for having assisted in the tedious task of copying documents and for having shared so many of the burdens attendant upon the writing of this book.

G. D. F.

Berkeley, California
July 1965

Contents

Illustrations

All the illustrations originally appeared in the magazine *Simplicissimus* on the date given in parentheses. The author is grateful to the following for permission to reprint copyrighted material: Frau Professor Dagny Gulbransson for "War Contractors" and "To the Rescue" by Gulbransson; Herr Erich Seemann for "A Magic Trick," "In the Service of England," and "Two Types of Strikers" by Th. Th. Heine; and Frau Professor Ruth Thöny for "Auxiliary Service" by E. Thöny.

Abbreviations

IN THE TEXT

AEG	Allgemeine Elektrizitäts Gesellschaft (General Electric Company)
a.v.	arbeitsverwendungsfähig (liable to work duty)
AZS	Abteilung für Zurückstellungswesen (Section for Exemptions Questions)
g.v.	garnisonverwendungsfähig (liable to garrison duty)
KEA	Kriegsernährungsamt (War Food Office)
KRA	Kriegsrohstoffabteilung (Raw Materials Section)
k.v.	kriegsverwendungsfähig (liable to field duty)
OHL	Oberste Heeresleitung (Supreme Command)
RWA	Reichswirtschaftsamt (Imperial Economic Office)
SAZ	Ständige Ausschuss für Zusammenlegungen (Standing Committee on Consolidations)
WUMBA	Waffen und Munitions Beschaffungsamt (Weapons and Munitions Procurement Agency)

IN THE FOOTNOTES

AGSOD	Leo Stern, ed., *Die Auswirkungen der Grossen Sozialistischen Oktoberrevolution auf Deutschland*, 4 vols., Berlin, 1959.
BA	Bundesarchiv Koblenz
BBS Reports	Berichte des Büros für Sozialpolitik (Reports of the Bureau for Social Policy)
BHStA, Abt. I	Bayerisches Hauptstaatsarchiv München, Abteilung Allgemeines Staatsarchiv
BHStA, Abt. II	Bayerisches Hauptstaatsarchiv München, Abteilung Geheimes Staatsarchiv

BHStA, Abt. IV	Bayerisches Hauptstaatsarchiv München, Abteilung Kriegsarchiv
DZA Potsdam	Deutsches Zentralarchiv Potsdam
DZA Merseburg	Deutsches Zentralarchiv Merseburg
HStASt	Hauptstaatsarchiv Stuttgart
IISH	International Institute for Social History, Amsterdam
MF	Militärgeschichtliches Forschungsamt, Freiburg im Breisgau
PrGStA	Hauptarchiv, Berlin-Dahlem (Preussisches Geheimes Staatsarchiv)
StADü	Staatsarchiv Düsseldorf
StAMü	Staatsarchiv Münster in Westfalen
VdESI	Verein deutscher Eisen- und Stahlindustrieller (Association of German Iron and Steel Industrialists)
ZMG Reports	Zusammenstellungen der Monatsberichte der stellvertretenden Generalkommandos (Compilations of the Reports of the Deputy Commanding Generals)

ARMY, INDUSTRY, AND LABOR IN GERMANY, 1914-1918

THE MIDDLE CLASS 1918

Introduction

BEFORE the First World War, the officers corps and the leaders of heavy industry were mainstays of the authoritarian political and social system of the German Empire. They functioned as defenders of the prerogatives of the crown and of a social order which deprived the German working class of political and social equality. In the Revolution of November 1918 which terminated the war, the army joined forces with the Social Democratic Party and the industrialists joined forces with the trade unions. In this manner both the officer corps and the great industrialists were able to preserve their authority and influence, and the leaders of organized labor were able to restrict the revolution which they had always preached and which they then found inopportune. This remarkable reversal of fronts was more than a momentary response to the chaos of 1918. It was made possible by the pattern of relationships developed among the leaders of army, industry, and labor during the war.

These relationships were largely determined by the nature of the war, a war which tested not merely the military prowess, but also the economic strength and social stability of the belligerent nations. They were forced to mobilize their material and human resources on an unparalleled scale and secure the active participation of all social groups in the war effort. Under such conditions a high level of industrialization and specialized social organization were of fundamental importance. Organization, however, was not enough. Social cohesion was equally essential. The industrialization that gave nations their external strength also burdened them with social problems that produced internal divisiveness and weakness.

The organizations representing industry and labor, whose participation in the war effort was to be essential, were the chief combatants in the social conflict. The industrial strife of the prewar period had led to a growing fear of revolution. The Triple Industrial Alliance in England, the Syndicalists in

France, and the Social Democrats in Germany, Austria-Hungary, and Russia threatened to become the gravediggers of governments and ruling classes. Dangerous in peace, they were potentially even more dangerous in war. Thus, if war was not to be transformed into revolution, the governments and ruling classes would have to demonstrate a high degree of adaptability. They would have to utilize the organized forces of society and at the same time minimize differences. Above all, they would have to make such concessions as were necessary to insure the cooperation of formerly dissatisfied groups. Every such concession, however, necessarily threatened to change or modify the existing order. The significance of such adjustments to the necessities of war, therefore, lay in the possibility that they might become permanent. The struggle for political and social advantage in the wartime economy was a struggle over the structure of society after the war.[1]

This struggle was particularly severe in Germany. The deprivations caused by the war coupled with the exceptional demands made on the workers intensified their discontent and compelled the authorities to give way to many of their demands. Although a similar process may be observed in all the belligerent countries, the manner in which it was resolved in Germany was singularly ambiguous. In contrast to Russia, which succumbed to total revolution, and Britain and France, whose social system and political institutions survived the war relatively unscathed, the German Revolution of 1918-1919 degenerated into a consolidation of political and social changes made under the impress of the war. Although it required military defeat and revolutionary danger to compel the representatives of the old order to accept the two chief gains of the revolution, parliamentarization and collective bargaining, there can be no question about the fact that the entire pattern of wartime political and social relations moved in this direction.

[1] On the problems of war, revolution, and reform, see Elie Halévy, *The World Crisis of 1914-1918*, Oxford, 1930, and Arno J. Mayer, *The Political Origins of the New Diplomacy, 1917-1918*, New Haven, 1959.

The political and social equality of the working class was tentatively won in war and was finally sanctified in defeat, and therein lay one of the great tragedies of German democracy. In contrast to the Bolsheviks, who eliminated the social groups which might have accused them of profiting from the war and stabbing the nation in the back, the leaders of organized labor in Germany, unwilling and unable to find a "third way" between Bolshevism and parliamentary democracy, felt compelled to ally with the old order and thus helped to preserve the power of those groups which were to accuse the Social Democrats of treason. This development, however, was implicit in the wartime situation, for throughout the war the leaders of labor were accused of profiting from the war at the expense of their brothers on the battlefield and the other classes of German society.

This charge, while certainly distorted, was not completely unfounded. Organized labor did use the war to increase its social, political, and economic power. The same charge, however, may also be made against industry, and particularly heavy industry. The supremacy of these two groups during the war was the basis for their alliance after the war, an alliance which found expression in the agreement between the industrialist Hugo Stinnes and the leader of the Socialist Free Trade Unions, Carl Legien, on November 15, 1918. This agreement formally established collective bargaining in Germany and, at the same time, did much to protect the industrialists from social revolution.

The most extraordinary aspect of these developments was the decisive role of the army in their promotion. It was Ludendorff's acceptance of a "revolution from above" to provide a satisfactory internal basis for his armistice request which inadvertently triggered the limited constitutional reforms of October 1918.[2] Far less well known, however, is the fact that

[2] See Wolfgang Sauer's forthcoming *Militär- und Zivilgewalt in der Revolution. Das Bündnis Groener-Ebert November-Dezember 1918*. Sauer has demonstrated that Ludendorff had no intention of handing "power

it was the German army which was largely responsible for the establishment of collective bargaining in Germany. In contrast to Ludendorff's revolution from above, the army's interference in industrial relations in favor of the workers began in 1914, when the chances of a German victory seemed bright, and its influence did much to erode employer resistance to recognition of the unions. The social policies of the military authorities and the collaboration between the army and the trade unions during the war form an important part of the background of the agreement of November 10, 1918, between General Wilhelm Groener and the Socialist leader, Friedrich Ebert, an agreement which preserved the old officer corps and prevented the extension of the Revolution.

The army's interference in labor-management relations and the surprising forms which it took are part of the larger story of the most continuous and pervasive form of military intervention in civil affairs during the war, namely, the army's management of the wartime economy. This intervention was neither anticipated nor planned by the army. Indeed, Germany's prewar military leaders had clung tenaciously to the view that modern, industrialized states were incapable of fighting long wars. In 1909 the former chief of the German General Staff, Count von Schlieffen, noted that "such wars are impossible in an age when the existence of the nation is founded upon the uninterrupted continuation of trade and industry. . . . A strategy of exhaustion cannot be conducted when the maintenance of millions depends upon the expenditure of billions."[3] Schlieffen could not understand that it was precisely the industrial might of nations which made lengthy, "total" wars possible. The Schlieffen Plan, which required the violation of Belgian neutrality in order to insure the speedy

---

over to his rival . . . the Reichstag" when he supported the "revolution from above." For the older interpretation, see Arthur Rosenberg, *The Birth of the German Republic*, New York, 1962, pp. 241ff.

[3] Reichsarchiv, *Der Weltkrieg 1914-1918. Kriegsrüstung und Kriegswirtschaft*, Berlin, 1930, p. 328.

subjugation of France, reflected Schlieffen's conviction that Germany could not sustain a long war. Schlieffen's successor, the younger Moltke, adhered to this plan. In Moltke's view the chief economic functions of government during wartime were to relieve unemployment and prevent hunger, thus eliminating domestic unrest that might disturb the morale of the troops. What was deemed necessary was not the economic mobilization of the productive forces of the nation but rather stabilization and quiet so that the army might do its work without interference. Although Moltke and other members of the General Staff did have pessimistic moments in which they suspected that the war could last as long as two years and expressed some interest in proposals calling for the establishment of an "Economic General Staff" and the preparation of measures to defend Germany against a long blockade, their practical planning demonstrated that they continued to consider the short, mobile wars of the nineteenth century, and particularly the Franco-Prussian War, the norm for all future armed encounters. Germany's preparations for the First World War were thus fated to rest on the twin pillars of military mobilization and civil immobilization.[4]

Germany was not alone in her failure to prepare for a long and total war. It was an error committed by all of the belligerent powers, and it alone cannot explain why the army assumed such a dominant role in the economic mobilization process in Germany, came to control raw materials, involve itself in the management of the food supply, interfere so decisively in labor-management relations, and establish agencies for the control of the war economy. In Britain the economic mobilization was directed by a civilian authority, the Munitions Ministry, and in France after a brief period of military dominance there was a restoration of parliamentary and civilian control.[5] The explanation for the German army's control

[4] *Ibid.*, pp. 329-331, and Arthur Dix, *Wirtschaftskrieg und Kriegswirtschaft*, Berlin, 1920, pp. 161ff.

[5] Samuel J. Hurwitz, *State Intervention in Great Britain. A Study of*

of the wartime economy is closely bound up with the explanation for the collaboration of army, industry, and labor at the end of the war. Both of these phenomena reflected the failure of the Imperial bureaucracy and the failure of the Reichstag to cope with the problems of modern war and, in a broader sense, of a modern industrial society. The army and the interest groups won their decisive positions by default.

1. The Sociopolitical Background

The Imperial German government's reputation for organizational talent and efficiency is a classic example of the degree to which human beings are impressed by labyrinthine complexity and painstaking devotion to narrow tasks. In reality the complexity of the German governmental edifice was a reflection of the nation's retarded constitutional development, and the notable achievements of its bureaucrats in the management of the particular problems falling within their competence veiled their complete incapacity to solve the major problems confronting German society. Politically Germany was an unstable compound of federalism, autocracy, and constitutional monarchy. The formal executive authority rested in the hands of the federal states represented in the Bundesrat. It was the Bundesrat which presented legislation to the Reichstag, passed upon the Reichstag's decisions, and issued the regulations concerning the implementation of legislation. Legislation was usually drawn up by the Chancellor and his state secretaries for presentation to the Bundesrat. These Imperial officials were responsible to the Emperor, not to the Reichstag. Furthermore, they had no executive authority of their own and had to rely upon the officialdom of the various states for the actual implementation of legislation. The real power, therefore, rested in the states and particularly in the largest and

---

Economic and Social Response, 1914-1919, New York, 1949, pp. 93ff., and Jere Clemens King, *Generals and Politicians. Conflict between France's High Command, Parliament and Government, 1914-1918*, Berkeley, 1951, pp. 34ff.

most powerful of these, Prussia. Prussia controlled a majority of votes in the Bundesrat, and the policy of the Reich was largely determined by the Prussian Cabinet (*Staatsministerium*). The Chancellor's power was based on his position as Minister-President of Prussia, and the Emperor's power was based on his position as King of Prussia. Although the Minister-President of Prussia did not formally depend upon the Prussian Landtag for his continuation in office, he could hardly ignore the fact that the Landtag controlled the Prussian purse strings. Unlike the Reichstag, which was elected by universal suffrage, the lower house of the Prussian Landtag was elected by a three-class voting system which gave a conservative clique of East Elbian Junkers and Rhenish-Westphalian industrial magnates an overwhelming majority. From such classes, and particularly from the nobility, were drawn the bureaucrats and officers who dominated the state apparatus.[6]

This system, devised by Bismarck at a time when Germany was a predominantly agricultural state, became increasingly obsolete in the course of her rapid industrialization. As the functions of the central government multiplied with the growing expenditure for national defense, the expansion of foreign trade, and the social problems created by industrialization, the administrative decentralization of the Empire became a barrier to efficient government. The right to levy direct taxes was monopolized by the states, and the Imperial government was forced to rely on the state authorities for the collection of indirect taxes. Despite the fact that the economic problems of the Empire had become national in scope, very little had been done to create national agencies capable of handling these increased burdens. The Imperial Office of the Interior, the chief national agency for the management of economic and social problems, was permitted to grow in a helter-skelter fashion until it became a caricature of bureaucratic organization. At the same time its capacity for effective action was hampered by the

[6] Klaus Epstein, *Matthias Erzberger and the Dilemma of German Democracy*, Princeton, 1959, pp. 19-37.

existence of the well-organized Prussian Ministry for Commerce and Industry, which jealously guarded its position as protector of the economic interests of Germany's most populous and industrialized state.[7]

The stunted development of centralized administration in Germany was the product of political design, not bureaucratic inertia. As the responsibilities of the central government grew, so did the importance of the Reichstag. Unlike Prussia, where the three-class voting system produced a Landtag whose composition in no way reflected the rapid industrialization and urbanization of Germany, universal suffrage in the Reich had, by 1912, produced a Reichstag controlled by Social Democrats, Catholic Centrists, and Progressives. The establishment of an Imperial administration independent of the administrations of the states would necessarily have increased the power and the influence of the Reichstag. The government would have been required to increase the size of the budget and request new taxes, but it would have denied the government a most convenient means of evading responsibility for the implementation of legislation, as it could no longer claim that the execution of laws was the sole province of the state administrations. Finally, the abandonment of the principle of delegated administration would have endangered the social composition of the Prussian bureaucracy, since the staffing of an imperial field administration would have required the greater utilization of nonnoble elements from the non-Prussian states.[8]

The impotence of the Reichstag, which was always justified by the superiority of the German administrative machine and the nonpartisan character of the bureaucratic experts who ran it, thus required the retention of an antediluvian administrative structure staffed by personnel drawn largely from the most politically backward elements of German society. Needless to

[7] Friedrich Facius, *Wirtschaft und Staat. Die Entwicklung der staatlichen Wirtschaftsverwaltung in Deutschland vom 17. Jahrhundert bis 1945*, Boppard am Rhein, 1959, pp. 65-78.

[8] Herbert Jacobs, *German Administration since Bismarck, Central Authority versus Local Autonomy*, New Haven, 1963, pp. 26-30.

say, what had proved inadequate in peace was bound to prove doubly inadequate in war. The threat to the efficient functioning of the central authorities under wartime conditions was twofold. First, the absence of a well-developed central administration would compound the problems involved in establishing the many new central agencies to be required by the war. Second, the dependence of the central government on state agencies in the implementation of national policy carried with it the implicit danger that these agencies might seek to assert particularistic interests in the performance of their executive functions and might therefore sabotage the goals of the national administration.

The Bismarckian constitutional compromise between authoritarianism and parliamentarism not only stifled the administrative development of the Empire, it also inhibited the maturation of parliamentary institutions and practices. The deliberate exclusion of parliamentarians from positions of administrative responsibility deprived them of executive experience and encouraged habits of political irresponsibility. The parties oscillated between a stubborn attachment to ideology which prevented the formation of viable coalitions and an opportunistic pursuit of special interests. The government encouraged both of these tendencies by basing its parliamentary support upon shifting political alliances.[9]

The Reichstag was powerful because it could vote down legislation, but it was impotent because it could not impose its will on the Prussian Landtag, Bundesrat, and Chancellor. Although the Reichstag's role in bringing down Chancellor Bülow in 1909 and the Reichstag elections of 1912 which gave the Social Democrats 110 seats and the antigovernment forces a vast majority demonstrated that the political system of the Empire was severely strained, the aftermath of these events did not bode well for the future of German parliamentarism.

[9] Ernst Fraenkel, "Historische Vorbelastungen des deutschen Parlamentarismus," *Vierteljahreshefte für Zeitgeschichte*, 8, Oct. 1960, pp. 523-540.

They neither led to reforms nor to the creation of a permanent coalition capable of reconciling party differences and maintaining a united front. The liberal parties were too fearful of the red specter to cooperate with the Socialists, and the Catholic Center Party sought to maintain its tactical alliance with the Conservatives in the defense of particularistic and clerical interests.[10] Thus, if the administration was unprepared for a sustained emergency, so was the Reichstag. The Bismarckian system gave Germany a Reichstag which was unable either to act as an agent for the integration of German society or to provide a cadre of leaders capable of assuming the direction of the nation.

The incapacity of Germany to make the complete transition from an authoritarian to a parliamentary system and the failure of both the bureaucracy and the Reichstag to act as integrating elements in German society encouraged the search for a third alternative, the corporatist solution. Although corporatist ideas took on many forms, their continuing significance in German political thought reflected the traumatic nature of the nation's transition from what the sociologist Tönnies called the "community" (*Gemeinschaft*) of the preindustrial era to the "society" (*Gesellschaft*) of the industrial era. The sudden severing of familial and geographical bonds, the loosening of rigid social patterns, the increasing separation of men from the tools and products of their labor were sources of anxiety and discontent. The belated unification and industrialization of the nation created an almost artificial break with the past. Germany became a mass society before she overcame her feudal past and before the liberal-individualistic period of early capitalism had created those institutions of self-government and ideas of liberty which make possible the existence of a mass society capable of organizing for the collective defense of their interests as free men.

The German conceptions of liberty and self-government

[10] Walter Koch, *Volk und Staatsführung vor dem Weltkriege*, Stuttgart, 1935, p. 122.

continued to move along the treadworn paths marked out during her prolonged history of national disunity and princely despotism. Liberty was a benefice handed down by authority guaranteeing the prerogatives of powerful individuals and corporative groups, not the reward garnered from the overthrow of established authority and the smashing of antiquated forms of social organization. Self-government was restricted to communal and corporative affairs and not associated with the higher and ultimately controlling functions of the state. This dualism between the spheres of liberty and authority, between society and state, was maintained by Bismarck when he gave the liberals the national unity and constitution which they were unable to attain by themselves and deprived them of the political power which would have made liberty and self-government a reality. The political debates of the Reichstag thus seemed useless and even trivial as economic and social problems became more pressing. The interest groups began to insist upon the "objectification" of politics, namely, the establishment of parties based on clear-cut economic and social interests. Implicit in this demand was the idea that the interest groups themselves should regulate economic and social questions.[11]

Under such conditions it was natural to confuse the interest groups with the old estates of the preindustrial era and to consider the establishment of corporative institutions as a restoration of the old sense of community destroyed by parliamentary "cattle trading" and bureaucratic arbitrariness. Bismarck sought to implement a corporatist and antiparliamentary scheme during the lengthy economic crisis which began in 1873. Taking advantage of the demands of heavy industry and agriculture for high tariffs, he encouraged their alliance and sought, in the early 1880's, to establish a People's Economic Council representing the various interest groups to

[11] Wolfgang Sauer, "Das Problem des deutschen Nationalstaates," *Politische Vierteljahresschrift*, 3, June 1962, pp. 159-186; Leonard Krieger, *The German Idea of Freedom, History of a Political Tradition*, Boston, 1957; Heinrich Heffter, *Die deutsche Selbstverwaltung im 19. Jahrhundert. Geschichte der Ideen und Institutionen*, Stuttgart, 1950.

advise the government on socioeconomic matters. This program failed because the Reichstag refused to support the further diminution of its powers by granting funds for this project.[12]

If the proposed institutionalization of interest politics along corporate lines failed to materialize, however, the events of the late 1870's did give the decisive push to the politicalization of the interest groups and encouraged their proliferation. The Junker-industrialist alliance, which Bismarck had cemented, lived on to dominate Prussian politics, promote high tariffs, support the imperialistic naval building program of the Wilhelmian era, and fight for the suppression of the labor movement. It corrupted the conservatives and split the bourgeois liberals. The Junkers stripped their conservatism of its ethical content and degenerated into an agrarian interest group. The German upper bourgeoisie, and particularly the leaders of German heavy industry, shed the feeble vestiges of their liberalism and became "feudalized." They aped the manners and sought to share the titles of their agrarian allies. The state encouraged this assimilation to Junker values by opening the bureaucracy and the army to upper class bourgeois elements with the "proper" attitude.

There were, to be sure, important differences between the Junkers and the big industrialists. The Junkers disliked the rapid pace of industrialism which diminished their power, suspected and disdained the methods of industrial capitalism, and were uninterested in overseas expansion. The industrialists suffered from the high agrarian tariffs which created foreign trade difficulties and raised the domestic price of food and, as a consequence, wages. These divergent economic interests became particularly marked in the 1890's when the industrial depression ended and the industrialists became less fearful of

[12] Gerhard Schulz, "Über Entstehung und Formen von Interessengruppen in Deutschland seit Beginn der Industrialisierung," *Politische Vierteljahresschrift*, 2, July 1961, pp. 124-154, and Heffter, *Deutsche Selbstverwaltung*, pp. 681-682.

foreign competition. Nevertheless, the alliance persisted because both groups continued to find it necessary to gain one another's support on tariff questions and, above all, because the alliance gave them dominance in Prussia and great influence over the policies of the Empire. The Junkers feared political isolation; the great industrialists feared being driven into alliance with the left wing liberals and, ultimately, into concessions to the Social Democrats and trade unions. The economically unnatural alliance between the Junkers and industrialists demonstrated the potentially decisive role which a coalition of competing interest groups could play as a third force between the government and the political parties.[13]

The relationship between the interest groups and the political parties was by no means clear. This was less true of the leading agrarian organization, the League of German Farmers, than of the major industrial group, the Central Association of German Industrialists. The league dominated the policies of the Conservative Party and had considerable influence on the agrarian elements in the National Liberal and Center parties. The Central Association, however, had very poor control over the Empire's leading bourgeoisie party, the National Liberals. This lack of coordination between the most important industrialist interest group and the National Liberal Party reflected the deep divisions within the business community and the "middle class." The policies of the Central Association were largely determined by the iron, steel, and coal industrialists, who were well-organized in special organizations such as the mighty Association of German Iron and Steel Industrialists and whose economic power increased immensely due to the cartelization and syndicalization policies they pursued after 1890.

If this group ruled over the greatest concentration of industrial power and resources in Germany, however, its claim to represent the interests of all of German industry was very

[13] Eckart Kehr, *Schlachtflottenbau und Parteipolitik 1894-1901*, Berlin, 1930.

dubious. The new chemical and electrotechnical industries and the great mass of small and middle-sized manufacturers of finished goods did not wholly agree with either the economic or the political policies of heavy industry. They objected to high tariffs and giant cartels which created difficulties for German exporters and which increased the domestic prices of basic raw materials. They disliked the alliance with agriculture for similar economic reasons, and although fearful of the rising power of the Social Democrats, they resented the political predominance of the Junkers. Driven into an alliance with the leaders of heavy industry during the economic downswing of the 1870's and 1880's, they began to break away from the Central Association of German Industrialists as business conditions improved in the 1890's. In 1889 the chemical industry formed a separate association of its own, and in 1895 a new League of German Industrialists was established to unite the various branches of the manufacturing and export industries in opposition to heavy industry and the Junkers. The National Liberal Party was split between the supporters of the Central Association and the supporters of the league. Although led by league supporters, Ernst Bassermann and Gustav Stresemann, the party was compelled to follow a wavering course because of the strong heavy industrialist element in the party.[14]

The growing importance of political and constitutional questions following the *Daily Telegraph* Affair of 1908 and the dismissal of Bülow in 1909, however, did lead to important changes in the sphere of interest-group politics. The interest groups began to combine along political lines. In 1909 the more liberal interest groups entered into a loose coalition, the Hansa League for Manufacture, Trade, and Industry, in an effort to mobilize these forces against the continuing predominance of Junker-agrarian power. In 1913 heavy industry, agriculture, and the right wing organizations of craftsmen and

[14] Thomas Nipperdey, "Interessenverbände und Parteien in Deutschland vor dem Ersten Weltkrieg," *Politische Vierteljahresschrift*, 2, Sept. 1961, pp. 262-280.

ialists was not entirely shared by the business elements ouped in the League of German Industrialists. Although the tter opposed the "constitutional factory system" that would ive permitted the workers to participate in the determination factory methods and work rules and in questions of hiring id firing, and although they supported legislation to protect e right of unorganized workers and members of yellow iions to break through the picket lines, they recognized the evitability of unions and accepted the right to strike. Some the smaller industries, either because of their strong craft adition or because they were too weak financially to sustain ng strikes, had actually concluded collective wage agreeents with the unions. Indeed, when viewed from a long perective, the establishment of employer unity in 1913 may also regarded as a step in the direction of large-scale collective irgaining, for such bargaining required the organization of th of the "social partners." In the immediate sense, however, is employer cooperation was incited by the growth of the ide union movement, the increasing number of strikes, the mands of social reformers for a more liberal policy, and the terference of the state in labor-management relations.[15]

The spectacular rise of the Social Democratic Party and the ee Trade Unions in Wilhelmian Germany was yet another ample of the Empire's incapacity to resolve the authoritariannstitutional dualism upon which is was based. Unwilling ther to forcefully suppress organized labor or to grant it cial and political equality, the government pursued a vacilting course. As a consequence, German Social Democracy came a state within the state, a subculture alienated from e dominant institutions and culture. In the course of its delopment, however, the Social Democrats came to suffer from polarity of alternatives which paralleled that of the state. though formally committed to a Marxist, republican, and

[15] *Der Weg zum industriellen Spitzenverband*, Frankfurt a.M., 1956, . 26ff., and Fritz Tänzler, *Die deutschen Arbeitgeberverbände 1904-29*, n.p., 1929.

white collar workers established a counter coaliti
of the Producing Estates," a political hodge-pod
technically advanced elements and those mos
industrialization and technology united in the de
cal and social reaction. However loosely held t
combinations of interest groups demonstrated t
to form "secondary systems of political power"
bureaucracy and the political parties.

If the economic prosperity of Wilhelmian
encouraged the overt expression of the political
conflicts within the business community, howeve
created, in somewhat contradictory fashion, inten
ration in the field of social policy. As the depress
of the Bismarckian era had caused the industria
up their differences and band together to dema
tection, so the prosperity of the post-Bismarckian
its concomitant growth of labor unions, recurri
mands, and strikes, drove the industrialists to
employer organizations. No less than 208 new em
zations were founded between 1890 and 1902.
began to consolidate. The Central Association o
dustrialists established a Central Agency of Gern
Associations while the League of German Indust
lished an Association of German Employer Orga
two groups collaborated, and by 1913 they were
into an Association of German Employer Organ
mutually satisfactory basis. As might be expect
tional unity was no proof of ideological unanimity
of heavy industry were extreme proponents of t
the employer should remain "master in his own
insisted that the state had no right to violate th
"natural" relationship between worker and emplo
ing with their attitude, they sought to solve the sc
by a combination of individual patriarchal welfa
and black lists, lockouts, strike breakers, and yello

The completely intransigent position of the

internationalist ideology, the Social Democrats became increasingly reformist and nationalist. In its positive aspect this reformist tendency reflected the improved conditions of the working class and the growing integration of the working class into German society on the local level, a phenomenon which found expression in the cooperation between the Social Democrats and the bourgeoisie parties in South Germany, the participation of trade union officials in the administration of the nation's social insurance system, and the collaboration between factory inspectors and Socialist trade union officials in certain parts of Prussia. In its negative aspect it reflected the fear that abortive attempts to implement the revolutionary program would lead to the destruction of the organizations which had proved so difficult to create.[16]

The Free Trade Unions were at the forefront of the struggle against radical tactics. Thanks to the exceptional organizational talents of the chairman of the General Commission of the German Free Trade Unions, Carl Legien, they had increased their membership from 680,000 in 1900 to 2,574,000 in 1913. With this extraordinary growth came wealth, bureaucratization, and a decisive influence on the policies of the Social Democratic Party. The union leaders were practical men who knew the difficulties involved in breaking through worker apathy and understood how easily the workers could be brought to defect by the failure of a strike, employer and police reprisals, and even a brief economic crisis. They did not wish to compound their difficulties by being taken into the tow of the party radicals. Thus the General Commission led the struggle against the party radicals and fought against political mass strikes. In fact the General Commission opposed every overt expression of the revolutionary ideology that might

[16] Carl E. Schorske, *German Social Democracy 1905-1917. The Development of the Great Schism*, Cambridge, Mass., 1955; Gerhard A. Ritter, *Die Arbeiterbewegung in Wilhelminischen Reich*, Berlin-Dahlem, 1963, pp. 176ff.; Guenther Roth, *The Social Democrats in Imperial Germany. A Study in Working Class Isolation and National Integration*, Totowa, N.J., 1963, pp. 212ff.

wastefully deplete its economic resources or subject the unions to dissolution by the state. The preservation and strengthening of the unions tended to become ends in themselves for the union leaders, and they devoted all their energies to relieving the immediate hardships of the workers and trying to create an established niche for the unions within the framework of the existing social order. Their major objectives were complete freedom to organize and recognition of the unions by the employers and the government. They wished an end to the treatment of the unions as political organizations and the annulment of such irritating exceptional laws as Paragraph 153 of the Industrial Ordinance which was used to protect strikebreaking. The union leaders fought with particular vigor for the establishment of collective agreements on wages and working conditions (*Tarifverträge*) between employer and worker organizations and the recognition of such agreements in public law. By this means the unions expected to achieve recognition, avoid expensive strikes, and protect both the organizations and the workers from depressions. For similar reasons they supported the establishment of compulsory worker committees in the factories, public labor exchanges based on the principle of parity between labor and management, and similarly organized conciliation bureaus for the mediation of industrial conflicts.

Neither the party nor the unions ever resolved the contradiction between their revolutionary ideology and their reformist practice. In using the former to stir up the masses and radicalize them, they created a discrepancy between promise and performance and frequently had cause to fear the effects of their agitation. This was all the more the case because advancing industrialization was breaking down the craft traditions upon which the spirit and structure of the Socialist labor movement had actually been based. The development of proletarian class consciousness and radical sentiment was particularly pronounced among the metal workers in the great urban centers, where the transition from the craft union to the industrial union had made the greatest progress. While a similar process may be observed in England, the problems thus created in Germany were particularly serious because proletarian protest still awaited legitimation by the state and ruling classes. This created a far greater sense of alienation among the more class conscious segments of the German working class. In striving to awaken the masses and to control them, the moderate leadership of the Socialist labor movement had the vexing tasks of preventing the development of schisms within their own ranks, fighting the lethargy created by unfulfilled promises, and competing with other parties and labor organizations.[17]

The Association of Christian Trade Unions and the Hirsch-Duncker Worker Associations, which competed with the Free Trade Unions for the loyalty of the workers, were much less imposing in size. The former, led by Adam Stegerwald, had 343,000 members in 1913. Although the practical goals of the Christians and the Free Trade Unions were similar, the Christian unions rejected the class struggle and were nationalist and Catholic in ideology. They were closely associated with the Center Party. The Hirsch-Duncker Associations, which boasted 107,000 members in 1913, were associated with the Progressive Party and sought, under the banner of liberalism, complete freedom of coalition and political equality for the workers. In the years immediately preceding the war, the Christian and Hirsch-Duncker unions became more radical in their methods because of the economic hardships faced by their members and the persistent refusal of the majority of the employers to deal with their organizations. Also, they had to

[17] Gerhard Bry, *Wages in Germany, 1871-1945*, Princeton, 1960, p. 32; Heinz Josef Varain, *Freie Gewerkschaften, Sozialdemokratie und Staat. Der Politik der Generalkommission unter der Führung Carl Legiens 1890-1920*, Düsseldorf, 1956, pp. 36ff.; Robert Michels, *Zur Soziologie des Parteiwesens in der Modernen Demokratie*, Leipzig, 1911, pp. 255-277; Peter von Oertzen, *Betriebsräte in der Novemberrevolution. Eine politikwissenschaftliche Untersuchung über Ideengehalt und Struktur der betrieblichen und wirtschaftlichen Arbeiterräte in der deutschen Revolution 1918/19*, Düsseldorf, 1963, pp. 27ff.; Gaston V. Rimlinger, "The Legitimation of Protest: A Comparative Study in Labor History," *Comparative Studies in Society and History*, II, April 1960, pp. 329-343.

become more radical in order to compete with the Free Trade Unions. Thus they joined with the latter in some of the serious strikes of the immediate prewar period. Although ideological differences and competition for members persisted, the three unions had an increasingly sound, if officially unrecognized, basis for collaboration. On the one hand, the Free Trade Unions were becoming more reformist and nationalist in practice, if not in ideology. On the other hand, the Christian and Hirsch-Duncker unions were more willing to use the strike as a means of achieving their ends.[18]

The trade union cause received support from a very important group of middle-class reformers which had been organized into a Society for Social Reform since 1872. Led by a number of distinguished professors, the most important of whom were Gustav Schmoller, Adolf Wagner, and Lujo Brentano, the Society opposed Manchesterian economics and supported state intervention in economic and social affairs. These "socialists of the chair" (*Kathedersozialisten*) sought to protect the workers and other lower orders of society against the ravages of the business cycle and the hardships of industrial society. At the same time they hoped to win the workers over to the state and monarchy by giving their organizations a recognized place within the social order. Most of the society's leading members were convinced that even the Free Trade Unions and the Socialist Party could be won over to the support of the state provided that they were treated in an understanding manner by the government and the employers. The society's influence was of exceptional importance. Its membership included not only noted academicians but influential government officials, among whom were the Prussian Minister of Trade and Commerce from 1889 to 1896, Freiherr von Berlepsch, and the State Secretary of the Interior from 1899 to 1907, Count von Posadowsky.

[18] Bry, *Wages in Germany*, p. 32; Karl Erich Born, *Staat und Sozialpolitik seit Bismarcks Sturz. Ein Beitrag zur Geschichte der innenpolitischen Entwicklung des Deutschen Reiches, 1890-1894*, Wiesbaden, 1957, p. 74.

The vast amount of literature produced by the society provided the government with material of a scientific character on social and economic problems. In the years before the war there was some collaboration between the General Commission and the society. Unlike the Christian and Hirsch-Duncker unions, however, the Free Trade Unions always maintained a certain reserve in dealing with the society. The society was detested and violently attacked by heavy industry because its reformist policies provided the government with a very real alternative to the policy of repression supported by heavy industry and the Junkers.[19]

The notion that the political discontent of dissatisfied classes could be channeled into the supposedly less threatening economic sphere had been the stock and trade of the Prussian bureaucracy for over a century. The liberal economic policy of the first three quarters of the nineteenth century, the Bismarckian unification of Germany, and the protectionist policy pursued since the late 1870's had all been part of that continuous "revolution from above" and that system of socioeconomic bribery by which the authoritarian state preserved itself in a rapidly changing world. Bismarck's attempt to compensate the workers for their political impotence and social subservience by means of a paternalistic social policy was at once a reflection of his Christian-pietist approach to social problems and a continuation of this political tradition. Through the introduction of an extensive system of social insurance, he sought to take the wind out of the Social Democratic Party's sails; but his efforts to bribe the workers with social legislation and suppress their party with anti-Socialist laws failed. By 1890 he had come to the conclusion that only the use of force and the creation of a new constitution could solve the problem. Neither the Emperor nor the dominant elements in the bureaucracy, however, were willing to see Germany transformed into a police state.[20]

19 Born, *Staat und Sozialpolitik*, pp. 34-47.

20 See Sauer's brilliant analysis of reform from above in *Politische*

After 1890 the anti-Socialist laws were permitted to lapse. Bismarck's successors, however, continued to use social legislation as a means of trying to win the workers away from the Social Democrats. Freiherr von Berlepsch and Count von Posadowsky promoted social reform measures which went much further than those of Bismarck because they challenged the absolute rule of the employers in the factories. The social insurance system was greatly extended, as were the protective laws governing the employment of women and children. Industrial courts were established to mediate conflicts between employers and workers. Funds were allocated for the housing of the workers. A system of factory inspection was established. After a major strike in the coal mines in 1905, a system of compulsory worker committees was set up in the mining industry, and the miners were thus provided with some means of presenting their collective complaints to the employers. Theobold von Bethmann Hollweg, who replaced Posadowsky as State Secretary of the Interior in 1907 and who became Chancellor of the Empire in 1909, carried on the social policies of his predecessor. He improved the social insurance system, introduced an imperial associations bill and sought, without success, to establish worker chambers (*Arbeitskammer*) in which employers and workers might collaborate in the regulation of industrial questions.

The failure of the worker chambers bill and the dissatisfaction with the Imperial Associations Law, however, reflected the fact that the government's social policy was heading toward a dead end. The worker chambers bill failed because the government refused to allow the election of union secretaries to the chambers. The Associations Law provoked opposition because it lent itself to juridical interpretations which placed the trade unions in the category of political associations. The unions were thus required to submit their membership lists

---

Vierteljahresschrift, 3 pp. 166-179, and Egmont Zechlin, *Staatsstreichpläne Bismarcks und Wilhelm II, 1890-1894*, Stuttgart and Berlin, 1929.

to the police, and the employers, who had access to the lists, could use them as a means of acting against workers who joined unions. Also, youths under eighteen were barred from joining the unions or attending union meetings. The social policy of the government always stopped short of recognizing the trade unions, of treating them as representatives of the workers, and of giving the workers complete freedom of coalition. Agricultural workers and workers in the state railways did not have this freedom of coalition. Workers in private industry did, but collective agreements between labor and management organizations were not recognized in public law.

The danger of this bureaucratic reform from above was that it accelerated the unleashing of those forces which it was trying to control. The unions sought to use these reforms to strengthen their hold on the workers and secure new concessions from the government. As one union leader pointed out, "The worker committees can and must do the preparatory work for the legal enactment of more rights. They must skillfully use those rights which they already have and through their work demonstrate again and again that the privileges of the worker committees can and must be extended."[21] The employers clearly perceived the dangers implicit in the work of the bureaucratic reformers. They warned the government that "in the worker chambers, whatever the election methods may be, the majority of the worker representatives will be under the influence of the union organizations which . . . have as their chief goal the attainment of political power."[22] Gustav Krupp von Bohlen und Halbach warned the Emperor that "every social-political law, whether it is made with the Social Democrats or against them, strengthens their position and heightens the aura about them, for the masses consider it to be their success."[23] Who could deny the truth of this statement

[21] Hans Jürgen Teuteberg, *Geschichte der industriellen Mitbestimmung in Deutschland*, Tübingen, 1961, p. 463.

[22] Peter Rassow and Karl Erich Born, *Akten zur Staatlichen Sozialpolitik in Deutschland, 1890-1914*, Wiesbaden, 1959, p. 386.

[23] Dieter Fricks, "Eine Denkschrift Krupps aus dem Jahre 1912 über

when 110 Social Democrats were occupying seats in the Reichstag?

Further social reform meant treating the trade unions, including those alligned to the Social Democratic Party, as the social partners of the employers. It was impossible, however, to grant social and economic equality without also granting political equality, and the latter would have ultimately necessitated the abandonment of the three-class voting system in Prussia. The government was simply unwilling to sacrifice the support of the Junker-industrialist alliance, and these groups were unwilling to surrender their political preponderance. In 1910 Bethmann had presented a moderate proposal for the reform of the Prussian suffrage. Despite the fact that it did not do away with the three-class voting system, it was defeated by the Landtag. A series of major strikes in 1912, the Socialist triumph in the elections of that year, and the intensified pressure from the employer organizations brought a halt to the government's policy of social reform. In a speech of January 1914 Clemens von Delbrück, the Imperial State Secretary of the Interior, demonstrated that the pendulum of government favor had now swung in favor of the conservative forces when he declared that a "sensible social policy" was one which gave the employer "that measure of economic and moral elbow room which he needs in order to fulfill the great tasks which our industry has previously fulfilled and which it must fulfill to a yet greater degree in the future in order to maintain its proud position in the world."[24] In May of the same year, the Society for Social Reform, joined by the Christian and Hirsch-Duncker unions, held a giant meeting in Berlin to protest the government's new course.

On the eve of the war the political and social issues had become completely intermeshed, but the efforts to solve them had reached a point of stagnation. Prosperity and widespread complacency seemed to promise protection against any major

den Schutz der Arbeitswilligen," *Zeitschrift für Geschichtswissenschaft*, 5, 1957, p. 1249.

[24] Born, *Staat und Sozialpolitik*, p. 246.

internal upheavals, but Germany was poorly prepared to suffer the sustained crisis which the war would bring. The nation's murky political waters were filled with competing interest groups forming coalitions on differing sets of issues and parties incapable of either integrating the interest groups seeking to influence them or joining together in a common effort. Bethmann Hollweg, plagued by right wing elements who wanted a belligerent foreign policy and a repressive internal policy and by left wing groups demanding moderation abroad and reform at home, sought a magical middle ground which would satisfy everyone. His life was made all the more difficult by an impatient and unstable Emperor and by his own growing conviction that Germany could not thus go on forever.[25]

2. *"Burgfrieden" and the Law of Siege*

The sudden establishment of political harmony which marked the outbreak of the First World War was bound to give rise to the hope that a new age had dawned for German politics. The economist Emil Lederer declared in 1914 that "We can say that on the day of mobilization the *society* which existed until then was transformed into a *community*."[26] The illusion that war could solve internal political problems was not uniquely German. Austria-Hungary had gone to war to save herself from internal disintegration and even the liberal British Prime Minister Asquith felt that the war "would 'settle' many of the outstanding domestic problems."[27] In Germany, however, the identification of war and reform constituted a veritable historical tradition. The Prussian reform movement of the Napoleonic period and the creation of a united Germany were the products of war. Would not this war, whose internal political history had formally begun on August 4, 1914, with a Social Democratic vote for war credits and a declaration by

[25] Hans-Günther Zmarzlik, *Bethmann Hollweg als Reichskanzler 1909-1914. Studien zur Möglichkeiten und Grenzen seiner innerpolitischen Machtstellung*, Düsseldorf, 1957, pp. 140-144.

[26] Emil Lederer, "Zur Soziologie des Weltkriegs," *Archiv für Sozialwissenschaft und Sozialpolitik*, 39, 1914-1915, p. 349.

[27] Hurwitz, *State Intervention in Britain*, p. 48.

the Emperor that he no longer recognized parties or classes, carry on that often interrupted process of reform so closely associated with the battlefield?

In reality the *Burgfrieden* (Truce of the Fortress) concluded among the competing political parties and pressure groups on August 4 was a far cry from the "community" it was made out to be. The Social Democrats were by no means unanimous in their decision to support the war effort. As might be expected, the trade union leaders stood at the forefront of those Socialists desiring to support the war. Legien had no use for the mass strike as a means of preventing war: "In a land with universal conscription, where one third of the men who are to take part in the mass strike will be taken into the army and another third will be unemployed, the thought of a mass strike is simply absurd." The union leaders also considered the war to be a defensive struggle against a reactionary and imperialist Russia. No less important was their conviction that Germany's defeat would wipe out the progress made by the German workers and their organizations during the previous decades and would place the German economy at the mercy of the Entente's imperialism. In their meetings of August 1 and 2, the chairmen of the Free Trade Unions decided to support the war effort, terminate all strikes and wage movements, refuse to give financial support to strikers during the war, and collaborate with the government's efforts to relieve unemployment.[28]

The party, however, was slower in coming to a decision. The radical leaders—Haase, Kautsky, Liebknecht, and Ledebour—maintained an internationalist position and demanded that the party refuse to support war credits. The moderate and right wing leaders, Ebert and Scheidemann typifying the former, Südekum and David representing the latter, felt either that the party had to vote for the credits or actually desired the party to do so. Fear, as always, played an important role in keeping the majority of the party leaders from pursuing a radical

[28] Varain, *Gewerkschaften*, pp. 71ff.

course. The government was prepared to dissolve the Socialist organizations, suppress their newspapers, and place their leaders in protective custody at the outbreak of war. At the same time, however, the government hoped to avoid open conflict with the Social Democrats for obvious internal and diplomatic reasons. In the last days of July and the first days of August, Südekum was in constant contact with the Chancellor. Bethmann assured Südekum that the government would not act against the party or its press if they did not oppose the war. Indeed, the government was very pleased to have "large organizations of the working class upon which the government can rely in taking the necessary ameliorative actions." Südekum, in turn, assured Bethmann that the party would support the government. Despite Südekum's optimism, however, the conflict within the party was quite bitter. Finally, on August 3 the party caucus voted 96 to 14 to support the war. The influence of the trade union leaders, who composed a quarter of the Socialist Reichstag delegation and who threatened to defect from the party, had much to do with this decision. The patriots within the party had thus triumphed, but the cleavage between them and the radicals remained. David, for example, felt that Haase's opposition demonstrated a "lack of national feeling" and that Haase "quietly hopes for a defeat . . . as the way to social revolution." The unanimous Socialist vote for war credits on August 4 was a reflection of party discipline, not party unanimity.[29]

Sharing the government's illusion that the war would be short, the Socialists went beyond the mere support of war credits. On August 4 they also agreed to an Enabling Act which empowered the Bundesrat to enact emergency economic legislation during the war without the consent of the Reichstag. The Reichstag maintained a right to veto or revise such legislation retroactively, but this presumptive right was not used once during the entire war.

[29] *Ibid.*; Schorske, *German Social Democracy*, pp. 285ff.; BA, Nachlass David, Nr. 3.

The *Burgfrieden* was given a measure of practical application by increased consolidation within the industrialist and trade union camps and by collaboration between them. Thus the Central Association of German Industrialists and the League of German Industrialists, while maintaining their separate organizations, joined together to form the German Industry War Committee. The Socialist, Christian, and Hirsch-Duncker unions also formed a cartel, although somewhat more slowly than the industrialist groups. At the same time the employer and worker organizations engaged in a limited form of collaboration for the purpose of relieving unemployment, and the government made use of both groups for this purpose. A typical example of the Spirit of 1914 was the long visit made by high-ranking government and military officials to the headquarters of the Free Trade Unions in Berlin.

In essence the *Burgfrieden* was a reduction of the Bismarckian state to its ideal form. The parties had terminated their political debates and the interest groups had joined together in the solution of practical economic problems. This momentary realization of the dream that a society could maintain itself in a state of political and social paralysis, however, was fated to give way to the nightmare of intensified political conflict. The superficial harmony of 1914 merely veiled those first indications of the domestic strife to come. In late August Deputy David had a discussion with State Secretary Delbrück concerning the political implications of the Social Democrats' decision to support the war. David pointed out that "the hundreds of thousands of convinced Social Democrats, who are giving all for their Fatherland, expect that consideration will be given to their ideals and dreams." They demanded "political deeds," not merely words, and David warned that if their hopes remained unfulfilled, "a chasm will be created among the people which will not be bridged for decades."[30] Ostensibly a victory for the authoritarian state, the *Burgfrieden*

[30] Jürgen Kuczynski, *Der Ausbruch des Ersten Weltkrieges und die deutsche Sozialdemokratie*, Berlin, 1957, pp. 208-209.

was really the death blow to every mode of argument which had previously been employed to justify the nonintegration of the working class into German society.

There was, however, yet another sense in which the Bismarckian state had been reduced to its "ideal" form, for if the parties had abdicated their power and responsibility to the government, the government, in turn, had abdicated much of its authority to the army. The Bismarckian revolution from above which had created the German Empire was the work of the army, and it was now the army which was given the task of being the chief guardian of its internal as well as external security. On the day of mobilization the Prussian Law of Siege of June 4, 1851, was placed in operation in each of the twenty-four army corps districts into which the Empire was divided. The method used to proclaim this law was symptomatic of its antiquated character. In each district an officer read the law following three blasts of the trumpet. These proclamations were usually greeted by cheers from the public, cheers which reflected the great enthusiasm of August 1914 and the general ignorance of the public concerning the Law of Siege. Under this law the Deputy Commanding Generals placed at the head of each army corps district were given virtually dictatorial power in their respective districts. Acting as agents of the Emperor and responsible to him alone, they were assigned the task of maintaining the "public safety" in their areas of command.[31]

The phrase "public safety" is extraordinarily vague, and it was not long before it came to include everything pertaining to the political, economic, cultural, and social life of the country. Since the law contained no provisions for the coordination of policy among the Deputy Commanding Generals,

[31] Ernst von Wrisberg, *Wehr und Waffen 1914-1918*, Leipzig, 1932, pp. 132-133, and Albrecht Mendelssohn-Bartholdy, *The War and German Society. The Testament of a Liberal*, New Haven, 1937, pp. 108-112. The title "Deputy Commanding General" was used because the actual commanding generals were sent to the front at the head of their respective army corps.

Germany was turned into a group of dictatorships, each of which conducted its own policy. The results were tragicomic. The handling of protective custody and censorship questions was a compound of injustice and caprice, and the Law of Siege became the despair of even the most conservative of men. The law did much to demoralize the civil bureaucracy. To the initial confusion created by the fact that the army corps districts did not coincide geographically with the provinces was added the continuous confusion created by the constant interference of the deputy commanding generals with the work of the local authorities. Only in Bavaria, where a special law existed, were they subject to the authority of the Bavarian War Minister and thus compelled to follow a common policy. The situation in the rest of the country was well described by Crown Prince Rupprecht of Bavaria:

> The censorship lies in the hands of the Deputy Commanding Generals! They have become twenty-odd shadow governments placed alongside the . . . provinces and even the states, and in this manner work is duplicated, not in collaboration, but rather alongside or even against each other. Their actual task, besides the regulation of army reserves and the training of troops, should be the maintenance of order; but their areas of operation are continually being widened and their staffs are continually being expanded. . . . Instead of order, there is a maze of ordinances and, as a consequence, disorder![32]

The subjugation of Germany to this incredible Law of Siege, however, merely marked the beginning of the process of military interference in internal affairs during the war. It was simply assumed that all matters connected with the conduct of war fell within the exclusive domain of the military authorities. They were placed in a position from which it was relatively easy for them and even necessary for them to expand

[32] Kronprinz Rupprecht von Bayern, *In Treue fest. Mein Kriegstagebuch*, 3 vols., Munich, 1929, I, p. 457.

their power. The vague prerogatives of the Deputy Commanding Generals inevitably involved them in economic and social affairs the moment such questions assumed major importance for the war effort. Furthermore, the procurement of men, munitions, weapons, and other supplies for the field army was the sole responsibility of the Prussian War Ministry, a ministry which, in contrast to Britain and France, was under military, not civilian, control. At the same time the poorly developed central administration of the Empire and the lack of preparation of the civil authorities to assume responsibility for the economic mobilization were open invitations to military intervention.

The Law of Siege, however, also demonstrated that the military apparatus was by no means ideally organized to meet the needs of modern war. The extreme decentralization represented by the Law of Siege and the lack of responsibility of the Deputy Commanding Generals to the War Ministry were the military counterparts of the administrative decentralization of the Empire in peacetime, and they arose from the same causes. The government leaders were well aware of the inadequacies of the Law of Siege and were conscious of the need for new legislation which would insure unity of command and practice. They also knew how easily the coexistence of military and civilian administrations led to conflict and abuse since a situation analogous to that created by the Law of Siege had caused a succession of scandals in Alsace-Lorraine before the war. Nevertheless the government had refrained from presenting a new Law of Siege to the Reichstag just as it had refrained from correcting the abuses in Alsace-Lorraine during the notorious Zabern Affair of 1913. It feared that the presentation of basic questions affecting the organization and powers of the army to the Reichstag would lead to interference with the Emperor's "power of command" (*Kommandogewalt*). As in the case of the civil administration, so in the case of the army, the safeguarding of authoritarian prerogatives could only be accomplished at the cost of increasing obsolescence and absurdity.[33]

Indeed the administrative muddle necessitated by the protection of the Emperor's power of command was evident throughout the military apparatus. There was no clear chain of command in the top echelons of the army. The War Minister, the Chief of the General Staff, the Chief of the Military Cabinet, and all of the Commanding Generals had the right to report directly to the Emperor (*Immediatbericht*). The War Minister, who had the task of defending the army's policies before the Reichstag, was thus denied a position as sole adviser to the Emperor on military affairs. His situation was made all the more unenviable by the deliberate efforts of the Emperor and the General Staff to deprive him of a role in the formulation of policy in order to keep the Reichstag from interfering in military matters. That this effort to reduce the War Minister to the role of instrument and defender of the actions of other agencies created a highly disturbing fragmentation of responsibility in Germany's military organization and that it did considerable harm to the formulation of a unified military policy was regarded as secondary to the struggle against parliamentary control of the army.[34]

The anachronistic organizational policy of the army was complemented by an equally anachronistic personnel policy. Despite the fact that the German army was a mass army based upon universal military training, the composition of the officer corps was determined by those same class prejudices which were so important in the recruitment of the bureaucracy. Although it had been impossible to retain the numerical preponderance of the Junker element because of the large number of bourgeois officers in the South German contingents and because of the growth of the army, the Junkers were still

[33] Clemens von Delbrück, *Die wirtschaftliche Mobilmachung in Deutschland 1914*, Munich, 1924, pp. 96ff.

[34] Gordon Craig, *The Politics of the Prussian Army, 1640-1945*, Oxford, 1955, pp. 228-232.

favored with the best regiments and the aristocratic spirit was widely inculcated. The recruitment of bourgeois elements for the regular officers corps was done almost exclusively from "reliable" groups, i.e., the sons of officers, bureaucrats, pastors, landowners, and businessmen. The institution of the reserve officer provided Germany's rulers with one of their most effective means of "feudalizing" the bourgeoisie. Here, again, selective recruitment was coupled with indoctrination in the ethos and values of the aristocratic officer. These policies led not only to ludicrously exaggerated behaviour on the part of the parvenue bourgeois officers, but also to a serious disregard of military considerations. In 1913 the War Ministry actually went so far as to justify a refusal to create three new army corps on the grounds that it could not find the "proper" type of officer to staff them![35]

While the army made use of the technological discoveries of modern science and employed the products of modern industry, the officer corps was by no means imbued with their spirit. Generally speaking, the German army officer was poorly trained in scientific and economic matters and felt a very aristocratic disdain for mercenary pursuits. Similarly, he had contempt for politics and, while usually identifying himself as a conservative, was singularly ignorant of political and social problems. Thus, measured in terms of social composition, education, and ethos, the officer corps of the German army was poorly prepared to assume the directing role in internal affairs which it was to be given during the war and inherently reluctant to demand the full mobilization of the civilian sector of society. If it had accommodated itself to the mass army, it still retained the notion that "calm is the first duty of the citizen" during a military crisis.[36]

[35] Karl Demeter, *Das deutsche Offizierkorps in Gesellschaft und Staat, 1650-1945*, 2d edn., Frankfurt a.M., 1962, pp. 14ff., and Eckart Kehr, "Zur Genesis des Kgl. Preussischen Reserveoffiziers," *Die Gesellschaft*, 1928, II, pp. 492-502.

[36] The famous proclamation of the Commander of Berlin after the battle of Jena. On the problem of officer education and ideology, see

German "militarism," properly understood, involved much more than simply the primacy of military over political considerations. Indeed, German militarism had very little to do with the maintenance of the army as an effective instrument for the defense of the nation. It was above all a social phenomenon whose fundamental characteristics were the preservation of those retarded social attitudes and authoritarian institutions associated with the officer corps and the development of a feeling of respect and admiration for these attitudes and institutions in the public at large. The officer was placed at the pinnacle of society and the barracks were regarded as the school of the nation. The inflated social status of the officer corps encouraged the military men to have contempt for the civilian authorities and encouraged large segments of the public to share this attitude and expect miracles from the army.[37]

Under conditions of total mobilization, these tendencies would threaten to radicalize German militarism. In its traditional form, this militarism was conservative in that it formed an integral part of an authoritarian state structure which separated large segments of German society from active participation in the affairs of the state. Even before the war, however, there were signs that a radical brand of militarism was developing in Germany. Significantly, this type of militarism made its most marked appearance in the navy, where officers of middle-class origin were in the vast majority. The agitation for the naval building program was accompanied by the use of modern propaganda techniques, lobbying in the Reichstag, and close collaboration between the navy and industrial pressure groups. This "democratization" of militarism and imperialism was as fateful for Germany's internal politics as it was for her

---

Demeter, *Deutsche Offizierkorps*, pp. 69ff., and F. C. Endres, "Soziologische Struktur und ihre entsprechende Ideologien des deutschen Offizierkorps vor dem Weltkriege," *Archiv für Sozialwissenschaft und Sozialpolitik*, 58, 1927, pp. 282-319.

[37] Wolfgang Sauer, "Militarismus," in Ernst Fraenkel and Karl Dietrich Bracher, eds., *Staat und Politik*, Frankfurt a.M., 1957, pp. 190-192.

foreign policy. It demonstrated that a more popular brand of militarism could be used to divert the nation from pressing internal problems and lead it on a policy of adventure. Similar tendencies, however, were also evident among non-Junker elements in the General Staff of the army, where the head of the Operations Section, Colonel Erich Ludendorff and the heavy artillery expert, Major Max Bauer, agitated in 1912-1913 for more troops and technical improvements with the aid of the Pan-German press and the support of industrialists in defiance of the War Ministry. There were men, in short, who were prepared to break the traditional bonds of German militarism. Such men would not find total war alien. On the contrary, their ignorance of all that lay outside the military problems to which they had narrowly devoted their lives and their lack of emotional attachment to older forms and traditions would lead them to idealize total war, to make of total mobilization a vision of the society of the future.[38]

In 1914, however, the enormously important role which the army would play in social and economic affairs was not realized by anyone, and the relationship between the army, on the one side, and the government, the parties, and the pressure groups, on the other, was not defined. If the army leadership had a certain contempt for the civilian bureaucrats, it was not without a bureaucracy and bureaucratic attitudes of its own, and the military and civilian leaders shared the same social origins and political attitudes. Although the army had always found the partisan conflict in the Reichstag extremely irritating, the unanimity of August 4, 1914, left the future relationship between the army and the Reichstag an open question. Lastly, the attitude of the army toward the social question was as unclear as it was untested. Many German employers made a practice of modeling factory discipline upon military discipline and of refusing to hire workers until they had served in the army. The army officers may have shared many of the con-

[38] Eckart Kehr, "Klassenkämpfe und Rüstungspolitik im Kaiserlichen Deutschland," *Die Gesellschaft*, 1932, I, pp. 391-414.

servative proclivities of the industrialists, but they were by no means formally committed to the capitalistic system as it existed in prewar Germany. As mentioned above, the ethos of the officer corps had its roots in a precapitalistic age, and this ethos could open the way toward a policy of paternalistic concern, fair play, and noblesse oblige toward the workers. Furthermore, there is some evidence that many officers were aware of the need to adapt the army to the needs of a mass industrial society. Although unalterably opposed to the internationalism of the Socialists, they were potentially receptive to a more nationally oriented "Prussian socialism." Finally, it would not be impossible for the officer corps to come to terms with the Social Democratic Party under such a system, a party whose exceptional discipline and organization owed much to the son of a noncommissioned officer, August Bebel, and which was not as far removed from the Prussian military tradition as its leaders wished to think.[39]

The sudden catapulting of the army into its totally unanticipated position as director of Germany's economic life and arbiter of the nation's social and political conflicts placed on the army the burden of mastering and overcoming a dismal heritage of administrative confusion, political bitterness, and social tension. As in the Wars of Liberation and the Wars of Unification, so in the World War, the army became an agent of revolution from above in order to prevent revolution from below, an agent linking the old order and the new.

[39] Christian Helfer, "Über militärische Einflüsse auf die industrielle Entwicklung in Deutschland," *Schmollers Jahrbuch für Gesetzgebung, Verwaltung und Volkswirtschaft*, 83, 1963, pp. 597-609; Otto-Ernst Schüddekopf, *Das Heer und die Republik. Quellen zur Politik der Reichswehrführung 1918 bis 1933*, Hannover and Frankfurt, a.M., 1955, pp. 9-11; Oswald Spengler, *Preussentum und Sozialismus*, Munich, 1920, p. 91.

PART ONE

The Old Regime and the Dilemmas of Total War

I

The Production, Manpower, and Social Policies of the Prussian War Ministry, 1914-1916

1. The War Ministry and Its Leaders

THE ANALYSIS of the German army's role in social and economic affairs during the war, and particularly during the first two years of the war, requires concentration upon the activities of the Prussian War Ministry, since it was there that the economic and social policies of the army were first defined. In the baffling mélange of secretariats, ministries, and cabinets which administered the Empire, the position of the War Ministry was particularly confusing. The War Ministry was at once a bureaucratic and a military organization. These two characteristics interacted in peculiar ways at different times. The military passion for organization and inflexible lines of authority served to intensify bureaucratic tendencies. At the same time military insistence upon decisive action and the absolute priority of its own demands also encouraged breaking through bureaucratic reservations. Yet in being a ministry among ministries, in its constant contact with a wider range of considerations and problems than was usual for military organizations, the War Ministry was forced to harmonize its military concerns with the broader demands made by and upon those managing the state.

In the prewar period the power and prestige of the War Ministry had suffered because of the influence and independence of the General Staff. This situation might have gone unchanged had it not been for the appointment of the Prussian War Minister, Erich von Falkenhayn, as Deputy Chief of the General Staff to replace the ailing Moltke on October 25, 1914, and his subsequent appointment as Chief of the General Staff on December 9, 1914. While the failure of the Schlieffen Plan at the First Battle of the Marne in September meant a lengthening of the war and hence the need for greater coordination between the General Staff and the War Ministry in matters of manpower and munitions, the appointment and views of General von Falkenhayn necessarily raised this question in its sharpest form.

Erich von Falkenhayn was fifty-three years old when appointed Chief of the General Staff, a remarkably young age for this position. He had, in fact, outpaced thirty older men in securing the highest position in the German army, and this in itself is some reflection of his considerable abilities. What distinguished Falkenhayn from the vast majority of his fellow officers was his grasp of political problems and his conviction that Clausewitz' teaching of the primacy of politics in warfare was not simply to be prated, but rather to be acted upon. He combined this with a belief in the need for complete unity of direction in the conduct of modern warfare. Falkenhayn's views did not receive much support, and he always felt isolated. This loneliness was intensified by his cool, oversensitive, and somewhat vain personality. That Falkenhayn, when appointed Chief of the General Staff, should have sought to continue in his position as War Minister was thus the natural consequence of his belief in a coordinated military policy and of his personal desire to do the coordinating.[1]

As General von Roon had gone to General Headquarters in 1870 to make sure that no important decisions were made without the cooperation of the War Minister, so Falkenhayn, consciously emulating Roon, left for the front in August 1914. On August 31 he appointed the military governor of Cologne, General von Wandel, as Deputy War Minister. This arrangement was continued when Falkenhayn replaced Moltke. In this way he hoped to insure the rapid satisfaction of the needs

[1] Heinz Kraft, "Das Problem Falkenhayn. Eine Würdigung der Kriegführung des Generalstabschefs," *Die Welt als Geschichte*, 21, 1962, pp. 51, 68-77; Freiherr von Freytag-Loringhoven, *Menschen und Dinge wie ich sie in meinem Leben sah*, Berlin, 1932, p. 282.

of the field army and cut through bureaucratic procedures. Neither the Chancellor nor highly placed individuals in military circles showed much enthusiasm for the arrangement. Bethmann objected on constitutional grounds, pointing out that the combination of an office responsible to the Reichstag with an office responsible to the Emperor was dangerous to the Emperor's power of command. Falkenhayn himself recognized the validity of this argument. The situation was much aggravated, however, by attacks on Falkenhayn's military leadership. General von Moltke, now in charge of General Staff headquarters in Berlin, accused Falkenhayn of letting operations bog down in the West, a judgment widely held in the offensive-minded officer corps. The great victories of Hindenburg and Ludendorff were used to make Falkenhayn appear a sluggard. Hindenburg had already launched his two and a half year struggle with Falkenhayn over manpower for the Eastern Command's projected campaigns. In fact an atmosphere charged with intrigue had developed in which the dismissal of Falkenhayn as Chief of the General Staff and his replacement by Hindenburg, with Ludendorff as Quartermaster General, might have been seriously considered had it not been for the general agreement that Hindenburg and Ludendorff were indispensable in the East.[2]

On January 11, 1915, Falkenhayn, at the Chancellor's behest, surrendered his position as Prussian War Minister to his First Quartermaster General, Wild von Hohenborn. The latter appeared a fine choice, not only because of his experience in the War Ministry, where he had served as Director of the General War Department, but also because of his closeness to the Emperor, whose schoolmate he had been. Wild von Hohen-

[2] Erich von Falkenhayn, *Die Oberste Heeresleitung 1914-1916*, Berlin, 1920, p. 2; Rudolf Schmidt-Bückeburg, *Das Militärkabinett der preussischen Könige und deutschen Kaiser*, Berlin, 1933, pp. 254-255; Helmuth von Moltke, *Erinnerungen, Briefe und Dokumente, 1877-1916*, Stuttgart, 1922, pp. 395-398; Walther Görlitz, ed., *Regierte der Kaiser? Kriegstagebücher, Aufzeichnungen und Briefe des Chefs des Marinekabinetts Admiral Georg Alexander von Müller 1914 bis 1918*, Göttingen, 1959, pp. 79-82.

born had Falkenhayn's complete confidence and shared the view that the War Minister belonged at General Headquarters, not in Berlin:

> The view that the War Minister is a domestic administrative chief is false. Certainly the activity at home is *greater in scope*, but the activity at General Headquarters is *no less* important. It is just because the work that has to be done at home is so great that the head of business there cannot at the same time judge the great Whole [*grosse Ganze*]. And no War Minister ought to shut himself off from a judgment of the entire situation. He has not only to advise his King in common with the Chief of the General Staff, but he must also have a certain influence on the conduct of the war in general, to prevent the impossible, to set the bounds of the possible, and, as the most intimate representative of the Chief of the General Staff, to anticipate his intentions and prepare at a distance for their fulfillment. Berlin *carries out* what is *conceived* and recognized as possible at General Headquarters.[3]

Wild knew that his ability to play such a role was dependent upon the closeness of his relationship with Falkenhayn:

> We discussed *everything*, operational questions, politics, personnel: there was no holding back of intentions and views. I had set up my wigwam in the building of the General Staff; each came into the other's room without appointment, we took our meals in common—in short, the strange spectacle of a complete fusion of General Staff and War Ministry was a fact.[4]

The relationship between the two men was based neither on personal friendship nor upon a complete harmony of views, but rather on the belief that a bridging of the gap between General Staff and War Ministry was vital to the war effort.

[3] Notation of Jan. 20, 1916, BA, Nachlass Wild von Hohenborn, Nr. 2.
[4] Wild von Hohenborn to Prof. Zorn, Jan. 1, 1916, *ibid.*, Nr. 6. See also

Wild would never have been able to remain at Falkenhayn's side, however, had it not been for their confidence in General von Wandel. The latter's reliability, skill, and energy insured that business would be well-managed in Berlin. An ex-officer in the War Ministry has left a fine portrait of this rather anonymous administrator:

> . . . large, extremely tall, a typical Prussian military figure of the old style, a man of unshakable calm. He seemed at first uncivil, but that was only appearance. In reality he possessed, beneath his initial impassiveness, not only eager interest in the material being presented by the reporter, but also personal interest. To report to him was not easy. He demanded the greatest brevity and was so precisely oriented about completely diverse things that at the conclusion one had the feeling many times of having said absolutely nothing new to the Minister. One can only measure the meaning of this overall view which extended down to the particular by the almost tropical growth of the Ministry during the war.[5]

2. *The KRA*

The growth of the War Ministry was greatly accelerated by the establishment of a Raw Materials Section (*Kriegsrohstoffabteilung* [KRA]) in August 1914, an organization which saved the German war effort from disaster and which, particularly in the later years of the war, was to have a profound influence on Germany's wartime economy. The state of Germany's raw materials supply in August 1914 was incredibly precarious. In a questionnaire sent out by the Imperial Office of the Interior to nine hundred large firms, it was discovered that they had, on the average, stores of raw materials for a half year of war.[6] While the problematic nature of Germany's

Freytag-Loringhoven, *Menschen und Dinge*, p. 273, and Falkenhayn, *Oberste Heeresleitung*, pp. 2-3.

[5] Heinrich Spiero, *Schicksal und Anteil. Ein Lebensweg in deutscher Wendezeit*, Berlin, 1929, p. 235.

[6] Alfred Müller, *Die Kriegsrohstoffbewirtschaftung 1914-1918 im Dienste des deutschen Monopolkapitals*, Berlin, 1955, p. 14n3.

raw materials supply had been recognized before the war, the expectation that the war would be short and that large stores could be seized in occupied areas resulted in a total lack of preparation. It was due to the initiative of two men outside of the government, Wichard von Moellendorff and Walther Rathenau, that the emergency was recognized and the KRA established.

It is no accident that the proposal for a careful investigation and centralized control of raw materials stores came from ranking members of the General Electric Company (*Allgemeine Elektrizitäts Gesellschaft* [AEG]), one of Germany's greatest cartels, in which the centralized procurement of a wide variety of raw materials was essential to the conduct of operations. Nor is it an accident that the form which the KRA took reflected the AEG's organization and Moellendorff's and Rathenau's belief in an economy in which centralized state planning was combined with large-scale private industrial organization. Moellendorff, an engineer by profession and a high official in the AEG's metals division, tended to be the more radical of the two. A disciple of the American efficiency expert, Frederick W. Taylor, Moellendorff believed that a radical reorganization of industry was needed to insure the maximum utilization of industrial technology. Rathenau, the head of AEG, was of a more philosophical bent and regarded industrial reorganization as the key to attacking sterile mechanization and poverty and to solving the dilemmas created by the increasing separation of ownership from control. Finally, both the engineer of Prussian noble family Moellendorff and the Jewish industrialist Rathenau shared an intense admiration for Prussia and the Prussian spirit of self-sacrifice, discipline, and conservative reform.[7]

Moellendorff, whose work gave him an intimate knowledge

[7] Ralph H. Bowen, *German Theories of the Corporative State. With Special Reference to the Period 1870-1890*, New York and London, 1947, pp. 164-218; Fritz Redlich, "German Economic Planning for War and Peace," *Review of Politics*, VI, July 1944, pp. 319-326; Mendelssohn-Bartholdy, *War and German Society*, pp. 223-230.

of the metals supply, was the first to warn of the dangers Germany faced if the English established a tight blockade. On August 8, 1914, he sent a note to Rathenau asking that the War Ministry be made aware of the situation and proposing that the raw materials supply be statistically determined and that controls be established through a central authority. Although Rathenau placed great hope in what could be found in Belgium, he shared Moellendorff's concern and discussed the situation with Colonel Scheüch, the head of the General War Department, on the evening of the same day. Scheüch must have been impressed because Rathenau was summoned to an interview with the War Minister on August 9. At the close of the interview Falkenhayn not only agreed to establish an organization in his Ministry, but also insisted that Rathenau be its leader. In so doing Falkenhayn demonstrated a flexibility and modernity quite at odds with the bureaucratic and conservative reputation of the War Ministry, for not only did he declare himself ready to intervene in an area falling within the competence of the Interior Office, but he also offered the leadership of the new section to a civilian and a Jew. Falkenhayn did run into some difficulties with conservative members of his own ministry, but he prevailed, and the KRA was set up a few days after the interview.[8]

The organization thus established was completely novel in both its personnel and methods. Rathenau not only asked his two closest collaborators in the AEG, Professor Klingenberg and Moellendorff, but also invited other leading industrial and financial leaders to take part in the KRA's administration. The KRA, in short, was staffed by many men closely connected with the industries using the raw materials which were to be controlled. For Rathenau, "conflict of interest" was never an issue. His entire object was to combine compulsion with industrial

[8] Otto Goebel, *Deutschlands Rohstoffwirtschaft im Weltkrieg*, Stuttgart, 1930, p. 20; Walther Rathenau, *Politische Briefe*, Dresden, 1929, pp. 7-8; Walther Rathenau, "Germany's Provisions for Raw Materials," translated in R. H. Lutz, ed., *Fall of the German Empire*, 2 vols., Stanford, Stanford University Press, 1932, II, pp. 77-79.

self-government and to have industrial experts serve as the instruments of a national policy. On the less idealistic side, the control of raw materials could only be accomplished by individuals who had the experience and skill to manage such an operation. Also, the fact that an industrialist of Rathenau's prestige headed the organization and that industrialists served in its administration undoubtedly smoothed the way for accomplishing the difficult tasks ahead.[9]

Although the necessity of compulsion was clear, the method had to be one which did not bring industry into a condition of utter chaos. The KRA had neither the time, the facilities, nor the personnel to sequester, account for, and reapportion raw materials. Instead, a modified system of requisitioning was adopted. Not ownership, but right of disposal, was regulated. Scarce raw materials could only be distributed to those firms producing goods directly or indirectly of service to the war effort on the basis of a system of priorities.

Rathenau and his colleagues had a hard time finding a legal basis for this system. Thanks to the enthusiasm of the early days of the war, they were able to secure the permission of the Bavarian, Saxon, and Württemberg war ministries to centralize the control of raw materials in the Prussian War Ministry. In relying upon the Law of Siege, however, many of the benefits of centralization were lost due to the independent and inconsistent policies of the Deputy Commanding Generals. Considerable improvement was made on July 24, 1915, by a Bundesrat decree officially centralizing the control of raw materials in the War Ministry.[10]

The ultimate purpose of the KRA's work was to insure that the raw materials were distributed to the firms needing them. The process of collecting and distributing raw materials had to be centralized and efficiently organized. To accomplish this

[9] Werner Richter, *Gewerkschaften, Monopolkapital und Staat im ersten Weltkrieg und in der Novemberrevolution*, Berlin, 1959, pp. 82-83; Lutz, *Fall of the German Empire*, II, pp. 83-84.

[10] Lutz, *Fall of the German Empire*, II, pp. 80-81; Goebel, *Deutschlands Rohstoffwirtschaft*, pp. 102-106.

end, a system of War Raw Materials Corporations (*Kriegsrohstoffgesellschaften*) was created, a system of private stock companies established under government auspices to buy, store, and distribute raw materials. That this system was an application of Rathenau's philosophy of industrial reorganization may be seen from his own description:

> On the one hand, it meant a step in the direction of state socialism. For commerce was no longer free, but had become restricted.
>
> On the other hand, it meant the attempt to encourage self-administration of our industries. How were such contradictory doctrines to be made to agree? . . .
>
> The system of war corporations is based upon self-administration; yet that does not signify unrestricted freedom. The War Raw Materials Corporation was established under strict government supervision. The corporations serve the interests of the public at large; they neither distribute dividends nor apportion profits; in addition to the usual organs of stock companies, a board of governors and a supervising committee, they have another independent organ, a committee of appraisement and distribution, made up of members selected from various chambers of commerce, or of government officials. This committee serves as an intermediary between the stock companies, representing capitalism, and the government—an economic innovation which may be destined to become generally accepted in future times.[11]

The system was not quite as ideal as Rathenau indicated. If the industrialists who invested in the war corporations received no dividends or direct profits from their investments, they still expected a reward in the form of a preferred position for their firms in raw materials distribution. Since only the largest firms could afford to invest in the war corporations, the system necessarily favored their interests. Rathenau fought

[11] Lutz, *Fall of the German Empire*, II, p. 84. I have changed the translation by using the term "war corporations" instead of "war boards."

the tendency to use the war corporations for personal advantage. His chief weapon was the corporations' financial need, for the investors were incapable of financing the societies by themselves and the banks were unwilling to invest large sums in ventures that could suddenly collapse due to a quick peace. In return for a government guarantee of their loans from the banks, the war corporations were forced to accept committees of appraisement and distribution, which they had initially opposed, and government commissars to watch over their activities.[12]

Rathenau's term of office in the KRA was, indeed, filled with difficulty. Industrialists objected to restrictions on many raw materials, and the civil authorities were not easy to deal with. The sharp rise of textile and metal prices in the fall of 1914 made the control of prices imperative, but the Imperial Office of the Interior declared this impossible. Rathenau then proceeded to arrange price ceilings with the industrialists themselves and, in early December, established the first such prices in Germany. Negotiations over prices, however, did not always run smoothly.[13]

On April 1, 1915, Rathenau resigned his position as head of the KRA. In his letter of resignation he pointed out that the organizational work was now complete and the time had come to integrate the KRA, which had attained the size of a normal ministry, with the rest of the War Ministry by placing it under military leadership. While there is evidence that Rathenau in fact had always expected to resign once his organization had been firmly established, there is also some evidence that his resignation was "not quite voluntary." That Rathenau had difficulties with the more bureaucratic elements in the War Ministry, with resistant industrialists, and with uncomprehending Deputy Commanding Generals is unquestionable.[14]

[12] Otto Wiedenfeld, *Rohstoffversorgung*, Berlin, 1917, pp. 7-8; Müller, *Kriegsrohstoffbewirtschaftung*, pp. 38-39.

[13] Lutz, *Fall of the German Empire*, II, p. 85; Rathenau, *Politische Briefe*, pp. 164-165.

[14] Rathenau, *Politische Briefe*, pp. 37-38; Spiero, *Schicksal*, p. 243;

It is equally certain, however, that Rathenau was very pleased with his successor, Major Josef Koeth. The son of a South German lawyer, Koeth had begun his military career in the Bavarian army. Despite an extraordinary record, he was not promoted to the Bavarian General Staff, and his disappointment led him to seek service in the Prussian army in 1899. He worked in the Prussian War Ministry from 1910 to August 1914, when he was sent to the front. In November 1914 he was called back to the War Ministry in connection with the serious munitions crisis, of which more will be said later. What undoubtedly made Koeth most appealing to Rathenau was Koeth's understanding of and sympathy for Rathenau's ideas. Koeth in fact shared many of Rathenau's philosophical concerns and was himself on intimate terms with scholars and scientists. These qualities, combined with considerable personal warmth, politeness, and humor, were to earn Koeth a respect and admiration that would serve him well in his position as one of the most powerful and feared men in German economic life.[15]

The KRA was undoubtedly the most successful economic organization created by Germany during the war. It demonstrated that lack of economic preparation did not preclude a successful meeting of difficulties during the war, provided that the needs were quickly recognized and that measures were taken without excessive delays. The prescience of Moellendorff and Rathenau and the receptivity of Falkenhayn saved Germany from a raw materials crisis which might have meant defeat. This was particularly the case in the critical area of nitrates production. At the same time, the establishment of raw materials controls was an important step in the direction of mobilization for total war, for the denial of scarce raw materials for production judged to be nonvital necessarily accel-

---

W. F. Bruck, *Economic and Social History of Germany from William II to Hitler, 1888-1938*, Cardiff, 1938, p. 140; Redlich, *Review of Politics*, VI, pp. 316-317.

15 Redlich, *Review of Politics*, VI, pp. 317-319.

erated the efforts of affected industries to produce wartime products. In the early years of the war, the KRA's powers were only partially applied because of government policy and the availability of coal and iron. But by establishing the KRA the War Ministry now had the capacity to maim or even to strangle nonessential industries should the need arise.

3. *Production Policy and Procurement*

It cannot be said that the War Ministry mastered the problems of procuring matériel for the army with quite the effectiveness which it had displayed in managing the raw materials situation. Here, again, the problems were not anticipated before the war. The consumption of ammunition in the Russo-Japanese War had impressed German observers, and the General Staff and War Ministry had set up a new munitions production program in 1912. This program was only partially completed in 1914, the remainder being either in production or delayed for financial reasons. Assuming, however, that the 1912 program had been fulfilled, it would still have proved totally inadequate. None of the belligerents had even approximately anticipated the amount of ammunition that was to be expended in the first months of the war.[16]

General Sieger, the head of the Field Army Munitions Service, had warned at the very beginning of the campaign that ammunition had to be saved, but "he was told by the Great General Staff that the campaign would not last so long and that it was unnecessary to save."[17] By October 1914 all the reserves were used up, and the army was left completely dependent upon new production. This munitions crisis, which was intensified in November, had a very negative effect on the conduct of military operations. It rendered the resumption of offensive operations in the West impossible and intensified Falkenhayn's

[16] Ludwig Wurtzbacher, "Die Versorgung des Heeres mit Waffen und Munition," Max Schwarte, ed., *Der Grosse Krieg 1914-1918*, 10 vols., Berlin, 1921-1933, VIII, p. 71.

[17] Görlitz, *Regierte der Kaiser?*, p. 66.

resistance to the pressure of Hindenburg and Ludendorff for a big campaign in the East.[18]

The task of formulating munitions policy belonged to the Army Section of the General War Department of the Prussian War Ministry, which in 1914 was headed by Colonel Ernst von Wrisberg. Wrisberg appears to have been only vaguely informed of what was happening at the front due to the speed of events. The need was clear enough, however, for the Department to have set up a new program on October 12. This program, which was designed on the basis of the shortage in raw materials, particularly saltpeter, was declared totally insufficient by Falkenhayn on October 22. He demanded that as many factories as possible be called upon to produce weapons and munitions. At a meeting in Berlin on October 30, however, Falkenhayn was forced to moderate his demands and accept the War Ministry program, for the shortage of explosives made an unlimited munitions program impossible.[19]

Falkenhayn did not rely completely on War Ministry machinery, but also took measures of his own by sending personal representatives to negotiate with the big industrialists. He made particular use of Major Max Bauer, the artillery expert on the General Staff, who had good connections with the industrialists because of his work. In November, Bauer negotiated with Professor Rausenberger of the Krupp firm, Dr. Schrödter of the Association of German Iron and Steel Industrialists, and Privy Councilor Carl Duisberg of the Bayer Dye Factories in Leverküsen. The success of Bauer's efforts may be measured by a letter Duisberg sent to him on July 24, 1915:

"If you were now to see how things are here in Leverküsen, how the whole factory is turned upside down and reorganized so that it produces almost nothing but military contracts, . . .

[18] Reichsarchiv, *Der Weltkrieg 1914-1918*, 14 vols., Berlin, 1925ff., V, pp. 560-561.

[19] Ernst von Wrisberg, *Wehr und Waffen 1914-1918*, Leipzig, 1922, pp. 84-86. In April 1915 Wrisberg replaced Scheüch as head of the entire General War Department.

then you, as father and initiator of this production, would be filled with great joy."[20]

Duisberg's patriotism is unquestionable, but it would not be unfair to conclude that this man, who was "a strange mixture of chemical training and commercial sharpness," was more than happy to accept a new market that would substitute for the old foreign markets that had consumed 85 percent of his production.[21] Bauer's work received more disinterested praise in the form of an honorary doctorate from the University of Berlin for the development of certain types of heavy artillery in conjunction with Krupp. Generals Sieger and von Wrisberg were much less enthralled with Bauer. Both felt that he had intruded upon their areas of authority. The War Ministry had a particular distaste for the younger General Staff officers led by Bauer, the "demigods" with a penchant for circumventing channels in the promotion of their immoderate programs. There can be little doubt, given the evidence to be presented about Bauer's later career, that he was the chief proponent of the massive production program Falkenhayn had initially demanded of the War Ministry.[22]

The Ministry had very good reasons for disliking such programs. Germany's saltpeter supply was completely dependent upon imports from Chile, and these had been cut off by the war. Both munitions production and agricultural production depended upon nitrates and were thus threatened with disaster unless Germany could make herself independent in the production of nitrates. In one of the truly great accomplishments of German technology, the basis for this independence was laid

[20] Duisberg to Bauer, July 21, 1915, BA, Nachlass Bauer, Nr. 11.

[21] Wild von Hohenborn's characterization of Duisberg in a notation of Feb. 29, 1916, BA, Nachlass Wild von Hohenborn, Nr. 2; Carl Duisberg, *Abhandlungen, Vorträge und Reden aus dem Jahren 1882-1921*, Berlin and Leipzig, 1923, pp. 268-270.

[22] Falkenhayn, *Oberste Heeresleitung*, p. 38; Max Bauer, *Der Grosse Krieg im Feld und Heimat. Erinnerungen und Betrachtungen*, 3d ed., Tübingen, 1922, pp. 61, 85; Max Bauer, *Könnten wir den Krieg vermeiden, gewinnen, abbrechen? Drei Fragen beantwortet von Oberst Bauer*, Berlin, 1919, p. 17; Wrisberg, *Wehr und Waffen*, p. 73.

by Professor Fritz Haber and Dr. Robert Bosch under the pressure of the 1914 munitions crisis. It is no exaggeration to say that their mass utilization of the nitrogen fixation process, which they had discovered before the war, saved the German war effort. Rathenau and Haber persuaded the government to subsidize the building of the large plants needed to utilize the process. A "Bureau Haber" was set up in the War Ministry, which was soon to be expanded into the Chemicals Section of the KRA. A War Chemicals Corporation, set up by the KRA and headed by Wichard von Moellendorff, brought the various chemical industrialists into a powerful syndicate. Both the process and the organizations were new, however, and previous experience was nil. The production of sufficient quantities of nitrates would take time.[23]

It is absolutely essential for the understanding of the munitions policy of the War Ministry to recognize that, until 1918, weapons production had to have as its measure powder production, and that powder production depended upon nitrates production. Yet the situation was even more complex. Conditions at the front varied and needs changed. This introduced an element of uncertainty into the contracts given for the manufacture of artillery, shells, and fuses, for changes in demands from the front necessitated changes in the types ordered. The only way this uncertainty might have been eliminated was by the establishment of a program for the massive and continuous production of all types of artillery, shells, and fuses. Obviously such a program would have been expensive and wasteful, as it would have created a large inventory of weapons rendered useless by the insufficient powder supply. Such a program would also have been dangerous, for it would have required a large-scale exemption of skilled workers from military service. The alternative, which the War Ministry chose, was a policy which strove, on the one hand, for a steady increase in

[23] Schwarte, *Grosse Krieg*, VIII, pp. 79-81; Karl Helfferich, *Der Weltkrieg*, 3 vols., Berlin 1919, II, pp. 201-208; Walther Rathenau, *Briefe*, 2 vols., Dresden, 1926, II, p. 166.

powder production and, on the other hand, for a delicately balanced increase of weapons and ammunition production that would satisfy immediate needs and provide some reserves to meet shifts in the situation at the front.[24]

This policy was a source of continuous conflict with the industrialists. Most of them had not expected to produce for the army and, at the beginning, were not very happy about being requested to do so. The process of converting to war production for a short war was not regarded as a profitable venture. Spurred on by patriotism and substantial price increases, however, they had hearkened to Major Bauer's call.[25] But they were businessmen, and they wanted a steady customer. This the army was not:

> It has always been incomprehensible why the same fuses, the same grenades, had to be ordered from different firms at the same time, while these same firms were in the position to produce much more if they had to occupy themselves with only *one* sort of fuse or grenade. Our own firm, which previously had nothing to do with ammunition, had, when in the fall of 1914 a horrible munitions shortage developed and although the greatest speed was desired, to occupy itself with two different types of fuses. This was the case with many firms. Then our continuity was greatly damaged because for three quarters of a year we received no contracts, although we had repeatedly declared that we had created the facilities to produce 10,000 fuses a day. Three quarters of a year we lay completely unused and then we were called upon again . . . and again for two different types of fuses and, to be sure, not for those we had made earlier, but for completely *different* ones.[26]

[24] Schwarte, *Grosse Krieg*, VIII, p. 83.

[25] Bauer, *Grosse Krieg*, p. 61; Hermann Cron, *Inventar des Reichsarchivs. Die Kriegseisenwirtschaft*, Potsdam, 1929 (unpublished manuscript in the BHStA, Abt. IV), pp. 6-7.

[26] Statement by Dr. Waldschmidt of the Ludwig Löwe firm at a meeting in the War Ministry, Sept. 16, 1916, BHStA, Abt. IV, MK, K Mob 6, Bd. I, Bl. zu 12.

To such complaints the military authorities could only reply that they had to have the flexibility to meet changes at the front.

Even more bad blood was caused by changes in the army's demands for the types of steel to be used in producing weapons and ammunition. The need for ammunition and artillery in 1914 had led to the employment of an inferior grade of steel, the mass utilization of which had been made possible by the inventiveness of Major Koeth. This could only be a temporary measure, however, as such ammunition was not as effective as that manufactured from Thomas process and Martin process steel. By early 1915 the capacity to produce Thomas process steel had been vastly increased and contracts for the inferior type were cancelled. The industrialists were infuriated. They complained bitterly that they could supply the army with grenades, shells, and cannon in enormous quantities if only the War Ministry would let them. They accused the Ministry of depriving the men in the trenches of the weapons and munitions they needed.[27]

Industrialists' complaints about the utter chaos and confusion in the structure and operation of the procurement agencies were far more justified. There were over forty of them, and coordination was primitive in the extreme. Procurement directives for the most important military materials came from the General War Department, which also carried on some procurement itself. Most of the actual procurement, however, was in the hands of the Ordnance Master's Office (*Feldzeugmeisterei*), which was responsible to the General War Department. Lieutenant General Franke, as head of this organization, supervised the work of the weapons and munitions factories owned by the Prussian state and the contracting with private firms done through these factories. In addition each of the three other German war ministries had its own Ordnance Master's Office, and, while following Prussian War Ministry directives,

[27] Schwarte, *Grosse Krieg*, VIII, p. 83; Redlich, *Review of Politics*, VI, p. 317.

they did their own procuring. Procurement for the Pioneers (barbed wire, sand sacks, materials for building positions), communications services, air force, and navy were handled independently of the War Ministry by the branches concerned. Finally, individual army units engaged in limited amounts of procurement on their own.[28]

The only justification that one can find for this situation is that the military authorities expected to do very little private contracting in wartime, despite the fact that 60 percent of all military production was being produced by private firms before the war. A small number of firms which specialized in military production, such as Krupp, had large contracts, but by and large it was expected that maximum utilization of the state factories would be sufficient to satisfy the army's needs in wartime. Only shortly before the war did the Ministry think it advisable to investigate what firms might be brought into war production, but this investigation was in its infancy when the war broke out. Even worse, many of the trained personnel that the procurement agencies did have were sent into the field in August 1914.[29]

Procurement during the first months of the war was thus fated to be a financial disaster. The untrained personnel in the procurement agencies had only the vaguest idea as to where to turn when suddenly ordered to get as many firms as possible to produce war goods. The extent of the corruption is illustrated by an advertisement in one of Berlin's most respectable newspapers: "Army contracts secured under the most favorable terms by a gentleman who has the best possible connections with the authorities in question."[30] Unscrupulous middle-

[28] Wilhelm Dieckmann, *Die Behördenorganisation in der deutschen Kriegswirtschaft*, Hamburg, 1937, pp. 16-35.

[29] Reichsarchiv, *Kriegsrüstung und Kriegswirtschaft*, pp. 389-394. An exceptionally important study of procurement methods was made by Captain Büsselburg of the War Ministry in 1917; see Nachlass Groener, Nr. 198. See also Richard Sichler and Joachim Tiburtius, *Die Arbeiterfrage eine Kernfrage des Weltkrieges. Ein Beitrag zur Erklärung des Kriegsausgangs*, Berlin, 1925, pp. 5-6, 8-9.

[30] Quoted in Herbert Dierkopf, *Vorgeschichte, Entstehung und Aus-*

men and firms seeking quick profits took advantage of the ignorance and, in certain cases, veniality of procurement officials. The results were ludicrous. Firms producing elegant female clothing, for example, sought and received contracts to make knapsacks, cartridge cases, pistol holders, and the like. Business was done by telephone or by word of mouth, seldom in writing. Prices were not always stated and contracts were signed which were of the most unfavorable nature to the government. The proclivity of the procurement officials to agree to any price under the stress of emergency was complemented by an artificial forcing upward of prices due to the competition among the myriad of procurement agencies. In short, procurement at the beginning of the war was chaotic and corrupt.[31]

With the end of the initial emergency period, however, the army began to take energetic measures to correct the situation. Pressure from the Imperial Treasury Office, from industrialists angry at the chaos which had led to the giving of contracts to incompetent firms instead of their own, and from Reichstag deputies spurred the Ministry on in its own housecleaning operation. The Ordnance Master's Office set up an agency to review prices and contracts (*Preisprüfungsstelle*) in early 1915, and many of the abuses of the previous months were corrected. Clothing procurement for the army was centralized in the War Ministry. The Ministry went so far as to ban all use of middlemen in military contracting. This last measure, if anything, went too far and at times led to results the reverse of those the Ministry sought to achieve. In banning the legitimate as well as the illegitimate middlemen, the Ministry deprived itself of the services of just those individuals who had the best knowledge of where and by whom certain articles might have best been produced. As a result the Ministry tended to rely upon the best known firms, whether or not they actually had the labor and facilities to produce ever-increasing quan-

---

wirkungen des vaterländischen Hilfsdienstgesetzes vom 5. Dezember 1916, Halle, 1937, p. 86n44.

[31] Sichler and Tiburtius, *Arbeiterfrage*, p. 10.

tities of goods most efficiently and economically. Deserving firms of lesser reputation were overlooked, and the larger firms received undeserved benefits from this practice.[32]

If industrialists had cause to complain about the laxity of the procurement agencies at the beginning of the war, it did not take long before they were singing a different tune. The Ministry introduced a more stringent system of war contracts in 1915. Old ones were revised and new ones provided for the examination of company accounts, the sending of Ministry representatives to investigate company operations, and limitations on profits. Billions of marks were thus saved. The army's efforts to cut costs, however, were made extremely difficult by the fact that there was a shortage of producers. A system of competitive bidding was thus impossible. Furthermore, producers felt entitled to a high premium for the risk they were taking in producing for a war that might end any day and under changing military conditions that might lead to a sudden cancellation of their contracts. The War Ministry had to find a means of providing industry with the incentive to produce for the war effort and yet had to limit profits to maintain the financial solvency of the Empire and the equanimity of the Reichstag. The solution found satisfied no one. The War Ministry generally favored a contract under which the army paid for costs (such as material, risk, and overhead) and labor, and then paid a 5 or 10 percent profit on the total cost. That this form of contract did not favor cost reduction is obvious. In fact, by its willingness to pay a fixed percentage fee on the costs, the Ministry seemed to encourage high cost calculations and expenditures. It was to counteract this disadvantage that the Ministry introduced provisions for the examination of accounts and the sending of inspectors. Contracts were loaded down with clauses concerning the punishments to be incurred in case of miscalculation of costs or late delivery. In signing these contracts, industrialists were compelled to have visions

[32] Wrisberg, *Wehr und Waffen*, p. 123; Helfferich, *Weltkrieg*, II, pp. 213-214; Sichler and Tiburtius, *Arbeiterfrage*, pp. 10-11, 49-61.

not only of high profits, but also of heavy fines and even imprisonment.[33]

When representatives of the War Ministry told the Reichstag that industrialists were finding the Ministry's price policies "impossible" and its contracts "insulting," they were telling the truth. Industrialists complained bitterly about the Ministry's contract provisions and argued that a "careful businessman" was surrendering his reputation when he signed them. The Ministry was accused of ruining the ability and willingness of industry to produce for the war effort. Meetings between industrialist representatives and the War Minister were far from pleasant affairs. The Ministry was accused of conducting too much "price policy" and not enough "production policy." One industrialist went so far as to tell Wild straight to his face that the "tendency dominating the War Ministry is the root of all evil."[34]

The industrialists accused the War Ministry, and particularly the KRA, of totally disregarding the views of the civil authorities in their price policies. They were particularly prone to seeking support from Dr. Karl Helfferich, a former Director of the Deutsche Bank, who as State Secretary of the Treasury and, after May 1916, as State Secretary of the Interior was sympathetic to high profits on the grounds that this would benefit Germany's ability to compete on world markets after the war and keep the treasury supplied with tax money. Industrialists knew precisely where to go when the War Ministry issued an order stating that wartime was not the time for high profits:

> I would like to suggest . . . that the passage in the War

[33] Ernst von Wrisberg, *Heer und Heimat 1914-1918*, Berlin, 1921, pp. 102, 123.

[34] Wild von Hohenborn found these statements "somewhat one-sided." On the conflict between the Ministry and the industrialists, see BHStA, Abt. IV, MK, K Mob 6, Bd. I, Bl. zu 12; Nachlass Stresemann, 6865, frames H129495-H129496; Dierkopf, *Hilfsdienstgesetz*, p. 34. Also, see Wild's defense of his policies before the Reichstag Budget Committee on Oct. 21, 1916, HStASt, E, 130, V, X^{a}.30, hereinafter cited without archival reference.

WAR CONTRACTORS

My heart bleeds when I think that I must make so much money out of this horrible war!

Chin up, my dear friend—pocket it and do not despair!

Ministry's order stating that the factories are not to make large profits be made the occasion of a little petition to State Secretary Dr. Helfferich, asking the questions as to who then is supposed to pay all the taxes (very true!) and how our communities are supposed to exist, when the industrial firms are no longer able to pay taxes. . . . It will be very good when Herr Dr. Helfferich and Herr Dr. Havenstein [the President of the Reichsbank] are again and again presented with these views of the War Ministry, so that they can see what forces are at work to make it impossible for us to earn anything even for the state and communities.[35]

[35] Dr. Beumer at a VdESI meeting, March 24, 1916, BA, R 13I/148.

Major Koeth could not help expressing irritation at this continuous running "to the great, all-encompassing aunt of the Empire, the Imperial Office of the Interior, . . . which must have a bon-bon for everybody."[36]

It would be incorrect to say that there was no point to the arguments of the industrialists and to Helfferich's reservations concerning the War Ministry's methods. The calculation of costs and profits was, in fact, extremely difficult. Costs varied from location to location and from time to time. The actual long-range profits of firms which had reorganized their plants for war production could only be truly calculated after the war, when the value of newly built facilities for peacetime production could be ascertained. It was equally true that German industry would need a store of capital with which to reconquer its old markets. The War Ministry and the Imperial Office of the Interior were, in fact, in agreement that the actual prevention of excess war profits ultimately depended upon the success of the war profits tax passed by the Reichstag in 1915, which forced corporations to put fifty per cent of their profits into a reserve fund subject to future taxation. There is no question, however, that this law was totally inadequate, that it was full of loopholes, and that it in no way prevented the payment of large dividends or the building up of great silent reserves. The real issue for the War Ministry lay elsewhere. The War Ministry was less interested in stopping high profits than in keeping them within the bounds of the reasonable. The Ministry's arguments that reports of high dividends in the newspapers caused social bitterness, that high profits raised wages to dangerous levels, and that they ultimately burdened the economy by creating an inflationary situation made no impression on the industrialists. As the industrialists argued for massive weapons and munitions programs, so they argued that "He who performs extraordinarily under exceptional conditions has a right to exceptional compensation! High war profits are

[36] Reichstag Budget Committee meeting, Oct. 21, 1916.

thus thoroughly justified."[37] In the eyes of the War Ministry these demands were nothing less than an insistence that the war be run for industry's comfort and pleasure. They could find no justification, either military or political, for letting industry run wild with the nation's purse, morale, and manpower.

4. *The Battle for Manpower*

The War Ministry had made no provision for a planned distribution of manpower between front and factory. The war was expected both to disrupt international trade and to reduce domestic consumption and thus to create severe unemployment. Few recognized that this unemployment would be temporary and that it would be followed by a shortage of skilled workers in the factories producing for the war effort. Here again, the expectation of a short war and the complete reliance upon the initial campaign resulted in a miscalculation. In the effort to pour as much strength as possible into the field army, the question of providing skilled labor for the war industries was almost totally disregarded.[38]

The munitions crisis in the fall of 1914 thus created a serious labor problem. The use of unemployed textile workers, unskilled youths, and women could provide no immediate substitute for the skilled labor needed by the factories to meet the crisis. The result was a flood of demands from industry for the preservation of their labor force and the return of skilled workers from the front. Firms refused to accept contracts unless these conditions were met, and the hard-pressed procurement agencies were willing to support such demands before the Deputy Commanding Generals, who had the power of decision in these matters. The results were unsatisfactory because the procedure was chaotic. In some cases the field army, in other cases the factories, were suddenly deprived of vitally needed manpower.

[37] Speech by the business manager of the VdESI, Dr. Reichert, Nov. 16, 1916, BA, R 131/149. For the remaining material, see Reichstag Budget Committee, Oct. 21, 1916; Reichstag Debates, 306, Dec. 20, 1916, p. 484; Helfferich, *Weltkrieg*, II, pp. 224-231; Nachlass Stresemann, 6865, frame H129491.

[38] Dix, *Wirtschaftskrieg und Kriegswirtschaft*, p. 190.

At the end of 1914 the War Ministry decided to do something about the situation, and a discussion was held with representatives of the German Industry War Committee on exemption policy. The industrialists proposed that a committee of factory owners handle the problem, and the General War Department was inclined to agree with this solution. Nothing better illustrates the fog in which many of the military men found themselves at the beginning of the war than this willingness to hand the manpower question over to the industrialists. They demonstrated no understanding of the fact that industry and army were now competitors for manpower and that the problem of exemptions was intimately connected with the question of supplying reserves to the army. To have given industry the decisive voice in exemptions policy would have meant giving industry a decisive voice in reserves policy as well. Acting upon better advice, General von Wandel decided to set up a special agency in the War Ministry to deal with exemptions. To head the agency, Wandel chose Richard Sichler, a businessman not connected with the industries engaged in war production. Sichler was recommended to Wandel by private persons as a man of great organizational ability who would be certain to carry out his duties in a disinterested fashion.[39]

The organizational history of this agency is important because it demonstrates how long it took before the nature of the manpower problem was clearly recognized, and the problems involved in breaking through the anticivilian prejudices of the military men. In January 1915 Sichler's office was attached to the Factory Section (B 5), the section in charge of

[39] Sichler and Tiburtius, *Arbeiterfrage*, pp. 10-12. Before entering the Ministry, Sichler was in charge of recruitment for Kathreiners Malzkaffeefabriken. The late Dr. Tiburtius was West Berlin Senator for Education, and the information concerning Sichler is based on a letter from Dr. Tiburtius to the author of Nov. 19, 1962.

It should be noted that there were two categories of exempted workers: (1) the *Reklamierte*, those who had been released from the army for service in industry, and (2) the *Zurückgestellte*, those liable to military service who had never been drafted because they were needed at home.

worker questions in the state-owned factories. Thus the labor and economic questions arising from the war were still seen as an extension of the problems of these factories, upon whom the war production was supposed to rest. In April 1915 Sichler was forced into an unwanted merger with the Imports and Exports Section, and his agency thereafter became known as the "Exports and Exemptions Office," or AZS. This transfer was the result of a report Sichler had given in which he happened to mention that the labor question was complicated by the problems of exports and imports.

The next two organizational measures taken were much more realistic. By May 1915 the Ministry had recognized that the completely decentralized drafting of men for the army through the Deputy Commanding Generals was impossible in a long war. Population composition varied in each corps district, and because of the need to affect a more equitable distribution in the draft and to insure uniform composition in each call-up, the Ministry was granted a general right of disposal over all men of draftable age. The Deputy Commanding Generals were required to report on a monthly or more frequent basis the number of men they were obligated to supply the field army, reserve units, and industry, and the number of men available in their districts. The Reserves Section of the Ministry (Clb) then organized the actual distribution schedule for each call-up. It must not be forgotten, however, that the actual decision as to who was to be drafted and who was to be exempted still rested with the Deputy Commanding Generals.

The fact that the Reserves Section now had this strengthened position in the handling of the manpower situation made its union with AZS all the more desirable. Sichler, recognizing the close connection between the reserves and exemptions questions, had desired such a union from the beginning. On January 19, 1916, the two agencies were placed side by side under the leadership of Colonel Ritter und Edler von Braun. Collaboration between the two offices was far from what it should have been, however. Although the officers in the Ministry gave both support and recognition to the work of AZS, "they did not carry their respect so far as to forgive the leader of AZS for his civilian character and give him the position of a Section Head."[40] The union, in short, was formal, and the two agencies did not collaborate on a common manpower plan. Sichler's efforts to promote collaboration on such a plan and to bring representatives of the Supreme Command into the discussions was flatly turned down with the comment that "the General Staff did not have to trouble itself with the internal economic situation." In the development of exemptions policy, therefore, AZS was subjected to important limitations. It could not act upon but only react to the decisions made concerning the drafting of men for the army. While overseeing the establishment of exemptions policy, it did not have the power to insure its implementation. AZS could "suggest" or "request" that the Deputy Commanding Generals do something, but it could not compel them to obey. Finally, the control of three important categories of labor—prisoners of war, wounded soldiers, and foreign workers—lay in other sections of the War Ministry.[41]

The relations between AZS and industry were bound to be tense, but Sichler's personality was not designed to smooth away the difficulties. "A distinguished businessman and organizer, who demanded the utmost of himself and others, and who carried this to the point of want of consideration,"[42] Sichler did not suffer nonsense easily and completely disregarded polite usage when irritated. It did not take him long to have grounds for irritation. In a conference with Dr. Schrödter of the Association of German Iron and Steel Industrialists on March 20, 1915, Sichler warned that the massive recall from service of iron ore miners recently carried out at the Association's request could only be a temporary measure and inquired as to the possibility of increased employment of unskilled

40 Sichler and Tiburtius, *Arbeiterfrage*, pp. 12-13, 15.

41 Wrisberg, *Heer und Heimat*, pp. 105-106.

42 Letter from Senator Tiburtius to the author, Nov. 19, 1962.

labor, prisoners of war, women, and youth. Dr. Schrödter's reply was completely negative, and Sichler was forced to conclude that this answer was not completely honest, as many mines were already employing prisoners of war with success.[43]

This is not to say that the industrialists, and particularly the coal, iron, and steel industrialists, were not faced with difficult manpower problems. One of their greatest achievements had been the creation of a skilled and disciplined labor force in a relatively short period of time. They ruthlessly competed with one another for workers and at the same time sent agents to eastern Germany and eastern Europe who enticed entire villages to serve in the mines, foundries, and rolling mills of the Ruhr and Upper Silesia. The success of their efforts was very much endangered by the war. The mobilization had already robbed them of many of their best workers, and a War Ministry directive of April 1915 threatened to complete the process. Until this time the Ministry had pursued a policy of sending older, trained men to the front first on the theory that the war would be short and that the country would have greater need for younger men in the coming peace than for older ones who had already performed their functions as citizens and fathers. By spring 1915 the deficiences of this policy were recognized and both the army and industry were compelled to undergo a major change of personnel. The new directives compelled industry to surrender young, strong workers for older and weaker ones, for exemptions were now to be based upon ascending physical fitness. First to be exempted were men "liable to work duty" (a.v.), then those "liable to garrison duty" (g.v.), and finally those "liable to field duty" (k.v.) who were over thirty-nine years of age. Only in the most extreme cases were k.v. men below this age to be exempted.[44]

[43] Wrisberg, *Heer und Heimat*, pp. 105-106.

[44] On the labor problems of German heavy industry, see Otto Neuloh, *Die Deutsche Betriebsverfassung und ihre Sozialformen bis zur Mitbestimmung*, Tübingen, 1956, pp. 129-130. The directive of April 11, 1915, is reprinted as Anlage 7 of the "Richtlinien für die Behandlung der Arbeiterfrage in den für Kriegsbedarf tätigen Gewerbezweigen" sent to

While not blind to industry's difficulties, Sichler's position was that industry could be more flexible in the way it met its manpower needs than the army and had, therefore, to make the sacrifices. On June 15, 1915, "Guidelines" were sent out to the Deputy Commanding Generals for the handling of the worker question. They were told that before granting exemptions they were to make every attempt to find other forms of labor. Exempted workers were not to be employed in production designated for export or the consumer market, as many were in fact being employed. Before exemptions were made, the industrial inspectors were to be asked to investigate whether or not the requested workers were really needed and whether or not the number requested was excessive. Within this framework, everything possible was to be done to assist industry. If the generals did not have enough workers in their own districts, they were to get help from a neighboring district or contact AZS. In the general process of exchanging younger for older workers, no workers in the former category were to be removed from the more important factories until adequate substitutes had been found.[45]

Sichler was convinced that a major cause of the labor difficulty stemmed from the methods of the procurement agencies. The granting of contracts in excess of needs and for such vague periods as "for the length of the war" or "until one year after the conclusion of peace" had created an artificial need for labor. He called on the procurement agencies to revise such contracts. Most important, however, was that the procurement agencies often gave new contracts to firms which lacked both the labor and the facilities to fulfill them instead of turning to other firms which might have fulfilled the contracts without raising new demands for labor. Sichler was the strongest proponent of the reintroduction of legitimate middlemen into war

---

the Deputy Commanding Generals on June 15, 1915, BHStA, Abt. IV, MK, Kriegswirtschaft 77 (Sammlung Knorr), hereinafter cited as "Richtlinien" without archival reference. See also Sichler and Tiburtius, *Arbeiterfrage*, pp. 14-15.

[45] Richtlinien, June 15, 1915.

contracting for this reason. Although unsuccessful in this effort, he did persuade General von Wandel to issue a decree on August 20, 1915, ordering that future contracts require the firms to state their ability to fulfill the terms without the use of additional k.v. manpower. In this manner it was hoped that the firms themselves would see the necessity for training unskilled labor, and the procurement agencies would be forced to look elsewhere in giving contracts. At the same time it was made clear that this provision could not apply to certain firms such as Krupp and Zeiss, whose work could not be duplicated elsewhere.[46]

The members of the Association of German Iron and Steel Industrialists were particularly incensed over the decree of August 20. In a discussion with their representatives on September 28, Sichler accused them of not doing enough to train substitutes for their k.v. workers, told them that the Ministry was willing to provide money for the establishment of training facilities, and warned that no consideration would be given to "Fatherlandless industrialists." The industrialists accused Sichler of being an "overburdened and nervous man, who in both tone and individual expressions forgets himself," and decided to appeal to Wandel on October 10. In a petition of November 5 they attacked the new contract provisions and accused the procurement agencies of lack of fairness in carrying out the new orders. No provisions were being made for firms producing from unfinished goods, although such manufacture required stronger and more skilled workers than other types. The petition went on to deny that the industrialists were not trying to find other types of labor and to defend the use of exempted workers for the manufacture of peacetime products. This was coupled with the usual criticism of the Ministry's procurement policy:

> If the producer is to be prepared for army contracts and to fulfill his obligations at the right time, then he must not

[46] *Ibid.*, and Sichler and Tiburtius, *Arbeiterfrage*, pp. 62-65.

set himself up on the basis of the lean period. In the irregular and only limited granting of war contracts is to be found the actual reason why our industry—if a factory generally capable of production and profit is to be maintained—must continue the production of peacetime products. Only a very few works are so richly supplied with war contracts that they can renounce peacetime deliveries.[47]

The logic of this argument must appear somewhat bizarre to the neutral observer. The army was being told that it had to permit exempted workers to produce peacetime products because the army was not providing a sufficient number of war contracts! Although this was justified by the argument that this was the only means of keeping the factories prepared to meet a sudden increase in war contracts, it completely neglected the fact that one of the reasons the army was keeping its contracts limited was because it could not afford to sacrifice the manpower.

In a meeting between representatives of the association and members of the War Ministry headed by General von Wandel on November 10, the latter was forced to admit that the decree concerning new contract provisions had been wrongly interpreted in certain instances and that distinctions had to be made between the needs of various types of industries. The industrialists, in turn, agreed to the basic idea of the decree, namely, that those who could perform contracts without k.v. workers were to be given preference over those who could not. In reality the meeting closed on a complete misunderstanding. The iron and steel industrialists now assumed that they would be exempt from the new contract provisions. The War Ministry regarded no group of industrialists as exempt, but only particular firms. The association thus felt compelled to remind Wandel of his supposed promise two months later and ask him for another interview. This time Wandel refused to discuss the matter and insisted that military interests had to

47 "Die Arbeiterfrage im Kriege, insbesondere das Zurückstellungswesen," Nov. 5, 1915, BA, R 131/184.

precede those of the iron and steel industrialists. He also turned down the repeated demand that industrialist advisers be placed in AZS and sent to the Deputy Commanding Generals. Advisers had been sent to the latter at the end of 1915 at the request of AZS, but these were chosen on the basis of their nonpartisan character.[48]

That the burdens of the new contract clause and AZS policies were not as great as the iron and steel industrialists wanted others to believe may be gathered from their own testimony. In a meeting of the Association leadership on March 24, 1916, Dr. Reichert reported that the Munitions Ordnance Master, General Franke, had been proving most helpful and that petitions for release from the clause were being quickly granted. Another industrialist confessed that he had had little difficulty and pointed out that "One must seek out the right people in order to get on with the military authorities in the right way."[49] One of the "right people" was certainly General Franke, who had advised the industrialists to speak "energetically" about the policies of AZS. What most distressed the industrialists at this point was that the army, due to military needs, was preparing to become even tougher in its exemptions policy. The army had now decided that no distinction was to be made any longer between k.v. men over and under thirty-nine years of age. They planned to try to stop the flow of k.v. men to industry. Furthermore, g.v. workers were not being exempted without k.v. men being given in return. The army's pressure for the use and training of other types of labor was increasing, and roving War Ministry commissions were proving difficult to deal with. The association had tried to collect statistics to prove its case before the War Ministry, but it refrained from sending them because the statistics demonstrated that the actual number of workers had slightly increased over the

[48] "Besprechung mit dem stellvertretenden Kriegsminister über die Arbeiterfragen im Kriege am 10. November 1915," *ibid.* See also, the VdESI letter to Wandel, Jan. 20, 1916, R 13I/185, and Wandel's reply, Feb. 23, 1916, R 13I/87.

[49] *Ibid.*, R 13I/148.

peacetime figure. To be sure, many of these workers were not as skilled or productive as the old ones, but the statistics by no means demonstrated a crying need.

Indeed, the army's statistics demonstrate that the number of k.v. men in industry increased from 600,000 at the end of 1915 to 740,000 in early 1916, the total number of exempted workers increasing from 1 million to 1.2 million. The last figure was to remain constant until the early fall of 1916. This shows that AZS policy was designed to provide a check on increasing exemptions rather than to institute a wholesale attack on the exempted labor force. By keeping this number constant, the Ministry was able to achieve a relative increase in the size of the army of considerable proportions. At the same time, AZS pressure resulted in a continuous increase in the utilization of female labor, youth, and prisoners of war. The partial resistance of industry to the use of such labor was based on both technical and social considerations. Training was difficult and exemptions from restrictions upon the working conditions for women and children were not always easy to come by. There was considerable reluctance to train prisoners of war on the grounds that this would lead to higher wage demands for them. Industry was not blind, however, to the value of female labor as a means of depressing wages, and this policy kept many women from entering war work. AZS was opposed to such misuse of female labor and insisted that industry provide more incentive for women to engage in war work. In fact the running battle between industry and AZS over exemptions policy was coupled with a conflict over social policy, for AZS saw a better social attitude on the part of the industrialists as one of the most important means of increasing the efficient utilization of manpower and production.[50]

5. *The Conflict over Social Policy*

An ill wind was blowing out of the War Ministry in the

[50] For the army's statistics, see Reichsarchiv, *Weltkrieg*, IX, pp. 370-373, X, pp. 626-628, XI, p. 41. On the social aspects, see the VdESI meeting, Dec. 9, 1915, BA, R 131/147.

opinion of the industrialists. "It comes from Mr. AZS, Sichler, who has an adjutant in a Dr. Tiburtius, who in civil life is an assistant of the well-known social politician Professor Dr. Francke. These people are making social policy there in the War Ministry."[51] The enemy had, indeed, been pinpointed. The twenty-six-year-old labor expert, Dr. Tiburtius, who entered the War Ministry as an assistant to Sichler in January 1915, was summoned largely because of his connections with the Society for Social Reform. A student of Professors Franz Oppenheimer and Adolf Wagner, and an assistant to Professor Max Sering (not Francke), Tiburtius had been recommended by Oppenheimer to serve as Sichler's assistant. The army needed expert advice on labor and union matters, and the Society for Social Reform was the only organization capable of providing advice that was at once "respectable" and informed. The use of one of its members, however, was bound to give a particular coloring to the War Ministry's social policies. Throughout his stay in the Ministry, Tiburtius sought the guidance of Professor Franke, the most important leader in the Society, and the social policies of AZS expressed his views: "I placed the basic views of the Society for Social Reform at the root of all our social-political measures in the War Ministry, thus the setting up of arbitration committees based on parity by the military commanders, the building up of labor exchanges on the basis of parity, . . . and the general principle of close collaboration with unions and employer associations."[52] The principle of parity was anathema to the vast majority of the industrialists. It is rather ironic that the favorite image of the industrialists for describing the proper relationship between labor and management was a military one: "A colonel in the trenches can no more permit negotiations with his troops than [a factory owner] can permit his

[51] Comment by Privy Councilor Hilger, a leader of Upper Silesian heavy industry, VdESI meeting, Nov. 16, 1916, BA, R 13I/149.

[52] Senator Tiburtius to the author, Nov. 19, 1962.

workers to make decisions about basic factory questions."[53]

To Sichler and Tiburtius the analogy between the army and the factory was false in every sense. From the outset they had to resist the wishes of General von Falkenhayn for the introduction of military or legal compulsion to work and to persuade General von Wandel to accept and defend their viewpoint:

> The workers are now fulfilling their war duty . . . with the greatest willingness. In this they are being strengthened and driven on by their unions. A military or legal compulsion to work will have a laming and destructive effect upon the readiness of the unions to help out. Pointing to the brilliant success of compulsory military discipline in the army misses the fundamental difference between service in the defense of one's country, in which all members work for the common good without personal benefit, and the capitalistic work relationship, in which there is a profit for the employer from the performance of the worker. To intervene in this relationship, which . . . was to be seen as a consequence of the historical development of the workers as a fighting class, in the manner that one group should be forced to perform by *official order*, while the other receives the highest remuneration from the same authority, would be felt by the workers and other classes of the people as a partisan stand in favor of the employers and would place at stake the further confidence in the military authorities of a class decisive for the carrying on of the war.[54]

The first practical application of AZS policy was an order of March 1915 requiring that all returned workers be completely released from military service for the period of their exemption and be paid at the normal rate. They were not to be put on leave and paid a low military salary, as had been the practice in certain areas. In this manner the employers were deprived

[53] Reichert speech, Nov. 16, 1916, BA, R 13I/149.
[54] Sichler and Tiburtius, *Arbeiterfrage*, pp. 13-14.

of an easy means of depressing wages, and the state was relieved of an unnecessary expenditure.[55]

The issue which raised the question of using compulsion against labor in its sharpest form was the control of the free movement of labor. The sudden flood of army contracts at the beginning of the war combined with the shortage of skilled labor produced a state of virtual anarchy in certain industrial areas. This was particularly the case in the Berlin metal industry, where a large number of the newer and smaller firms went over to war production even though they did not have the labor needed to fulfill their contracts. By demanding a high price as a reward for taking the contracts and then offering high wages, these firms were able to win away workers from other firms. The workers took advantage of this competition to sell their labor to the highest bidder. The result was an abnormal growth of wages and a disturbing loss of labor on the part of the older and larger firms.

The leaders of the Berlin metal industry, headed by Privy Councilor von Borsig, went to the Imperial Office of the Interior and proposed that the Austrian system of compulsion be introduced, whereby a worker could not change his job without the permission of his employer. A decree to this effect had already been drawn up by General Franke at the industrialists' request, but both the Interior Office and the War Ministry opposed such a far-reaching step. Although black lists were normally proscribed, the Interior Office suggested that the metal industrialists help themselves by getting together and agreeing not to hire workers who changed jobs without permission. It proved impossible to get an agreement among the three hundred metal firms in Greater Berlin, however, let alone among the eight hundred firms in Berlin who had war contracts. Borsig and his friends therefore once again turned to General Franke and asked him to issue a decree refusing to award contracts to any firm that employed a new

[55] Anlage 3, Richtlinien of June 15, 1915.

worker without the permission of the previous employer. General Franke complied on January 11, 1915.[56]

This decree was conspicuously hung in the factories and patriotically bedecked with the imperial colors by the owners. The italicized last paragraph—"It will be taken as self-understood, that in cases where workers bring just complaints about low wages to the employers, these will be examined and adjusted with the sense of equity suitable to this great time"[57] —was always omitted. The Berlin metal workers, the most organized and, despite the conservative leadership of Alexander Schlicke and Adolf Cohen, the most radical workers in Germany, were not in the mood for such games. They regarded the decree as arbitrary and the omission of the paragraph as a piece of added crassness. General Franke was warned by Cohen that the union leadership would not accept any responsibility for the consequences of the decree. Strong protests were made to Sichler's office, and the War Ministry prepared a decree abolishing Franke's order. Borsig, who knew his Berlin workers and had doubted that the order would hold up under union protest, prevented its revocation by agreeing to negotiations between the Association of Berlin Metal Industrialists and the German Metalworkers Union.

The result of these negotiations was the establishment of the War Board for the Metal Industry of Greater Berlin (*Kriegsausschuss für die Metallbetriebe Gross-Berlins*) in February 1915. This board, which was composed of three representatives of each group, met weekly to judge whether or not workers who wished to change employment against the wishes of their employers should be permitted to do so. A representative of

[56] Most of the description in this and the following paragraphs is based on Borsig's remarks at the VdESI meetings of March 24 and Nov. 16, 1916, BA, R 13I/148-149.

[57] The decree is reprinted in *Der Deutsche Metallarbeiterverband im Jahre 1915. Jahr und Handbuch für Verbandsmitglieder*, Stuttgart, 1916, p. 16. For the union reaction, see also *Die zwölfte ordentliche Generalversammlung des Deutschen Metallarbeiter-Verbandes in Berlin. Abgehalten vom 28. Juni bis 3. Juli 1915 im Gewerkschaftshaus*, Stuttgart, 1915.

the Ordnance Master's Office witnessed the proceedings, and a representative of the employers served as chairman. If a worker's complaint was found to be just and the employer refused to give him satisfaction, then he was given the "leaving certificate" (*Abkehrschein*) which permitted other employers to hire him. If the worker's complaint was not found to be just, then the certificate was refused. In actual practice the majority of cases were settled by a compromise in which some of the worker's demands were met in return for his staying on the job. The interesting thing about the agreement is that both sides were prepared to disregard basic questions in setting up this institution. The chairmanship was simply handed to the employers. No provision was made for a decisive majority in contested cases, and no detailed guidelines were laid down for settling cases.[58]

That the employers were quite ready to reach a quick, if vague, understanding was natural given the closure of all other avenues to the accomplishment of their purpose. The willingness on the part of labor, however, requires closer attention, for the agreement represented a practical surrender of the worker's prized right to freely dispose of his labor. The agreement, however, also represented the fulfillment of one of the great aims of the labor leaders, as the industrialists had negotiated with the union leaders and, by setting up the War Board, had agreed to continue to settle grievances with the unions by direct negotiation and collaboration. To be sure, the agreement was limited to the duration of the war, but it might also serve as a precedent for relations with management in peacetime. In asking its members to support the work of the War Board, the union was quick to point this out: "If the members and all concerned are conscientious in maintaining the agreement, then later the enemies of collaboration with the unions will have to keep silent."[59] But the Berlin union leaders had yet

[58] For the agreement, see BHStA, Abt. IV, MK, K Mob 11, Bd. I, Bl. zu 1.

[59] *Metallarbeiter-Zeitung*, Feb. 27, 1915.

another very special reason for wanting a quick agreement. They had to have an agreement with the employers if they were to keep the demands of the membership from getting out of hand. This is clearly demonstrated by an account Borsig gave to his fellow industrialists on November 16, 1916:

> Insofar as the unions are concerned . . . I can only say that they have worked hand in hand with us during the war. I can tell you confidentially that I was even recently called by the union and was told . . . that it was amazed at the demands made upon a firm by the workers and we should take every care that the firm made no further concessions to the workers. The wages were already so high and the unions couldn't rescue themselves from these demands. Thus I have the impression that the unions are here in actuality finally following the principle that the demands of the workers should not climb in an uncalled-for way, and I believe that if we did not establish our War Board, unbearable conditions would have developed.[60]

The sort of chaos that could develop from the competition between firms for skilled labor is demonstrated by the situation in the shipbuilding industry, an industry which relied almost completely on highly trained and practiced personnel. As early as December 1914 the Vulcan-Werke, which was the largest producer of vessels for the navy, was complaining that it was losing workers to competitors. It asked that all exempted workers who left their jobs be redrafted and expressed regret that the Military Service Law did not permit the mustering of all Germans over forty-five years of age to serve in the war industry. How the military authorities on the local level could themselves contribute to the difficulties was demonstrated a few days after the firm's first complaint. The District Commander in Hamburg had suddenly informed many of Vulcan's workers that they had a choice between entering the army or going to work for Krupp in Essen. Since Krupp paid better

[60] VdESI meeting, Nov. 16, 1916, BA R 13I/149.

wages, little persuasion was needed. The officer's zeal for solving the worker shortage at Krupp was quickly ended, but its effects were long felt. It must be said that the Vulcan firm was by no means averse to stealing workers for itself and expressed great irritation when its agents were thrown out of the Ruhr by the military authorities for conducting raiding expeditions there. As in Berlin the competition within the shipbuilding industry for workers was particularly harmful to the firms with longstanding contracts with the navy, as these could not profitably meet the large wage offers of their competitors. It was thus natural for some of them to seek a solution to the problem in an extension of the Berlin War Board to the entire metal industry.[61]

The War Ministry's policy in 1915 was extremely cautious. The Berlin War Board had as its basis the willingness of both labor and management to come together. It was, in short, a private agreement. Whatever the personal views of the leading members of AZS, they did not feel capable of immediately taking a stand that would involve them in conflicts of principle between labor and management. They did wish to limit the excessive movement of labor so far as this was within their power. An order of December 19, 1914, required that both exempted workers and the firms that had requested their exemption report any change of employment. Given the shortage of workers, this did not necessarily mean that exempted workers would immediately be taken into the army if they changed jobs, but it did create the basis for control over this class of workers and for private agreements between firms and the Deputy Commanding Generals. In issuing this order the War Ministry warned against using the "threat of the trenches" and turning military service into a form of punishment for workers found distasteful by employers.[62] That this order was

[61] MF, Marine Archiv, 6448, Bd. I, Bl. 2-10, 18, 40-41. A proposal for the extension of the Berlin War Board system was made by the Germaniawerft (Krupp) on Feb. 4, 1916, *ibid.*, Bl. 267-269.

[62] Anlage 2, Richtlinien of June 15, 1915.

both used and abused is demonstrated by this confession on the part of one industrialist:

> Gentlemen, I have kept the free movement of the workers rather within bounds by coming to an agreement with the Deputy Commanding General. As soon as a worker wanted to go away or in some other way behaved himself in a disorderly manner, I reported him to the Deputy Commanding General and he was immediately drafted and put in uniform. It was done very quickly. Then everything went along very peacefully; then the men were completely reasonable.[63]

The War Ministry tried to get industry to take upon itself the burden of alleviating a situation for which it was largely responsible. This was made clear in a decree of March 31, 1915, in which the Deputy Commanding Generals were told to ask the Chambers of Commerce to get the firms to agree among themselves, first, not to try to win workers away from each other, second, not to advertise for workers by offering high wages and exemption from military service, and third, not to hire workers who left jobs where they were getting a decent wage. At the same time, however, the industrialists were to be warned against making black-listing agreements as this would deny the worker his fundamental right to choose his own job. Nor would the Ministry recommend the establishment of conciliation agencies (*Einigungsämter*) composed of an equal number of employer and employee representatives to settle disputes. Use of the industrial courts was recommended instead. This decree was completely evasive. It advised industry to help itself, but warned against any attempt to apply compulsion to either employers or employees. In refusing to support the establishment of conciliation agencies for the adjustment of differences, AZS seemed to be contradicting the beliefs of its leaders.[64]

[63] Remark of Privy Councilor Ziese of the Schichau firm, VdESI meeting, March 24, 1916, BA, R 13I/148.

[64] Anlage 1, Richtlinien of June 15, 1915. The directive was sent to

The reasoning behind this vague decree may be found in the inherent difficulties of AZS's socially progressive position. Sichler and Tiburtius were convinced that wages in the war industry had to grow because of the high cost of living and because of the shortage of labor. This increase in wages, in their view, was compensated for and justified by the increase in profits. The demands of the unions had so far been kept within the bounds of the reasonable. The surest means of keeping the workers from changing jobs was by giving them wages that would make it undesirable for them to do so. There was, therefore, no reason to support any agreement among employers that might encourage an unnatural holding down of wages. Since, as shall be demonstrated shortly, the vast majority of the industrialists did not want to set up war boards of the Berlin type or conciliation agencies, AZS could do no more than tell the industrialists to at least put an end to their own contributions to job changing and excessive wage increases.[65]

This was all the more the case because AZS was unwilling to defy the policies of the civil government, particularly those of the Prussian Minister of Commerce, Sydow. The idea of setting up conciliation agencies had first been proposed by the Centrist deputy Giesberts, who represented the interests of the Christian trade unions in the Reichstag, to the then Deputy Commanding General in the Rhenish-Westphalian district (VII Army Corps), Freiherr von Bissing. The proposal was particularly designed to alleviate tension in the Ruhr coal mines, where the practices of the mineowners led by Emil Kirdorf, Hugo Stinnes, and Alfred Hugenberg had led to major strikes and lockouts before the war. Bissing took to the idea, which was presented by Giesberts in October 1914, and inquired among the civilian authorities as to its feasibility. The Royal Mine Bureau, which managed the government coal

the Germaniawerft in reply to its letter of Feb. 4 (see note 62), MF, Marine Archiv, 6448, Bd. I, Bl. 270-273.

[65] Richtlinien of June 15, 1915.

mines and watched over conditions in the private ones, took a completely negative stand, arguing that there was no need for such an institution and that it would permit the growth of union power. This view was shared by the Government President (*Regierungspräsident*) in Arnsberg, Bake, who thought the plan "a highly dangerous experiment." Only the Government President in Düsseldorf, Kruse, felt that a revision of thinking was necessitated by union collaboration with the war effort. In a letter to Bissing, he pointed out that he had been trying to impress the industrialists with the fact that "in industry also the absolute monarchy will have to give way to the constitutional one."[66]

Sydow, while also tending to feel that some sort of new attitude would have to be taken, was sympathetic to the mineowners' argument that such institutions would be used by the unions to increase their membership and power. Above all, he was most unwilling to force the mineowners to relent, as such a step might harm coal production. The replacement of General von Bissing by General von Gayl, who was very friendly to the views of the industrialists, further strengthened the resistance of the mineowners. Sydow ordered on March 22, 1915, therefore, that the idea of setting up conciliation agencies be dropped, but that the Royal Mine Office mediate all dangerous situations whether asked to do so or not, and that the workers committees in the mines be treated with every possible consideration. This, then, was the basis of AZS's refusal to recommend officially the establishment of conciliation agencies or war boards in its own decree of March 31, 1915.[67]

Where AZS's real sympathies lay was demonstrated by the "Guidelines for the Handling of the Worker Question" it sent

[66] For the correspondence, see Bissing to the Government President in Münster, Count von Merveldt, Nov. 24, 1914, and the Royal Mine Bureau to Bissing, Dec. 1, 1914, StADü, Reg. Dü., 33608. Also, see StAMü, Oberbergamt Dortmund B, Gruppe 119, Nr. 250 for the Giesberts proposal of Nov. 19, 1914, Kruse to Bissing, Dec. 24, 1914, and Bake's note of Dec. 24, 1914.

[67] Sydow directive of March 22, 1915, StAMü, Oberbergamt Dortmund B, Gruppe 119, Nr. 250.

to the Deputy Commanding Generals on June 15, 1915. Although the decree of March 31 giving the official position on conciliation agencies was printed as an appendix, Kruse's letter of December 24, 1914, was also reprinted as a demonstration of the great value placed on the role of the unions in the war by a "high government personage." There was thus a considerable difference of emphasis between AZS and Sydow. Both recognized the importance of the unions to the war effort and sought union collaboration, but AZS took a much more positive attitude toward negotiations on the basis of parity and was more willing to encourage union development. This becomes clear in the instructions given to the Deputy Commanding Generals for the handling of dangerous labor disputes. They were to intervene in such disputes, not as arbitrators, but rather to bring the two parties together through mutual agreement. They were to ask for expert advice from the factory inspectors, but themselves take no sides in the technical issues in the dispute. Where union members were involved, the unions were to be consulted so that any agreement reached would have at least a morally binding effect upon the unions. In this way the workers would feel responsible to their unions for the maintenance of the agreement, and the unions would feel obligated to refuse to support a strike. Great emphasis was placed on bringing representatives of both management and labor organizations to the conference table: "The participation of representatives of the employer organizations in such discussions is desired."[68]

It did not take long for the AZS "Guidelines" to anger the industrialists. The German Industry War Committee had already complained to the Interior Office in April 1915 that a "Section for Social Policy" had been created by Sichler in the War Ministry. This was denied by the Ministry, but the "Guidelines" of June 15 seemed to prove that such a section did in fact exist. When the military governor of Cologne, General

[68] Anlage 4, Richtlinien of June 15, 1915. Kruse's name was omitted.

von Held, passed wage demands of the metalworker unions to the metal industrialist organization there and called for negotiations, the industrialists linked this action to the "Guidelines." The German Industry War Committee sent a protest to General von Wandel and an angry petition to the Imperial Office of the Interior on July 20, 1915. Particular exception was taken to the printing of Kruse's letter. AZS was accused of taking a one-sided stand in favor of the unions. The decision to advise measures which interfered so basically with existing conditions without consulting industry was attacked as a disturbance of the work of industry which damaged the good relations between employers and workers. Above all, the "Guidelines" would have a prejudicial effect upon the future position of the employers:

> For it will hardly be contested that the *consequences* of the intervention of the military authorities in the relationship between employers and workers will also remain when those authorities are no longer competent after the end of the war. Above all the Imperial Office of the Interior, the appointed central agency for the regulation of German social policy, ought not to permit serious difficulties to develop from the social-political "Guidelines" written by the War Ministry for the Deputy Commanding Generals.[69]

A revision of the "Guidelines" was demanded, as well as the assurance that the War Ministry would make no more decisions about social policy without consulting the Interior Office.

These efforts to get the War Ministry to change its social policy by an appeal to the Interior Office were no more successful than appeals made by certain industrialists to Generals von Falkenhayn and Wild von Hohenborn at Supreme Headquarters to promote the introduction of compulsory labor for the civilian population. On June 19, 1915, Wild inquired as to

[69] German Industry War Committee to Wandel, July 16, 1915, and to Delbrück, July 20, 1915, Nachlass Stresemann, 6844, frames H127895-H127860 and H127885-H127888.

the desirability of such a step in view of the labor shortage in the armaments industry. General von Wandel's reply of July 31 was a lengthy defense of the policies of AZS.[70] The efforts of the War Ministry to supply industry with workers were clearly outlined, as were the measures taken to control turnover. At the same time it was pointed out that many workers changed jobs "from reasons whose justification is perhaps not always to be denied," and that these changes frequently "have their roots in the ruthless competition among the employers" for labor. Wandel denied that there was a large body of workers outside of the war industries. Where such groups of workers existed, they were being forced into war work by the lack of a market for peacetime products and the shortage of raw materials. Most important, the workers would regard the introduction of compulsion as an "unearned answer" to their efforts and patriotism, and this would ruin their will to give their utmost. An increase in productivity was to be sought by two means. First, a continuous appeal had to be made to the patriotism of the workers and their identification with the national interest, particularly through the unions. Second, the workers had to be given adequate wages. Wandel declared that the industrialists' desire to extend the working day by compulsion was both wrong and undesirable. Modern industrial experience, particularly the implementation of the Taylor system at the Bethlehem steel works in the United States, had demonstrated that increasing the working day increased productivity only up to a certain point. Compulsion was characterized by Wandel as an invitation to strikes, sabotage, and noncooperation by the unions. In this stand Wandel received the wholehearted support of the Imperial Office of the Interior, which opposed any measures that might create internal friction.

The support received by AZS from General von Wandel enabled it to act more effectively in 1916 by directly supporting the establishment of war boards throughout Germany on the

[70] Wrisberg, *Heer und Heimat*, pp. 229-233.

Berlin model. Sichler and Tiburtius recognized a double advantage to such institutions. They at once satisfied union desire for a means by which disputes might be settled in direct and equal collaboration with the employers and satisfied the need to control turnover of industrial labor which caused inefficiency and excessive wage increases. Strictly speaking, the Giesberts proposal for conciliation agencies and the Berlin War Board had no direct relationship with each other, but labor leaders increasingly identified them as representing the same basic idea. They saw in both types of institutions a means of bringing about recognition of the unions and collective bargaining. They felt also that such institutions would give exempted workers an agency before which to bring their complaints and justify their desires to change employers. They would no longer be completely at the mercy of the employers and Deputy Commanding Generals.[71]

AZS's intensified pressure for the establishment of war boards had its first success in Dresden, where an agreement was concluded between labor and management organizations from all the major industries—not only the metal industry—under the aegis of the Saxon Ordnance Master's Office on January 5, 1916. The agreement, while similar to that made in Berlin, was both more formal and more detailed. Specific mention was made of the rights of exempted workers to protection by the War Board; the chairmanship was given to an employer representative, the secretaryship to a representative of the unions; the worker was given the right to appoint someone to present his case; the agreement was to terminate three months after the conclusion of peace.[72]

In January 1916 the German Metalworkers Union petitioned the War Ministry and the Ordnance Master's Office in Berlin

[71] See the statement of Deputy Huë, the Socialist mine union leader, Prussian Landtag Debates, Feb. 25, 1915, VII, pp. 8536-8538.

[72] BHStA, Abt. IV, MK, K Mob 11, Bd. I, Bl. zu 1. Professor Franke seems to have played a role in the establishment of the Dresden War Board as indicated by the VdESI discussion, March 24, 1916, BA, R 13I/148.

for the creation of war boards for the metal industry throughout the Empire. This proposal was turned down by the metal industrialists in discussions conducted by General Franke on January 18, on the grounds that conditions in Berlin were very special and that what was applicable in Berlin was not necessarily applicable elsewhere. Franke presented this view to the metalworkers union in a letter of February 4, but promised that an effort to set up war boards would be made through the Deputy Commanding Generals. A copy of this letter was sent to the metal industrialists with the additional comment that official mediation agencies would be set up where employer resistance made it impossible to set up war boards. On February 10 the actual position of the War Ministry was put in no uncertain terms to the metal industrialists:

> The War Ministry regards it as desirable to satisfy in some way the wishes of the workers and create war boards for the settlement of differences arising from the changing of places of employment for the duration of the war.
>
> This need steps into the foreground more at the present time because a greater increase of turnover is to be expected due to the increased calling up of workers liable to field service.
>
> In view of the decreased worker supply resulting from call-ups, the military authorities must place more value than before upon the workers staying on their jobs and the utilization of all available manpower. But if the worker is to be kept on his job, then his right to move freely is restricted, and he must be given the possibility of turning to a nonpartisan agency in disputes concerning wages, etc.
>
> This is particularly necessary for exempted workers.
>
> For these reasons, the War Ministry sees itself as given reason to consider the establishment of mediation agencies wherever the setting up of war boards meets with the resistance of the associations.[73]

[73]BHStA, Abt. IV, MK, K Mob 11, Bd. I, Bl. zu 1.

The metal industrialists were asked to take the initiative in this matter and, perhaps through the use of the Association of German Employer Organizations, break down opposition to the measure. The note concluded by stressing that the boards were to be regarded as nothing more than a wartime measure.

Attached to the letter of February 10 were "Theses for the Establishment of War Boards."[74] These repeated the principles expounded in the letter and advised that the Berlin-type organization be used elsewhere. The prounion attitude, however, was even more sharply intoned. The importance of strong unions for the establishment of Boards was openly stated: "The precondition for the creation of boards is the existence of employer and employee organs, which are in the position to take over representation and possess sufficient influence." A new justification was added for the right of the workers to have a place to bring complaints. This right was "also particularly to be recognized when the worker representatives agree—as did the chairmen of the unions immediately after the outbreak of the war—to renounce the use of strikes during the war." While such renunciations were highly desirable, it was warned against making them a precondition for the establishment of war boards or, indeed, letting the negotiations break down over small points.

In a meeting with Dr. Hoff of the Association of German Employer Associations and Dr. Tänzler of the Northwest Group of the Association of German Iron and Steel Industrialists on March 11, Franke reiterated the War Ministry's position and stressed the need to give the unions some compensation for the renunciation of strikes. The industrialists argued that no one had a right to a reward for sacrifices made for the Fatherland. They objected to the generalization of the Berlin War Board on the grounds that Berlin was not typical of the rest of Germany. There the majority of the workers were unionized. In the Ruhr the unions had lost much of their membership, while in Silesia they never had any to start with. The

[74] *Ibid.*

boards would lead to an unjustifiable strengthening of the unions. Franke replied that nonunion members could be elected to the boards and stressed that the employers had to make sacrifices for the war effort. Hoff and Tänzler went away with the distinct impression that the matter had already been decided and that they were being given the option of voluntarily cooperating or being faced with unilateral actions on the part of the military authorities.[75]

The most violent resistance to the war boards came from the Association of German Iron and Steel Industrialists, which saw the war boards as nothing but a plot on the part of union officials and social reformers to gain their aims through the back door. Borsig, who shared their view insofar as the areas outside of Berlin were concerned, resented being treated as the father of the idea by the members of the association: "For us it was pure self-help, a measure that has worked well, and I can do nothing about the stupidity of the authorities—I ask that this expression not be used in the protocol—when they, despite all my resistance, do not understand this and generalize such things."[76] During the previous thirty years the association had fought health insurance, accident insurance, and every other kind of measure involving the establishment of worker committees on the grounds that all such measures would lead to an interference of the workers in the management of the plants. Now the desire of the unions to have war boards to discuss questions of wages, hours, and working conditions seemed to demonstrate that their fears had been well-founded. In fact the unions seemed to be nearing their goal, for the war boards meant nothing less than a "parliamentary factory system." Nor could the industrialists see any objective reasons for setting up war boards, as turnover in the Ruhr was lower than before the war and the workers were making few complaints thanks to the high wages being paid in war plants. They feared that once these boards were introduced, they would be over-

[75] VdESI meeting, March 24, 1916, BA, R 13I/148.
[76] *Ibid.*, Nov. 16, 1916, R 13I/149.

whelmed by demands from union secretaries that the workers themselves never would have dreamed of making. In this way the unions would agitate their way into an increase of membership. The less unionized the industrial area they came from, the more violent the objections of the industrialist. It was thus no accident that Privy Councilor Hilger from Upper Silesia, where only 2 percent of the workers were unionized, should have expressed the fears of the industrialists most bluntly: "I see in these arbitration agencies an extraordinarily great danger. They will not be terminated after the end of the war. That is a belief in miracles. I am completely convinced that when we once have them we will never be rid of them, and then a breach is shot through our social position."[77] At a meeting on March 24, 1916, the association decided to marshal the various industrial organizations together and open a "small barrage" upon the War Ministry.

The Ministry remained impervious to the industrialist attack. On April 4 General von Wandel issued a decree to the Deputy Commanding Generals asking them to support the establishment of war boards. Where their efforts failed, they were to establish mediation agencies composed of an officer and a representative each of labor and management. In areas where workers belonged to different unions, the unions were to be brought together to agree upon a representative. In a meeting with the industrialists on May 1, Wandel assured them that he would not compel them to set up war boards, but asked that they support their establishment in areas where they were needed and where local employers had no objections. He refused in any way to revise his instructions of April 4.[78]

The last hope of the industrialists now lay with the Deputy Commanding Generals, for they did not have to obey the War Ministry and their social attitudes tended to vary. Efforts to persuade the Deputy Commanding General in Frankfurt am

[77] *Ibid.*

[78] Wandel to Deputy Commanding Generals, April 4, 1916, BHStA, Abt. IV, MK, K Mob 11, Bd. I, Bl. zu 1; Reichert to VdESI membership, May 2, 1916, BA, R 13I/186.

Main to forget the matter broke down because he felt obligated to apply the policies decided in Berlin. He did agree, however, to have representatives of the yellow unions sit on the local war board, which was set up in September. War boards were established in Bavaria on July 1 and in Baden on October 1. Yellow union members were not permitted to sit on the latter. Boards were also set up in Kassel and Erfurt in August. In their struggle against the boards the industrialists faced great union pressure for them and for representation on them. How clear union aims were is demonstrated by union propaganda:

> Since these arbitration committees will probably remain on after the war, it is of pressing necessity that the union cartels make sure that there is union representation on them.
>
> The unions and union cartels are everywhere, also in the army corps districts, to come out in support of the establishment of these arbitration committees.[79]

Not all the generals, however, were unwilling to listen to the industrialists. The general in Saarbrücken refused to set up boards on the grounds that they would disturb labor relations in his district. The industrialists received their most important support from General von Gayl in the Rhenish-Westphalian district. He was in complete agreement with the industrialists but, as he told their representative, Dr. Beumer, "We are being so colossally pressed by Berlin that we simply must propose something positive."[80] Beumer suggested that a way out might be found in the use of workers committees in the factories. Such committees already existed by law in the mining industry, and the other industries might now set them up as a means of warding off the boards. In this way the employers would not have to negotiate with union secretaries, but rather with repre-

[79] *Correspondenzblatt der Generalkommission der Gewerkschaften*, hereinafter cited as *Correspondenzblatt*, Sept. 30, 1916. For information on the various war boards, see *Metallarbeiter-Zeitung*, Oct. 14, 1916, BHStA, Abt. IV, MK, K Mob 11, Bd. I, Bl. zu 1c.

[80] Report by Beumer, VdESI meeting, Nov. 16, 1916, BA, R 131/149.

sentatives of their own workers. Gayl took to the idea and, on October 19, sent a note to the chambers of commerce pointing out that the pressure for the establishment of war boards was very great and that the War Ministry was insisting that the workers have some kind of representative organization to make complaints. Workers committees were an ideal way to solve the problem, and it was time that the factories which did not have such committees establish them. The note concluded: "It is not to be denied that the increasingly strong strivings of the unions to take part in negotiations with the employers find strong support in the absence of workers committees." This "strictly confidential" letter was angrily read by Deputy Cohn (Nordhausen) before the Reichstag on November 3 and assailed as an example of how the industrialists were trying to shift from the war boards to the "dead rail" of workers committees. He pointed out that workers committee members, as shown by past experience in the mining industry, were always subject to threats and reprisals from the employers and were thus no substitute for the war boards.[81] Cohn attacked the War Ministry for being incapable of fighting employer resistance. This charge, as the history of the war boards demonstrates, was not altogether fair. The Ministry could defy the industrialists, but it could not compel the Deputy Commanding Generals. So long as the Ruhr and Silesian industrialists had the generals in their pockets, the War Ministry was powerless. By November 1916, therefore, a deadlock had been reached in many key industrial areas.

To the already bitter conflict between industry and the War Ministry over production policy and price policy was thus added an extremely sharp conflict over social policy. Army contracts contained clauses obligating firms to pay decent wages and, insofar as they existed, to pay the rates specified by jointly negotiated wage contracts. The sending of factory inspectors

[81] Reichstag Debates, Nov. 3, 1916, 308, pp. 2038-2039. Cohn also read a letter of Oct. 24, 1916, from the Essen Chamber of Commerce to its members supporting the Gayl proposal.

to examine wage lists, a favorite method of the Ministry and the more progressive Deputy Commanding Generals, met with passive resistance. Hilger would provide them with the lists, "a more or less well-warmed room," but no help in finding their way through the complicated records. Yet even he had to admit the effectiveness of the pressure: "I give way in things where I would not have before, not out of consideration for public opinion—at that I whistle—but because the Royal government and the entire military administration stands behind it."[82] There seemed to be almost no limit to the War Ministry's capacity for social ideas in the opinion of the employers. In September 1916 AZS began supporting a union proposal, warmly seconded by the Society for Social Reform, that workers be given a week or more vacation to recuperate from the strains of hard work and insufficient food. The industrialists replied that production demands and worker shortages made this possible only for sick workers. They were really quite disgusted: "Over and over one comes to the conclusion in viewing such official intervention that *certain responsible agencies conduct too much social policy and not enough production policy*."[83]

A close examination of the relations between the War Ministry and the industrialists during the first two years of the war thus leads to a conclusion as inescapable as it is surprising. Their relations were extremely unsatisfactory. Some of the tension was attributable to the unavoidable fumbling attendant upon the adjustment to an unanticipated kind of war. Far more important, however, was that the War Ministry and the industrialists approached the war in entirely different terms. The Ministry's major concern was winning the war, and the productive forces of the nation were important instruments in the

[82] VdESI meeting, Dec. 9, 1915, BA, R 13I/147.

[83] Reichert speech, Nov. 16, 1916, BA, R 131/147. On the vacation question, see *Berichte des Büros für Sozialpolitik*, July 1916, BHStA, Abt. IV, MK, XIV Mob 2c, hereinafter cited as BBS reports without archival reference, and the VdESI circular letter of Sept. 26, 1916, BA, R 13I/186.

service of this goal. The demands of the industrialists, therefore, had to be balanced off against the manpower needs of the army, the financial problems of the state, and the interests of the workers. In concentrating on this limited goal the Ministry had, in effect, ceased to be the bulwark of an obsolete social system incapable of providing the social efficiency required by modern war. It had picked up where the bureaucratic social reformers of the prewar period had left off and was completing the process of destroying the authoritarian factory system that left the employer complete master in his own house.

The concerns of the industrialists were broader, but their vision was narrower. Once they were compelled to go into the business of war production, they demanded that the manpower, price, and social policies of the War Ministry be made subsidiary to "production policy." As the high tariff policy and the suppression of the trade unions had once been identified with the "protection of national labor," so now the unrestrained promotion of business interests was identified with the defense of the nation at war. What lay at the root of the industrialists' struggle with the War Ministry, however, was their desire to keep their stock of skilled workers, maximize their profits, and maintain their social power.

It should thus come as no surprise that the chief support for the policies of the War Ministry, once regarded as the center of militarism and reaction, came from the left rather than the right. Only the War Ministry had proved itself capable of ignoring the taboos prohibiting interference with the sacred principles that lay at the root of industrialist power. If the chief credit for the Ministry's measures belongs to Sichler and Tiburtius, it must not be forgotten that they could have accomplished nothing without the support and understanding of the leading military men in the Ministry, particularly General von Wandel. Deputy Gustav Bauer, Vice-Chairman of the General Commission of the Free Trade Unions, provided only one of the many songs of praise sung to the Ministry by labor leaders:

In all the negotiations that have been conducted from the union side with the War Ministry, the War Ministry has always shown the greatest possible willingness to meet the wishes of the workers. (Bravo! from the Social Democrats.) I want expressly to establish that here the gentlemen have shown understanding for the needs of the workers and have honorably sought, insofar as it has stood within their power, to create recognition for the justified demands of the workers. Gentlemen, if a similar attitude was also present among the civil authorities, then much in Germany would be different, then the judgment of the union-organized workers would in many matters finally have to be subject to a revision. But Gentlemen, that today is still not the case. In the civil authorities there is demonstrated a monstrous anxiety of coming in any way into unpleasant collisions with the employers. (Hear! Hear! from the Social Democrats.)[84]

[84] Reichstag Debates, Aug. 26, 1915, 306, p. 362.

II

The Army and the Internal Crisis, 1914-1916: Image and Reality

DEPUTY BAUER's praise of the War Ministry and his deprecation of the feeble policies of the civil government raise problems of considerable importance. While the tendency of the political right to seek military support for its immoderate war aims and conservative policies is well known, the faith of the political left in the army has received scant attention. Social Democratic and trade union newspapers and speakers continuously made invidious comparisons between the army and the civil bureaucracy. They called for the intervention of the former to undo the mistakes of the latter and praised the military authorities for being more atune to the times than their civilian counterparts. How valid were these claims? The words of Deputy Bauer would almost make one believe that the reforming spirit of Scharnhorst and Boyen had been revived and that the army was consciously locked in struggle with stodgy bureaucrats and reactionary cliques. Was the army more efficient and progressive than the civil government? Whether or not this really was the case, the vast majority of the German people believed it to be true. It is therefore necessary to explore the most practical results of this exaltation of the army, namely, the increasing interference of the army in civil affairs under the pressure of public opinion and the effort of the civil authorities to cover their unpalatable policies with the prestige of military personalities.

1. The Food Problem

To enter into the bureaucratic bungling, selfish interest, and shady practice that characterized the management of Germany's wartime food supply is to understand why so many thought that only a military food dictator could clean up the mess. But the army bore considerable responsibility for the situation. Although Germany had been dependent upon imports for a third of her prewar food supply, the danger that there would not be enough food for the civilian population in wartime was virtually ignored by the military authorities. No effort was made to control army rations in terms of the general food supply, and army procurement policy, thanks to the competition among agencies, helped prices to skyrocket.[1]

The chief responsibility for the inadequate measures and poor organization, however, must rest on the Imperial State Secretary of the Interior, Clemens von Delbrück. Ill and overburdened by an office whose tasks were a standing challenge to the principle of the division of labor, Delbrück was not the man to bear successfully the new strains imposed by war. His greatest fear had been that Germany would find herself at war between the spring planting and the fall harvest, when the previous year's harvest had been consumed or exported and the population was totally dependent upon imports. In 1911 he had proposed that the government buy up a large store of wheat to meet such an eventuality. Until July 1914, however, he did not gather up the energy to override the budgetary objections of the Imperial State Secretary of the Treasury, Kühn, and by then it was too late. The immediate problem was solved by the existence of wheat stores in some West German mills and the proximity of the next harvest. Also, thanks to the initiative of the head of the Hamburg-America Line, Albert Ballin, a private corporation was set up to purchase wheat abroad. In general, however, no plans had been made to meet future difficulties. All that Delbrück had prepared was the Enabling Act and a decree permitting the establishment of price ceilings on the local level. In short, there was a certain amount of legal machinery available if he decided to do something.[2]

[1] Sichler and Tiburtius, *Arbeiterfrage*, pp. 24-25.

[2] Delbrück, *Wirtschaftliche Mobilmachung*, pp. 94-97, 101-102. Ini-

Delbrück would be less subject to criticism if he had awakened to the dangers in time. He was, after all, as much a victim of the military plans for a quick victory as was the military itself. Fearing panic and unrest, however, Delbrück remained silent and inactive. Lulled by optimistic press reports on the food situation, the public consumed more cake in late 1914 than before the war. But at the same time mounting food prices produced unrest, and Socialist demands for price ceilings and controls on producers were the result. In November 1914 the Social Democrats ordered their local organizations to engage in a full scale agitation on the food question.[3]

Appeals to the army were not long in coming, although they first came from other sources. As early as August 1914 Rathenau suggested that the War Ministry control food in the same manner as it was then preparing to control raw materials, but Falkenhayn refused on the grounds that this lay completely outside his sphere of authority. In November Undersecretary Göppert of the Prussian Ministry of Commerce, after a vain effort to persuade Delbrück to control the distribution of wheat and to prevent the use of wheat and rye for fodder, establish price ceilings, and introduce rationing, also turned to the army. During Christmas 1914 he appealed to the head of the Field Railways Section of the General Staff, Major General Wilhelm Groener. The latter had shown some concern about the food supply before the war when he made provisions for the transport of food to the cities in the mobilization plan. Furthermore, Groener had enormous prestige due to the brilliant success of the German mobilization. It was, therefore, natural for Göp-

---

tially a private corporation which reflected Ballin's economic liberalism, the Reichseinkauf GmbH was removed from Hamburg to Berlin in December 1914 and, in January 1915, was transformed into the Zentral-Einkaufs-Gesellschaft mbH. Ballin gave up his leadership at this time, and the new corporation was modeled on the war corporations which had been created in connection with the KRA. See Facius, *Wirtschaft und Staat*, pp. 79-80.

[3] Georg Michaelis, *Für Staat und Volk. Eine Lebensgeschichte*, Berlin, 1922, p. 269, and circular note of the Executive Committee of the Social Democratic Party, Nov. 12, 1914, IISH, Nachlass Vollmar, Nr. 3566.

pert to have expected an understanding response from Groener to his plea for military intervention. Göppert, however, was to be disappointed, for while Groener passed the letter on to Wild von Hohenborn, both generals felt that the situation had been too darkly painted by Göppert and that the army was not the proper agency to handle such questions.[4]

The desire to force Delbrück to take action was not limited to Social Democrats and perceptive bureaucrats of Göppert's stamp. In September 1914 the industrialists Alfred Hugenberg and Hugo Stinnes and some of the mayors in the Ruhr sought government aid for the establishment of a corporation to buy up two million tons of wheat. The plan suddenly to remove large quantities of wheat from the market was designed to raise prices and compel reduced consumption so that food would be on hand for the spring and summer of 1915. When Delbrück rejected this plan, its supporters turned to the Prussian Ministry of Finance. Here they found acceptance for their idea, particularly from Undersecretary Georg Michaelis. A War Wheat Corporation was set up on November 17, 1914, with Michaelis as head of the supervisory committee and officials of the Hamburg-America Line and the North German Lloyd in charge of business operations.[5]

It is interesting that the agrarian leaders opposed the Hugenberg-Stinnes solution, which would have left the food supply and prices subject to the unrestricted development of the market. Dr. Roesicke, the head of the League of German Farmers, feared that an unrestricted development of prices would subject agriculture to charges of profiteering and thus multiply the old attacks leveled against it for its tariff policies.

[4] Rathenau, *Briefe*, p. 213; Wilhelm Groener, *Lebenserinnerungen: Jugend, Generalstab, Weltkrieg*, ed. Friedrich Freiherr Hiller von Gaertringen, Göttingen, 1957, p. 210.

[5] The Kriegsgetreide-Gesellschaft is not to be confused with the Zentral-Einkaufs-Gesellschaft. The sole function of the latter was to purchase wheat from abroad. Originally, both of these corporations were supposed to help maintain the free market economy, but they ended up as government agencies for the control of the food supply. Michaelis, *Staat und Volk*, pp. 269-273.

Roesicke won over the other Conservative leaders, Count Westarp, Freiherr von Wangenhein, and Count von Schwerin-Löwitz, to his point of view. While they agreed with Hugenberg and Stinnes that the workers might be able to meet higher prices through wage increases and government help, they feared an alienation of the lower middle class, to whom such help was not so readily accessible. Political and social considerations thus led the agrarians to support moderate price ceilings on wheat, while the state of the food supply led them to support the sequestration of wheat stores.[6]

Both the industrialists and the agrarians, however, were agreed that action would have to be taken by the Imperial government. The former group was upset by the inability of the War Wheat Corporation to secure the two million tons of wheat it had set out to purchase, and they wanted more government support. The latter feared leftist agitation and the consequences of further delay. Both groups, accompanied by the famous agricultural expert Professor Max Sering, turned to General von Moltke at the end of December 1914. Despite his military failure and displacement to General Staff Headquarters in Berlin, Moltke still had influence with the Chancellor and the Emperor. To the great irritation of Falkenhayn, who disliked independent political activity on the part of his subordinates, Moltke sent an appeal to Bethmann on January 10, 1915, calling for thoroughgoing measures to remedy the food situation. By now, however, Delbrück was prepared to act, for the Social Democratic leaders, Ebert and Scheidemann, and the head of the Free Trade Unions, Legien, had warned him that they could not maintain the *Burgfrieden* if prices continued their uncontrolled rise.[7]

In late January and early February 1915 a series of orders

[6] Kuno Graf von Westarp, *Konservative Politik im letzten Jahrzehnt des Kaiserreiches*, 2 vols., Berlin, 1935, II, pp. 397-385.

[7] *Ibid.*, pp. 383-385; Moltke, *Erinnerungen*, pp. 399-401; Count von Lerchenfeld, Bavarian ambassador to Berlin to Count Hertling, Minister President of Bavaria, Jan. 19, 1915, BHStA, Abt. II, MA 1, Nr. 909.

were passed by the Bundesrat which put wheat production under government control. All wheat was placed at the disposal of the government, and farmers were required to declare their stores. Heavy fines were stipulated for false declarations. The use of wheat and rye for fodder was prohibited. The War Wheat Corporation was ordered to buy up the wheat and maximum prices were imposed. An Imperial Allocation Office was set up to distribute the wheat. This was later joined to the War Wheat Corporation. Bread rationing was introduced in Berlin in January and extended to the rest of the Empire in June. Thus began the government organization of the wheat supply, the "compulsory economy" (*Zwangswirtschaft*), that was to serve as a model for all subsequent developments in the organization of the food supply.[8]

Controls on other food items were slower in coming for both political and technical reasons. The farmers, who were forced to engage in a massive pig slaughter in early 1915 due to the fear of a potato shortage, held on tenaciously to their remaining livestock and looked askance at further efforts to cut the fodder supply. They resented the price ceilings set by the government and tended either to produce noncontrolled products or to go over to black marketeering. In the control of wheat, however, the government had been dealing with a relatively uniform and storable product. Potatoes, other vegetables, milk, and eggs did not present such advantages. The agrarian leaders, who wanted only moderate price ceilings on wheat and opposed the extension of the compulsory economy, were soon completely at odds with the urban consumer groups, who wanted the compulsory system extended to almost all food products and prices kept as low as possible. Urban pressure increasingly proved the stronger, and Delbrück was forced to set up an Imperial Potato Office in October 1915. This Office had the right to sequester potato stores and to ban the use of

[8] August Skalweit, *Die Deutsche Kriegsernährungswirtschaft*, Berlin, Leipzig, Stuttgart, 1927, pp. 146-161.

Something must be done to relieve the bureaucratic hemorrhoidism. The food supply is drowning in a huge flood of ink.

potatoes for fodder. An Imperial Price Examination Agency and price examination agencies for all cities with over ten thousand inhabitants were also established in the fall of 1915. Both the Imperial Price Examination Agency and its local branches lacked all executive power, however, and they were merely advisory bodies.[9]

Most deleterious to the government's efforts was the clumsy machinery through which it had to operate. The Interior Office had no administrative apparatus of its own and was thus forced to rely upon the officialdom of the various states. Between the Interior Office and the implementation of its directives stood the special interests of ministries and local officials. In Prussia the Minister of the Interior, Loebell, and the Minister for Agriculture, Schorlemer, were in complete disagreement. The former supported consumer interests, while the latter demanded high prices and minimum controls. Loebell was supported by Minister of Public Works Breitenbach and the Commerce Minister, Sydow. Both men were naturally most interested in the problems of the industrial workers. Breitenbach felt that "the most important task of the government is to bring about an equitable regulation of prices."[10] Sydow, in direct opposition to the views of Hugenberg and Stinnes, argued that the miners cared more about cheap potato prices than about wage increases. Although the Prussian prefects (*Landräte*) were under the direction of Loebell, they tended to carry out their orders in the spirit of Schorlemer. Sympathetic to the farmers because of class ties and personal interest, it is no wonder that they were allied with Schorlemer in sabotaging the compulsory system.

The non-Prussian states were not easy to deal with either. Bavaria, a primarily agricultural state, was loathe to obey the orders of Berlin and serve the interests of the urban consumers. Count Hertling, the Minister-President, was a strong opponent of the sequestration of wheat, which he regarded as a surrender to "socialist principles." As an official observer remarked:

[9] *Ibid.*, pp. 120-133; Westarp, *Konservative Politik*, II, pp. 397-398.

[10] Prussian Cabinet meeting, Sept. 21, 1915, BA, Nachlass Heinrichs, Nr. 14, and notation of Nov. 23, 1915, BA, Nachlass Wild von Hohenborn, Nr. 2.

He believes that the carrying out of these measures will cause great difficulties and that they will not have the desired success, since there will certainly be successful efforts to evade the regulations. He only hopes that the measures will have a frightening effect, namely, that the people will see what happens when one fulfills the demands of the Social Democrats.[11]

If the efforts of the Interior Office foundered upon the passive resistance of the state authorities, they were also hampered by the actions of many Deputy Commanding Generals. Where the former were inclined to serve agrarian interests, the latter had consumer interests uppermost in mind. Since the food situation was the chief source of public agitation, it constituted a menace to public security and many generals were quick to intervene with arbitrarily instituted price ceilings and threats to farmers who seemed to be holding back food or not producing enough. Such actions called forth Social Democratic praise in the Reichstag and irritation in the Interior Office. In many cases they only increased agricultural resistance and made life all the more difficult for the harried civil officials. The effect of the local price ceilings was usually one of driving food into areas where higher prices were paid. The speed with which the military authorities acted, however, seemed to provide a welcome contrast to the oscillation of the civil authorities between consumer and producer interests.[12]

The cry for a military solution to the food situation found its most concrete expression in proposals for a military food dictator and an economic general staff. General von Moltke actually went so far as to appeal to the Emperor directly. The universal loss of faith in the government led both consumer and producer groups to support the creation of a military agency advised by "experts" to solve the food problem in an

[11] Von Möser, Württemberg ambassador to Munich, to Weizsäcker, Minister-President of Württemberg, Jan. 28, 1915, HStASt, E, 73, 42e, $12g^1$.

[12] Reichstag Debates, Jan. 11, 1916, 307, p. 520, and Westarp, *Konservative Politik*, II, p. 392.

"independent" fashion. General von Falkenhayn was constantly appealed to, and he had some inclination to intervene. His efforts were blocked by the Prussian Cabinet and, particularly, by the War Ministry. While willing to consider the appointment of an advisory council of experts to help the government, the Prussian Cabinet was opposed to the establishment of an independent executive authority under military leadership. In a meeting of the Cabinet on May 1, 1915, Breitenbach expressed the viewpoint of all present:

> The state government is responsible to the King and the Parliament and must therefore defend itself against the lately repeated attempts of the General Staff of the army to interfere in the regulation of economic questions. The General Staff of the army is a commanding authority [*Kommandobehorde*] without parliamentary responsibility and can, therefore, deal with the government on the problems here in question only through the War Ministry.[13]

General von Wandel also felt that the idea of granting a decisive voice in economic questions to the General Staff was "insupportable in public law." For a change even Schorlemer and Loebell were in agreement on something.

Wandel's objections were of a practical as well as of a constitutional nature, however. In a letter to the Deputy Commanding Generals on November 24, 1915, he pointed out,

> A Deputy Commanding General sees the possibility of eliminating all difficulties in the passage of an Imperial law that would put all the existing agencies into one Imperial agency (economic dictator). It goes without saying that the War Ministry would welcome this with regard to many matters. But it would only be realizable if such an agency had been prepared and organized in peacetime. If one wants

[13] Prussian Cabinet meeting, May 1, 1915, BA, P 135/1782. See also the Deutsche Wehrverein memorandum of Aug. 17, 1915, HStASt, E, 130, X^{a}.38, Bl. 78, and the VdESI discussion, Dec. 9, 1915, BA, R 13I/147.

> to create this now, then—aside from constitutional barriers—more costly time would be lost until it was capable of operating. I believe, therefore, that one must do with what is at hand and direct one's efforts toward recognizing the food problems quickly and then decisively meeting them.[14]

While admitting that many of the measures taken by the civil authorities had come too late and that this had caused "sinking confidence on the part of the population in the civil authorities," he warned the generals against promoting this tendency by arbitrary measures either at variance with or duplicating those ordered by the civil authorities. The generals were to collaborate with the responsible food agencies and to report problems to the War Ministry so that the Ministry might seek their adjustment at the highest level.

The decision to try to make do with the organization at hand and to pragmatically respond to immediate situations as they arose met with little sympathy as the food situation took a decisive turn for the worse in 1916. The army had placed as much labor as possible at the disposal of the farmers in 1915, but nothing could compensate for the miserable weather. To a bad potato crop was added the deliberate holding back of potatoes by the farmers in order to secure higher prices. In January 1916 the Reichstag irritability forced the government to establish an Advisory Food Council (*Ernährungsbeirat*) of Reichstag members to watch over the work of the Interior Office.[15] The Council had purely advisory functions and satisfied no one. Industrial areas were particularly hard hit by the potato shortage, and war production began to suffer. Disgusted with the government's impotence, many firms engaged in what was euphemistically called self-help, i.e., buying food for the workers on the black market. As one industrialist reluctantly admitted,

> We have been robbing the strength of our workers and

[14] BHStA, Abt. IV, MK, I Mob zu 4, Allg. U.-A. 2, Bd. I.
[15] Prussian Cabinet meeting, Dec. 11, 1915, BA, P 135/1783, Bl. 58.

> officials for two years, and it can't go on forever, especially since the workers are getting much less food than in peacetime. It may be that too much was eaten in peacetime; I'll grant that. But now they are so far at the limit of their strength that it is really to be taken seriously when they say: we cannot work more than nine hours.[16]

In 1916, and particularly during the last half of that year, there was a marked increase of food riots, disturbances before food stores, and small strikes. The Deputy Commanding Generals reported growing discontent among housewives and workers and increasing concern on the part of employers. At the same time the farmers felt persecuted and maligned. Rising tension between city and country found its only relief in a joint, albeit discordant, execration of the government.[17]

The growing seriousness of the situation heightened the demands for a military food dictator. Falkenhayn was bombarded with demands for help, demands he resisted under the pressure of the War Ministry and the Operations Section of the General Staff. The latter, headed by the very influential Colonel von Tappen, wanted the General Staff free of economic distractions. Wichard von Moellendorff sought to enlist the influence of Fritz Haber for the appointment of Field Marshal von Hindenburg as food dictator in the hope that the magic of Hindenburg's name might break through the bureaucratic tangle and the obstinacy of the farmers. The Reichstag debates were filled with attacks on Delbrück and demands for a food dictator and centralization of the government organization. On January 1, 1916, the Socialist trade union organ, the *Correspondenzblatt*, commented:

16 Comment by Dr. Waldschmidt at War Ministry meeting, Sept. 16, 1916, BHStA, Abt. IV, MK, K Mob 6, Bd. I, Bl. zu 12.

17 The number of strikes increased from 137 in 1915 to 240 in 1916, Wrisberg, *Heer und Heimat*, p. 116. On strikes, riots, and disturbances, see the "Zusammenstellungen aus den Monats-Berichten der stellvertretenden Generalkommandos, BHStA, Abt. IV, MK, I Mob zu 4, Allg. U.-A. 2, Bd. I-III, hereinafter cited as ZMG Reports without archival reference.

> The *military dictatorship* has in many cases shown more understanding for the needs of the people than the bureaucracy. It is more competent in mass supply and requisitioning and knows also how to evaluate the conditions for the successful conduct of war . . . better than the civil administrative people, for whom the landowner and the commercial councilors are still individuals to be regarded more highly than the average man of the people.[18]

In May the same paper called for the establishment of an Imperial food office "armed with military force" that would control the food supply of the country.

The most ardent supporter of unified food administration in government circles was Undersecretary Michaelis. Although he originally favored an economic general staff under military leadership, Michaelis gave up this idea due to the War Ministry's resistance. He proposed instead the establishment of a war food office to control the food supply for both the civilian population and the army. Military cooperation, therefore, was essential. Michaelis' work in the Imperial Wheat Office brought him into constant contact with General Groener, who was very much involved in the transport of food, particularly from Rumania. By 1916 Groener had had ample opportunity to revise the light-hearted reception he had given to Undersecretary Göppert's gloomy prognostications in 1914, and he brought Michaelis' proposals directly to Falkenhayn. In early April Falkenhayn told Groener that he was willing to send a personal representative to serve in a war food office and, on April 20, informed Groener that he would be appointed were such an institution created. Falkenhayn insisted, however, that the civil authorities take the initiative and make the proposals.[19]

[18] *Correspondenzblatt,* Jan. 1 and May 13, 1916. For the preceding material, see Groener, *Lebenserinnerungen*, p. 332; Moellendorff to Haber, May 11, 1916, BA, Nachlass Moellendorff, Nr. 6; Reichstag Debates, Jan. 11-14, 1916, 307, pp. 514ff.

[19] Michaelis to Finance Minister Lentze, April 25, 1916, BA, P 135/1783, Bl. 129 and Groener, *Lebenserinnerungen*, p. 333.

For a change matters were now moving swiftly in Berlin. Delbrück, surrendering to both illness and universal antagonism, resigned on May 7. One of his last decisions was to support the establishment of a war food office. Bethmann agreed that something had to be done to satisfy Reichstag opinion and was even prepared to place a military officer at the head of the new organization. On May 15 he sent a telegram to Falkenhayn asking whether Groener was suitable and available for this position. He insisted, however, that Groener surrender his position on the General Staff. Groener, in short, was to receive his powers from the Chancellor and to be responsible to him alone. When Falkenhayn discussed the question with Groener, the latter objected to giving up his position as head of the field railways. Groener's stubborn insistence stemmed not only from his personal attachment to his work, "but above all because my personal power in every other activity stood or fell with this office and its extraordinarily wide powers. And it was above all necessary for the new agency that . . . one could command with resolution and have power."[20] Falkenhayn was inclined to agree with Groener's reasoning, and he sent Groener to Berlin to present these views to the Chancellor on May 16.

While traveling to Berlin, Groener developed proposals for the Chancellor. He favored placing the War Food Office (*Kriegsernährungsamt* [KEA]) under a military leader empowered to command all military authorities in the homeland, including the War Ministry and the Deputy Commanding Generals, on food questions. As an alternative, an officer from the General Staff might be attached to the KEA with such powers. Groener wanted real power for the military leader or representative of the KEA. He had long regarded the War Ministry as excessively bureaucratic, and he disliked the slow-moving machinery of the civil government. As head of the field railways he had grown used to wide powers over both civil

[20] Groener, *Lebenserinnerungen*, pp. 333-334.

and military agencies and now wished to extend this kind of authority into the food area.[21]

In Berlin he found nothing but resistance to his ideas. Wild von Hohenborn was irritated by Groener's "pretensions to power" and rejected the idea that Groener enter the KEA as "an organ of the Supreme Command." The War Minister was particularly insistent that only he be empowered to give orders to the Deputy Commanding Generals. Wandel was in complete agreement with Wild. It was thus clear that the KEA was not to have a military leader. Wandel was willing to make one concession to Groener's wishes, however. He agreed that Groener could remain head of the field railways while representing the army on the KEA. In return Groener was forced to promise that he would consult with the War Ministry before taking any measures requiring the cooperation of the Deputy Commanding Generals.[22]

Groener was angered by what he regarded as the narrow bureaucratic mentality of the War Ministry and disgusted by the ultimate form of the KEA, which he called a "bloodless creation of the Holy St. Compromise."[23] Formally established by the Bundesrat on May 22, 1916, the KEA was anything but a dictatorial agency. The Bundesrat vested all control of the food supply in the Chancellor, who in turn passed his powers to the President of the KEA. All previous regulations of the Bundesrat concerning the food supply, however, remained in force. The army remained independent of the KEA in its own food procurement. The KEA, like the Interior Office, was dependent upon the various state ministries for the enforcement of its directives. Only two organizational improvements can be singled out. First, a centralized agency solely concerned with the food supply and unburdened by other areas of competence had finally been created. Second, by a royal order of May 27,

[21] For his notes on this question, see Nachlass Groener, 192-I.

[22] Notation, June 4, 1916, BA, Nachlass Wild von Hohenborn, Nr. 2; Groener, *Lebenserinnerungen*, pp. 333-334; Generalobersten von Einem, *Ein Armeeführer erlebt den Weltkrieg*, Leipzig, 1938, p. 229.

[23] Groener, *Lebenserinnerungen*, p. 550.

the Deputy Commanding Generals were henceforth to issue no orders concerning the food supply and prices without the approval of the War Ministry. Groener's presence in the KEA insured closer collaboration between the civil and the military authorities and laid the foundation for cooperation between the KEA and the Deputy Commanding Generals.[24]

The man appointed President of the KEA, Freiherr von Batocki, had distinguished himself as High President of East Prussia, where he had successfully led the reconstruction following the Russian retreat. Although a Conservative with close ties to the agrarian leaders, Batocki was critical of their policies and sensitive to consumer interests. Like Delbrück, Batocki wanted to please everyone. Groener recognized immediately that "He lacked the necessary hardness and lack of consideration to be a dictator."[25] Relations between Groener and Batocki, however, were always of the best. Both men placed national interests above all else and both felt victimized by the lumbering administrative apparatus of the Empire. The desire to secure national unanimity in the management of the food supply led to the appointment of a KEA Executive Committee reflecting all shades of opinion. Labor was represented by the head of the Christian Trade Union Movement, Adam Stegerwald, and the Social Democrat, Dr. August Müller. The appointment of the latter was largely due to the insistence of Groener that a Social Democrat be taken into the KEA. The Reichstag Advisory Council was now attached to the KEA. The various interest groups were thus well ensconced in the new organization.[26]

The KEA may be judged either in terms of public expectations or in terms of what it managed to accomplish under very

[24] Skalweit, *Kriegsernährungswirtschaft*, pp. 179-185; Royal Cabinet Order, May 27, 1916, BHStA, Abt. IV, MK, 1 Mob 4c, Bd. I, Bl. zu 1.

[25] Groener, *Lebenserinnerungen*, p. 335.

[26] *Ibid.* Commercial Councilor Reusch represented industry; Commercial Councilor Manasse represented commerce; Undersecretary von Falkenhausen represented the Prussian Ministry of Agriculture; the Mayor of Plauen, Dr. Dehne, represented the cities; and the Bavarian Ministerial Director, Edler von Braun, represented South German interests.

difficult circumstances. In the first case it was an utter failure. In the second it was moderately successful. Batocki and Groener had as hard a fight with Schorlemer as had Delbrück. Bavarian officialdom and peasantry were no easier to deal with than before. Coordination with the army continued to present difficulties. Having reconciled himself to a Food Office directed by civilians, Groener took the view that it was now the task of the military authorities to serve the new organization. Groener's desire to direct the Deputy Commanding Generals in this sense and without much prior consultation with the War Ministry led to many conflicts with Wild von Hohenborn, who felt that "The cutting out of the War Ministry seems to be the chief point of his [Groener's] program!"[27]

At the same time, the KEA attacked the problem of feeding the industrial workers with more vigor than had been demonstrated by its predecessor. A system of special food premiums for "hard-working" and "hardest-working" laborers (*Schwer- und Schwerstarbeiterzulagen*) was introduced. The system was far from perfect, but it was an important step in the direction of food allocation according to physiological need. The KEA recognized also that it was impossible for workers to queue up in the infamous "polonaise" that assembled before food stores every morning, and the communal authorities were ordered to supply food directly to the factories. Such improvements, however, could only mitigate the effects of actual shortage. The old conflict between city and country remained, and the organization of the KEA was not likely to end demands for military control of the food supply.[28]

Yet the army had demonstrated neither the desire to manage the food supply nor the aptitude for doing so. The War Ministry was absolutely opposed to military direction of the food supply, and Falkenhayn certainly never displayed a pas-

[27] Notation of July 26, 1916, BA, Nachlass Hohenborn, Nr. 2 and Groener, *Lebenserinnerungen*, p. 553.

[28] Skalweit, *Kriegsernährungswirtschaft*, pp. 184-185, and Batocki to the Federated Governments, June 14, 1916, BHStA, Abt. IV, MK, 1 Mob 4c, Bl. zu 8.

sionate desire to respond to pleas for his intervention. The army's performance in the food question was not exactly exemplary. The unwillingness of the military authorities to coordinate their food supply administration with that of the civil authorities was certainly most bureaucratic, while the arbitrary measures of the Deputy Commanding Generals demonstrated that the men in military uniform were just as capable of adding confusion to the situation as were those in civil garb. Shortly after entering the KEA, Groener himself was forced to admit the futility of establishing a military food organization in the midst of the war:

> The difficulty lies in the many-sidedness of our administrative apparatus. To me, as an officer, the relationships seem like a labyrinth which is so confused that one cannot find one's way. But we cannot get away from this administrative apparatus, cannot set up something new in its place, above all not a military organization. There has been much talk of a military food dictatorship, but the way things stand, I do not know what a military apparatus is supposed to create. Speed is necessary. It would be another matter if this had been prepared in the mobilization plans before the war.[29]

Indeed, it would seem as if the War Ministry's opposition to military control of the food supply reflected a modesty all the more praiseworthy because it was felt at a time when public opinion was convinced that the army could work miracles.

Furthermore, we must ask whether the army was able to present anything new by way of a program. Here, again, the answer is negative. The reasons for this were made clear in a memorandum written in October 1916 by Groener's adjutant, Captain Richard Merton, a memorandum which Groener circulated widely in military and government circles.[30] In this

[29] From an undated statement to the press, BHStA, Abt. IV, MK, XIV Mob 2, Bd. XXVII, Bl. 59.

[30] For the text, see Richard Merton, *Erinnernswertes aus meinem Leben, das über das persönliche hinausgeht*, Frankfurt a.M., 1955, pp. 12-22.

memorandum Merton stressed the actual food shortage as the heart of the problem. The government's procrastination had exacerbated the difficulties, but difficulties would have been present in any case, and the KEA would never be able to eliminate them. Turning to the debate between supporters of the compulsory system and the supporters of the free market system, Merton first defended the former system on purely economic grounds. Production and price controls were absolutely necessary if the urban consumers were to have enough to eat and be able to pay for their food. The farmers might complain, but they would always have enough food for themselves and, given the food shortage, they would also be guaranteed some profit. For the consumers, the question was one of life or death.

Far more interesting, however, was Merton's analysis of the political aspect of the food question. The measures taken by the government had a distinctly "socialist" flavor and thus appeared as a harbinger for the future. This seemed all the more the case because the government was promising a "new orientation" after the war. Thus the Socialists were using the food issue as a test of the sincerity of the government's promises of internal reform, and the Junker conservatives were attacking the government's food system precisely because it represented concessions to the left.[31] While recognizing the bad effect this had on the morale of the farmers, Merton argued that a retreat from or reversal of the compulsory system was impossible. From a theoretical standpoint, such a change might be worthy of discussion, "but politically it is already harmful and practically the attempt would lead to the collapse of morale." In short, however much the compulsory system led to black marketeering, overorganization, and demoralization of producers, there was no escaping it. So long as the urban masses were vital to the war effort and so long as their collabo-

[31] For an illustration of the connection between the debates over the food question and the new orientation, see the remarks of the Socialist deputy Hoffmann and the agrarian leader Roesicke, Reichstag Debates, June 7-8, 1916, 308, pp. 1622-1623, 1643-1653.

ration was threatened by the tendencies of the industrial workers in the direction of an internationalist and republican ideology, so long would it be necessary to give their interests primary consideration. The path chosen by the civil authorities was inescapable, and the army, by implication, would always be bound by the same social and political necessities.

2. *Bureaucracy, Army, and the Social Consequences of the War*

The concern of the government and the army with the care and satisfaction of the industrial workers in the distribution of food is only one important indication of the shifting balance of political and social power that becomes clearly discernible by 1916. Although the general tendency toward the preponderance of producers' goods industries and the industrial workers in Germany's economic structure was evident before the war, the war had a catalytic effect upon this development. After the initial period of economic contraction, a contraction which had begun in May 1913 but which had been very much intensified by the military mobilization of 1914, the first phases of economic mobilization had created the foundation for a period of economic expansion which began in the summer of 1915, when employment returned to prewar levels. This expansion, however, did not benefit all sectors of the industrial economy. Those industries producing primarily for the war effort and having access to raw materials at home or in the occupied territories were the chief gainers. The civilian industries, which were incapable of easily converting to war production and which were dependent upon foreign trade necessarily suffered. The war was disastrous to the German commercial interests because of the blockade and was very harmful to the textile industry because of the raw materials shortage. Government efforts to keep the textile companies in business and maintain their stock of workers by stretching policies—cutting working hours, banning the use of laborsaving devices, supporting unemployed textile workers to keep them from seeking employment elsewhere—were only partially successful. The South German states complained bitterly that they were being ruined by the war while the great industries of Prussia were being richly supplied with war contracts.[32]

The war greatly increased the importance and attractiveness of employment in heavy industry. Wages in the war industries, as compared with other sectors of employment, rose rapidly. To these relatively higher wages were added food premiums of various kinds. As a result, agricultural workers and workers engaged in less lucrative forms of employment tended to drift into the armaments industry or other branches of heavy industry. The situation in agriculture became so serious that Deputy Commanding Generals had to issue orders forbidding agricultural workers from going into industry on the grounds that this threatened the food supply. Workers in war industries were better able to meet the rise in the cost of living than craftsmen, white collar workers, and lower officials.

The wartime expansion, however, did not bring prosperity to the workers. The average daily real wages of workers in the war industries had dropped 21.6 percent between March 1914 and September 1916, while the real wages of workers in the civilian industries had decreased 42.1 percent during the same period.[33] This loss of purchasing power, coupled as it was with a growing scarcity of food, inevitably produced great discontent. At the same time, the shortage of labor gave the workers considerable leverage when it came to making their demands felt. These developments encouraged the unions to collaborate with one another to improve the economic conditions of the workers and to take advantage of the favorable labor market to promote the union cause. The unions sought to keep the workers loyal to the war effort, but they warned the government that this loyalty could not be taken for granted: "The

[32] Bry, *Wages in Germany*, pp. 191-192, and Heinz Henning, "Der Aufbau der deutschen Kriegswirtschaft im ersten Weltkrieg," *Wehrwissenschaftliche Rundschau*, VI, 1956, pp. 49-65. There will be a more detailed analysis of the socioeconomic effects of the war in Chapter IX.

[33] Bry, *Wages in Germany*, pp. 200-211.

masses of the workers cannot in the long run bear the lessening of their otherwise unsatisfactory income. They must and will demand wage premiums, and the carefully guarded *Burgfrieden* between employers and workers will thereby founder."[34]

The ever-increasing union demands for higher wages led to growing conflict with the employers. It is important to understand what was really at stake in these conflicts. Employers were usually willing to grant wage increases. They needed the labor and they had to keep up the physical strength of the workers. What they feared was the precedent these wages were setting for the future. As early as November 1914, the *Arbeitgeberzeitung*, the most important employer newspaper, was warning that the maintenance of wartime wages after the war would ruin Germany's ability to compete on world markets. A bitter postwar struggle with labor was anticipated over this issue. By February 1916 the same paper was taking an even harsher tone by stating that a reduction of wartime wages was "to be expected with certainty."[35]

The unions feared the coming struggle, particularly since the demobilization would probably create unemployment and thus render strikes ineffective. Union support for the establishment of an Imperial conciliation bureau to settle postwar wage conflicts grew out of these fears.[36] This demand raised the even more basic issue of negotiations between labor and management on the basis of parity. We have already seen the role played by this question in the conflict over war boards. It is thus clear that the struggle over the political and social equality of the working class lay at the root of the various conflicts between labor and management during the war and that both sides were seeking to secure the best possible position for themselves during the crucial demobilization period. As a consequence, both the labor and the employer organizations tended to draw closer together within each of their respective camps.

[34] *Correspondenzblatt*, July 24, 1915.
[35] *Arbeitgeberzeitung*, Jan. 11, 1914, and Feb. 13, 1916.
[36] *Correspondenzblatt*, Nov. 22, 1916.

The *Burgfrieden* concluded among the Free, Christian, and Hirsch-Duncker unions found expression not only in their collaboration in the government-assigned tasks of relieving unemployment and caring for the war wounded, but also in joint petitions for the establishment of public labor exchanges and the improvement in the food supply system. Most important, preliminary discussions had been held on the continuation of such cooperative efforts after the war. Similarly, on October 26, 1916, the Central Association of German Industrialists and the League of German Industrialists decided to found a German Industrial Council to maintain that unity which had its wartime expression in the German Industry War Committee. A comparison of the social policies of the army and the civil authorities during wartime, therefore, must be measured in terms of the fundamental conflicts which had divided German society in the past and which seemed to promise to divide it even more in the future.[37]

The policy of the government toward organized labor was extremely ambivalent. An Imperial Chancellery memorandum of October 27, 1914, raised the question of "drawing upon broader classes for the tasks of the state" along with the problem of the "transformation of the labor movement":

> There is no doubt that the common danger has won the German workers for the nation. It offers perhaps the last opportunity to win them not only for the nation, but also for the state. The workers who return home as soldiers crowned with victory will not be disposed to follow a Social Democracy that is an enemy of the Fatherland and revolutionary. But they will remain workers. The state must seek to avoid treating the labor movement as an enemy. It must call upon the unions and avoid giving the antistate dogmatists of the old Social Democracy slogans under which they can again lead the workers against the state.[38]

[37] Varain, *Gewerkschaften*, p. 91; *industriellen Spitzenverband*, pp. 83-85.

[38] Werner Richter, *Gewerkschaften, Monopolkapital und Staat im*

The necessity of internal reform was recognized, but the problem of reconciling such reform with the authoritarian state remained as difficult as ever. In the early months of the war Bethmann did not feel that reforms could be made until "the Social Democratic leaders clearly understand that the German Empire and the Prussian State can never shake the firm basis upon which they have grown and the firm sense of the state and that system which the Social Democrats have previously branded as militarism." The government thus adopted a policy of promising a "new orientation," while putting off reforms until the end of the war. An effort was made to gain the collaboration of the Socialist organizations, but the government strove equally hard to avoid having this collaboration lead to immediate legislative consequences.[39]

The patriots in the union and Socialist movements were most anxious to establish an entirely new relationship with the government. Indeed, in a confidential discussion with Undersecretary of State Wahnschaffe in October 1914, Deputy Cohen went so far as to speak of a "movement of the Social Democratic Party in a monarchical direction" as a possibility for the future.[40] Such a transformation of objectives, however, had to be justified to the masses of workers who had been indoctrinated in a revolutionary and republican ideology. The alliance with the government had to bring concrete results. Those most in favor of supporting the war effort were thus compelled to agitate for reforms that would win the masses over to their policy, a necessity that became all the more pressing with the growing split in the party in 1915. Ostensibly caused by the question of voting for war credits, this split was actually the culmination of many years of conflict within the party.[41] As desirable as this split was in the eyes of the government, it was

---

ersten Weltkrieg und in der Novemberrevolution, 1914-1919, Berlin, 1959, p. 50.

[39] *Ibid.*, pp. 48-49.

[40] Kuczynski, *Ausbruch des ersten Weltkrieges*, p. 210.

[41] Schorske, *German Social Democracy*, pp. 269-301.

certain to create difficulties. The pressure for reform of the Prussian suffrage, the Associations Law and the other laws affecting the social order gathered momentum as the struggle between the competing wings of the party for the control of the masses achieved overt expression.

It was the length of the war that destroyed the government's ability to delay reforms until the coming of peace. Cordial visits to union headquarters and praise for union contributions to the war effort were no longer enough. The government had to prove its sincerity by deeds. The unions were particularly insistent upon a reform of the Imperial Associations Law of 1909 under which, thanks to the interpretation of the courts, unions were regarded as political associations. Young men under eighteen were thus prohibited from joining the unions and attending union meetings. The government had tried to evade the settlement of this issue by promising to treat the unions as nonpolitical associations during the war and eventually to revise the law. The unions declared that this was unsatisfactory, as it provided no guarantee against independent judicial decisions running contrary to government policy. By December 1915 Bethmann decided to give in to this union demand. As he told the Prussian Cabinet,

> As a result of the long duration of the war, the attitude of the radical wing of the Social Democrats becomes ever harsher. The radicals use the existing food problems and the increasing war-weariness to make propaganda for their aims. They fight the revisionists by reproaching them for being pacified by the pretty words of the government without actually getting any concessions. The situation had become very serious, and it will hardly be possible to keep the revisionist wing on the previous track if one does not create some relief for them through some success in internal politics.[42]

Despite the government's apparent desire for speed, it took six

[42] Institut für Marxismus-Leninismus, *Dokumente und Materialien zur Geschichte der deutschen Arbeiterbewegung*, Reihe II: 1914-1945, 2 vols., Berlin, 1957-1958, I, pp. 258-259.

months of tedious negotiation before the matter was settled. In June 1916 the party finally settled for its minimum demands, and a law was passed declaring that unions were not to be regarded as political associations. The union leaders, who were most anxious to win over the large number of young people engaged in war work, regarded this as an important victory. It certainly was a major defeat for the industrialists and conservatives, who feared a radicalization of Germany's youth.[43]

One of the major quarrels holding up revision of the Association Law was the Socialist demand that the law be amended to include a provision guaranteeing the unrestricted right of coalition for railroad workers. Before being employed, railroad workers had to take an oath that they did not belong to any union whose constitution did not expressly prohibit strikes. The Free Trade Unions were trying to form a new German Railroad Workers Union. On principle it had to maintain the right of unions to strike, and Breitenbach refused to permit his workers to join the union. The General Commission sought to resolve the issue by publicly declaring that it would not support railroad worker strikes, but Breitenbach insisted that this be stated in writing in the union's constitution. The result was an acrimonious debate, the Social Democrats making a particular point of contrasting Breitenbach's "formalism" with the flexibility of the military authorities.[44]

The most important issue of the new orientation was the reform of the Prussian suffrage. Here Socialist agitation was matched by a fervent government effort to delay facing this issue. By 1916, however, the same considerations that had made action on the Associations Law necessary were operative in the case of the suffrage question. Despite the violent objections of the conservative members of the Prussian Cabinet, Bethmann had persuaded the Emperor to indicate, in his

[43] Westarp, *Konservative Politik*, II, pp. 222-227; *Arbeitgeberzeitung*, Aug. 29, 1915; IISH, SPK Fraktionssitzung, May 19, 1916; Reichstag Debates, June 5, 1916, 307, pp. 1473ff.

[44] Paul Umbreit, *Der Krieg und die Arbeitsverhältnisse: Die deutschen Gewerkschaften im Kriege*, Stuttgart, Berlin, Leipzig, 1928, pp. 137-141.

Speech from the Throne of January 13, 1916, that there would be a change in "the basis for the representation of the people in the law-giving bodies" after the war. The promise was vague enough, as there were many types of undemocratic suffrage systems that could replace the bizarre one then employed in Prussia. Yet it was an important sign of the growing tendency of the government to make concessions to the left in order to relieve the strains of the long war.[45]

That the government moved slowly in making these concessions was to be expected. As an employer, as the ultimate guardian of the old social order, and as the repository of its power, the government could not respond with measures affecting the social and political structure of Germany in peace time with the same alacrity with which the War Ministry responded to the immediate demands of war. It was one thing "to draw upon broad classes for the tasks of the state," it was another to permit those classes to define the tasks of the state and determine its mode of operation. The Socialists clearly recognized what lay at the core of Breitenbach's refusal to recognize their railroad union: "Herr von Breitenbach is by no means what one calls a typical reactionary. As a minister concerned with technical matters he has more than once demonstrated an undeniable sense for the needs of modern life. But he can no more escape the authoritarian traditions of the Prussian bureaucracy than someone can jump over his shadow."[46]

Breitenbach sincerely feared that substantive concessions made under the pressure of war would revenge themselves in peacetime. He would not permit "outside groups" to participate in the management of the railroads which were so vital to Germany's economy and defense. Needless to say, the maintenance of this bureaucratic power and the power of the traditional ruling classes made it all the more imperative for the ministers to be cautious in taking measures which might lead to the parliamentarization of Germany. A Socialist majority in

[45] Westarp, *Konservative Politik*, II, pp. 255-260.
[46] *Internationale Korrespondenz*, Feb. 6, 1917.

the Prussian Landtag would inevitably impose restraints on the independent functioning of the bureaucracy. In contrast to the army, the civil authorities were in a position to make permanent substantive concessions, and they were very conscious of the ultimate implications of their actions. They were thus more inclined to hesitate and to weigh every step in the direction of reform with a view toward its long-term significance.

It is revealing to note that General Wild von Hohenborn voted against a reform of the Associations Law and expressed the greatest reservations in voting for a statement by the Emperor on the suffrage question. The same man who defended the policies of AZS before the industrialists was opposed to political and social concessions of a substantive nature! Wild was a conservative intimately associated with the leaders of the Conservative Party. While there is no evidence that he consciously deliberated in his own mind the contradiction between his own views and the policies of his Ministry, he certainly must have been aware that such a contradiction existed. The industrialists were not exactly silent about AZS. The simplest explanation is that Wild was able to rationalize the contradiction away by considering the measures taken by AZS to be purely temporary and limited to the war period. He was no fool, however, and he certainly must have realized the dangerous postwar implications of the War Ministry's social concessions. Furthermore, Hohenborn did not face this dilemma alone. General von Wrisberg, also a supporter of AZS, was a conservative. The Deputy Commanding Generals were almost all conservative, when not blatantly reactionary. Yet they, too, acted in ways at variance with their convictions. The only two leaders in the War Ministry who appear to have had real sympathy for the ideas of the Society for Social Reform were Wandel and Koeth.[47]

[47] For Wild's votes, see Westarp, *Konservative Politik*, II, pp. 224, 257; in a meeting with the industrialists on Oct. 14, 1916, he vigorously defended AZS and Sichler, Nachlass Stresemann, 6865, frames H129489-H129496. Wrisberg's postwar memoirs demonstrate his conservatism. The information on Wandel and Koeth is derived from Senator Tiburtius'

Explanations of both a psychological and a practical nature can be given for this behavior. The former type of explanation is most applicable to the Deputy Commanding Generals. A goodly number of them were old soldiers taken out of retirement. They were monarchists and conservatives by tradition, but it is very doubtful whether they had ever given very serious consideration to political and economic questions. Indeed, it was traditional in the Prussian army to regard such questions and the people who devoted their energies to them with a certain disdain. They felt that they were above special interests and had an idealistic attachment to the spirit of the *Burgfrieden.* Many of them sincerely sought to give the Emperor's declaration that there were no longer parties or classes practical application. Being conservatives, they had a keen sense of honor and responsibility and a patriarchal concern with those placed in their charge. General von Kessel, or Papa Kessel, as he was affectionately called by his friends, had strong family and personal ties with leading members of the Conservative Party. In his capacity as High Commander in the Mark (*Oberkommando in den Marken*), however, he urgently recommended that the government pay close attention to Social Democratic ideas on the management of the food supply. His agrarian ties were no barrier to a sincere concern with the plight of the urban populace and an objective appraisal of what needed to be done. So, too, many a general was willing to treat union secretaries as men of good will united in the common effort.[48]

Less flattering, however, were the number of instances in

---

letter to the author of Nov. 19, 1962. The best source of information on the Deputy Commanding Generals is the ZMG Reports.

48 Theobold von Bethmann Hollweg, *Betrachtungen zum Weltkrieg*, 2 vols., Berlin, 1919-1922, II, pp. 38-41; Wrisberg, *Heer und Heimat*, p. 6. For Kessel's views, see his ZMG Report, Aug. 23, 1916. Finally, see the very interesting article on the Deputy Commanding Generals in the *Zentralblatt der christlichen Gewerkschaften Deutschlands* (hereinafter cited as *Zentralblatt*), April 23, 1917. The High Commander in the Mark was the Deputy Commanding General for Berlin and its environs.

which military officers took "social" measures out of a narrow concern with the solution of their own immediate problems. An interesting illustration of this is the methods used by Captain Count Oppersdorff of the Airplane Section of the War Ministry when dealing with a dangerous labor dispute in the Berlin airplane industry. In the fall of 1916 a compromise wage agreement was reached between the employers and the union. The workers, however, were dissatisfied, and one of them went to Count Oppersdorff to complain. The latter immediately summoned management and union representatives to his office. Neither side had the slightest idea why the meeting had been called, and they were shocked to find out that Oppersdorff was demanding that further concessions be made to the workers despite the fact that an agreement had already been reached. When the industrialists pointed out that further concessions to the 7,000 workers in the airplane industry would necessarily lead to new wage demands on the part of the 160,000 other workers engaged in similar types of work in Berlin, Oppersdorff made the startling reply that he had to have the airplanes and "what the rest of industry does is a matter of indifference to us."[49]

One must be very cautious in speaking of a "military attitude toward social problems," however. The wartime army, particularly on the homefront, was not a very homogeneous organization. It was filled with reserve officers, who had pursued professional careers in government, industry, and scholarship. The professional soldiers rarely had experience with economic and political problems, and they were very dependent upon the reserve officers on their staffs for advice. These influences were not always salutory. Many a reactionary industrialist-turned-soldier exerted a very insidious influence upon his military superiors. Yet many of the reserve officers also played a very positive role, as has already been demonstrated

[49] Report by Borsig at the Nov. 16, 1916, VdESI meeting, BA, R 13I/149.

in the case of Tiburtius, who was a captain in the reserve.[50]

The common denominator determining the social policies of both the military and the civil authorities was the dangerous social situation they confronted. The unions were needed to control the workers. Thus in January 1915 the Prussian Minister of the Interior, Loebell, asked the local Prussian officials to seek out suitable speakers to "enlighten" the population about the food situation. He made a particular point of the need to find union leaders to volunteer for such work. A training course was given to those selected. Following this the speakers were asked to hold meetings at which the workers were to be enlightened after having "ventilated" their grievances. Under the Law of Siege such public meetings required the approval of the Deputy Commanding Generals. Generally speaking, they collaborated wholeheartedly with the government's efforts and even took the initiative themselves in promoting union meetings for propaganda purposes. There was one notable case of resistance. The Deputy Commanding General in Stettin, Freiherr von Vietinghoff, firmly opposed the holding of such meetings. Despite the efforts of Loebell and Wandel to bring him to terms, he remained recalcitrant. The Deputy Commanding General in the Ruhr, General von Gayl, was also a known conservative. Yet he encouraged union enlightenment work. These contrasting attitudes have an interesting parallel in the Prussian Cabinet. Loebell numbered among the most conservative of its members, and his views differed very little from those of Schorlemer. Yet the former felt impelled to make concessions to labor, where the latter refused to consider any. Similarly, Loebell and Gayl defended the consumer viewpoint in matters pertaining to the food supply, while Schorlemer and Vietinghoff were outspoken representatives of agrarian interests. The difference between Loebell and Gayl, on the one hand, and Vietinghoff and Schorlemer, on the other, lay in what we might call their clientele. The first two had authority over large numbers of industrial workers,

[50] *Zentralblatt*, April 23, 1917.

and they could not afford the luxury of disregarding the unions. The latter two did not face the same difficulty, and they could engage in reactionary fulminations at their leisure.[51]

The use of Social Democratic and trade union speakers to calm the workers grew in importance as the number of strikes increased during 1916. Until that year there had been very few strikes, and the number of workers involved was extremely small. They were almost always expressions of dissatisfaction with wages and the food supply. The three day strike of 55,000 Berlin workers that occurred in June 1916, however, was of an entirely different nature. It was a political protest strike against the sentencing of Karl Liebknecht to imprisonment for leading a May Day demonstration against the war. It was organized by a small group of radical shop stewards (*Obleute*), the most vociferous of whom was Richard Müller, who had great influence in certain of the larger Berlin factories. A similar protest strike broke out in Braunschweig, another important center of radicalism. The German Metalworkers Union leaders, who had always attacked "mass strike apostles" like Müller, maintained complete silence on the strikes in the hope of keeping the news from spreading to the rest of Germany. Richard Müller accused the union leaders of reporting many of the instigators of the strikes to the military authorities in order to have them drafted.

While Richard Müller's charge cannot be proved in this particular instance, it is interesting to note that there is documentary evidence demonstrating that the right wing Socialist trade union leader and KEA member August Müller reported the names of strike agitators to the War Ministry in July 1916. He took advantage of this occasion to warn the authorities that the Socialist trade union movement was in danger of splitting and that it was short of the money needed to counter this

[51] Loebell to the Landräte, Jan. 22, 1915, and his note to Wandel concerning Vietinghoff, March 23, 1915, and other material pertaining to the propaganda question in PrGStA, Reg. Bromberg I, Bd. 779.

threat. He concluded by suggesting that the unions receive some financial support from the government![52]

It is also significant that General von Kessel was full of praise for the attitude of the union leaders during the May 1916 strike. The implications of the strikes for union control of the workers, however, were quite clear. A serious danger now existed that strikes over economic grievances could be turned into political strikes by the radicals. A report by the Deputy Commanding General in Magdeburg demonstrates the difficulties the union leaders were facing: "The union leaders pointed out that they were doing everything to prevent such unrest and strikes arising from the food problem, but that they do not have their people in their hands anymore; besides this there were many unorganized workers among the strikers over whom they had no influence."[53] The peculiarity of this situation deserves to be noted. On the one hand, the unions were losing control of those already in their ranks. On the other, the unions were blaming the strikes on the unorganized workers, who were not subject to union discipline, and then using the specter of further strikes as a demonstration of the necessity of increased organization of the workers.

The general policy of the War Ministry was to use the unions to prevent strikes and to bring those that took place to a speedy conclusion. This policy was reconfirmed in a directive issued to the Deputy Commanding Generals in July 1916. They were told to act cautiously in handling strikes so as to avoid creating martyrs. Strike leaders were to be arrested immediately and, depending on the individual case, either tried for treason or drafted into the army. Then the workers were to be ordered to return to work, punishment being threatened in cases of refusal. Finally, "after implementation of these measures, the

[52] Peter von Oertzen, *Betriebsräte in der Novemberrevolution*, p. 63n2.

[53] See the ZMG Report of July 15, 1916, for this and other reports by the Deputy Commanding Generals. On the strikes in general, see Fritz Opel, *Der Deutsche Metallarbeiter-Verband während des ersten Weltkrieges und der Revolution*, Hannover and Frankfurt a.M., 1962, pp. 54-56, and Richard Müller, *Vom Kaiserreich zur Republik*, 2 vols., Vienna, 1924-1925, I, pp. 63-64.

leaders of the Social Democrats (excluding the Haase group) and the unions are to be called to the military commander so that the necessity of these measures might be made clear to them and thus, where possible, their influence on the workers secured."[54] Even the irascible General von Vietinghoff was willing to use union secretaries to settle strikes. Thus he permitted them to hold worker meetings to settle a strike on the Stettin docks. What he opposed was the use of union secretaries to prevent strikes, and when the latter requested that they be allowed to hold meetings in the future to enable the workers to air their grievances, Vietinghoff refused. It was a great mistake, in his view, to be fooled by the "reasonable" attitude of the union leaders during the war. They were trying to "win and maintain power" by establishing themselves as an "indispensable connecting link between employers and employees." To permit them to hold meetings would be to destroy industrial peace in his area, as they would be certain to agitate: "It would be naïve to believe that even these moderate leaders of the Social Democrats have given up any of their final goals."[55]

The views expressed by Vietinghoff, however short-sighted, deserve careful consideration. Just as the government was striving to reconcile its authoritarian character with the utilization of the trade unions, so the latter were seeking to reconcile their traditional goals with their newly acquired status as quasi-agents of the regime. In 1916 the unions were experiencing two types of difficulties. First, they had suffered a serious loss of membership and income. The military draft had cut deeply into their membership, while their loyalty to the war effort did not permit them to agitate in quite the old way for new members.[56] Second, the combination of growing eco-

[54] E. O. Volkmann, *Der Marxismus und das deutsche Heer im Weltkriege*, Berlin, 1925, pp. 277-278.

[55] ZMG Report, Aug. 23, 1916.

[56] Free Trade Unions membership had dropped from 2,076,000 members in 1914 to 967,000 members in 1916, Bry, *Wages in Germany*, p. 32.

nomic hardship and radical agitation endangered their control of the remaining members. From a purely practical standpoint the union leaders could not appear before worker meetings as mouthpieces of the government. This would only have alienated the workers and helped the radicals. Also it was unreasonable to expect the union leaders to be hypocrites. There were very good reasons to agree with the complaints of the workers. Both self-preservation and self-respect, therefore, required that the union leaders state their views. They had to be militant and at the same time keep the workers loyal to the war effort.

The problems of the unions, however, did not end here. The unions wanted to increase their power, and they had ambitions. They had not given up their aims, and they never claimed they had. They wanted the recognition of the employers and the support of the government. These goals could never be attained if the unions did not grow in size and strength. The temptation to use worker meetings aimed at preventing strikes or ending them for purposes of increasing union membership were very great indeed. The line between "enlightenment" and "agitation" could thus be very thin. Furthermore, a strike, if easily brought under control, could be rather useful to the unions. Such strikes gave the unions an opportunity to demonstrate the value of their organizations to both the army and the workers. The army was reminded that the best way to end a strike peacefully was through union assistance. The striking workers were shown that the unions could wrest concessions before the army employed harsh measures to end the strike. All this is not to impugn the loyalty of the unions to the war effort, but only to point out that they did seek and find means of continuing to function as militant organizations and of taking advantage of the wartime situation to increase their power. Nevertheless it must be said that the tactics adopted to keep the workers loyal to the war effort and to increase union strength were not always in consonance with one another.

An illustration of this complex situation is the role played by the unions in the Ruhr coal mine strikes of August 1916.[57] The immediate causes of the strikes were the food shortage and the failure of wages to keep up with prices. There was considerable evidence, however, that the local union leaders had done much to incite the disturbances both directly and indirectly, and there can be no question about the fact that they used the unrest among the miners for their own purposes. In the period prior to the strikes union secretaries had held meetings with the miners under the benevolent gaze of the military authorities. In these meetings there had been continuous discussion of government inefficiency in the management of the food supply and the high price of food. Just before the strikes broke out, the unions presented new wage demands to the employers. Also, the Social Democratic *Bergarbeiterzeitung* made a special point of publishing statistics indicating the high profits being made by the mining companies and the high dividends being paid to stockholders. Finally, union agitators were going from house to house to stir up sentiment concerning these matters and win new members.

Although the union secretaries claimed that the strikes were completely spontaneous and denied any prior knowledge of their outbreak, the authorities had good reason to suspect the truth of these claims. When questioned, the heads of the workers committees either repeated the latest union demands and complained about the high profits of the companies or were extremely vague in explaining their cause and insisted that union secretaries be brought in to clarify the situation. Workers committee representatives in Erkenschwick, for example, seemed embarrassed by the strike there and were visibly relieved when union secretaries entered the negotiations with the authorities. The union secretaries also experienced some difficulty in making good their claim that they had known nothing about the strike. One made the faux pas of admitting that he had heard about the strike on the day before

[57] The documents on this strike are to be found in StAMü, Reg. Münster 17, Bd. I.

it broke out. Another union secretary was known to have remarked that "things are going to break loose in Erkenschwick also" two days before the strike there.[58] For men caught unawares, the union secretaries certainly managed to arrive on the scene and pacify the workers with remarkable speed, and they were equally quick in taking advantage of the situation. In the meetings held with the strikers, union agents were sent around to sign up new members, and the union proclamation against the strike included an appeal to all miners to join the unions so that the unions could represent the workers' demands with real strength. While calling for an end to the strike, they demanded not only more food and higher wages for the workers, but also that the employers negotiate with the unions. Given the evidence, it is very clear that at the very least the unions contributed to the development of these strikes through agitation, that they knew they were going to take place, and that they used the strike to increase their membership and prestige.

General von Gayl, whom the Ruhr industrialists were fond of calling their "devoted father" and the "right man in the right place,"[59] might have been expected to join forces with Vietinghoff at this point. The Ruhr, however, was not Pomerania. Gayl refused to obey the demands of Hugenberg's Mineowners Association; he would not ban all worker meetings and bar union speakers. While willing to cut down the number of these meetings, to place them under sharp surveillance, to exclude known agitators, and to draft restless workers, he refused to take the sharpest measures. Worker meetings were necessary to give the men a chance "to talk about those questions closest to their hearts," and the loss of such opportunities could only have "the most adverse effect upon the morale of the workers." The workers needed a "safety valve" to express their grievances. Similarly, a ban on union speakers was undesirable because "the union secretaries have great influence and

[58] See especially Count von Merveldt to General von Gayl, Aug. 19, 1916, *ibid.*

[59] Duisberg, *Abhandlungen*, p. 808.

have actually employed this influence in the recently ended strike in favor of a return to work."[60]

Nevertheless, Gayl did admonish the unions. In a letter of August 28, 1916, he told them that "with every strike the workers stab their fighting brothers out there in the back." It was the task of the union leaders to prevent strikes, not simply to show up for their pacification. The unions were to give the workers a chance to express their grievances concerning the food situation, but these grievances were not to be used to agitate about other questions. It was the task of the unions to explain how sincerely the government was trying to improve the food supply.[61]

On the same day Gayl wrote to the Mineowners Association insisting that they, too, cooperate in the national effort.[62] While pointing to the fundamentally loyal attitude of the unions during the war, Gayl assured the mineowners that he would not permit the unions to use the war situation to decide questions of principle in their favor. At the same time he reminded them that the unions had to support the justified demands of the workers. Not all the mineowners had demonstrated a very "humane viewpoint" in meeting these demands. But Gayl did not stop here. Even if many of the miners, as the mineowners claimed, did not belong to the unions, nonetheless the unions "had the confidence of the greater part of the unorganized workers." This being the case, the mineowners would have to make some concessions:

> It is neither my task nor my intention to bring to the fore the great questions of principle between employers and workers. My only obligation is to maintain and guard peace and order, so that the production which is so terribly needed is harmed as little as possible. For this purpose, as in the first two years of the war, so also in the third, a compromise

[60] Gayl to Merveldt, Aug. 19, 1916, and his report on the meeting with the mineowners, Aug. 23, 1916, StAMü, Reg. Münster 17, Bd. I.
[61] Gayl to the unions, Aug. 28, 1916, *ibid.*
[62] Gayl to the mineowners, Aug. 28, 1916, *ibid.*

> by all sides is necessary, and my pressing appeal therefore is also directed to the Mineowners Association to give up, under present conditions, its sharply negative stand against the unions . . . at least so far as is possible without surrendering the question of principle.

Specifically, Gayl asked them to reply to union petitions to the Mineowners Association. Such replies in no way forced the owners to negotiate with the unions, but only provided a response to the more general demands of the workers. In so doing the owners would make things easier for the union leaders and thus contribute to the industrial peace so fatally endangered by the continuation of the war.

General von Gayl was performing a juggling act. He needed union help to quell unrest even though union agitation had contributed mightily to that unrest. He had no intention of interfering in questions of principle, but he demanded a relaxation of principles. In the last analysis, General von Gayl, his fellow Deputy Commanding Generals in the industrial districts, the War Ministry, and the civil authorities were all responding to the fact that the war had given the workers the upper hand. As the Social Democratic deputy Eduard David pointed out in the Reichstag, this war differed from the War of 1870 in being the "first technical-industrial war." The war had demonstrated the absolute necessity of a "highly developed industrial working class," and the "political consequences" of this fact could scarcely be escaped:

> Gentlemen, the race of trench fighters will return home with this consciousness, and it would be bad . . . if one said: Now then, you were gallant; you did your duty; now you can go; the old has proved itself; the old will remain. That will lead us, I believe, into political catastrophes . . . the likes of which we have never had in Germany.[63]

3. *The New Supreme Command*

Much of the rabid annexationism of the industrialists and

[63] Reichstag Debates, Oct. 11, 1916, 308, p. 1740.

landowners may be explained by a fear of those very political consequences of the war described by David. Hugenberg, with his usual brutality, made the connection between the war aims problem and the internal political problem very clear to his fellow industrialists as early as November 7, 1914:

> The consequences of the war will in themselves be unfavorable for the employers and industry in many ways. There can be no doubt that the capacity and willingness of the workers returning from the front to produce will suffer considerably when they are subordinated to factory discipline. One will probably have to count on a very increased sense of power on the part of the workers and labor unions, which will also find expression in increased demands on the employers and for legislation. It would therefore be well advised, in order to avoid internal difficulties, to distract the attention of the people and to give phantasies concerning the extension of German territory room to play.[64]

Hugenberg's views were widely shared by the leaders of heavy industry. Only a small group of National Liberals led by Gustav Stresemann, who spoke for smaller and less reactionary industrial groups, made a rather different connection between war aims and internal reform. Stresemann was an annexationist because he believed that annexations and indemnities were necessary for the economic prosperity and security of Germany. He wanted to win over the workers to his war aims by a program of moderate social reforms.

In his own peculiar way, Bethmann Hollweg was implementing Stresemann's ideas with his "policy of the diagonal," a policy of intimating that there would be annexations and a new orientation with one and the same breath. There was thus going to be something for everyone. The industrialists and Junkers were going to get annexations in line with their eco-

[64] "Aufzeichnung über die Sitzung des Unterausschusses des Kriegsausschusses der deutschen Industrie am 7. November 1914," Nachlass Stresemann, 6839, frames H126925-H116927.

nomic interests; the Socialists were going to get some measure of internal reform.[65]

In his public utterances Bethmann had been very vague about both annexations and internal reforms. With the passage of time, however, he became more specific about the latter, while he remained very ambiguous about the former. This was in response to the growing war weariness of the masses and Socialist demands for a peace of understanding and internal reforms. Bethmann found it extremely difficult to remain deaf to these demands and utterly impossible to ignore his own growing conviction that a total victory was impossible. As a temporary solution he sought to impose silence insofar as the war aims problem was concerned. The Deputy Commanding Generals were instructed to ban all public discussion of this issue in the name of the *Burgfrieden*. The use of the censors, however, only served as an irritant, and nothing prevented the Reichstag deputies from venting their feelings from the rostrum. Both sides employed Bethmann's vague statements to prove that the government supported their policies, and yet everyone complained, not without justification, that nobody knew what Germany was fighting for. The policy of making concessions to the right to pacify the left and concessions to the left to pacify the right made sense only if Bethmann could keep his promises to everyone. This was impossible because both the military and the internal situation made the external, as well as the internal, aims of the right untenable. Bethmann had to make his concessions to the left, and he needed to end the war on more moderate terms than the annexationists were prepared to accept.[66] He sought to escape from this dilemma by finding a great military personality to act as a cover for a peace concluded on moderate terms:

That such a peace will meet with the sharpest resistance

[65] On Bethmann's early war aims, see Fritz Fischer, *Griff nach der Weltmacht. Die Kriegszielpolitik des Kaisserlichen Deutschland 1914/1918*, Düsseldorf, 1961, pp. 107-114.

[66] Rosenberg, *Birth of the German Republic*, pp. 96ff; Bethmann, *Betrachtungen*, II, pp. 33-35.

from certain circles is sure, and it must therefore be covered by the authority of the most popular man in the German Empire. That is today Field Marshal von Hindenburg. The latter must conduct the peace negotiations with the Chancellor. The people will believe him when he says: This and no more was to be achieved.[67]

Ironically enough, many of the Junker and industrialist annexationists also wanted to replace Falkenhayn with Hindenburg. This was only one part of their program, however, as a good many of them also wanted to replace Bethmann with Falkenhayn. The annexationists detested Bethmann's weak policies. They wanted open government support of their war aims and the introduction of unrestricted submarine warfare. While not thinking much of Falkenhayn's military talents, they were certain that he would be the "Bismarck" Germany needed for the peace negotiations. With little subtlety and great enthusiasm they called for the appointment of a man with "falcon's eyes" (*Falkenaugen*) who would know how to bang his fist on the conference table.[68]

The annexationists who wanted a Falkenhayn Chancellorship were laboring under some serious misconceptions. Falkenhayn would have gladly satisfied their war aims if they were attainable, but he believed, along with Bethmann, that Germany could not defeat all her enemies. Falkenhayn was too conscious of the limits of Germany's power to share in the

[67] Lerchenfeld to Hertling, Oct. 24, 1916, BHStA, Abt. II, MA 1, Nr. 912. See also the report of Colonel Holland to the Württemberg War Minister, General Marchtaler, Sept. 6, 1916, HStASt, Nachlass Marchtaler, Nr. 5, and Bethmann, *Betrachtungen*, II, pp. 45-46. The thesis that Bethmann promoted Hindenburg's cause in order to gain popular support for a "moderate" peace is ably argued by Carl Heinz Janssen, "Der Wechsel in der Obersten Heeresleitung 1916," *Vierteljahreshefte für Zeitgeschichte*, VII, Oct. 1959, pp. 337-371. Fritz Fischer disagrees with Janssen and argues that Bethmann supported Hindenburg's plans for a major offensive in the East in order to force Russia to sue for peace, *Griff nach der Weltmacht*, pp. 301-302. This is true, but it neglects Bethmann's other motives and does not fully account for the very significant evidence supporting the motive emphasized here.

[68] Duisberg, *Abhandlungen*, p. 812.

phantasies of the Pan-Germans. Recognizing that Germany's most dangerous enemies were the Western Powers, he desired a speedy negotiated peace with Russia. Indeed, much of Falkenhayn's quarreling with Bethmann and the Foreign Office arose from his insistence that Germany take the initiative in opening peace negotiations with the Russians rather than wait until the Russians made the first move. Falkenhayn's opposition to the grandiose plans of the Eastern Command was due in large measure to his fear that a major offensive in the East would create political commitments precluding a speedy settlement in that area.[69]

It might be imagined that Bethmann would have given complete support to so moderate a soldier as Falkenhayn. The contrary was the case. Bethmann resented Falkenhayn's influence on the Emperor, his interference in foreign policy questions, and his unquestionable political ambitions. He shared the widely held opinion that Falkenhayn's military strategy was unsound and felt that only a great offensive in the East would bring Russia to terms. Above all, he needed Hindenburg's name behind any negotiated peace he concluded. He thus allied himself with the almost two-year intrigue to overthrow Falkenhayn. He maintained close contact with Hindenburg and Ludendorff and other army officers plotting against Falkenhayn and fanned the flames of anti-Falkenhayn sentiment in the Bavarian and Württemberg state ministries.[70]

Until 1916 the *fronde* against Falkenhayn was completely unsuccessful. In that year, however, Falkenhayn began to lose his grip. The chief cause was his abortive effort to bleed France to death at Verdun. In early 1916 he suddenly dropped his opposition to unrestricted submarine warfare despite the obvious danger that this would bring America into the war. The military situation seriously deteriorated in the summer.

[69] Heinz Kraft, *Welt als Geschichte*, XXI, pp. 54-58, and Fischer, *Griff nach der Weltmacht*, pp. 217-219.

[70] Janssen, *Vierteljahreshefte für Zeitgeschichte*, VII, pp. 337-371, for the description of Falkenhayn's fall.

The English offensive on the Somme, which began in July, revealed great enemy superiority in men and matériel. The Brusilov Offensive in July caused a veritable collapse of the Austro-Hungarian forces in the East. At this point Falkenhayn began to support the idea of setting up an independent Kingdom of Poland in the hope that Polish manpower would then rally to the German cause. Needless to say, this stood in contradiction to his desire to bring about a speedy peace with Russia.

The chief barrier to the dismissal of Falkenhayn was the Emperor. On the one hand, the Emperor had great confidence in his Chief of Staff. On the other, he was envious of Hindenburg's popularity and often referred to the great popular hero as another Wallenstein. To this attitude was added Wilhelm's absolute loathing for Ludendorff. Until the summer of 1916 Falkenhayn also received very strong support from General Wild von Hohenborn and the Chief of the Military Cabinet, General von Lyncker. The latter was particularly influenced by one of his aides, Colonel von Marschall, who detested Ludendorff. Both Wild and Lyncker changed their views, however, with the deterioration of the military situation in the summer of 1916. The support they gave to the appointment of Hindenburg as commander of both the German and the Austrian forces in the East spelled the beginning of the end for Falkenhayn.

In fighting Falkenhayn, Bethmann had to find military supporters because the Emperor placed little stock in what civilians had to say. This was difficult because it was not customary for officers to plot against their superiors. In the summer of 1916, however, the military opposition to Falkenhayn became more overt. Bethmann received important support from Crown Prince Rupprecht of Bavaria, who commanded the German forces on the Somme. The "demigods" on the General Staff were also hard at work. Colonel Bauer, repeating a role he had played in the dismissal of Moltke, went to the Emperor's adjutant, General von Plessen, and informed him that Falkenhayn "no longer had the confidence of the army."[71] A major blow was struck at Falkenhayn from yet another source. For reasons which shall be discussed in greater detail later, the Association of German Iron and Steel Industrialists sent a memorandum to General von Lyncker complaining about Falkenhayn's munitions policies. The *coup de grâce*, however, was provided by Rumania's entry into the war on the side of the Entente in August 1916. Put into a state of panic by this sudden addition to Germany's foes, the Emperor decided to make Falkenhayn the scapegoat. Falkenhayn was reproached for failing to predict the Rumanian attack and for making insufficient preparations to meet it. At this point, all Falkenhayn's opponents, old or newly acquired, swooped down upon the Emperor, and, with expressions of great regret and displeasure, the Emperor surrendered. On August 28, 1916, Hindenburg was made Chief of the General Staff. Ludendorff was appointed First Quartermaster General. While nominally subordinate to Hindenburg, Ludendorff was given equal voice and responsibility in all operative decisions.

Never were more popular appointments made. The Chancellor rejoiced because he could now undertake his peace program. The army and the annexationists rejoiced because they now had military leaders who were certain to bring victory. The Social Democrats expressed jubilation as well. Hindenburg was praised for achieving victories with the least possible expenditure of human lives. Ludendorff was portrayed as a man "immune from political and court influences of every kind." The Society for Social Reform reported that

> The naming of the General Field Marshal . . . von Hindenburg as Chief of the General Staff has been received with joy by the workers. . . . Even before numerous Socialist leaders and newspapers had expressed themselves in the warmest tones concerning the new Chief of the General Staff. . . . Even the most radical papers have always ex-

[71] Bauer, *Grosse Krieg*, p. 104.

> pressed the most complete confidence in his brilliant leadership. . . . "That Ludendorff remains at Hindenburg's side," the Stuttgart [Socialist] paper points out, "helps to strengthen the confidence which the people have in the new Chief of the General Staff."[72]

Strange indeed was the lonely dissent of Colonel von Marschall: "He, Marschall, feared that Ludendorff in his measureless vanity and pride would conduct the war until the German people were completely exhausted and would then let the monarchy bear the damages. He has set his views down in a memorandum, since he cannot take any responsibility for the change in the Supreme Command."[73]

It is difficult to explain the confusion of mind which led Bethmann to struggle so hard to place the shirt of Nessus on his back and appoint the men who were to bring about his downfall ten months later. Yet the facts were as readily available to him as they were to Marschall. Two years before, the then sixty-six-year-old Hindenburg had been taken out of retirement to serve as the senior officer under whose paternal eye Ludendorff was to rescue East Prussia from the Russian offensive. Thanks to the latter's brilliance and the government's desire to distract attention from the debacle on the Marne, Hindenburg, who had been chosen in the most accidental fashion, was turned into the national hero. In reality he was a soldier of average abilities with a very traditional and correct abhorrence of all things political and bureaucratic. His most distinguishing characteristics were an impenetrable calmness and confidence. To point out that these qualities had their origins in a certain dullness of mind, a primordial satisfaction in the fulfillment of a narrowly conceived duty, and, perhaps, a complacency derived from the arrival of unexpected fame, is in no way to detract from their significance. At Tannenburg, and on many another occasion, Hindenburg kept Ludendorff from falling prey to his highly nervous temperament. The patri-

[72] BBS Reports of Sept. 1916.
[73] Quoted in Groener, *Lebenserinnerungen*, p. 316.

archal Field Marshal aroused hope and confidence in all who encountered him. Typical was the reaction of the Prussian Commerce Minister, Sydow, who was overwhelmed by Hindenburg's personality, "above all, by the glance of his great blue eyes, from which streamed calmness, clarity, assuredness, decisiveness, and at the same time friendliness."[74] The sums paid in war bond drives for the strange pleasure of driving nails into gigantic wooden statues of Hindenburg attest to how general and fanatical was this obeisance before the legend. It is not impossible that Bethmann had fallen victim to this legend himself. Furthermore, Hindenburg's distaste for political questions undoubtedly made him quite suitable for Bethmann's purposes.

Such explanations would only be acceptable, however, if one could accept the idea that Bethmann was unaware of Ludendorff's domination of Hindenburg. Yet it was well known that Hindenburg had almost always yielded before the more dynamic personality of the man whose talents had brought him fame. Surely Bethmann knew that Ludendorff had been the driving force in the plot to oust Falkenhayn. Ludendorff had thus demonstrated himself capable of defying the most elementary traditions of Prussian military subordination. Furthermore, Ludendorff had demonstrated a penchant for very dubious forms of political activity. The odium attached to the way Ludendorff conducted business was largely responsible for the fact that he did not receive an appointment to the staff at Supreme Headquarters at the beginning of the war.[75] The fifty-one-year-old Ludendorff had triumphed despite the dislike of the Military Cabinet. He owed his career to unquestionable genius for organization, a blind addiction to work, and ruthless ambition. There was certainly nothing about his brutal face or arrogant and vain personality that was likely to

[74] BA, Nachlass Sydow, p. 13; On Hindenburg and Ludendorff, see J. W. Wheeler-Bennett, *Wooden Titan, Hindenburg in Twenty Years of German History*, New York, 1936, and Karl Tschuppik, *Ludendorff. Die Tragödie des Fachmanns*, Leipzig, 1931.

[75] Groener to von Reischach, June 22, 1925, Nachlass Groener, 36.

send men into raptures. How could Bethmann believe that Ludendorff would be more tractable than Falkenhayn?

The answer may lie in the peculiar ambiguities of Ludendorff's character. Although always regarded as the "strong man," Ludendorff was really very dependent upon others for advice. His range of knowledge was very limited because his entire education and career had been dominated by military concerns. He was, therefore, easily impressed by men more knowledgeable than himself. Possessing a strong inclination to interfere in matters which were none of his business, he was nevertheless dependent upon others for guidance as to the direction which this interference was to take. General Groener, for example, had an extremely difficult time with the Eastern Command on railroad questions. The tone of some of the telegrams Groener received made him wonder if Ludendorff wasn't "ripe for the crazy house." In personal conversation with Ludendorff, however, Groener found him to be quite "reasonable." After some investigation, Groener discovered that much of the harshness of the telegrams was directly attributable to the influence of Ludendorff's subordinates.[76]

Groener was not the only person to come away from a personal conversation with Ludendorff with a positive impression. Count Hertling was "pleasantly disappointed" by his first personal encounter with Ludendorff. He had expected to find a "rough, insolent man." Instead he found him to be very "agreeable and understanding." The Württemberg military representative at General Headquarters had a similar reaction to his first meeting with Ludendorff.[77] It is very likely that Ludendorff had made a similar impression on Bethmann Hollweg, particularly since Bethmann shared Ludendorff's chief passion during the first two years of the war, getting rid of Falkenhayn. Bethmann might have been less sanguine if he had known what had

[76] Groener, *Lebenserinnerungen*, pp. 243-244, 271, 279.

[77] Möser to Weizsäcker, Dec. 12, 1916, HStASt, E, 73, 42e, 12i, and report of the Württemberg military representative to General Headquarters, Oct. 1, 1916, *ibid.*, Persönliche Angelegenheiten der württembergische Kriegsminister, Bd. 114, Bl. 37-43.

taken place at another of Ludendorff's personal interviews, this one with the former Secretary of the Navy, Admiral von Tirpitz, one of Bethmann's chief opponents. Tirpitz went away from the interview with the impression that "he was not the only one whose abilities and deeds were not getting proper recognition."[78] The bond between the two men was cemented by a memorandum Ludendorff gave to Tirpitz containing his political views. In it Ludendorff declared his support of unrestricted submarine warfare, dismissed the importance of American entry into the war, and placed himself in favor of the most far-reaching war aims.

What is really important, however, is that Bethmann *wanted* to believe that Germany could be saved by Hindenburg and Ludendorff. The most damning criticism that can be made of a statesman is that he shares the illusions of the society he is supposed to govern. Bethmann is all the more to be condemned because he had willfully promoted these illusions by encouraging the public to believe that the war was going well. As the public believed that only the army could solve the food problem, and as the Social Democrats looked to the army for social reform, so Bethmann sought through the army a means of evading full responsibility for his own actions. This search for military saviors in nonmilitary matters was symptomatic of a sick society in which the intermingling of new and old ills had created a demand for total cures and heightened the inclination of men to seek out quack doctors and quack remedies.

[78] Report of Admiral von Mann, Aug. 14, 1915, MF, Marine Archiv, Nr. 8766.

PART TWO

Total Mobilization and Interest-Group Politics

III

Hindenburg Program and War Office: The Triumph of Heavy Industry

THE APPOINTMENT of Hindenburg and Ludendorff to the Supreme Command placed the future German conduct of the war in the hands of the radical militarists. During their first three months in office the new Supreme Command reversed the policies of the previous military leaders. They abandoned the old munitions and manpower policies of the War Ministry and sought, through the so-called Hindenburg Program, to create an extraordinary increase in the supply of weapons and munitions within an arbitrarily fixed period of time. They terminated the close collaboration between the War Ministry and the General Staff and went on to deprive the Ministry of most of its social and economic functions by establishing a mammoth organization, the War Office, for the control of the economy. Finally, they forced the government and the Reichstag to pass a law compelling the civil population to serve the war effort, the Auxiliary Service Law of December 5, 1916.

It is not very useful to interpret these measures in terms of the slogan "total mobilization," and thereby lend support to the view so successfully propagandized by Ludendorff and his supporters that the new Supreme Command was responsible for rescuing Germany from antiquated economic mobilization policies and finally forcing the homefront to think and act in terms of fearsome military necessities. In reality the radical militarism of the new Supreme Command was even less determined by objective military considerations than the conservative militarism of the older school had been. If the economic and social prejudices of the conservative militarists had blinded them to the possibility of a long war and inhibited the modernization of the army before the war, the same susceptibilities also kept them from making an exaggerated effort to correct the mistakes of the past. The policies of Falkenhayn, Wild von Hohenborn, and Wandel, while not very imaginative, did have the virtue of paying some heed to the limits of Germany's economic and human resources and to the tenuousness of the nation's social stability.

The new Supreme Command represented the triumph, not of imagination, but of fantasy. In his pursuit of an ill-conceived total mobilization for the attainment of irrational goals, Ludendorff undermined the strength of the army, promoted economic instability, created administrative chaos, and set loose an orgy of interest politics. His program represented the victory of heavy industry and the general staff over the War Ministry, and its chief architects were self-seeking industrialists and a ruthless military intriguer.

1. *The Hindenburg Program*

Colonel Max Bauer, unlike Bethmann Hollweg, had good reason to rejoice over the appointment of Ludendorff. Bauer and Ludendorff were old friends with a great deal in common. Both were of middle-class origin, and their professional success exemplified the growing importance of technical and organizational skills in modern warfare. Bauer had served under Ludendorff in the Operations Section of the General Staff from 1908 to 1912, and they had fought against the War Ministry together. They were men who did not shy away from the use of radical means to serve reactionary purposes. In this tendency they contrasted sharply with officers of more aristocratic pedigree, upon whom feudal loyalty to the Emperor, religion, and tradition imposed a certain concern with means as well as ends. Bauer and Ludendorff were thus most akin to the industrial barons, who had assimilated to Junker values for reasons of interest and social aspiration.[1]

[1] The portrait of Bauer is based on the author's study of the Bauer papers in the BA. See also Bauer, *Grosse Krieg*, pp. vi-vii, and Rüdt von Collenberg, "Oberst Bauer," *Deutsches Biographisches Jahrbuch*, XI, pp. 16-32.

There were important differences between Ludendorff and Bauer, however. What was potential in the former had become actual in the latter. Where Ludendorff had merely become acquainted with many industrialists while serving as regimental commander in Düsseldorf in 1913, Bauer had deliberately sought out and cultivated the industrialists. Ludendorff had a tendency to pontificate about and interfere in questions about which he knew nothing. Bauer had already developed a bizarre hodgepodge of ideas in which such a sundry assortment of concerns as antifeminism, anti-Semitism, and increasing the birthrate were given due regard. Ludendorff sought programs; Bauer made programs. Although given to intrigue, Ludendorff was not always sure of himself. Bauer, like Iago, had intrigue in his blood and never faltered in his objectives or found himself at a loss for a "solution." Little wonder that Ludendorff once referred to Bauer as the "cleverest man in the army," for Bauer was able to give the uninformed and unstable Ludendorff both ideas and direction.[2]

Bauer had not prospered under Falkenhayn. The latter had given Bauer's considerable technical abilities their due, but he had rejected Bauer's grandiose projects. The War Ministry had blocked Bauer's efforts to introduce the massive munitions program desired by heavy industry, and Falkenhayn certainly did not need Bauer's advice on political questions. Ludendorff felt differently. Bauer's heavy artillery section was given greatly increased responsibility in all questions of weapons and munitions. Of far greater significance, however, was the fact that Bauer was now given a stamp bearing the words, "By Command of Ludendorff."[3] This, indeed, was power.

The military situation in the summer of 1916 was ideally suited to a man of Colonel Bauer's talents and inclinations. On

[2] *Berliner Lokal Anzeiger*, April 15, 1918, in BA, Nachlass Mentzel, Nr. 7. See also Sichler and Tiburtius, *Arbeiterfrage*, p. 31, and Wilhelm Breucker, *Die Tragik Ludendorffs. Eine kritische Studie auf Grund persönlicher Erinnerungen an den General und seine Zeit*, Stollhamm, 1953, pp. 29-31.

[3] Merton, *Erinnernswertes aus meinem Leben*, p. 47, and Wrisberg, *Heer und Heimat*, pp. 165-166.

July 1 the British had opened a major offensive on the Somme. Despite its ultimate failure, this offensive was a clear demonstration of Allied superiority in men and matériel. General Wild von Hohenborn was forced to confess that "I have fooled myself enormously concerning the English," and in mid-July he ordered an increase in the munitions program.[4] As in November 1914, so now again, Germany was in the midst of a munitions shortage, only now the dead numbered in the millions and the homeland suffered from a catastrophic food shortage and renewed political strife. There was, however, yet another important point of contrast between the two munitions crises. In 1914 the War Ministry had been successful in persuading the General Staff to reject the great munitions program advocated by Colonel Bauer and the leaders of heavy industry. In 1916 the policies of the War Ministry were to suffer a decisive defeat.

Since 1914 the Ministry had undertaken a step by step increase of powder production. Thus in December 1914 a monthly production goal of 6,000 tons had been set. When two thirds of this goal had been achieved a year later, it was raised to 8,000 tons. In July 1916 three quarters of this program, or 6,000 tons, had been achieved, and because of events on the Somme a 10,000-ton program was established. As in the case of the previous powder programs, the new program required a relative increase in the production of munitions and artillery.[5]

The War Ministry's munitions program was abandoned two days after Hindenburg and Ludendorff took office. On August 31 Hindenburg sent a letter to Wild outlining the munitions program which was to bear his name. Hindenburg demanded that the supply of munitions be doubled and that the supply of machine guns and artillery be tripled by the spring of 1917. He justified these demands on the basis of the enemy superiority revealed on the Somme. Even greater enemy offensives

[4] Notations of July 1916, BA, Nachlass Wild von Hohenborn, Nr. 2.
[5] Wrisberg, *Wehr und Waffen*, pp. 285-288.

were anticipated for the spring, and Germany had to undertake immediate measures if she was to be capable of beating them back. Given the enemy's irredeemable superiority in manpower, Germany would have to compensate for her shortage of men by having "machines." While recognizing that the War Ministry had already increased its munitions program, Hindenburg argued that still greater increases were necessary and that the desired production would have to be achieved quickly. Wild was instructed to promote the new program with the greatest energy and with the understanding that "financial and other reservations can no longer be considered."[6]

How did the Hindenburg Program differ from the program of the War Ministry? In the irresponsible propaganda employed in support of the former, Hindenburg's demand for a doubling of the munitions supply was fraudulently portrayed as a radical improvement over the insufficient programs developed by the War Ministry. In reality the Hindenburg Program represented an increase of only one sixth over Wild's goal of 10,000 tons monthly powder production established in July 1916. Actual powder production in August 1916 was 6,000 tons, and the doubling of the powder supply meant the establishment of a 12,000 ton program. In short, the Hindenburg Program called for a doubling of the munitions *supply*, not the munitions *program.*[7]

Where the Hindenburg Program did markedly differ from the War Ministry's programs was not so much in the size of the demands made as in the new principles employed in determining production goals. In the words of Wichard von Moellendorff, the Hindenburg Program demanded not "as much as is attainable, but rather definite increases of production by a definite time and at any price."[8] At a time when the internal war loans which had formed the chief basis for the financing

[6] Erich Ludendorff, *Urkunden der Obersten Heeresleitung über ihre Tätigkeit*, Berlin, 1920, pp. 63-65.

[7] Wrisberg, *Wehr und Waffen*, pp. 284-286.

[8] Moellendorff to Haber, Sept. 5, 1916, BA, Nachlass Moellendorff, Nr. 6.

of the war effort had ceased to cover expenditures, the Supreme Command decided to dismiss all financial considerations and to embark upon a program whose practical feasibility, as shall later be demonstrated, had never been seriously investigated. The deadline for the fulfillment of the program, May 1917, was based upon purely military calculations. The production quotas for weapons was set in a purely ad hoc fashion without any regard for the state of the powder supply. The dependence of weapon production upon powder production had thus ceased to be the guiding principle of Germany's munitions policy. Where the War Ministry had emphasized the utilization of existing plant facilities in an effort to save raw materials and manpower, the Hindenburg Program required an extraordinary amount of new plant construction. The effort to balance the manpower needs of the army and the homeland were, at least for the moment, abandoned. In devising his July program, Wild had considered the losses at the front, the manpower required by the coming harvest, and the needs of industry. Hindenburg cut through these tortuous calculations by simply informing Wild that the Supreme Command was prepared to release large numbers of skilled workers to serve in industry. The Hindenburg Program, in short, was a gamble in which the nation's finances and resources were recklessly exposed to exhaustion on the basis of unfounded expectations and in defiance of the objections raised by General Franke, Major Koeth, and other experienced experts in the War Ministry.[9]

The Hindenburg Program had very little to do with either sound military planning or rational economics. In the months preceding the establishment of the program, the two year struggle between heavy industry and the War Ministry reached its culmination, and the new munitions program was the direct consequence of its outcome. In July 1916 the War Ministry turned to the iron and steel industrialists for help in accom-

[9] Sichler and Tiburtius, *Arbeiterfrage*, p. 37; Spiero, *Schicksal*, p. 269.

plishing the tasks created by the munitions crisis, and this led to an intensification of their old conflicts. The Ministry had always sought to have all shells made out of Martin process steel, which was the hardest type of steel and hence the most effective. In the spring of 1916 this seemed possible, and the Ministry had refused to renew contracts for the inferior Thomas process steel scheduled to expire on June 30. The situation on the Somme caused a reversal of this policy on July 16. The old contracts were renewed and increased quantities of Thomas steel were placed on order. The industrialists were exasperated. First their contracts had been canceled, and now they were being flooded with orders. As usual, these orders came from a multitude of competing procurement agencies, and they had no idea as to which of them was to be given priority. Also, they claimed that the new orders exceeded their capacity to perform. The industrialists were willing to meet the new demands, however, and even to cut back exports, provided that they were given the workers they needed and that steel production for "nonmilitary" purposes—railroad tracks, for example—could be cut back. These demands were presented to representatives of the War Ministry in a meeting on August 18. Unhappily, the young major leading the discussion was not in a position to make basic policy decisions, and the meeting had no positive results.[10]

At this point the angry industrialists turned to the State Secretary of the Interior, Karl Helfferich. He advised them to appeal directly to Wild, but the latter, who was touring the Eastern front at the time, answered their telegram by referring them to General von Wandel. Wandel was the last person they wanted to see, since they held him responsible for their difficulties. Instead, on August 23, they sent a memorandum to the War Minister, the Chief of the Military Cabinet, Helfferich, and many other military and civilian officials. In this memorandum Falkenhayn and the War Ministry were accused of not doing enough to promote war production. The cutback of

[10] Helfferich, *Weltkrieg*, II, pp. 277-279.

orders for Thomas steel at the end of June was cited as evidence for this accusation. The industrialists demanded an end to the bureaucratic practices of the Ministry, the unification of the procurement agencies, a satisfactory supply of labor, and a munitions program that was large enough in scale to satisfy the needs of the front.[11]

The industrialists' arguments deserve careful examination. The treatment of the industrialists in the meeting of August 18 had been clumsy, and it was high time that the procurement agencies were placed under unified direction. Wild himself recognized this last need and, on August 5, asked Major Koeth to draw up the necessary organizational plans.[12] The argument that Falkenhayn and Wild were lax in supplying the army with matériel, however, was not only erroneous but also insidious, for it gave rise to the myth that the War Ministry had cut back the munitions program before the battle of the Somme. This was absolutely untrue. The powder program, which was the basis of all war production, had never been cut back. The termination of the Thomas steel contracts was, if anything, a favorable sign of the progress that had been made in the production of Martin steel and represented an effort to improve the quality of the steel being used in the production of munitions. The military authorities had made a mistake, but it was primarily a military error. After having wasted enormous numbers of men and quantities of matériel at Verdun, Falkenhayn underestimated what the English were capable of achieving in an offensive of their own.[13]

Events on the Somme demonstrated the necessity of increasing the munitions program, but they in no way justified a departure from the War Ministry's previous principle, that is, the dependence of weapons production upon the capacity for powder production. The essence of the War Ministry's policy

[11] *Ibid.*; Dierkopf, *Hilfsdienstgesetz*, p. 24; Cron, *Kriegseisenwirtschaft*, pp. 16-18.

[12] Notation of Aug. 5, 1916, BA, Nachlass Wild von Hohenborn, Nr. 2.

[13] Wrisberg, *Wehr und Waffen*, pp. 285-288.

was a careful husbanding of Germany's resources, and it was to this that the industrialists had objected from the very start. Wild, in language more suitable to a Social Democrat than to a conservative, had very good reasons for exclaiming that "apparently the iron and steel people haven't earned enough yet!"[14]

In fact, a close examination of the production and price policies of the iron and steel industrialists demonstrates that they were being hypocritical.[15] At the beginning of the war they had persuaded the Interior Office to leave the control of exports to self-regulation by the industrialists. As a result, tons of German steel reached France and Italy through Switzerland. As if this were not bad enough, the export policies of the industrialists also deprived the army of steel. In 1916 Britain banned the export of iron and steel to neutrals in order to increase her munitions program. The demand for German iron and steel was thus enormously increased. To profit from this situation and improve Germany's balance of payments, the Interior Office asked the industrialists to stop competing with each other and band together to raise their export prices. Had the additional profit flowed into the Imperial Treasury, the policy would have been a sound one. Instead, the extraordinary profits being made from exports flowed into the pockets of the industrialists, and they began to prefer producing for export.

The result was chaos in the internal market, great delays in the fulfillment of war contracts, and a sharp increase in the domestic price of steel. The situation became so bad that in June 1916 the KRA was called on to control the allocation of iron. A special section was set up under the leadership of Alfons Horten, a government mining expert with wide experience in the operation of iron and steel works and with a very expert knowledge of cost accounting. Horten immediately put his knowledge to good use. When the army called on the industrialists to increase Thomas steel production in July, the latter

[14] Marginal notation on a letter from Deputy Roesicke of April 23, 1917, BA, Nachlass Wild von Hohenborn, Nr. 7.

[15] See the important memorandum on these policies by Alfons Horten, BA, Nachlass Mentzel, Nr. 8.

demanded an outrageous price increase which Horten compelled them to reduce. At the same time he made an important discovery. In November 1914 the industrialists had blackmailed General Franke into paying a scandalously high price for Martin steel by threatening to break off negotiations. When Horten compared the price allowed for Thomas steel with the price that the army had been paying for Martin steel, the completely unjustified price of the latter became obvious. The KRA immediately called on six of the largest firms to state their costs, and the firms replied with a strong refusal. Since the same firms had previously supplied cost statistics to justify a price increase in certain types of lower quality steel, it was impossible to escape the conclusion that they had much to hide with regard to Martin steel prices.[16]

The industrialists thus found themselves in a rather unpleasant situation in the summer of 1916. On the one hand, they had to reduce their very profitable exports due to the military situation. On the other hand, they were now being threatened with an attack on the profits they had been making from the sale of Martin steel to the army. Would not a massive munitions program compensate for the losses incurred due to the restrictions being placed upon imports, and would not such a program distract attention from the price question? It is difficult, indeed, not to conclude that such motives played an important role in the industrialists' decision to send their memorandum of August 23.

Before Bethmann left for General Headquarters on August 28 to take counsel with the new Supreme Command, Helfferich gave him a copy of the industrialists' memorandum. Hindenburg and Ludendorff did not need to be enlightened, however. The memorandum was in their hands already and, as demonstrated by their letter to Wild of August 31 outlining the

[16] A reasonable price for Martin steel in 1915 would have been 160-180 marks per ton, but the army was forced to pay 260-300 marks. The industrialists thus received a monthly excess profit of 10 million marks. A justifiable price differential between Martin and Thomas steel in 1916 would have been 40 marks per ton. Instead, it was 140 marks, *ibid.*

Hindenburg Program, they took immediate action.[17] There can be no question that the Hindenburg Program was the handiwork of Colonel Bauer, since Ludendorff gave him the credit for it, and Bauer readily accepted responsibility for the program. The new program was a direct response to the industrialists' memorandum of August 23, and it is very likely that Bauer had inspired this memorandum as well.[18]

Before the OHL (*Oberste Heeresleitung* [Supreme Command]) left General Headquarters for a consultation with the chiefs of staff of the various army groups at Cambrai on September 8, yet another of Bauer's goals was achieved. General Wild von Hohenborn was ordered by the Emperor to go to Berlin and to stay there. His task was to implement the new program, and the new OHL was convinced that the place of the War Minister was in Berlin, not at General Headquarters. Bauer could now be certain that no one would stand between himself and Ludendorff. The discussions with the chiefs of staff at Cambrai served to strengthen Ludendorff's support of Bauer's views, as they painted the military situation in the blackest terms and stressed the shortage of munitions. Despite the fact that Ludendorff had spent two years fighting for a great eastern campaign and had achieved power by this means, he now dropped the idea and agreed to concentrate upon the west. Hindenburg reassured the officers that something would be done about the munitions shortage.[19]

[17] Helfferich, *Weltkrieg*, II, p. 278.

[18] Bauer called himself the "father of the program" in his *Grosse Krieg*, p. 120. Groener, in his "Bemerkungen zu dem Kapital 'Hilfsdienstgesetz und Hindenburg Programm' in den 2. Band Der Weltkrieg von Karl Helfferich" indicates that Bauer was responsible for the memorandum of Aug. 23, Nachlass Groener, 192-I. We might know more about the way Bauer collaborated with the industrialists in devising the Hindenburg Program if Bauer's aide, Major von Harbou, had not taken the most important documents in 1918, Groener to Reichsarchiv, Oct. 29, 1919, *ibid.*, 196.

[19] Erich Ludendorff, *Meine Kriegserinnerungen, 1914-1918*, Berlin, 1919, p. 267, and Reichsarchiv, *Weltkrieg*, XI, pp. 30-31. Hindenburg created much glee when he told the assembled officers that Wild had been sent home "um Wandel zu schaffen," Einem, *Armeeführer*, p. 256.

After the meetings at Cambrai, Hindenburg and Ludendorff traveled with Bauer to meet the latter's industrialist friends, Carl Duisberg and Gustav Krupp von Bohlen und Halbach. The industrialists were certain that the Hindenburg Program could be fulfilled if the labor problem was solved. It is highly likely that the OHL were inspired by the industrialists' optimism to go beyond even the Hindenburg Program at this time, for the War Ministry was instructed to begin work on yet another program. Where the object of the Hindenburg Program was 12,000 tons of powder production per month by spring, the OHL now hoped that 14,000 tons production could be achieved. The OHL did have some doubts about the feasibility of this program, however, and its calculations continued to be based on the "old" Hindenburg Program.[20] In any case it is certain that the industrialists came away from the meeting with a feeling of satisfaction. On the day following the meeting, Duisberg sent his thanks to Bauer in a letter filled with sentimentality and Byzantine effusiveness:

> It was so kind and nice of you . . . to have given me the opportunity not only to see you again, but also to become personally acquainted with the popular hero, Hindenburg, and the Moltke of this war, Ludendorff. The ninth day of the ninth month of 1916 was an eventful day in my life and one which I will not soon forget. It was similar to that time after the Battle of the Marne. . . . Then also it was a munitions shortage, and a much more threatening one than today's, which brought us together, and which not only permitted us to become closer personally, but which also permitted us to seize, in a practical sense, upon the spokes of the wheels of war.[21]

See also Notation of Oct. 29, 1916, BA, Nachlass Wild von Hohenborn, Nr. 2.

[20] Ludendorff, *Kriegserinnerungen*, p. 267, and *Urkunden*, p. 63; Cron, *Kriegseisenwirtschaft*, p. 35.

[21] Duisberg to Bauer, Sept. 10, 1916, BA, Nachlass Bauer, Nr. 11.

The two year battle between the War Ministry and the industrialists over production and manpower policy had thus been decided by the new OHL in favor of the industrialists in two weeks. In contrast to Falkenhayn, Hindenburg and Ludendorff had not even consulted with Wild about the munitions problem. They had simply accepted the munitions program favored by Colonel Bauer and the industrialists. The significance of Bauer's influence was further demonstrated by the fact that Ludendorff had decided to launch the Hindenburg Program before meeting with the chiefs of staff at Cambrai, and the continuation of this influence was assured by Wild's forced return to Berlin. The Hindenburg Program, in short, was as much determined by the industrialists' desire for profit and by Bauer's yearning for power as it was by the desire for victory in the war of production, and it was the former two goals which were decisive in determining the actual nature of the program.

Having justified the faith of his friends, Bauer now justified the fears of his enemies. The War Ministry was on the defensive, and Bauer meant to keep it at bay. As in 1912, so in 1916, Bauer and Ludendorff sought to mobilize public opinion against the Ministry. In a meeting with an influential member of the National Liberal Party shortly after the interviews with Gustav Krupp von Bohlen und Halbach and Carl Duisberg, Ludendorff "complained bitterly that there was a munitions shortage. The deputies should energetically force the War Ministry to do its duty in this connection."[22] In early October the munitions situation was made the subject of a special investigation by a subcommittee of the Reichstag Budget Committee at which vigorous attacks were launched against the War Ministry by Stresemann and others.

Wild was justly angered by these attacks. Despite his own reservations and the strong objections of his colleagues in the

22 Notation by Stresemann, Sept. 16, 1916, Nachlass Stresemann, 6872, frames H130653-H130656. On the Reichstag investigation, see the notes of Oct. 2 and Oct. 5, 1916, BHStA, Abt. II, MA 1, Nr. 916.

Ministry, he had decided to support the Hindenburg Program. The OHL's use of the new program as a means of inciting the Reichstag against the War Ministry seemed poor recompense for his collaboration. In so doing the OHL left everyone with the impression that the Ministry had been negligent and needed to be flogged into performance.

This dim view of the War Ministry was shared to some extent by State Secretary Helfferich. In a letter to Ludendorff of September 3, he supported industrialist demands for more workers, placing industrial advisers in the procurement agencies and centralization of procurement. In his conclusion he espoused the general subordination of the War Ministry then underway: "I find it to be a great relief from a pressing care that the Supreme Command has now taken this important matter into its hands. The Supreme Command is the only agency that can work upon the War Ministry concerning this question with certainty of success."[23] Actually, Wild and Koeth had been working on the reorganization of procurement since August 5, and a new Weapons and Munitions Procurement Office (WUMBA) was being established during the first two weeks of September. WUMBA was to replace the old Ordnance Master's Office. General Franke, as an opponent of the Hindenburg Program, was completely unsuited for continued leadership of procurement, and he was replaced by the head of the Technical Institute of Artillery, Major General Coupette. Coupette was universally admired for his technical abilities, and he had played a major role in overcoming the munitions crisis of 1914. Despite all the fanfare attached to its creation, however, WUMBA was not really a radically new organization. It brought the procurement agencies of the Ordnance Master's Office, the General War Department, and the Engineer's Committee together and placed them under unified leadership. Representatives of the Saxon, Bavarian, and Württemberg war ministries were appointed to WUMBA to coor-

[23] Helfferich, *Weltkrieg*, II, p. 280.

dinate policy, but these ministries continued to have their own procurement agencies. This was not the fault of the War Ministry but rather of the federal structure of the Empire. The navy, air force, communications services, and railroads remained completely independent in their procurement. This was not the fault of the War Ministry either. It was the OHL that had approved their petitions for continued independence.[24]

Having thus established WUMBA, Wild now felt prepared to meet with the industrialists in accordance with the instructions he had received from the OHL. A secret conference was held in the splendid *Kaisersaal* of the War Ministry on September 16, 1916.[25] Present were thirty-nine of Germany's greatest industrial leaders and representatives of the civil authorities, the navy, and the War Ministry. As might be expected, Colonel Bauer represented the OHL. Wild opened the three hour long meeting with a speech in which, after reviewing the serious military situation, he expressed his support for the Hindenburg Program: "In agreement with the Supreme Command, I must state that the earlier program no longer suffices; it does not suffice for the present situation, it does not suffice for the situation that is to be anticipated." He was thus forced to demand "the *greatest* and *quickest* imaginable production of powder, iron, and steel." Without giving statistics, he simply stated that "*gigantic demands*" were going to be made.

The rest of the speech was an effort to conciliate the industrialists without surrendering to all of their wishes. Thus he promised, in the name of the OHL, that the skilled workers already exempted for industry, including those in the "liable to field duty" (k.v.) category, would not be taken away. Furthermore, many more skilled workers would be given up by the army. He did insist, however, that the industrialists

[24] WUMBA, which was officially established on Sept. 30, 1916, is analyzed in Captain Büsselburg's study, Nachlass Groener, 198.

[25] The discussion and quotations which follow are based on the protocol of the meeting, BHStA, Abt. IV, MK, K Mob 6, Bd. I, Bl. zu 12.

make greater use of labor not liable to military service. Above all, he absolutely refused the repeated demands of the industrialists that the exemptions question be turned over to the procurement agencies. In his view the procurement agencies would be partial to industry and neglect the need for reserves. He did promise to make AZS more effective. At the same time he defended AZS's social policies. The food shortage and the recent strikes made the conciliation of labor a "national as well as a social duty." Finally, Wild outlined the organization and tasks of WUMBA and concluded with a plea for a restoration of harmony between industry and the War Ministry.

Colonel Bauer then conveyed the greetings of the OHL and stressed both the necessity and the feasibility of the new munitions program. It was extremely difficult, he pointed out, for the army to give up the skilled workers needed by industry, and he begged them to take no more than they needed. His conclusion, however, left little doubt as to who now had the upper hand in the manpower question and, indeed, in every other question: "But place upon yourselves restrictions in this connection with your attention focused upon that which the War Minister has just said: the performance demanded must be achieved! Be clear that what industry must accomplish is just as important as what the army has to do. Only with your help can we march on to victory. It is a question of existence or nonexistence." A rather pleasant change after having been called "Fatherlandless industrialists" by Sichler!

The industrialists expressed great satisfaction with WUMBA, and they applauded heartily when Coupette promised to attach an industrialists' advisory council to the new organization. Despite Wild's plea, however, they were unprepared to dismiss the past. Duisberg led off with an attack on the "holy bureaucratism" of the Ministry. The program could not be fulfilled by spring if they had to run from one bureau to another and if the Ministry insisted upon helping the Imperial Treasury Office to "save a few pennies" instead of richly subsidizing new construction. Rathenau was almost insulting when he spoke of the way the Ministry had continuously changed its production demands: "Had we not had elasticity, had we not said we will work on because the gentlemen do not know what they need, but we know, then we would have caused immeasurable damage." Dr. Waldschmidt of the Ludwig Löwe firm demanded that the contracts be made more palatable to industry. Borsig pointed out that this was not the time for the factory inspectors to try to cut working hours for women and children, and he demanded greater support from the War Ministry against such efforts. Hilger insisted that industry be "spared social experiments" like war boards and vacations. The Saar industrialist Carl Röchling attacked the interference of factory inspectors and military officers in the running of their plants.

The replies of the War Ministry's representatives, although generally conciliatory, demonstrated that the Ministry was still not completely in accord with the spirit that was supposed to rule the day. Thus Major Koeth remarked that many of the industrial firms were even more bureaucratic and harder to deal with than the War Ministry. Coupette was certain that there would be greater continuity of production under the Hindenburg Program than previously, but he insisted that the War Ministry had to have the right to terminate or change contracts when demanded by the military situation. Coupette also made a particularly strong appeal that the workers be given vacations so that they might "feel human again."

The labor question was the main topic of conversation at the conference. The industrialists were particularly angry at the way in which field commanders and Deputy Commanding Generals had blocked their efforts to exempt workers. They continued to demand that the whole exemption question be put in the hands of WUMBA. Wild admitted the difficulties, but stressed the fact that he was personally powerless in dealing with both field commanders and Deputy Commanding Generals. He promised that every effort would be made to convince them of the need to supply industry with labor. At the same time, however, reserves had to be supplied to the army, and only the nonpartisan AZS could correctly render judgment in the competition between industry and army for manpower.

The problem of the free movement of labor was taken up in connection with the general discussion of the manpower problem. Commercial Councilor Reinecker, a Saxon machine tool manufacturer, stressed the importance of keeping the workers on their jobs and suggested that the Austrian system of commandeering soldiers to work in the factories be employed. A similar demand was voiced by others. Wild, however, remained noncommittal on this question and simply pointed out that exempted workers who left their jobs could be redrafted into the army.

Great concern was expressed concerning the food question. Duisberg denounced the recent seizure of food he had smuggled across the Dutch border for his workers. Previously the authorities had looked the other way, and now they were suddenly becoming "bureaucratic": ". . . it would be well if one of the gentlemen in the War Food Office was put into the War Ministry, so that each case is not handled rigidly. Bureaucracy can only be overcome through differentiation." Dr. Reusch, who was in the "less envious position" of being the industrialist representative on the KEA, objected to Duisberg's plea for the institutionalization of smuggling and black marketeering. He pointed out that the recent strikes were, in many cases, caused by the capacity of certain firms to feed their workers better than others.

A final issue of great importance raised in the course of the discussion was the significance of the Hindenburg Program for the industrial community itself. The new program demanded a type of industrial efficiency which only the largest and wealthiest firms could provide. Rathenau, while recognizing that it was socially desirable to keep smaller firms in business, pointed out that national concerns now had to precede social ones. The large firms functioned best when fully employed, and they utilized labor more efficiently. With the exception of the Bavarian industrialist Rieppel, who felt that the smaller firms should be saved through a system of subcontracting, the industrialists agreed with Rathenau. Coupette also agreed with Rathenau and warned that the army's efforts faced "shipwreck" if scarce labor and machinery were divided up among thousands of little firms. The new program demanded that heavy industry receive the lion's share of the contracts.[26]

The conference of September 16 presents a rather confusing picture. Through its new munitions program the OHL had given the upper hand to the big industrialists, and the latter had taken this opportunity to dredge up every old conflict with the War Ministry in an effort to decide those conflicts in their favor. The course of the discussion, however, demonstrated that the industrialists were completely dependent upon the OHL in achieving their aims. Thus the Hindenburg Program itself and the decision to favor industry in the allocation of manpower antedated the meeting. The unification of procurement was achieved by the common agreement of the OHL, the War Ministry, and industry. However, on every issue where the War Ministry was unwilling to make concessions and where the OHL had not forced them to do so—putting the procurement agencies in charge of exemptions, easing the terms of contracts, guaranteeing the continuity of contracts, showing less concern with social questions, restricting the free movement of labor—the representatives of the War Ministry replied either negatively or evasively. In short, the War Ministry was holding on tenaciously to those vestiges of independence remaining to it.

This was far from easy. Wild was both patriotic and attached to his position as Prussian War Minister. He felt bound to give the new OHL his utmost support. His entire conception of the role of the Prussian War Minister spoke against his rele-

[26] Another important demand raised at the meeting was for the use of compulsion against unemployed Belgian workers who refused to work in Germany. Duisberg asked the OHL to "open up the great Belgian labor basin," and Bauer promised to do so.

gation to Berlin, but he set aside his convictions. Similarly, he bore manfully the irritations that came with the growing subordination of his ministry to the OHL. The industrialists now felt that they could disregard the War Ministry, and they brought their demands directly to the OHL. The Ministry was flooded with orders stamped "By Command of Ludendorff." The real source of these orders was by no means a mystery. Members of Colonel Bauer's staff made a practice of turning up at ministerial meetings uninvited. How demoralizing an effect all this had on the officers serving in the Ministry can well be imagined. By the end of September, General von Wandel had had enough and, to Wild's chagrin, he resigned his post. "He felt my continuous presence in Berlin to be a *capitis diminuto* and took his leave. Since the Reichstag was standing before the door and the amount of work was enormous, I can only regard his departure as desertion. We are still at war! What value do personal patents have now?"[27] Probably it was not merely the loss of his own power, but also the general disintegration of the War Ministry's power that drove Wandel into retirement, but Wild's comment demonstrates the degree to which he was prepared to ignore his own feelings in his effort to aid the new OHL. The tests imposed upon Wild's endurance, however, were multiplying daily.

2. *Military Reorganization and Civilian Mobilization*

If the OHL was prepared to release thousands of skilled workers from the front despite the military disadvantages that this entailed, it still remained impossible to disregard the long-run dangers of this policy. Germany's inferiority in manpower demanded the most rational use of her human material. In his letter to Wild von Hohenborn of August 31, Hindenburg indicated some of the methods that would have to be used to accomplish this end. The army would have to purge its agencies in the occupied territories and at home of k.v. manpower.

[27] Notation of Oct. 29, 1916, BA, Nachlass Wild von Hohenborn, Nr. 2, and letter to Prof. Zorn, Jan. 1, 1917, *ibid.*, Nr. 6.

Furthermore, exempted workers would eventually have to be taken back into the army, and it was thus necessary to train unskilled labor employed in nonessential industries. Even this, however, might not suffice, and he pointed out that "if occasion should arise, we must use compulsory measures as in England."[28]

This intimation that compulsion might be employed to mobilize the civilian population demonstrated that the new leaders shared Falkenhayn's inclination to give way to industrialist proposals along these lines. The success of the British on the Somme seemed attributable to their economic mobilization. The British measures had a dual character. On the one hand, the British had established an extraordinarily effective centralized organization for the management of the war economy, the Munitions Ministry. On the other hand, they had introduced the national registration of labor and had legislated far-reaching controls on the free movement of labor in their Munitions Act of July 1915.[29] On August 31, however, the OHL did not seem to have been very clear as to the extent to which they wished to emulate the British. If they had been, Hindenburg's letter certainly would have been more definite. Yet two weeks later, on September 13, the OHL presented the Chancellor and the War Minister with concrete demands for compulsory civilian mobilization and for organizational changes within the War Ministry. The question thus arises as to what influences were at work between August 31 and September 13 that caused the OHL to come to a decision.

Once again it was Wichard von Moellendorff who provided the inspiration for the measures taken to master the problems of Germany's economic war effort. If any program demanded the organization of an economy for the national purpose, it was the Hindenburg Program, and it was natural for Moellendorff to want to take the opportunity it presented to give

[28] Ludendorff, *Urkunden*, pp. 63-65.

[29] The English system is discussed in G. D. H. Cole, *Trade Unionism and Munitions*, London, 1932, pp. 53ff.

practical application to his ideas. Moellendorff had been appointed technical adviser to WUMBA, which was in the process of creation at this time, and he was thus already devoting all his energies to the problems created by the Hindenburg Program. The passion with which he approached these problems, however, had its origin in his vision of the social reconstruction along corporatist lines for which the Hindenburg Program seemed to present such a marvelous opportunity:

> In my view Prussia is called upon by history to intervene. In her history there is a direct line from Frederick the Great to Stein, List, and Bismarck . . . to that which we must accomplish in the next few years if Germany is to remain economically and politically independent. I place great value on the historical connection, because I believe that a conscious national-aristocratic-corporative-socialist orientation as opposed to the antiquated internationalist-democratic-parliamentarian-capitalistic epoch will be most likely to be established internally.[30]

Such, then, were the grandiose foundations which underlay Moellendorff's practical work on the Hindenburg Program.

In the first days of September Moellendorff was approached by his close friend, the chemist and leading technical organizer of the wartime chemical industry, Fritz Haber, with a request for an organizational program designed to meet the needs of the Hindenburg Program. Moellendorff responded in a letter dated September 5. He proposed the establishment of a Labor Office in the War Ministry to control the Empire's manpower, including prisoners of war, soldiers working in the occupied territories, and the troops in the home garrisons. No labor was to be employed without the permission of the Labor Office. The need for labor was to be predetermined before contracts

[30] Moellendorff to Privy Finance Councilor Meydenbauer, Sept. 11, 1916, BA, Nachlass Moellendorff, Nr. 69a. Throughout the year, Moellendorff had been circulating a pamphlet containing his program for a planned postwar economy, Bowen, *Corporative State*, p. 184, and Wichard von Moellendorff, *Deutsche Gemeinwirtschaft*, Berlin, 1916.

were granted and duties assigned. Under this system all labor had to be legally bound to the orders of the Labor Office. Therefore, "Compulsory labor will be introduced for the entire population, perhaps in connection with the distribution of food."[31] Having all of Germany's labor within its power, the Labor Office would be able to exercise both quantitative and qualitative control of the labor force. On the one hand, it would gather statistics on the labor market each month and then make its decisions concerning the assignment and transplantation of workers accordingly. On the other hand, it would gather information on projected needs for different types of labor and then develop training programs and efficiency systems so that these demands might be met.

Through these measures Moellendorff hoped for the implementation of the Hindenburg Program and the unification of the agencies dealing with labor questions. While recognizing that many of the tasks to be solved were matters that one would normally expect to be handled by the civil authorities, Moellendorff pointed out that the entire history of the war had demonstrated the refusal of the civil government to accept its responsibilities and that "everything seems to point in the direction of having the entire land drawn together under unified military leadership and utilized like an arsenal."[32] He warned that every wasted month was an irredeemable loss because the labor shortage was certain to get progressively worse.

At the conclusion of his letter of September 5, Moellendorff asked Haber to make whatever use he thought best of the proposals contained in it. Haber had probably already indicated the use he intended to make of them when he first approached Moellendorff. The proposals were given to Colonel

[31] Moellendorff to Haber, Sept. 5, 1916, BA, Nachlass Moellendorff, Nr. 6. This letter is reprinted without any indication as to the sender or the recipient in Sichler and Tiburtius, *Arbeiterfrage*, pp. 101-104.

[32] Moellendorff to Dr. Bueb, Sept. 15, 1916, BA, Nachlass Moellendorff, Nr. 49. Bueb, the later Imperial Nitrates Commissar, received a copy of the letter to Haber.

Bauer, a man with whom Haber had frequent contact, and, on September 13, the Moellendorff letter was sent to General Wild von Hohenborn by the OHL. It was signed by Hindenburg and bore Ludendorff's characteristic "L."[33]

The OHL sent yet another letter on September 13, this one to the Chancellor,[34] although the War Minister also received a copy. It contained concrete proposals for the management of the manpower question. Turning first to the problem of getting reserves for the army, the OHL asked that the physically unfit and urban youth be sent to the country for health reasons. They also recommended that schools and factories be forced to provide time for the military training of boys over sixteen. Most important, Hindenburg demanded that the age of liability for military service be raised from forty-five to fifty. Older men could then be used to relieve younger personnel serving in the rear of the fighting forces.

The OHL then turned to industry's manpower problems. Combining the proposals that the industrialists had previously made to Falkenhayn with the technical considerations more recently outlined by Moellendorff, the OHL demanded an amendment to the War Production Law of 1872 enabling the government to transplant workers from industries suffering

[33] In the upper left-hand corner of the letter to Haber of Sept. 5, Moellendorff noted: "Sent on by Privy Councilor Haber to Lieutenant-Colonel Bauer (OHL) and from there, according to information from Bauer (29/9.16), it was sent out for evaluation," *ibid.*, Nr. 6. For a comparison of the original Moellendorff note and the version sent to Wild, see Sichler and Tiburtius, *Arbeiterfrage*, pp. 101-104. Nearly all of the important correspondence sent out by Hindenburg had "L" attached to the last line. This practice once provoked Count Lerchenfeld to ask if "Hindenburg, perhaps, is incapable of writing any letters by himself?" Lerchenfeld to Hertling, March 24, 1917, BHStA, Abt. II, MA 1, Nr. 958. At the same time, it is important to recognize that nearly all of the OHL memoranda discussed in this book came from Bauer's office, as demonstrated by the "op. II" in the upper right-hand corner. In general, therefore, it is safe to say that Bauer composed these important memoranda, Ludendorff initialed them, and Hindenburg signed them.

[34] The discussion and quotations which follow are based on Ludendorff, *Urkunden*, pp. 65-67.

from raw materials shortages and from nonessential industries to war plants. It would then also be legally possible to register the workers, as in England, and to utilize labor rationally.

The letter of September 13 was characterized by nastiness of tone and brutality of language. The proposed legislation was justified by the existence of universal suffrage in the Empire and the fact that one group of men—"and to be sure . . . the strongest and most useful to the state"—were risking their lives while the other group sat home in perfect security and sought profit. This was "screaming injustice." Even harsher was Hindenburg's justification for the application of compulsion to women: "There are untold thousands of childless soldiers' wives who just cost the state money. Also, thousands of women and girls are running around doing nothing or, at best, pursuing useless occupations. The principle 'He who does not work shall not eat' is, *also pertaining to women*, more justified than ever before in our present situation." With the exception of the medical schools, the universities were not to be spared either. They were to be shut down: "This also is an act of justice, so that men incapable of military service and women do not outstrip in rank and then take away the positions of the students now in the field. It is also in the interest of increasing the population that care should be taken to make it as easy as possible for the young men returning home to start families." It was, in short, "high time" that the "screamers and agitators" were shut up and the "search for profit and pleasure" was ended: "The entire German people should live only in the service of the Fatherland." The burning resentment of these lines demonstrates both the growing estrangement between front and homeland which the long war had brought and the tendency of the new OHL to give concrete expression to the *Frontsoldat's* bitterness. The OHL expressed great impatience in calling for a remedy: "To achieve success, quick action is necessary. *Every day is of importance.* The necessary measures are to be undertaken *immediately.*"

On September 14, the day after the letters discussed above

were sent, the OHL drove the spur yet deeper in another note to the War Ministry. Hindenburg informed Wild that the military situation demanded the summoning of all k.v. men, including those in the class of 1918, to the colors. Only exempted workers were to be excluded. Hindenburg pointed out that there was no reason to fear that such an acceleration of the draft would make it difficult to supply the reserves needed after the spring of 1917. The new munitions program was designed to solve this problem: "At the time when the number of available men will become smaller, the machines of war (machine guns, cannon, mine throwers) will have to be so numerous that we will be able to hold our lines with a decreased deployment of manpower." Finally, Hindenburg reminded Wild that the key to the reconciliation of his demands for both reserves and munitions was to be found in the OHL's proposals of the previous day.[35]

Both the Imperial Office of the Interior and the War Ministry had fought the proposals for compulsory civilian mobilization in Falkenhayn's day. How would they receive their revival on the part of the new OHL? Since the material contained in the OHL's letter of September 13 fell within the competence of the Interior Office, Bethmann passed the letter on to Helfferich for his comments, and the latter penned a memorandum expressing almost complete opposition to the OHL's demands.[36] He warned that the removal of manpower to the countryside and the military training of young boys would be harmful to industry. He objected to the extension of the military service requirement by pointing out that the males over forty-five capable of work were, almost without exception, already employed in the service of the war economy. The high wages paid by the war industries had induced nearly all of Germany's available male labor, including the students, to flock to those

[35] *Ibid.*, pp. 69-70.

[36] The discussion and quotations which follow are based on the original copy of the memorandum in DZA Potsdam, Kriegsakten 1, Bd. 8, Bl. 254-262.

industries. The government had contributed to this development by refusing to give contracts for nonessential production and limiting the distribution of raw materials. Helfferich praised the achievements of the German home front and stressed the degree to which German industry had already adjusted to the war economy. He warned against compulsory measures which would bring no results but only "disturb this healthy adjustment and bring the entire structure of our economy into confusion." The most that Helfferich would concede was that some limited success might be achieved through further restrictions on nonessential construction work, careful training of war wounded to restore their capacity to work, the drafting of seventeen- and eighteen-year-olds, and, in the last extremity, the extension of the draft age to fifty.

Helfferich was particularly adamant in his rejection of compulsory female labor. He based his argument upon the rather simple fact that the supply of women seeking employment exceeded the demand. For each 100 available jobs there were 80 men, but 160 women. The number of female workers employed in war work had increased enormously since the beginning of the war, but further increases depended upon the degree to which industrialists were prepared to make this possible. To introduce compulsory service for women would be "to put the cart before the horse." Furthermore, considerations of an economic, moral, and social nature also militated against such a measure, as considerations of a cultural nature militated against a closure of the German universities.

The application of the principle of compulsion to economic life was anathema to Helfferich, whose entire economic philosophy was based on the principle of economic freedom. He had long been an opponent of the corporatist ideas of men such as Moellendorff. At the same time, as a government leader constantly called on to deal with a disintegrating internal situation, Helfferich was bound to fear the internal effects of an effort to impose compulsion upon the workers in accordance with the wishes of certain industrialists. The OHL, by aligning itself with the ideas of both Moellendorff and those industrialists who wanted compulsion, had thus driven Helfferich into opposition. The conclusion of his memorandum reflected the depths of his antagonism to the OHL's labor program:

> All in all, I can only advise in the most urgent manner against the attempt to replace the freedom under which our economy, with the willing and enthusiastic collaboration of all its components, has transformed itself in such a marvelous way to meet the demands of war by a compulsion ruinous to the adaptability of our economic structure. An army permits itself to be commanded, but not an economy.

Bethmann must have been thrown into some consternation by the OHL's letter of September 13, which represented an effort to dictate to the government on questions lying completely outside the army's competence. Well-informed persons had warned Bethmann to establish clear distinctions of competence between himself and the new OHL, but he had refused to do so on the grounds that his relations with Hindenburg were of a very friendly nature.[37] He now had cause to repent his refusal, and he sought to correct the error. On September 17 he sent a short reply to the OHL's letter indicating that he had taken their proposals under advisement and reminding them that a distinction had to be made between purely military measures and "those questions in which my collaboration is necessary" and which, therefore, required "common consultations."[38] On September 20 Ludendorff replied in his most "reasonable" tone. He thanked the Chancellor for his willingness to consider his proposals and agreed that, aside from purely military measures, "all other questions lie within Your Excellency's competence."[39] Ludendorff did express the

[37] Lerchenfeld to Hertling, Nov. 22, 1916, BHStA, Abt. II, MA 1, Nr. 958.

[38] Bethmann to Hindenburg, Sept. 17, 1916, DZA Potsdam, Kriegsakten 1, Bd. 9, Bl. 3.

[39] Ludendorff to Bethmann, Sept. 20, 1916, *ibid.*, Bl. 4.

urgency of the questions he had raised and the hope that the Chancellor would see fit to discuss them with a representative of the OHL. Bethmann was undoubtedly impressed by Ludendorff's friendly tone. Since the OHL's proposals were being rejected, he refrained from asking for an interview with an OHL representative. Instead, he ordered that a written reply be sent based on the Helfferich memorandum.

On September 30 Bethmann signed and sent off his reply to the OHL. It was almost an exact copy of the Helfferich memorandum. The sharp tone of some of Helfferich's comments had been made milder, and Helfferich's stinging conclusion was omitted. The new conclusion, however, was in some ways even less at one with the spirit of the OHL's proposals than the old one. Bethmann opposed the indiscriminate shutting down of all factories not producing for the war effort. Such a measure might prove fatal to Germany's economy, "whose life and work cannot simply be replaced by authoritarian measures." The morale of the people was necessary for victory, and Bethmann warned against taking steps that would ruin it. At the same time he warned against destroying the foundations of the economic reconstruction that would have to follow the war.[40]

Ludendorff was convinced neither by the argument that there was little to be gained through his proposals nor by the broader economic and social arguments contained in the Chancellor's reply. Having gotten nowhere with the Chancellor, Ludendorff turned to the War Ministry, which still had not answered his proposals of September 13. On October 5 he sent another note to Wild, to which was appended the Chancellor's letter of September 30. In this note Ludendorff reiterated his demand for an amendment to the War Production Law and placed particular emphasis on the necessity of restricting the free movement of labor. What Ludendorff was really after, however, was the Ministry's support against Bethmann's arguments, for he asked the War Minister whether the measures

[40] Ludendorff, *Urkunden*, pp. 70-76.

he had proposed would bring the desired results. In short, Ludendorff was fairly sure of what he wanted but rather unsure of the reasons he should give for his desires. One gets a similar impression from his short reply to the Chancellor of October 7, in which he refused to accept the latter's arguments but also indicated that the Chancellor would have to wait momentarily for the OHL's counterarguments. Everything now seemed to hinge on what the War Ministry would have to say, not only about the idea of compulsory civilian mobilization, but also about the proposal for the establishment of a labor office.[41]

In reality the officers of the OHL were becoming increasingly uninterested in what the War Ministry would have to say about their organizational proposals. They had by no means lost interest in the labor office idea. How could they when Duisberg and the League of German Industrialists were sending them petitions demanding the establishment of just such an institution?[42] What really was happening was that the OHL was now beginning to take a much broader view of the organizational problem. This was largely due to Freiherr von Batocki and General Groener. As Duisberg wanted to overcome the resistance of the Deputy Commanding Generals to exemptions, so Batocki wanted greater control established over them in matters of food distribution. Also, after half a year of wrestling with the food problem, Batocki seems to have become convinced that the army would have to intervene. Thus on September 20 he sent a personal letter to General Groener proposing the establishment of a "supreme war economy command" (*Oberste Kriegswirtschaftsleitung*), which would be placed under the leadership of a general. Since the labor and food problems were so closely interrelated, the new institution would have a war labor office and the KEA as its constituent elements. By implication, the new institution would be inde-

[41] *Ibid.*, pp. 76-77.

[42] WUMBA Advisory Council meeting, Oct. 15, 1916, BA, Nachlass Moellendorff, Nr. 58, and Dierkopf, *Hilfsdienstgesetz*, pp. 33-34.

The Prussian War Ministry in August 1916

(*denotes a department or section subsequently transferred to the War Office.)

Minister of War

Deputy Minister of War

1. *Central Department* (ZD)
   a. Ministerial Section (Z1)
   b. Budgetary Section (Z2)
   c. Central Information Bureau (NB)

2. *General War Department* (AD)
   a. Army Section (A1)
   b. Reserves Section I (C1a) (officers and noncommissioned officers)
   c. Reserves Section II (C1b)* and Exemptions Section (AZS)*
   d. Infantry Section (A2)
   e. Cavalry Section (A3)
   f. Field Artillery Section (A4)
   g. Foot Artillery Section (A5)
   h. Engineer and Pioneer Section (A6)
   i. Communications Section (A7V)
   j. Imports and Exports Section (A8)*
   k. Factory Section (B5)*
   l. Chemicals Section (A10)

   Agencies Attached to the General War Department:

   Ordnance Master's Office (F2)* and
   Technical Institutes*

3. *Army Administration Department* (BD)
   a. War Supply Section (B1)
   b. Peace Supply Section (B2)
   c. Clothing Section (B3)
   d. Finance Section (B4)
   e. Food Supply Section (B6)*
   f. Captured War Material Section (ZK)

4. *Quartering Department* (UD)
   a. Quartering Section, Eastern Front (U1)
   b. Quartering Section, Western Front (U2)
   c. Training Grounds Section (U3)
   d. Works Section (U4)
   e. Section for the Protection of German Prisoners of War and for Breaches of International Law (U5)
   f. War Quartering Section (UK)

5. *Pensions and Justice Department* (CD)
   a. Pensions Section (C2P)
   b. Annuity Section (C2R)
   c. Assistance Section (C3V)
   d. Justice Section (C4)

6. *Raw Materials Section* (KRA)*
   Composed of nineteen sections charged with the allocation of vital raw materials

7. *Remount Inspection* (RI)

8. *Medical Section* (MA)

pendent of the War Ministry, and it would, of course, have the right to issue orders to the Deputy Commanding Generals. As we know, this sort of arrangement appealed very much to General Groener, and it was thus natural that he should have presented Batocki's ideas to the OHL in a very favorable light. It is equally understandable that Bauer and Ludendorff should have grasped at the new idea. The labor and food questions were uppermost in their minds, as was the connection Moellendorff had made between the two problems in his proposal for a compulsory labor law. In the course of the discussions that took place at Supreme Headquarters, the institution proposed by Batocki was gradually expanded to include other agencies dealing with the war economy. This reflected the desire to establish something comparable to the British Munitions Ministry. It also reflected Colonel Bauer's desire to have all questions relating to the war economy taken out of the hands of the War Ministry and placed under the direction of the OHL.[43]

During the period of October 7-10, Ludendorff and Groener had a number of conversations concerning the establishment of what was now being called a "supreme war office" (*Oberste Kriegsamt*). During these conversations Ludendorff indicated that he and Bauer were thinking of placing Groener at the head of the new organization. The choice of Groener was natural enough. Groener had considerable experience with economic matters and the men in Berlin, and his technical skills were widely admired. Groener had worked with Ludendorff and Bauer in the General Staff before the war. He shared their distaste for the bureaucratism of the War Ministry. Ludendorff had already used Groener in connection with the munitions crisis, as he had sent Groener to make a special survey of the situation on the Somme. To be sure, Groener was a Swabian, whose personality and inclinations differed markedly from

[43] Groener, *Lebenserinnerungen*, p. 553, and Bauer, *Grosse Krieg*, p. 120.

those of the humorless and rigid Ludendorff, but Groener had demonstrated his worth, and, in these days, he seemed to be in complete agreement with the OHL. For the moment, however, the leadership question was left undecided. Everything depended upon what the Chancellor would have to say, and Groener was sent to Berlin to report the OHL's organizational program to Bethmann.

On October 10 Groener was given a "secret and personal" letter to present to the Chancellor.[44] In it, the OHL pointed out that the organizational measures relating to the war economy that had been taken so far were insufficient. So long as the KRA, AZS, and WUMBA did not have the "necessary independence and power of command," they would never be capable of accomplishing the tasks assigned to them. The KEA was cited as an example of the deficiencies of the organizational forms being employed. The OHL could not permit such an insupportable situation to continue. Hindenburg warned that a failure to organize in such a way as to insure industry's capacity to produce and guarantee that the workers were properly fed could result in the loss of the war. A quick change was necessary, and there was no time to call on the legislative bodies for help. The matter would have to be settled by a decree of the Emperor.

Attached to the letter was the OHL's draft proposal for this decree. It established a supreme war office for the regulation of procurement, raw materials, labor and food. WUMBA, AZS, and the KRA were to be placed under the Supreme War Office. Also, it was to oversee the work of the KEA insofar as the feeding of the industrial workers was concerned. The supreme war office was to have the right to command the Deputy Commanding Generals to follow its orders on all economic questions. Finally, the methods and actions of the supreme war office were to be subject to the approval of the OHL.

[44] Nachlass Groener, 192-I, and DZA Potsdam, Kriegsakten 1, Bd. 9, Bl. 147-149.

This was an extraordinarily radical proposal. It deprived the War Ministry of any role in the war economy. Similarly, it represented an attack on the independent functioning of the various state war ministries, for the supreme war office was obviously meant to be an Imperial agency. At the same time, it meant an enormous increase of the OHL's power, for if the Deputy Commanding Generals were bound to follow the orders of the War Office, and the War Office's actions were subject to the approval of the OHL, then the OHL was in a position to supervise the most important military agencies in the homeland. For the moment, and evidently because of the legal questions involved, the OHL abstained from asking that the KEA be formally placed within the supreme war office. Given the role assigned to the latter in food questions, however, it is obvious that the new institution would be able to exert considerable control over the KEA. Batocki did not seem to mind this, and his office was a unique creation of the war anyway, so that the constitutional questions involved were not serious. The same conditions did not hold for the War Ministry, however. On the one hand, the Ministry was being emasculated. On the other hand, the War Minister would now have to answer before the Reichstag for the actions of an entirely new organization over which he had no control. Little wonder that the OHL had not informed Wild and had requested Bethmann in their letter to keep the matter a secret until a decision had been reached. The supreme war office was to be created behind the War Minister's back. The OHL planned to have Bethmann and Hindenburg present the idea to the Emperor together. Once the latter gave his approval, the War Minister would then be called upon to countersign the necessary decree.

On October 14 Groener presented the aforementioned letter to the Chancellor. On the same day, ironically enough, the War Ministry finally answered the OHL's letters of September

13 and October 5.[45] Wild rejected both the Labor Office and compulsory civilian mobilization. He pointed out that a "labor office" had been in existence for some time in the form of AZS. He agreed that the competence of AZS might be expanded to include prisoners of war and the military personnel in the occupied areas, but he pointed out that it was technically impossible for AZS to approve each specific case where labor was to be employed. This would require a mammoth organization quite beyond the Ministry's resources and would only create confusion. He reminded the OHL that the Ministry had required employers to state their labor needs before being given contracts since July 1915. More than this could not be expected. Thus Wild rejected Moellendorff's plan by arguing that a labor office already existed and that the new methods being proposed were technically impossible.

Wild's rejection of compulsory civilian mobilization was largely a repetition of the arguments the Ministry had first employed in July 1915. The Ministry enumerated the measures that had already been taken to train and procure labor, emphasized that there was little additional labor available, and stressed the need to maintain the morale of the German worker. The workers, Wild insisted, had to support the war effort out of inner conviction, not because they were being compelled to do so. He was, therefore, forced to agree with the objections of the civil government to the OHL's proposals. Like Helfferich, the only concession Wild was prepared to make was an extension of the age of military service liability from forty-five to fifty. He was careful to point out that this would yield little additional manpower and that it was not justified by the army's manpower needs. It might, however, provide a useful means of controlling this group of workers, since they could then be forced to work in war plants and be bound to their jobs. Finally, Wild suggested that the Law of Siege might be used as a means of restricting the free move-

[45] Wild to Hindenburg, Oct. 14, 1916, in Sichler and Tiburtius, *Arbeiterfrage*, pp. 109-118.

ment of labor in cases where this was particularly necessary.

The situation in mid-October was thus confusing indeed. The War Ministry had turned down already superseded organizational proposals. The new proposals were being made to the Chancellor without the Ministry's knowledge. At the same time the idea of compulsory civilian mobilization had been rejected by both the Chancellor and the War Minister. They were willing to consider an extension of the age of liability to military service, but it was clear that this would not yield much labor. In a meeting of the industrialist Advisory Council to WUMBA on October 15, Coupette asked whether the Hindenburg Program could be fulfilled without legislative measures concerning the labor question. The industrialists denied this possibility. They insisted that nonessential factories be shut down and that compulsion be employed to force young people into war industry. There was also considerable sentiment for restrictions upon the free movement of labor. On the same day Bethmann was telling Groener that such restrictions were unnecessary, and that "it would meet the sharpest resistance" from the Reichstag.[46]

The events of the next few days demonstrate that the OHL now embarked on a dual course of action. It launched a major offensive against the War Ministry, but it also conducted a temporary strategic retreat on the question of compulsory civilian mobilization. The reason for this was that the Chancellor seemed agreeable to the war office idea. In Bethmann's view, a war office would be established in two ways if one wished to follow the OHL's proposals exactly. The first would involve the organization of an Imperial war ministry. This, however, would require Imperial legislation because of the constitutional structure of the Empire. The second method would be to make the war office an Imperial office, like the Interior Office or Treasury Office. This last solution, however,

[46] WUMBA Advisory Council meeting, Oct. 15, 1916, BA, Nachlass Moellendorff, Nr. 58, and Bethmann to Hindenburg, Oct. 15, 1916, DZA Potsdam, Kriegsakten 1, Bd. 9, Bl. 160-163.

would make the Chancellor responsible for the actions of the War Office, and, since the War Office was to command the Deputy Commanding Generals, it would make the Chancellor responsible for their actions as well. This would be undesirable: "The principle which we have maintained until now—despite severe opposition—that the Emperor's power of command should in no way be touched upon or limited by the political responsibility of the Imperial Chancellor, would then no longer be possible to maintain."[47] In short, the Chancellor would have to answer for the actions of the war office and the Deputy Commanding Generals before the Reichstag. The problem, therefore, was to find a means of creating a war office that would not present either of the above-mentioned difficulties.

Bethmann's solution was to establish the war office within the framework of the Prussian War Ministry by royal decree. It would be independent of all the other sections of the War Ministry and, at the same time, be capable of fulfilling all the functions the OHL wished to assign to their war office. The War Minister would be the official head of the new agency, but he could assign his functions to a deputy minister. Furthermore, the War Minister could then be given the right to issue binding orders to the Deputy Commanding Generals, although special arrangements would have to be made with the non-Prussian states in this regard. Since the express statement of the dependence of the new agency's activities upon the approval of the OHL might create constitutional problems, Bethmann suggested that this simply be tacitly understood rather than specifically stated in the proposed royal decree. Finally, to avoid a conflict of competence with the KEA, Bethmann suggested that the new agency be responsible for the supplying of meats and fats to the industrial workers, but that the distribution of bread and potatoes, which was governed by a multitude of KEA regulations, remain in the hands of the latter agency.

[47] Bethmann to Hindenburg, Oct. 15, 1916, DZA Potsdam, Kriegsakten 1, Bd. 9, Bl. 160-163.

Evidently, Ludendorff was impressed with the Chancellor's arguments, for he immediately agreed to Bethmann's compromise solution. Ludendorff did lay down one condition: Wild had to go. As Groener noted in his diary: "The new War Minister must swear to the new program, otherwise the old bureaucratic spirit of the War Ministry will rule as before."[48] Bethmann was more than happy to get rid of Wild, who as a supporter of unrestricted U-boat warfare, a "creature of Falkenhayn," and an opponent of the projected German peace offer had done much to earn the Chancellor's enmity. In fact, Wild would have been disposed of much earlier had it not been for the Emperor's reluctance to have too many changes made at once.[49]

Thus by October 21 agreement had been reached between the OHL and the Chancellor on the new war office and on a change in the leadership of the War Ministry. During the period when this agreement was being worked out, from October 14 to October 21, the OHL's demands for compulsory civilian mobilization and a general restriction upon the free movement of labor seemed to be set aside. The events of October 17 demonstrated this. On that day a discussion of the labor question was held in the Interior Office in which both the representatives of the civil authorities and of the War Ministry once again rejected legislation controlling the free movement of labor. There was general agreement that the Reichstag would not accept such a bill and that a Bundesrat order would only serve to provoke difficulties with the Reichstag. Everyone agreed that the best solution to the problem was to encourage the establishment of more war boards. In cases of dire need, the Law of Siege could be used, as it had already been used to stop agricultural workers from fleeing to the cities. On the same day, Ludendorff sent a very strange

[48] Groener, *Lebenserinnerungen*, p. 554, and Ludendorff to Bethmann, Oct. 21, 1916, DZA, Potsdam, Kriegsakten 1, Bd. 9, Bl. 198-200.

[49] Wild to Prof. Zorn, Jan. 1, 1917, BA, Nachlass Wild von Hohenborn, Nr. 6 and Lerchenfeld to Hertling, Oct. 12, 1916, BHStA, Abt. II, MA 1, Nr. 958.

note to the War Minister. He expressed pleasure over the fact that there was so much agreement between them on the measures to be taken with regard to the labor question. He agreed that the extension of the age of liability for military service would solve the problem of restricting the free movement of labor, and he promised to answer the Chancellor's letter of September 30, "in the sense of Your Excellency's remarks." Ludendorff did say that he disagreed with the War Minister on the question of setting up a labor office, but he left unmentioned the reasons for his disagreement and what he intended to do about it.[50]

Ludendorff's letter to Wild of October 17 can only be interpreted as a cruel joke. He was deliberately vague about the labor office question because he was arranging to set up a war office and because he planned to have Wild dismissed. What he meant when he said that he intended to answer the Chancellor's letter of September 30 in the sense of Wild's remarks became clear on October 23. By then the organizational question was settled for all intents and purposes, and the OHL could return to the labor question with increased vigor.

In a letter to the Chancellor, Ludendorff demanded that all German males from age fifteen to sixty be made liable to military service. In other words, the age of liability was to be extended two years at the lower end of the age scale and fifteen years at the upper end. This, Ludendorff explained, would solve the problems of ending the free movement of labor, amending the War Production Law, closing the universities, and compelling the wounded to work. Ludendorff was twisting the War Minister's remarks to serve his own purposes. The War Minister had pointed out that a mere extension of the age of liability from forty-five to fifty would yield little new manpower. Ludendorff accepted this argument and decided that the ages of liability would then have to run from fifteen to sixty. Wild had pointed out that an extension of the age of

[50] Ludendorff, *Urkunden*, pp. 127-131, and Sichler and Tiburtius, *Arbeiterfrage*, pp. 129-130.

liability would certainly enable the army to control the free movement of those workers affected. Ludendorff took the unintended hint. By this one measure he eliminated the need for special legislation to mobilize the civilian population and limit the free movement of labor. In other words, the OHL had taken the one concession made by Bethmann and Wild and had used it as a means of reviving the entire OHL program. The question of using compulsion against female labor, however, did not admit of such a neat solution. Undaunted, Ludendorff revived this demand as well. The OHL had not surrendered any of its program. It warned against making public opinion an excuse for refusing the demands: the "depressed mood at home in my view will be improved and *not* further depressed by whole and decisive measures." There was no time for "lengthy discussions." The letter concluded in a very ominous tone. If the Reichstag failed to fulfill its duty, then it would, in so doing, reveal which elements were willing to safeguard the state and which were not. At this moment, however, "I do not need to express myself . . . on the measures to be taken in that eventuality." It was thus quite clear that the OHL meant business.[51]

Bethmann now realized this, and on October 26 he went to General Headquarters. Final arrangements had to be made for the establishment of the war office and the selection of its leader. Also, whether Bethmann liked it or not, the labor question was obviously reopened. The OHL had already been hard at work on the personnel problem. Groener was very reluctant to accept an appointment as head of the war office due to his unhappy experiences on the KEA and his strained relations with some of the bureaucrats in Berlin. He had asked Ludendorff to appoint General von Lochow instead, but Lochow refused. At this point, the OHL definitely decided that Groener was their man. Groener was officially informed of his appoint-

[51] Ludendorff, *Urkunden*, pp. 78-81.

Chief of the War Office: General Groener
Chief of the Military Staff: Major von Kretschmann
Chief of the Technical Staff: Dr. Kurt Sorge

STAFF

Group P1

(Capt. von Dewitz-Krebs)
Relations with the Bundesrat, Reichstag, and Landtag

Group P2

(Capt. Richard Merton)
Special assignments connected with industrial and labor questions; press relations; organization and recruitment of female labor

Group P3

(Lt. Count von Hülsen)
Communications and meetings

Group M1

(Capt. von Zabiensky)
Administration and personnel

Group M2

(Capt. von Heeringen)
Liaison with the War Food Office

Group M3

(Maj. von Ludwiger)
Organization of War Office bureaus; liaison with War Office bureaus; statistics and priority lists; intelligence and propaganda

Group M4

(Capt. Sartorius)
Auxiliary Service Law and liaison with Reichstag committee

Group M5

(Capt. Just)
Liaison with War Office departments

Group ML

(Lt.-Col. von Schwerin)
Agriculture

Technical Staff

(Dr. Kurt Sorge)
Liaison with the various branches of industry and the shutting down and consolidation of industries (SAZ)

Group WK

(Prof. Max Sering)
A Scientific Commission of over two hundred experts serving in an advisory capacity to the War Office

DEPARTMENTS

1. Reserves and Labor Department (E.D.)
   Chief: Col. Marquard
   Technical Adviser: Richard Sichler
   Reserves Section (AZSa): Col. von Braun
   Exemptions Section (AZSb): Col. Frodien

2. Weapons and Munitions Procurement Department (WUMBA)
   Chief: Maj.-Gen. Coupette
   Technical Adviser: Wickard von Moellendorff

3. Raw Materials Section (KRA)
   Chief: Col. Koeth

4. Clothing Procurement Agency (BBA)
   Chief: Lt.-Col. Ziegler

5. Imports and Exports Section (A8)
   Chief: Lt.-Col. Giessler

6. Food Section (B6)
   Chief: Col. Wilcke

ment and promotion to the rank of Lieutenant General during Bethmann's visit to Pless on October 26.[52]

The major topic of conversation at this conference was the OHL's latest demand for an extension of the ages of liability to military service. Bethmann and Groener had a long talk about this. Groener explained that he personally much preferred freedom to compulsion, but that there was not enough time left to mobilize the labor force on a voluntary basis. The manpower needs of both army and industry could be expected to rise rapidly in the immediate future. It was therefore necessary that older men, women, and high school students replace men now engaged in easy types of work. Also, soldiers had to be released from desk work to serve at the front and in the factories. Bethmann, however, was unalterably opposed to the extension of military service liability to men between fifty and sixty. This would create the impression that "Germany was whistling out of her last hole."[53] As an alternative Bethmann suggested that some sort of obligation to work (*Arbeitspflicht*) be imposed. Although no definite decision was reached, Bethmann did come to the conclusion that "We must somehow intervene and organize things."[54]

3. *The War Office*

With the conclusion of Bethmann's visit to Pless on October 26, a turning point was reached in the development of the OHL's program for total mobilization. From this date onward there was a common agreement between Bethmann and the OHL to introduce some form of compulsory civilian mobilization. The discussion of this question, therefore, now takes on an entirely new character and is best left to the next chapter. In contrast to the labor problem, however, the dismissal of

[52] Groener, *Lebenserinnerungen*, pp. 343, 554-555. The German *Generalleutnant* is approximately the equivalent of the American major general.

[53] Groener to the Reichsarchiv, April 9, 1923, Nachlass Groener, 196.

[54] Bethmann to Wahnschaffe (for Helfferich), Oct. 26, 1916, DZA Potsdam, Kriegsakten 1, Bd. 9, Bl. 227-228.

Wild and the establishment of a war office were matters which could be brought to a speedy settlement after October 26, and it is upon these events which we must now focus our attention.

Wild had never expected to remain long in office after the appointment of the new OHL. By now he was cognizant of the plans to establish a war office and to give its head command over the Deputy Commanding Generals. Needless to say, he regarded these plans as an effort to make the War Minister "a section head of the Operations Section of the General Staff."[55] It is very likely that he would have resigned rather than place his signature upon orders running so completely counter to his views. He was not given an opportunity to resign, however. On October 28 he received a curt notification from General von Lyncker that he was dismissed: "His Majesty, at the behest of Field Marshal von Hindenburg, finds it necessary to give someone else the position of Prussian War Minister. The desirable collaboration between the War Minister and the Supreme Command is no longer taking place. In giving this position to someone new, His Majesty will follow the advice of the Field Marshal."[56] The subordination of the War Ministry to the General Staff could hardly have been more clearly stated.

General Hermann von Stein was chosen to replace Wild. Stein had served with Ludendorff and Groener on the General Staff before the war and had been Moltke's First Quartermaster General in 1914. After Moltke's dismissal, he was given command of a division on the Western Front. The OHL liked the idea of appointing a *Frontsoldat* who had personally experienced the Battle of the Somme. Stein, in contrast to every other Prussian War Minister since the Ministry's creation, had never served in the Ministry. Given the OHL's attitude toward the War Ministry, however, this lack of experience may actually have been viewed favorably.[57]

[55] Notation of Oct. 29, 1916, BA, Nachlass Wild von Hohenborn, Nr. 2.
[56] *Ibid.*
[57] Groener, *Lebenserinnerungen*, p. 343; Spiero, *Schicksal*, pp. 267-

On November 1 General von Stein countersigned two royal decrees. The first created the War Office. The second placed the Deputy Commanding Generals under the authority of the War Ministry in all matters pertaining to economic mobilization. Stein then delegated this authority to the Chief of the War Office, General Groener. Groener's powers were further enhanced by his appointment as Deputy War Minister and as a Prussian representative to the Bundesrat. During the following weeks Groener developed the organizational structure of the War Office. In its upper levels, the War Office, unlike the War Ministry, was organized along military rather than bureaucratic lines. At its summit stood the Chief of the War Office. A Chief of the Military Staff and a Chief of the Technical Staff served as his immediate advisors. The first position was filled by Major von Kretschmann, who had previously served as one of Groener's aides in the Field Railroad Service. Dr. Kurt Sorge, the Director of the Krupp-Gruson Works in Magdeburg and the chairman of the German Society of Engineers, was appointed Chief of the Technical Staff. A series of "groups" were placed under each of the Chiefs of Staff. They had the task of handling specialized problems. Strictly speaking, the staffs had no executive functions. They were meant to act as planning and advisory bodies and as organs for the transmission of Groener's decisions. Thus the Military Staff was responsible for advising Groener on administrative and manpower problems and for conveying his decisions to the departments and sections responsible for their implementation. The Technical Staff performed the same duties with regard to technical and economic matters. The superstructure of the War Office, therefore, closely resembled that of an army group in the field. The Chief of the War Office, its "general," bore the ultimate responsibility for all decisions and operations,

268; Hermann von Stein, *Erlebnisse und Betrachtungen aus der Zeit des Weltkrieges*, Leipzig, 1919, p. 83.

while his Chiefs of Staff served as advisers and conveyors of commands.[58]

The substructure of the War Office, however, was bureaucratically organized. There were six major departments: (1) the Reserves and Labor Department (E.D.), (2) WUMBA, (3) the KRA, (4) the Clothing Procurement Agency (BBA), (5) the Imports and Exports Section (A8), and (6) the Food Section (B6). Of the departments, all of which had originally been located in the War Ministry, only the first underwent serious changes. Previously Colonel von Braun had directed the Labor Office, which was composed of two bureaus, one charged with reserves and the other with exemptions. Now these bureaus were transformed into departmental sections, Colonel von Braun becoming head of the Reserves Section and Colonel Frodien taking charge of AZS. Colonel Marquard, who had previously served as a staff officer on the Eastern Front and who was held in high regard by the OHL, became Director of the entire Reserves and Labor Department. Sichler, once the head of AZS, was now appointed as its chief economic adviser.

The new War Office was thus a compound of the military and bureaucratic types of organization. Its personnel were also quite variegated. The Technical Staff was filled with eminent scientists and industrialists. A good many of the military officers and civilians in the War Office had already been performing similar functions in the War Ministry, but there was a considerable increase in the numbers of both types of personnel. Needless to say, the War Office was an extremely large organization, so large, in fact, that a number of Berlin hotels had to be taken over by the army in order to provide it with adequate lodgings.

The establishment of the War Office required corresponding

[58] For Stein's orders, see BHStA, Abt. IV, MK, 11b, Bd. 6. On the organization and personnel of the War Office, see the Organization Manual, Nachlass Groener, 193, and Groener's press conference of Nov. 13, 1916, HStASt, KM, Abt. f. allg. Armee- u. f. pers. Angelegenheiten, Bd. 1272, Bl. 28-29.

organizational changes on the local level. On November 18 War Office Bureaus (*Kriegsamtstellen*) were set up in the district of each Deputy Commanding General to keep the Berlin War Office informed of local developments and to implement its orders. These bureaus were staffed by the personnel who had previously served as economic advisers to the Deputy Commanding Generals but, here too, a considerable number of additional personnel was needed. It is to be noted that both the War Office and the War Office Bureaus were set up within the framework of already existing military agencies, i.e., the War Ministry and the administrations of the Deputy Commanding Generals. A certain dualism was thus built into the entire military organizational structure existing in the homeland. Added to this was the dualism within the War Office itself, as represented by the coexistence of staffs and departments. Yet another complication was the position of the War Office vis-à-vis the non-Prussian war ministries. The latter insisted on a certain independence. Thus independent war offices were set up in the Bavarian, Saxon, and Württemberg war ministries, and they sent special representatives to the Prussian War Office. The states were particularly insistent that these representatives be consulted concerning all major decisions. Also, the Prussian War Office was prohibited from issuing orders of a general and far-reaching nature to the Bavarian Deputy Commanding Generals. The success of the War Office, therefore, would depend upon the degree to which it could resolve the dualisms within its own structure, within the military organization of Prussia, and within the military organization of the Empire.

For the moment, however, these problems were obscured by the general enthusiasm with which the new organization was greeted. As usual, the various interest groups were pleased for different reasons. The labor unions were hopeful that the War Office would see to it that the industrial workers were properly fed. The right wing Socialists were prepared to attach the most far-reaching implications to the new organization.

They referred to its creation as the "strongest measure of War Socialism"[59] yet undertaken because it implied centralized direction of the economy. Their hopes were raised to new heights when Groener promised that organized labor would be represented in the War Office. The industrialists, who had played such an important role in the establishment of the War Office, were, of course, quite pleased. Now that the Labor Office had been expanded and the Deputy Commanding Generals placed under the War Office's command, it seemed certain that the exemptions question would prove less troublesome. Furthermore, they felt sure that there would be less difficulty with AZS social policies, for as Dr. Reichert told the iron and steel industrialists, "You no longer need be frightened when you hear the letters AZS, for Sichler has been taken down a step or two."[60] This was true. Sichler was now subordinate to two officers, Colonel Marquard and Colonel von Braun. Above all, the industrialists were overjoyed at the high position given to Dr. Sorge. In a congratulatory letter they expressed the hope "that you, as General Groener's chief industrial adviser, will work in the sense of the industrialists, particularly the iron and steel industrialists."[61]

In early November 1916 the industrialists did, indeed, seem triumphant, and they owed everything to the OHL. The Hindenburg Program, the War Office, and the plans for compulsory civilian mobilization were all measures they had long desired. Similarly, the recently instituted policy of compelling unemployed Belgian workers to work in German industry represented yet another OHL concession to industry. The OHL also took the right attitude concerning social questions. When the industrialists complained to Ludendorff that the Socialists were trying to restore the protective laws governing the employment of women and children, it took only eight days

[59] *Internationale Correspondenz,* Nov. 17, 1916, and BBS Report, Nov. 11, 1916.

[60] VdESI meeting, Nov. 16, 1916, BA, R 13I/149.

[61] Reichert to Sorge, Nov. 18, 1916, *ibid.*, R 13I/88.

for Ludendorff to express his complete agreement with the employers' views. The contrast between Ludendorff's way of doing things and that of the War Ministry was not lost upon the industrialists:

> How valuable it would have been for industry if this . . . deep recognition of the necessity of maintaining and increasing our capacity to produce had been present earlier in the responsible agencies. But many of the war officials followed the ideas of the social politicians alone, as if we do not already have enough sections for social policy in the Imperial offices and other agencies.[62]

[62] Speech by Reichert, Nov. 16, 1916, *ibid.*, R 13I/149.

IV

The Auxiliary Service Bill and the Triumph of Labor

1. The Struggle with the Bureaucracy

ALTHOUGH Bethmann Hollweg had agreed to the introduction of some type of compulsory civilian mobilization during his visit to Pless on October 26, the actual form that this mobilization was to take had not been decided. Bethmann's remark to Groener about the possibility of instituting an obligation to work demonstrates that he was seeking a compromise between the extreme positions of Colonel Bauer and Secretary Helfferich. The former had inspired Ludendorff to demand a radical extension of the ages of liability to military service.[1] The latter, until October 26, had been successful in keeping Bethmann opposed to any form of compulsory civilian mobilization. The OHL, however, now had another adviser on labor questions in the person of the Chief of the new War Office, General Groener. If Groener joined Bethmann in an effort to arrange a compromise, then a very severe conflict between the Chancellor and the OHL could be avoided.

Groener had been convinced by Bethmann's arguments and was seeking a compromise. In Berlin, on the evening of October 28, Groener had an opportunity to present his views to Ludendorff without any interference from Bauer and under conditions requiring a quick decision. On the following morning Ludendorff was to return to Pless and Groener was to appear before a conference of the Prussian state ministers. This, therefore, was the last opportunity for the OHL to formulate a concrete proposal, and Groener handed Ludendorff the draft of a "Patriotic Auxiliary Service Law" which he had drawn up in the course of the day:

[1] Bauer, *Grosse Krieg*, pp. 22-23.

> Every German youth and male between the ages of fifteen and sixty who is not serving in the armed forces may, at the command of the War Minister, be called upon to perform Patriotic Auxiliary Service (*vaterländischer Hilfsdienst*) for the period of the war.
>
> Besides service in government offices and official institutions, work in war industry, in agriculture, and in every type of organization serving the war economy shall be considered Auxiliary Service.
>
> The training of youth over fifteen for military service shall also be included in the powers of the War Minister.[2]

Repeating Bethmann's arguments, Groener warned that an extension of the Military Service Law "would awaken great hopes in our enemies." An Auxiliary Service Law would "achieve the same results" as an extension of the Military Service Law while avoiding its disadvantages.[3] Evidently Groener also persuaded Ludendorff to drop his demand for the use of compulsion against female labor, for Ludendorff accepted Groener's draft.

Despite Groener's willingness to compromise, he did not have an easy time with the state ministers at their meeting on October 29.[4] Only Loebell and Breitenbach gave the Auxiliary Service bill warm support. Helfferich began by objecting to any form of compulsory labor and arguing that compulsion could be imposed indirectly by the shutting down of non-essential plants. In the face of a passionate appeal from Groener, who pointed out that the Hindenburg Program re-

[2] For the text and Groener's account of his discussion with Ludendorff on Oct. 28, see his letter to the Reichsarchiv of Apr. 9, 1923, Nachlass Groener, 196.

[3] Groener gave full expression to these views at a meeting with the Bundesrat delegates on Nov. 9, report of Dr. Wolf, representative of Sachsen-Meiningen, Nov. 9, 1916, BHStA, Abt. IV, MK, K Mob 14, Bd. I.

[4] Wahnschaffe's rather illegible notes are to be found in DZA Potsdam, Kriegsakten I, Bd. 9, Bl. 244-257. Groener described the meeting in a letter to Hindenburg of Oct. 29, 1916, Nachlass Groener, 192-I. See also Groener, *Lebenserinnerungen*, p. 555.

quired from two to three million more workers, Helfferich modified his views. He finally proposed that every male between seventeen and sixty be required to demonstrate employment in war work. If such employment could not be demonstrated, then compulsion could be used. Groener objected to such a "negative solution," which would force the government to engage in a lengthy examination of individual cases in order to determine whether or not a worker was serving in the Auxiliary Service. Furthermore, it would not give the War Office "the necessary bases for the free development of its activity."

Groener found Sydow, who "took a very bureaucratic proposal out of his pocket," even more difficult than Helfferich. Sydow feared that the shutting down of nonessential factories would have a ruinous effect on Germany's economy after the war. He wished, therefore, to limit the Auxiliary Service obligation to men between seventeen and forty-five, that is, to those already liable to military service. He was also willing to agree to the transplantation of male workers between fifteen and sixteen and between forty-five and sixty who were already working in factories employing an excessive number of workers. Groener did not have much use for Sydow's suggestions. The exercise of compulsion against workers liable to military service was superfluous. The provision for the control of workers in other age groups was of dubious value because it was limited to workers already engaged in war work.

Groener did pay more heed to the wishes of Bethmann and the Minister for Education and Culture, August von Trott zu Solz, concerning youths between fifteen and seventeen. He dropped the paragraph providing for military training and promised to refrain from a vigorous enforcement of the law in the case of youngsters. In general Groener sought to quiet the fears of the ministers by promising to seek the cooperation of the civil authorities in the general implementation of the law.

Bethmann said little at the meeting, but the fact that he gave no support either to Helfferich or Sydow was, in itself, helpful to Groener's cause. At the conclusion Bethmann accepted Groener's proposal in principle and ordered that a bill be drafted along the lines laid down by Groener. No decision, however, was made as to whether the bill was to be brought before the Reichstag or simply promulgated by the Bundesrat on the basis of the Enabling Act of August 4, 1914. The ministers preferred the latter solution. The government was having a very difficult time with the Reichstag, where both the civil and the military authorities were being attacked for abuses of the Law of Siege. The nonconservative deputies had so little confidence in the good will of the government that it seemed unlikely that they would treat a request for even greater governmental powers in a friendly manner. Indeed, as Groener noted, the fear of the Reichstag was probably the chief reason for the efforts of Helfferich and Sydow to water down his proposal.

Following the meeting Groener sent off a report to the OHL. In a reply of October 30 the OHL rejected the proposals of Helfferich and Sydow. The manner in which the OHL supported Groener's draft, however, suggests that Colonel Bauer was angry over the way Groener had persuaded Ludendorff to abandon the proposed extension of the Military Service Law, which in Bauer's view was the only "clear solution." Despite this objection, the OHL specifically supported Groener's draft. The only change demanded was in the direction of greater emphasis on the "duty" of the German people to serve. The bill was to state that every citizen was "obligated (*verpflichtet*) to do Auxiliary Service." The OHL was particularly adamant in their demand that the Reichstag accept responsibility for the passage of the bill. Unlike the ministers, the OHL was "certain that the Reichstag will not deny passage to this bill when it is made clear that the war cannot be won without the help of such a law."[5]

[5] Ludendorff, *Urkunden*, pp. 81-82. Bauer continued to think in terms of an extension of the Military Service Law, as is demonstrated by another letter sent by Hindenburg to Bethmann on Nov. 1, 1916, in

The ensuing week was filled with tedious discussions concerning the wording of the bill, discussions conducted under constant pressure from the OHL for the speedy passage of a short bill giving the War Office extensive powers. Although the OHL insisted that there was no time "for long deliberations" and expressed complete indifference as to how the problem was solved,[6] Bethmann knew that it was utterly impossible to present a bill to the Reichstag, however short, without careful preparation. Time was needed to draft the bill properly, to conduct negotiations with the interest groups, and to secure the approval of the Bundesrat. He felt compelled to insure that the military authorities would not be given excessive powers, to guarantee that the law would not be abused by the employers, and to take care that the state did not interfere in social questions in a manner offensive to the employers.

An example of the conjunction of such complex considerations was a section of the draft of the bill drawn up by Imperial Undersecretary of the Interior Richter and his colleagues on October 30. In an effort to at once reassure the workers and give the War Office the desired authority, the draft provided that "suitable conditions and suitable remuneration shall be established for work in the Auxiliary Service. The detailed regulations shall be issued by the War Office." Helfferich raised strong objections to this clause. He feared that a precedent was being established for the regulation of working conditions by the state and opposed giving the War Office such great powers. At the same time he was convinced that the Reichstag would still not be satisfied by such vague guarantees. Bethmann could

which he continues to write of an extension of the law despite the fact that this idea had been discarded, see *ibid.*, pp. 83-84. Since Hindenburg and Ludendorff placed their signature on this correspondence, it is highly likely, as Groener suggested to the Reichsarchiv after the war, that the two generals did not really understand the difference between changing the Military Service Law and creating an entirely new law, see Nachlass Groener, 196.

[6] Hindenburg to Bethmann, Nov. 1, 1916, Ludendorff, *Urkunden*, pp. 83-84.

not help agreeing that the "military desire to rule has greatly increased." As usual he hoped to find a way to please everyone. Thus he ordered that the War Office be given as much power as possible and instructed Helfferich and Groener to negotiate with labor and industry in order to ascertain their wishes.[7]

The Auxiliary Service bill, however, was not Bethmann's only major concern at this time. He was also preparing a peace offer, and he hoped that this effort to end the war could be made before the Auxiliary Service bill was presented to the Reichstag. Needing time to work on both of these tasks, Bethmann decided to adjourn the Reichstag on November 4. While officially scheduled to meet again on February 17, 1917, the deputies were informed that the Reichstag might be summoned sooner for a "pressing reason." At the same time he assured the OHL that the adjournment would not delay the passage of the bill.[8]

The OHL was not pacified, and an appeal was made to the Emperor. On November 6 Hindenburg was able to inform Bethmann that the Emperor had ordered that the bill be passed quickly and that all "other actions" be regarded as secondary.[9] The disagreement between Bethmann and the OHL as to the tempo with which the bill was to be pushed through thus spilled over into a more fundamental disagreement in matters of foreign policy. In fact, the honeymoon between Bethmann and the OHL was at an end. The Chancellor replied on the following day with a sharply worded note. While agreeing that speed was desirable, he warned that "nothing will bring a more annoying failure than an impractically and superficially worked out draft, whose implementation has not been thought through like a good strategic plan and which

[7] For the draft, see BA, Nachlass Bauer, Nr. 14, and for the discussion concerning it, see DZA Potsdam, Kriegsakten I, Bd. 10, Bl. 4.

[8] Bethmann to Hindenburg, Nov. 4, 1917, *ibid.*, Bl. 28.

[9] Grünau, Foreign Office representative to the OHL, to Bethmann, Nov. 6, 1916, *ibid.*, Bl. 33.

cannot be presented to the Reichstag with clarity."[10] Bethmann insisted that he had to have time to negotiate with the interest groups and concluded with the hope that Germany might make her peace offer either before the presentation of the bill to the Reichstag or simultaneously with it.

2. *The Demands of the Interest Groups*

The conflict between those who wished to mobilize the civilian population by means of an extension of the Military Service Law and those who wished to do so by means of a new law had important social implications. Restriction of the free movement of labor was implicit in both solutions. There was no point in compelling men to work and assigning them to particular factories if they could not be forced to stay on their jobs. Under a revised Military Service Law, however, this aim could have been achieved by the old device of the threat of the trenches. A greatly enlarged group of exempted workers would have been completely at the mercy of the military authorities. The decision to conduct the civilian mobilization on the basis of an entirely new law meant that a more formal mechanism for the restriction of the free movement of labor would have to be found. Since both the OHL and the government wanted the bill to be short and general in content, the restriction on free movement was not to be stated explicitly in the text of the bill. It was understood, however, that the regulations governing the implementation of the bill would restrict the free movement of labor, and it was this aspect of the bill which made negotiations with the leaders of industry and labor so necessary.

The events leading up to the establishment of the Berlin Metal Industry War Board had demonstrated that the unions would not accept a restriction on the free movement of labor without compensation. Specifically, they were certain to de-

[10] Bethmann to Hindenburg, Nov. 7, 1916, *ibid.*, Bl. 43-44. The OHL wanted to have the German people express their willingness to fight by passing the Auxiliary Service bill before the announcement of the peace offer, see Lerchenfeld to Hertling, Dec. 11, 1916, BHStA, Abt. II, MA 1, Nr. 916.

mand arbitration committees organized on the basis of parity between labor and management. It was equally certain that many of the industrialists would oppose such institutions. As shown earlier, the battle over war boards had been raging for two years and had reached a stalemate in October 1916 when the War Ministry's efforts to extend the system were frustrated by certain industrialists and Deputy Commanding Generals.[11] Bethmann, Helfferich, and Groener knew that the decision to bring the Auxiliary Service bill before the Reichstag was tantamount to breaking this stalemate in favor of labor. The industrialists, therefore, had to be forced to accept the general introduction of war boards. At the same time the unions might also demand other forms of compensation in return for their support of the bill.

Groener and Helfferich negotiated with the industrialists on November 7. Many of the industrialists invited to the meeting welcomed the bill and were willing to accept war boards. The Bavarian industrialist Rieppel was particularly enthusiastic and emphasized the good results that had been achieved in Bavaria, Berlin, and elsewhere. The representatives of heavy industry, Stinnes, Hilger, and Privy Councilor Beuckenberg, however, opposed both the bill and the war boards. As always, they were loathe to engage in "social experiments" which might have "disagreeable consequences." When General Groener tried to explain that the war boards were a wartime measure with no permanent political significance, Beuckenberg insisted that they had "enormous political significance" and irritatedly remarked "that we, who have been in the midst of this situation for decades and have to deal with it year in and year out, have a more accurate judgment than the gentlemen from the army, who are only concerned with it in exceptional cases and now only under the special conditions of war."[12] In Beuckenberg's view, the general introduction of

[11] See pp. 86ff.

[12] This account and the quotations in the paragraph are taken from a report given at the VdESI meeting of Nov. 16, 1916, BA, R 13I/149.

war boards would simply provide the union secretaries with a platform from which to agitate.

In an effort to pacify the industrialists, Groener suggested that union secretaries would not necessarily have to be appointed to the war boards. He forced the industrialists to admit, however, that the introduction of compulsion would increase the danger of conflicts and hence create the need for arbitration. The industrialist opponents of the measure were not really satisfied by this argument, but they now demanded that the war boards at least be placed under military chairmen so as to emphasize their temporary character. In general they hoped, as did the very sympathetic Helfferich, that compulsion would be used as little as possible.

One of the paradoxes of the wartime situation was that the trade unions, in contrast to the leaders of heavy industry, had a certain interest in the promotion of formal restrictions upon the free movement of labor. To be sure, they never publicly admitted this. In fact the German Socialist unions had bitterly assailed their English counterparts for supporting the Munitions Act. They accused the British unions of surrendering the gains of decades in the name of the war effort.[13] This criticism was by no means unjustified. The Munitions Act did represent an effort to limit the power of the trade unions. In England, unlike Germany, the unions had been very powerful before the war. The English employers had been forced to accept severe restrictions upon their right to employ unskilled workers and laborsaving devices. These restrictions ran counter to the English government's desire to "dilute" the wartime labor force with unskilled labor, and one of the major purposes of the Munitions Act was to suspend prewar union-management contracts. Furthermore, it is to be noted that England did not have military conscription until December 1916. The Munitions Act was the only means by which the government could exercise some control over the nation's manpower and insure

[13] *Correspondenzblatt*, April 3 and Dec. 11, 1915; *Metallarbeiter-Zeitung*, Aug. 7, 1915; *Internationale Correspondenz*, July 25, 1916.

efficient production. In short, the Munitions Act was the English government's reaction to the great strength of the labor unions and the inability to introduce conscription early in the war. It may be added here that the German admirers of the English law, among whom the OHL and Groener must be included, had a very poor understanding of the particular internal conditions which had led the English government to set up its system.[14]

Germany's internal conditions were of a completely different nature. The country had always known conscription and never known union control of working conditions. The army controlled exempted workers, and this had acted as an automatic brake upon turnover. The unions could not sabotage the efforts to dilute the labor force with unskilled labor. Indeed it was the German employers who resisted the use of unskilled labor. Because of their very different situation, the German unions, unlike their British counterparts, had something to gain from official limitations on the free movement of labor if such limitations were accompanied by war boards organized on the principle of parity between labor and management. In this way exempted workers received some measure of protection against being arbitrarily taken into the army if they wished to change their jobs and the unions were given some measure of recognition by the employers.[15]

[14] In the prewar period the English employers had accepted labor's demands "only under duress and protest," and "the war seemed a golden moment in which to destroy what seemed to them artificial barriers to efficient and cheap production," Hurwitz, *State Intervention in Great Britain*, p. 90. The War Office sought to follow the English model as much as possible, as is indicated by the many studies Groener requested concerning the English system, Nachlass Groener, 192-I. One of the few critics of this tendency was Koeth, who understood that the English Munitions Act was the only way "one could become lord over the workers again," and that the English and German systems could not be compared. See his remarks at the meeting of June 14, 1917, BA, Nachlass Mentzel, Nr. 6.

[15] Indeed, the Metalworkers Union leader Adolf Cohen actually took the initiative and proposed something analogous to the Auxiliary Service bill to the War Ministry in October 1916; see *Die dreizehnte ordentliche Generalversammlung des Deutschen Metallarbeiter-Verbandes in Köln*

It is thus not at all surprising that the heads of the General Commission, Legien and Bauer, raised no fundamental objections to the Auxiliary Service bill when Helfferich and Groener discussed it with them on November 8. Since basic rights of the workers were being restricted, however, they felt entitled to demand compensations. As might be expected, the union leaders demanded that war boards be set up throughout the country and that transplanted workers be given additional remuneration if they had to maintain a double household. These demands pertained directly to the provisions of the bill and were thus to be expected. The same cannot be said of the other demands raised by the union leaders. Legien and Bauer wanted workers committees established in all factories and conciliation bureaus set up throughout the country. The employers were to be compelled to negotiate with the workers through these institutions. Needless to say, this was an effort to use the bill as a means of achieving old union aims. Legien and Bauer insisted that labor's representatives on the war boards and conciliation bureaus be appointed on the basis of union suggestions. They wanted more than one representative of labor and one representative of management sitting on them so that the particular union and management organizations involved in any given case could play a role in the decision. Furthermore, Legien wanted to use the bill to protect union activity. He was incensed by a secret decree issued by Breitenbach on October 24 banning the employment of members of the recently organized Socialist German Railroad Workers Union because that union had not openly renounced strikes in its constitution. He therefore seized this opportunity to demand complete freedom of coalition for all workers affected by the bill. Lastly, he complained bitterly that union efforts to pacify the workers were being hampered by certain Deputy Commanding Generals and demanded that freedom of assembly be guaranteed. Groener and Helfferich did not dis-

---

a. Rh. Abgehalten vom 27. bis 30. Juni 1917 in Frankischen Hof, Stuttgart, 1917, pp. 77-80, 117.

cuss these demands in any detail, and they avoided making any commitments. It was very clear, however, that it was not going to be easy to get the government's draft of the bill through the Reichstag.[16]

Helfferich had suspected this all along. Since the OHL and the government were anxious to avoid an angry debate in the Reichstag, Helfferich and Groener held a meeting with the party leaders on November 7. Although Helfferich placed particular emphasis upon the fact that compulsion would only serve as the *ultima ratio* and that a speedy and unanimous passage of the bill was desirable for the impression it would have upon the enemy, the Socialist, Centrist, and Progressive leaders insisted that the details of the bill be carefully deliberated. The Socialist leader Ebert went so far as to doubt whether the whole question was really as pressing as the government suggested. An agreement was reached finally to try to settle all the controversial aspects of the bill in the Budget Committee and then pass the bill in one plenary meeting of the Reichstag. In this way a public debate would be avoided and the outside world would have the impression that everything had gone smoothly.[17]

The intensity of the debate, wherever it took place, would depend on the degree to which the government was willing to meet the demands of the union leaders. Helfferich and Groener came into sharp conflict over this issue. Helfferich wanted to concede as little as possible on the theory that the more one gave the unions, the more they would ask. He was thus deliberately reticent at the meeting with the union leaders on November 8. Groener, while not making any commitments, indicated a greater willingness to compromise and promised that one of their leaders would be taken into the War Office and sought to ingratiate himself with them. When informing

[16] Helfferich's report to the Prussian Cabinet, Nov. 10, 1916, BA, P 135/1810, Bl. 1. See also the exchange between Helfferich and Legien, Budget Committee, Nov. 24, 1916.

[17] DZA Potsdam, Kriegsakten 1, Bd. 10, Bl. 45-47.

the Bundesrat delegates of the bill on the following day, he stated his attitude quite bluntly: "The task is extraordinarily difficult. It can only be solved in the closest collaboration with industry and the workers. We can never win this war by fighting against the workers. Reservations of an internal political nature must be put aside, and all political attitudes must be geared to the problem of how we are going to bring the war to a victorious conclusion."[18]

This was not the only reason for Groener's desire to conciliate labor, however. He had another reason that he gave only private expression. Groener was no longer the "hurrah soldier" he had been during the first two years of the war. His work on the KEA had brought him into close contact with the problems of the home front, and he knew that the spirit of 1914 was little more than a memory. This is not to say that he had given up his hopes of victory, but he no longer refused to face the possibility of defeat. If Germany was defeated, the monarchy might still be saved if the unions had the workers under control. He wished, therefore, to meet union demands as much as possible in order to give the unions a reason to support the preservation of the state.[19]

The four paragraph draft of the Auxiliary Service bill presented to the Prussian State Cabinet at its meeting of November 10, however, reflected Helfferich's views, not Groener's.[20] The first stated the obligation of every German between sixteen and sixty to serve in the Auxiliary Service. The second generally defined the types of labor included in this concept. The third gave the Bundesrat the power to issue the directives

[18] BHStA, Abt. IV, MK, K Mob 14, Bd. I. Helfferich explained his reticence to the Prussian Cabinet on Nov. 10, 1916, BA, P 135/1810, Bl. 1.

[19] Lerchenfeld to Hertling, Nov. 12, 1916, BHStA, Abt. II, MA 1, Nr. 916; "Bemerkungen zu dem Broschüre 'Ludendorff,' Verfasser Dr. Wilhelm Spickernagel"; and "Bemerkungen zu dem Kapital 'Hilfsdienstgesetz und Hindenburg Program' . . . von Karl Helfferich," Nachlass Groener, 192-I.

[20] For the draft, see BA, Nachlass Bauer, Nr. 14, and for the Prussian Cabinet meeting of Nov. 10, 1916, upon which the discussion and quotations which follow are based, see BA, P 135/1810, Bl. 1.

necessary for the carrying out of the bill and to punish violators of the bill with fines and imprisonment. The fourth declared that the bill would go into force on the day of its proclamation and gave the Bundesrat the right to declare its date of expiration. The new draft, therefore, was designed to satisfy the OHL's desire for brevity and Helfferich's desire to provide some check on the powers of the War Office. It was tacitly understood that the War Office would draw up the decrees necessary for the implementation of the bill. By requiring that these decrees be subject to Bundesrat approval, however, Helfferich fitted the bill within the normal legislative pattern, for the Bundesrat normally directed the execution of all legislation.

Since Helfferich knew that the Reichstag would demand some indication of how the bill was going to be implemented and some measures to protect the rights of those engaged in Auxiliary Service, he appended a series of "Guidelines" to the bill. The Bundesrat would be obligated to implement the bill in accordance with these Guidelines. Although they were not actually part of the bill, Helfferich planned to submit them to the Reichstag for general approval. The Guidelines provided for three types of committees to implement the proposed law: determination committees (*Feststellungsausschüsse*), draft committees (*Einberufungsausschüsse*), and arbitration committees (*Schlichtungsausschüsse*).

The determination committees, one of which was to be set up in the district of each Deputy Commanding General, had the task of deciding whether or not a factory was essential to the war effort and determining whether or not factories were employing an excessive number of workers. The chairman of these committees, as of the other two types of committees, was to be an officer. In addition, two higher government officials, one of whom was to be a factory inspector, and a representative from labor and from management were to sit on the determination committees. The decisions of these committees could be appealed to a central agency of the War Office composed of two officers, one of whom was to serve as chairman, two representatives of the Interior Office, and one representative of the federal state in which the particular factory in question was located.

The draft committees, which were to be composed of an officer, an official, an employer, and a worker, were charged with calling up those not already employed in the Auxiliary Service and those who were superfluous in their present employment. Men thus summoned to join the Auxiliary Service would have two weeks to find employment themselves. If they did not do so, then the committees were to assign them to a specific job. In so doing, they were to take into account, "wherever possible," age, family situation, previous profession, and previous income. These committees were to be established in each of the districts where there was a reserves commission charged with selecting men for the army. The decisions of the draft committee could be appealed to the determination committee of the army corps district in which it was located and, finally, to the War Office.

The arbitration committees were to settle differences arising from the refusal of an employer to give his employee a "leaving certificate." No employer was allowed to hire someone who, within the previous two weeks, had left his job without this certificate. If an employee wished to leave his job and his employer refused him the certificate, then he had a right to appeal to the arbitration committee. If he left his job despite the refusal of the arbitration committee to give him a certificate, then he would have to wait two weeks before being able to find new employment. The draft was not very clear concerning the constitution of these committees. It stated that the arbitration committees were to be organized in the same manner as the draft committees. But it stated also that the arbitration committees were to be composed of an officer, an employer, and an employee. The difference is important because the draft committees were not organized on the principle of parity between labor and management. In any case, the members of this type of committee, as well as the other two, were to be appointed by the Deputy Commanding Generals and the civil authorities. The decisions of the arbitration committees could not be appealed.

Under the Guidelines, appeals from the decisions of the determination and draft committees and appeals to the arbitration committees did not constitute a reprieve for those making the appeals. Thus immediate action was to be taken on decisions to shut down a factory or assign a man to a specific job even though an appeal was in progress. Similarly, a worker who was denied a leaving certificate by his employer had to remain on his job until the arbitration committee rendered a decision. Finally, the Guidelines required employers to supply the War Office with whatever information concerning the number of workers they employed, working conditions, and wages that it requested.

The Cabinet was satisfied with Helfferich's work. The bill itself was accepted with little discussion. Only one change was made. The age of liability to Auxiliary Service, despite Groener's objections, was raised to seventeen. The Guidelines were accepted without change, but they received more detailed consideration. Bethmann was somewhat unclear as to the way the determination committees were supposed to work. To the general relief of all present, Groener explained that he had no intention of ruthlessly shutting down nonessential industries and factories. Most of the shutting down and consolidation of industries would be done in collaboration with the representatives of the industries concerned. Once they had reached an agreement, the determination committees would then remove workers from factories in accordance with it. Groener promised to spare as many small businesses as possible.

The one important concession which Helfferich had made to union demands was the provision for arbitration committees. These committees, he explained, would necessarily concern themselves with working conditions and wages and would thus also function somewhat in the manner of conciliation agencies.

While recognizing that the unions would greet these committees as a precedent for the future, Helfferich reminded the ministers that they were a natural result of the decision to restrict the free movement of labor. He expected objections from heavy industry, but he hoped to win it over by stressing the military and temporary character of the institution. Breitenbach reminded his colleagues that the interference of the arbitration committees in wage questions could prove terribly expensive, but he admitted that Helfferich was right. There was some discussion of the possibility of limiting the right of appeal to these committees to workers assigned to specific jobs by the draft committees. Helfferich pointed out that this was impractical since it was necessary to limit the free movement of both the old and new workers. Groener went even further:

> He also is of the opinion that this institution cannot be limited to people drafted under compulsion. One should not forget how much depends upon the steady and faithful labor of the workers. Conciliation agencies which they regard as nonpartisan and in which worker representatives help to make decisions are a safety valve for all expressions of unwillingness to work which are to be found among those workers already in the factories as well as those assigned to them. No one can know whether consequences for peacetime will arise from such institutions. It will depend, above all, on how the war ends and the kind of peace that we have.

The ministers were unanimously opposed to Legien's demand for complete freedom of coalition. Breitenbach declared that this was a "capital question," a clear indication that he would rather see the law defeated or resign than to make this concession. Schorlemer also insisted that the restrictions upon the coalition rights of agricultural workers remain in force. Loebell suggested that the Reichstag be made to understand that the government could have simply extended the Military Service Law and that no party had the right to use the Auxiliary Service bill to realize its special interests. Helfferich agreed, but felt that they would have to face the fact that disagreeable demands were going to be made in the Reichstag. If the Socialists forced through complete freedom of coalition, then the government would have to demand the inclusion of a ban on strikes in wartime. He hoped, however, to avoid such a disagreeable situation. Concessions might be made to the Reichstag in other areas. Helfferich had to admit that the manner in which the Law of Siege had been administered was "insupportable." He had fought against Reichstag demands that the Law of Siege be annulled, but he did feel that something might be done to make it milder, and he was now working on this question.

Needless to say, there was much concern about the reception the bill was going to get in the Reichstag. Groener and Loebell felt that the Reichstag might be more tractable if the OHL summoned some of the Reichstag leaders to Pless for a personal discussion. Groener had suggested this to the OHL and had received a favorable reply. Bethmann, however, vetoed the idea and informed the OHL that "he alone was responsible for guiding policy."[21] There is no definite evidence indicating why the Chancellor took such a sharp stand. It is very possible that a recent resolution passed by a majority of the Reichstag declaring that it would support unrestricted submarine warfare if the OHL regarded this to be necessary was very important in making Bethmann want to keep contacts between the Reichstag and the OHL to a minimum.[22]

The OHL gave way to Bethmann on the question of inviting deputies to Pless, but it continued its pressure for a speedy passage of the bill. This pressure reached its culmination in a telegram from Hindenburg to Bethmann, which was sent on November 16:

The solution of the labor question becomes more pressing

[21] Hindenburg to Groener, Nov. 11, 1916, BA, Nachlass Bauer, Nr. 14.
[22] Ernest R. May, *The World War and American Isolation, 1914-1917*, Cambridge, Mass., 1959, pp. 296-301.

> every day. The production of military equipment threatens to decline instead of rise. I will have to refuse responsibility for the continuation of the war if the homeland does not provide the necessary support. . . . Since my first proposals, months have been taken up, chiefly by *deliberations*, while our enemies, in model fashion, *act*. The establishment of the War Office can also only be fully effective when the Auxiliary Service bill gives it the essential legal foundation for its activity.[23]

Bethmann was angered by this latest assault. He replied that time was being taken for vital negotiations, not for deliberations, and that "I am not in the position to take responsibility for the consequences of a hopeless attempt to break the matter over my knee."[24]

The Bundesrat discussed the bill from November 16 to November 21. The delegates had already indicated that they would support the bill in a preliminary discussion on November 9. Particularist interests were at stake, however, and the Bundesrat demanded certain changes. Bavaria, Saxony, and Württemberg did not wish their military sovereignty impinged upon. Thus clauses were introduced requiring that the military chairmen of the various committees to be established in their states be appointed by the individual war ministries and that the War Office carry out the proposed law in collaboration with the war ministries. The state representatives were very concerned with the economic effects that the shutting down of nonessential plants would have on their home territories. The government draft was therefore changed to give the states a more important voice in such actions. The decisions of determination committees were no longer to take immediate effect if an appeal was made.[25]

[23] DZA Potsdam, Kriegsakten 1, Bd. 10, Bl. 130.

[24] Bethmann to Hindenburg, Nov. 17, 1916, BA, Nachlass Bauer, Nr. 14.

[25] On the Bundesrat discussions, see the report of the Bavarian delegate, Dr. von Meinel, of Nov. 22, 1916, BHStA, Abt. I, MH, Nr. 16018,

The delegates were very anxious to put the compulsory aspects of the bill into the background. The section of the Guidelines concerned with the method of treating those not already employed in some form of Auxiliary Service was amplified. Before such persons were individually summoned by the draft committees, they were to be given an opportunity to find work on the basis of a general appeal from the authorities for the various types of workers needed. Only after such an effort to secure workers on a completely voluntary basis had been totally exhausted would the draft committees set to work. The Bundesrat also decided that considerations of "previous income" in the assignment of men to Auxiliary Service would constitute an unfair class distinction, and these words were struck out.

The social aspects of the bill received considerable attention from the Bundesrat delegates. The representative of Alsace-Lorraine, where the civil administration was very liberal, pointed out that "workers should not be compelled to work in the war industry in order to bring the industrialists large profits" and suggested that provisions be made for the limitation of profits. Undersecretary Richter and Secretary Helfferich objected to "burdening the bill with such material." They felt that a fair and accurate method of determining excess profits could not be found and argued that the industrialists needed a strong incentive to fulfill the Hindenburg Program. As usual, Helfferich felt that the war profits tax would solve the problem.

During the discussion of the arbitration committees, Groener made a final effort to get concessions for the unions. He suggested that the union demands for an increase in the number of labor and management members of the committees, for the assignment of labor representatives to the committees on the basis of union proposals, and for the institution of compulsory

---

and the much fuller report of the Württemberg delegate, Dr. Schäffer, of Nov. 21, 1916, HStASt, E, 130, V, Xa.29, Bl. 17, upon which the discussion below is based.

workers committees in all factories be granted immediately. If these wishes were satisfied, then the government could take a firmer stand with regard to the more far-reaching union demands. Undersecretary Richter said that he had nothing against an increase in the size of the arbitration committees, but he opposed giving the unions the right to propose who should represent labor. Although he agreed that the establishment of workers committees was desirable, he insisted that this question had no relation to the bill under discussion and pointed out that the demand for these committees had to be rejected "out of consideration for the employers." Helfferich was not quite so negative in his approach. He was prepared to concede an increase in the size of the arbitration committees and the right of the organizations to propose the names of the members. In contrast to Groener, however, he was "of the view that these concessions are to be saved for the Reichstag." The only change Helfferich permitted the Bundesrat to make was in the form of an additional clause specifically indicating that the officials who served on the draft committees were not to serve on the arbitration committees. It was thus made clear that the arbitration committees would be organized on the principle of parity.

On November 21 the Bundesrat accepted the bill after having made the changes discussed above. The text was made public on the same day.

3. *The Budget Committee Transforms the Bill*

The situation on November 23, the day when the Budget Committee began to debate the Auxiliary Service bill, was depressing indeed. For all his protestations, Bethmann had permitted the OHL to rush him into bringing the bill before the Reichstag. The OHL, however, was not the only party responsible for this situation. With the exception of the arbitration committees, the government had made no real effort to meet the demands of the unions and left wing parties. To be sure, conferences had been held. In addition to the negotiations with the union leaders on November 8, Helfferich had discussed the bill with the Social Democratic Party leader, Scheidemann, a day or two before the Budget Committee debates began. No specific compromises had ever been worked out, however. This was most reprehensible because the Socialist, Center, and Progressive deputies were certain to be strongly influenced by, respectively, the Free Trade Unions, Christian Unions, and Hirsch-Duncker Unions. It was to be expected that the parties under their influence would form a bloc in the debate on the bill. Also, this bloc was bound to receive considerable support from Stresemann's wing of the National Liberal Party, which was committed to the pacification of the workers on social questions. It was, of course, most important that the Social Democrats and the Free Trade Unions support the bill, as this was the only way to insure the cooperation of the large body of workers they represented. Helfferich knew what most of the union demands were going to be, and he thus had an opportunity to take some of the wind out of their sails. Instead, he exacerbated the situation by presenting a bill which completely ignored everything the union leaders had said. On November 22 the executive committee of the General Commission took its revenge by officially rejecting the government's draft. The Social Democratic Party decided to follow suit on the following morning.[26]

The opening statements made by Helfferich and Groener before the Budget Committee were a combination of patriotic pleading and verbal reassurance. Helfferich emphasized Germany's serious economic and military plight and pointed out that the government was forced to abandon its previous policy of promoting the irrational use of labor and machinery in industries that were not essential or that suffered from short-

[26] On the meeting with Scheidemann, see Budget Committee debate, Nov. 23, 1916, and Deputy David's diary notations, Nov. 20-21, 1916, BA, Nachlass David, Nr. 7. On the decisions of the General Commission and the Socialist Party not to accept the bill as presented, see *Die dreizehnte . . . Generalversammlung des Deutschen Metallarbeiter-Verbandes*, p. 88 and IISH, SPD Fraktionssitzung Protokoll, Nov. 23, 1916.

ages of raw materials. He assured the deputies, however, that the shutting down and consolidation of industries would be carried out in collaboration with those affected. Similarly, he stressed the government's desire to secure labor by voluntary means. He also explained, in some detail, that conditions on the labor market were such as to make the inclusion of compulsory measures for women unnecessary.[27]

Groener related what he had seen during his personal survey of conditions on the Somme. He continually praised England's economic mobilization and pointed out that Germany lagged far behind her adversary in this respect. Passage of the Auxiliary Service bill, in his view, would be a moral, not a political act. It would demonstrate that all classes were prepared to fulfill their patriotic duty. He promised that the War Office would demonstrate its solidarity with the workers: "We all want to work and sweat together." He had no intention of ruthlessly transplanting workers. On the contrary, he would try "to bring the work to the workers." Groener pleaded with the deputies to give him their confidence, and he reminded them that he never could have organized the mobilization in 1914 if his authority had been restricted: "I simply commanded: It shall be done so—and it was done so, and that's why it succeeded." In the face of obvious disquiet on the part of the deputies, Groener declared that what mattered was not so much the bill in itself as the kind of freedom it would give him to act quickly in meeting the demands of constant crisis. He warned the deputies not to give "this emergency bill a character designed to hinder its implementation."

It is very likely that Groener knew that plans were afoot to give the Reichstag a voice in the implementation of the bill, but his efforts to dissuade the deputies were made in vain. The first deputy to speak, the Centrist, Gröber, launched an attack on the incompetent and arbitrary way in which the Law of

[27] Unless otherwise noted, the discussion of and quotations from the Budget Committee debates are taken from the debates of Nov. 23-28, 1916.

Siege had been implemented. The Reichstag could not continue to encourage this:

> One must protect oneself against such mistakes beforehand, and if complete confidence in the War Office is demanded, then the Reichstag should also display confidence in itself; and one must assume that it, too, wants the best for the Fatherland, but that it must also take care that mistakes are not made and that the energy and enthusiasm of the people are not ruined and destroyed. . . . The deputies can only do good when they have a complete opportunity to collaborate in the issuance of regulations and in the control of their implementation.

Ebert, the Progressive Party leader, Payer, and Stresemann expressed similar sentiments. Only the Conservative leader, Count Westarp, and the German Party leader, Freiherr von Gamp-Massaunen, were willing to give the government a free hand. If this pleased the government, however, their desire to include female labor under the compulsory measures of the bill was in no way helpful to the government's cause. Westarp emphasized the great need for female labor on the farms and warned against using the bill to take agricultural workers and put them in factories. Stresemann joined in this demand for the compulsory mobilization of female labor.

Most of the discussion on November 23 was sidetracked, however, by the unfortunate emphasis Groener had placed upon the "failures" of the past. The deputies were angry that the government had always painted a rosy picture of the munitions situation, and they insisted upon discussing the "guilt question." Helfferich was particularly annoyed at this because the deputies interpreted Groener's remarks to mean that financial considerations on the part of the civil authorities had played a role in creating the munitions problem. Groener had made a bad mistake in playing up this question, but the irritated former Treasury Secretary made an even greater mistake in pursuing it and choosing General von Stein, of all persons, as his instrument. Stein had no experience in dealing with the Reichstag and was given to oratory. Despite the fact that Helfferich supplied him with a carefully prepared statement to read at the beginning of the second session of the Budget Committee on November 24, Stein proceeded to speak

Ray of Hope

If only compulsory female service would come. Then perhaps the marriageable age would also be extended to fifty years.

extemporaneously.[28] What he said infuriated the deputies, for he implied that the Reichstag had been responsible for denying the General Staff the three army corps it had requested in

[28] Stein confesses his lack of Reichstag experience in his *Erlebnisse*, p. 107. On Helfferich's effort to prepare Stein, see Lerchenfeld to Hertling, Nov. 24, 1916, BHStA, Abt. II, MA 1, Nr. 958.

1912 and that the absence of these troops had caused the failure on the Marne. Even if this charge was true, this was hardly the time or place to make it. The result was an angry retort by the Centrist, Erzberger, a furious interchange between Stein and another deputy, and, finally, a weak effort by Stein to extricate himself from the situation. The detailed discussion of the bill, therefore, did not get off to a very pleasant start, and Groener was rather depressed over the way Stein had ruined his efforts to put the deputies in a good frame of mind.[29]

In this meeting and in the ensuing meetings of the Budget Committee on November 25, 27, and 28, the Auxiliary Service bill presented by the government was almost completely transformed. The Reichstag refused to accept a short bill. The Guidelines were to be incorporated into the bill itself, and, the bill was to contain a great many more concessions than the government was originally prepared to make. The Reichstag began the imposition of its demands by insisting that it be given power to control the implementation of the bill. Most interesting in this connection were the remarks of the Socialist deputy, David. In his view the Reichstag had made a "fateful mistake" in giving the Bundesrat a blank check on August 4, 1914, and it should not make the same mistake again. The Bundesrat, he pointed out, was nothing more than an instrument of the Prussian Cabinet, and the Reichstag could not place complete confidence in the administrative apparatus of the Empire, for "the war has shown that the German administrative machine is a completely old, rattling instrument which does not meet the needs of the times." Undoubtedly David had the management of the food supply very much in mind when he made this statement. Most of the deputies were thoroughly disgusted with the powerlessness of the Reichstag Advisory Council to the KEA. They wanted a more effective means of supervising the implementation of the Auxiliary Service bill.

There were three possible Reichstag agencies capable of

[29] Groener, *Lebenserinnerungen*, p. 347.

performing this function: the Reichstag itself, the Budget Committee, or a special committee. Both the Minority Socialist Party (at this time called the *Sozialdemokratische Arbeitsgemeinschaft*) and the Conservative Party were insistent that the Reichstag could not delegate its authority to a committee. But where the Minority Socialists wanted the Reichstag to pass on each Bundesrat order before it went into effect, the Conservatives wanted this right employed only when the Reichstag was dissatisfied with an order already issued and put into effect by the Bundesrat. In short, the Conservatives wanted the rights of the Reichstag to be presumptive, as was the case under the Enabling Act. There was general agreement among all the other parties that these solutions were unsatisfactory, the first because it would involve too much time and be too clumsy, the second because it would not give the Reichstag enough power. There was also general agreement that the Budget Committee was already too overburdened to take on yet another task.

The general consensus was for the establishment of a special standing committee. The exact powers of the committee were rather difficult to define. The deputies were certain that they wanted the committee to pass judgment on all the general regulations concerning the bill that the Bundesrat planned to issue. They also wished to have some check over the activities of the War Office, but not to get bogged down in petty administrative details. Groener felt impelled to resist efforts to give the committee a right to veto decrees issued by the War Office and angrily told the Budget Committee that "I have not accepted the leadership of the War Office to have my hands chained, gentlemen—not by anyone."

The objections of the civil authorities were of a more fundamental nature. The demand of the Reichstag for a voice in the execution and administration of the bill represented a dangerous incursion into the executive powers of the Bundesrat and government. It could become a precedent for future demands of a similar nature. In October the government had agreed to permit the Budget Committee to hold sessions even when the Reichstag was not in session.[30] Now an effort was being made to give yet more power to the Reichstag. Nevertheless, the Prussian Cabinet, in a meeting on November 26, decided to accept the demand for a special Auxiliary Service Law Committee. Bethmann pointed out that in normal times the Reichstag would never delegate legislative powers affecting the civil rights of citizens to the Bundesrat or to a government agency. The establishment of a special committee, in his view, was the best solution. This would help to emphasize that a precedent was not being established and would also keep the Budget Committee from "developing into a permanent welfare committee." The most important reason for the government's surrender, however, was stated by Helfferich: The Reichstag would not pass the bill without this concession.[31] There was to be much wrangling over the exact powers of the committee in the Budget Committee and the plenary sessions of the Reichstag, but the ultimate result demonstrated that the deputies had won an important victory:

> The Bundesrat issues the necessary instructions for carrying out this law. General regulations need the consent of a committee of fifteen members appointed by the Reichstag out of its own members.
>
> The War Office is bound to keep the committee well informed on all important events, to give it any desired information, to accept its resolutions, and to obtain its opinion before issuing important orders of a general nature.
>
> The committee is empowered to meet during the prorogation of the Reichstag.[32]

[30] Erich Matthias and Rudolf Morsey, *Der Interfraktionelle Ausschuss 1917/18. Quellen zur Geschichte des Parlamentarismus und der politischen Parteien. 1. Reihe. Von der Konstitutionellen Monarchie zur parlamentarischen Republik*, 2 vols., Düsseldorf, 1959, I, pp. xiv-xv.

[31] Prussian Cabinet meeting, Nov. 26, 1916, BA P 135/1810, Bl. 4a.

[32] Translation of the Auxiliary Service Law of Dec. 5, 1916, in Lutz, *Fall of the German Empire*, II, pp. 89-104.

This concession did not suffice, however. Legien was furious that so little had been done to implement the demands made by the unions in their preliminary negotiations with Helfferich. The latter's "fine declarations" were not enough. The workers had to have guarantees, and these guarantees had to be written into the law itself. On November 24 Legien launched a vigorous attack on the Interior Office before the Budget Committee: "The Imperial Office of the Interior, which should be an Imperial Office for social policy, but which is not, is responsible for the wording of this bill. If the war ends unfavorably for Germany, then a large part of the blame will fall upon the Imperial Office of the Interior, which has failed in all social and food problems." Legien then enumerated the union demands: obligatory workers committees in all factories employing over twenty workers, a network of conciliation agencies throughout the country, an increase in the size of the proposed arbitration committees, selection of the labor representatives on the arbitration committees on the basis of union proposals, and, finally, complete freedom of coalition for all workers. The acceptance of these guarantees was the "indispensable precondition" for union support of the bill.

The way in which Legien placed the entire blame for the government draft of the law on the Interior Office demonstrated that the union leaders were fully aware of the conflict between Helfferich and Groener. Groener, as he himself admitted, had established a "relationship of confidence" with the union leaders. Furthermore, and much to Helfferich's chagrin, Groener was privately informing the union leaders that the government would compromise.[33]

Helfferich now struck back by falsely associating Groener's position with his own. While admitting that Legien had voiced his demands in a general way in the meeting of November 8, Helfferich denied that either he or Groener had ever understood them to be a *conditio sine qua non* for the acceptance of

[33] Groener as much as confesses this in his "Bemerkungen zu dem Kapital 'Hilfsdienstgesetz und Hindenburg Program' . . . von Karl Helfferich," Nachlass Groener, 192-I.

the bill. He warned the deputies against raising "unacceptable" demands, expressed astonishment over the demand for complete freedom of coalition for railroad workers, and bluntly stated that it "cannot be conceded." Helfferich felt that the unions had every reason to be satisfied with the provisions he had made for arbitration committees. These committees were to have military officers as chairmen, and, as Helfferich sarcastically remarked, labor's experience with the military authorities was such that it could not be said that "they do not have the social feeling which you deny me." Lastly, Helfferich sought to dissuade the deputies from demanding obligatory workers committees. Such committees had not been set up in many factories because of "difficulties, which are as well known to the gentlemen as to myself." This was an obtuse way of saying that heavy industry would object. Also, factory elections held in connection with the establishment of the committees might cause unrest among the workers.

Helfferich's resistance was futile, and he knew it. In the Prussian Cabinet's meeting on November 26,[34] he admitted that he was prepared to accept workers committees and conciliation agencies. Sydow took a positive attitude toward workers committees and emphasized that they had done much good in the mining industry. He warned, however, against going beyond the provisions of the Prussian Mine Law. The Social Democrats wanted to compel the employers to discuss even the complaints of individual workers with the workers committees. In Sydow's view this could cause a breakdown of factory discipline. He warned also against making the committees obligatory for very small factories. In such factories the close relationship between employer and employees obviated the necessity of such institutions. Helfferich agreed with Sydow and proposed that the committees be required in factories employing a hundred or more workers.

While agreeing in principle to the establishment of concilia-

[34] For the discussion of and quotations from this meeting, see BA, P 135/1810, Bl. 4a.

tion agencies, the ministers were loathe to set up yet another type of committee in connection with the bill. Helfferich proposed, therefore, that the arbitration committees also be used as conciliation agencies. Thus, conflicts involving groups of workers which could not be settled in the workers committees could then be taken to the conciliation agencies. If no agreement was reached, or if the employer refused to accept the decision of the conciliation agency, then the employees as a group could demand the leaving certificate from the arbitration committee. Breitenbach and Schorlemer, while recognizing the necessity of establishing the above-discussed institutions in private industry, successfully fought to keep them out of the railroads and agriculture. Breitenbach feared that these institutions would lead to an increase in wages and a reduction of hours for the railroad workers. Schorlemer felt that they were not suited to the special conditions of agriculture. Bethmann agreed with Breitenbach and Schorlemer and instructed Helfferich to fight for the exclusion of the railroads and agriculture from the provisions under discussion. Finally, Helfferich was instructed to concede the right of the unions to propose the members of the arbitration committees but to oppose the assumption by the government of a formal obligation to follow union recommendations.

Two other issues, both of which had been the subject of considerable discussion in the Budget Committee, were taken up in the Cabinet's meeting of November 26. The first concerned the granting of compensation to the owners of nonessential factories who would lose their workers because of the bill. Many Centrist, Progressive, and National Liberal deputies were concerned that one group of employers would profit at the expense of the other, and they wanted the government to obligate itself to provide financial compensation to those who would suffer under the bill. Helfferich, with considerable justification, had rejected the proposal. He pointed out that it would be exorbitantly expensive and very unfair. Could the government assume an obligation toward these industrialists and then deny a similar responsibility toward craftsmen and shopkeepers who had lost their livelihood when drafted into the army? While expressing the hope that the shutting down and consolidation of industries would be accomplished with the cooperation of the industrialists and that compensation agreements would be reached between those who were going to continue in business and those who were going to shut down, Helfferich refused to accept any obligations. The Cabinet was in complete agreement with Helfferich on this issue.

It was much more difficult to achieve unanimity on the other question taken up during the Cabinet's meeting, the control of war profits. The Social Democrats, Centrists, and Progressives had continuously demanded that the bill be used to regulate war profits. They gave particular praise to the provision of the English Munitions Act limiting excess war profits to 20 percent of the profits made in peacetime. Helfferich correctly noted that the English had a very difficult time enforcing this regulation because so many new firms had been established during the war. Yet he was also hiding some very significant facts from the deputies. The industrialists were taking advantage of the Hindenburg Program to demand unjustifiable price increases. Two of the greatest producers of weapons, the German Weapons and Munitions Factory and the Krupp firm were making life very difficult for General Coupette and the State Secretary of the Treasury, Count Roedern. The first firm had increased the price of machine guns from 1500 to 2000 marks. Krupp was putting on a fine demonstration of the prices one could ask when one had a cannon monopoly.

On November 25 Coupette and Moellendorff had called on Count Roedern to discuss ways and means of compelling these and other firms to produce for reasonable profits. In fact, they were rather concerned about the way the industrialists were implying that they would go on strike if their demands were not met. The only legal means of doing anything about this was provided by the Law of Siege. The Deputy Commanding Generals could use the law to take over the factories, open their accounts, control their prices, forbid them to produce non-essential items, and punish disobedience. Use of this method, however, presented certain very serious disadvantages. The Deputy Commanding Generals would need experts to advise them in their control of the factories, and there were very few such experts available. Also, military control of the factories might have a very bad effect on the morale of the technical and managerial personnel. Even if these difficulties were surmounted, there was still no guarantee that the firms would not find devious ways to raise their prices. They could, for example, subcontract at high prices to associated or friendly firms. Coupette and Moellendorff wanted to know whether another means of solving the problem could be found. They were particularly interested in finding a way to use the Auxiliary Service bill for this purpose.[35]

The Prussian Ministry of Justice set to work on this problem and on November 26 presented the Cabinet with the draft of an addition to the law. Under the terms of this proposal, every firm would be required to produce in the amounts and within the time demanded by the War Office whether or not a final agreement on the price had been reached. Temporarily, it would have to produce at the price stated by the War Office. The final price would be settled by an arbitration commission composed of a chairman appointed by the War Office, a representative of the procurement agency involved, and a representative of the firm. Firms would be required to place their accounts at the disposal of the commission. Industrialists who refused to produce or to open their accounts could be punished by a year in prison, a fine up to 100,000 marks, or both.[36]

Helfferich was unalterably opposed to this proposal. Count Roedern disagreed with him. Roedern pointed out that the

[35] See Moellendorff's reports on this problem, Nov. 25 and 27, 1916, BA, Nachlass Moellendorff, Nr. 51a.

[36] For the draft of this proposal, see BA, P 135/1810, Bl. 4b.

industrialists' latest price demands were creating terrible financial problems. He completely rejected Helfferich's contention that an extension of the war profits tax would solve the problem. The industrialists escaped this tax by putting their profits into new enterprises and used every anticipated increase in the tax as an excuse to raise prices. Roedern assured Helfferich that he had no intention of revising already existing contracts. The Justice Minister, Lisco, supported Roedern and pointed out that the control of profits was a matter of equity:

> It is to be remembered that in the carrying out of the Auxiliary Service bill numerous workers will be removed from factories. For these workers, as for the firms involved, this is a heavy burden which is for the benefit of the entire community. On the other side, a small group of industrialists will have advantages from this law in that their profits will increase enormously. A measure which prevents these profits from being arbitrarily raised in an unjustified fashion by the industrialists must be regarded as a certain compensation for the shutting down of factories and the compulsory assignment of workers.

In reply, Helfferich cautioned against offending the industrialists, who were going to have difficult enough a time accommodating themselves to the social provisions of the bill. He warned against destroying the will of the industrialists to produce. An excess profit here and there was the "smaller evil." The Prussian Finance Minister, Lentze, agreed with Helfferich and argued that the industrialists could only overcome the difficulties involved in fulfilling the Hindenburg Program if they "were incited by the prospect of profit." General von Stein added that "the chief thing is quick production, and the cost question cannot be put into the foreground." At this point Lisco backed down, and Bethmann declared that they would have to rely on the war profits tax.

The profits question was thus settled when Helfferich once more defended his view before the Budget Committee during its last debate on the law on November 28. In the face of a charge by the Minority Socialist deputy, Dittmann, that "the capitalists are only ready to give their capital for the production of munitions if their great war profits are left to them," Helfferich replied that not the capitalists but their factories were being spared, i.e., it was important not to disturb production with such questions. He was certain that the War Office would be "man enough" to protect its interests against the industrialists. Groener assured the deputies that he was aware of the problem, but that production had to be put first. Helfferich and Groener begged the deputies not to stress the profits question from the floor of the Reichstag, as this would only create bitterness.

The deputies were by no means pleased by the way the government employed a dual standard in its presentation of the bill. Profits were not to be touched and the shutting down and consolidation of industries was to be done on the basis of voluntary agreements among the industrialists. But the workers were to be forcibly assigned to factories and to be compelled to stay on their jobs. The Social Democratic and trade union leaders could hardly accept the right of the employers to unrestrained profits without guaranteeing the workers a chance to improve their wages. They did not feel that it was enough to state, as did the draft that was emerging from the hearings, that the arbitration committees would give a worker a leaving certificate if he could demonstrate an "important reason" for wanting to leave his job. They therefore demanded that the bill explicitly state that the committees were especially to consider "the possibility of improving working conditions" as an "important reason." In other words, a worker was to be permitted to leave his job if he could demonstrate his ability to find better wages or working conditions elsewhere.

Needless to say, the government was very opposed to this proposal. This was particularly the case because the Social Democrats had already compelled Groener to agree that exempted workers would have all the benefits of the new law and thus no longer be subject to automatic drafting into the army if they left their jobs. Helfferich attacked the Social Democratic proposal with particular vehemence at the Budget Committee hearing of November 28:

> In my view, through such a regulation the men will actually be encouraged to reflect upon where they can get better working conditions. Instead of hindering job changing, I fear that through such a one-sided definition the opposite will be achieved in that the great mass of the workers who until now have not thought of changing jobs will now be made dissatisfied. We thus cut out the ground from beneath the bill and create something that will in many cases bring about confusion.

He reminded the deputies that the government could have simply brought in a request for an extension of the Military Service Law, and that this could hardly have been rejected. In that case there would have been no social protection at all. Yet the government did not choose this alternative because "we were convinced that the hardships that would have been thus created would have been much greater than those that could arise from this bill." This was not exactly an accurate portrayal of the real reasons for the government's decision, but Helfferich cannot be denied some grounds for self-righteousness on this point. Helfferich and Groener were willing to accept the Social Democratic amendment if the Social Democrats, in turn, were willing to permit the addition of another clause stating that the purposes of the bill would also be given due consideration by the arbitration committees. In this way, national as well as private interests would be safeguarded.

The government's opposition to the Social Democratic amendment received considerable support, not only from the Conservatives and National Liberals but also from the Progressives and right wing Centrists. A National Liberal deputy, Eugen Schiffer, warned that "every potato picker" would be encouraged to seek higher paid work in the munitions factories if the Social Democratic amendment was accepted without qualification. He proposed an amendment of his own: "In deciding the question as to whether an important reason exists, account is to be taken of the purposes of Patriotic Auxiliary Service. A suitable improvement of working conditions in the Patriotic Auxiliary Service shall be considered a particularly important reason." The Social Democrats and left Centrists, however, could not be won for such a compromise. Their minimum concession was a willingness to place the adjective "suitable" before "working conditions" so that not every slight possibility of a wage increase would be regarded as an "important reason." They would not permit the introduction of any clause which might be used as a means of depressing wages. Their motives are not only to be understood in terms of protecting the workers, but also in terms of a need to protect their own position. The Social Democratic Textile Union leader, Krätzig, was quite blunt about this necessity: "If the desired formulation regarding the improvement of wages is not accepted, then the union representatives will be in a difficult position vis-à-vis the workers. The asseverations of the government's representatives are no longer given very much credence by the workers."

When the Budget Committee concluded its hearings on November 28, this question, as well as a number of other important questions, were left unresolved. The government still refused to obligate itself to appoint worker representatives for the various Auxiliary Service committees on the basis of union proposals. The government refused also to establish worker committees and conciliation bureaus in the railroads and in agriculture. No definite agreement had been reached as to the number of workers a factory had to have before it was to be required to establish a workers committee. Another problem was the means by which the elections for workers committees were to be carried out. The Socialists wanted elections based on proportional representation and a reconstitution of those workers committees already existing on the basis of new elections. While willing to concede the former demand, the government opposed new elections for already existing committees. Finally, the Socialists had by no means spoken the last word on the protection of coalition and assembly rights for those serving in the Auxiliary Service. The continued existence of such unresolved issues meant that the government's desire to conclude the actual Reichstag debate on the bill in a single day could not be fulfilled.

Much had been accomplished in the Budget Committee, but the government could take little pleasure from these accomplishments. The bill was going to be long, and it was going to be filled with concessions to the left wing parties. The government had accepted the establishment of a special Reichstag committee to oversee the implementation of the bill. It had also agreed to the establishment of conciliation agencies and workers committees. Furthermore, there were to be both workers committees and white collar workers committees (*Angestelltenausschüsse*). The latter group of employees had been suffering terribly from the effects of low wages and high prices, and the deputies wanted to provide them with some means of collectively bringing their demands to the attention of the employers. In addition to the standing representatives of labor and management on the arbitration committees, the law was now to provide for an additional nonstanding representative from each side. The nonstanding representatives were to be taken from the particular industry involved in a given case. The unions were to have the right to suggest the names of the labor representatives for the various committees.

The government had also made a series of important oral promises. Exempted workers were to have all the benefits of the bill. The government promised to treat unions and newspapers as organizations vital to the war effort, and their functionaries were not to be forcibly assigned to other types of work. Above all, the government obligated itself to implement every aspect of the bill on as voluntary a basis as possible. One could be certain that the special Reichstag committee would not let the government forget these verbal guarantees.

Helfferich's greatest accomplishment had been the protection of unrestrained profit making, and he had paid dearly for it. The Conservatives, who were unenthusiastic about the bill to start with and feared that it would lead to a loss of agricultural workers, had the slight satisfaction of a clause prohibiting the drafting of agricultural workers into other forms of Auxiliary Service. This was pitifully little, and the Social Democratic demand that workers be permitted to seek higher paying jobs seemed to threaten the efficacy of even this very limited Conservative success.[37]

4. *The Reichstag Debate*

The Social Democratic Party Reichstag leaders met on November 29 to decide the policy they would follow in the plenary session of the Reichstag scheduled to begin that day. The middle-class parties had presented a new draft of the bill. This draft had served as the basis for the final discussion in the Budget Committee, and, as we have seen, it fulfilled many of the Social Democratic demands. The middle-class parties now wanted the Socialists to associate themselves with the draft. The Social Democrats, therefore, had to decide whether to support this draft and, furthermore, whether to declare publicly that they would vote for the law. The trade union leaders were prepared to take the latter step. Bauer felt that the law now presented great advantages for the workers. In his view, the Minority Socialist claim that it was a "bill for the enslavement of the workers" was nonsense. Ebert, speaking for the party, emphasized the great power that the Reichstag committee would have and was particularly pleased at the prospect of improving the lot of the exempted workers. He also noted that Groener had promised to appoint Alexan-

[37] Schorlemer indicated the lack of Conservative enthusiasm at the Prussian Cabinet meeting of Nov. 10, 1916, BA, P 135/1810, Bl. 1.

der Schlicke, the head of the Metalworkers Union, to represent labor's interests in the War Office. For the moment, however, the Social Democrats decided to withhold their support from the middle-class parties draft and to avoid publicly stating that they would vote for the bill. There was still serious opposition to the bill within the party and the unions. The Social Democrats did not want to give the Minority Socialists political capital by supporting the bill prematurely. Finally, since the Social Democrats hoped to wrest more concessions, it would have been tactically unwise to give in just yet.[38]

In the first reading of the law on November 29, the government and the parties restated their positions. Bethmann received considerable applause from the left when, in his introductory remarks, he stated that the bill required the cooperation of all occupational groups and, "above all, of their trusted organizations."[39] Helfferich made clear that the Federated Governments would agree to the inclusion of guarantees and protective measures within the bill. David, speaking for the Social Democrats, was less cordial. He attacked the government for having brought in its inadequate draft and vehemently denounced Breitenbach's ban of the German Railroad Workers Union. The workers had to have "real guarantees." David did touch upon the profits question, but his demand that the armaments industry be taken over by the state was a good demonstration of how unreal the whole question had become.[40]

The most interesting statements made during this session

[38] IISH, SPD Fraktionssitzung Protokoll, Nov. 29, 1916. The Berlin Metalworkers and the Shoemakers unions opposed the bill, as Dittmann noted at the Budget Committee meeting of Nov. 28, 1916.

[39] Reichstag Debates, Nov. 29, 1916, 308, p. 2156.

[40] *Ibid.*, pp. 2166ff. An amendment giving the War Office the right to take over factories that did not cooperate was voted down in the third reading of the bill on Dec. 2 because of Helfferich's strong opposition, *ibid.*, pp. 2314ff. Groener privately supported this amendment, "Bemerkungen zu dem Kapital 'Hilfsdienstgesetz und Hindenburg Programm' von Karl Helfferich" in Nachlass Groener, 192-I.

were those of the National Liberal and Progressive leaders, Bassermann and Payer, for they demonstrated the degree to which the middle-class parties had been forced into a coalition with the Socialists. Of the two parties, the National Liberals were the most split. Bassermann recognized that many of his colleagues in the party were opposed to workers committees, conciliation agencies, and arbitration committees. Basserman declared nevertheless that his party would support the bill anyway because the fulfillment of the Hindenburg Program required the collaboration of labor. Payer was more open and more positive in his approach. He admitted that the bill was being used to achieve old social demands and that it would bring more benefits to the workers than to the employers. He could not deny that because of the concessions being made to labor "the future development will, to a certain extent, be thereby influenced." Yet it might not be such a bad thing to use this occasion to cut through the "Gordian Knot," so as to "find out how things will go," and he concluded that "I think that the experiences will lead more to a setting aside of resistance and conflicts than the longest theoretical debates and conflicts of interest."[41]

The Minority Socialist Party was much less sanguine. It continued to regard the bill as an effort to enslave the workers and swamped the Reichstag with amendments to make it milder. The Conservatives were equally dissatisfied, and they sought to extend the liability to Auxiliary Service to women and youths. Above all, they wanted to rid the bill of its social provisions. Neither of these extreme views received support from the government or the Reichstag. The strange alliance of the radical Ledebour and the reactionary Heydebrand in opposition to the bill provoked much mirth, and the deputies jokingly referred to the new "coalition of Ledebrand and Heydebour."[42]

[41] Reichstag Debates, Nov. 29, 1916, 308, pp. 2175-2176.

[42] Lerchenfeld to Hertling, Nov. 30, 1916, BHStA, Abt. I MH, Nr. 16018.

The Social Democrats were favorably impressed by the way things were going, and they decided, before the second reading, to give their support to the draft that the middle-class parties had drawn up. They refused, however, to declare formally that they would vote for the bill, and they reserved the right to continue to add amendments. In other words, they wanted further concessions and knew they could not get them if they made a final commitment.[43]

On November 30 the Reichstag undertook the second reading of the bill, a process which lasted from noon to midnight. The first major quarrel arose over a Social Democratic amendment stating that the rights of coalition and assembly of those serving in the Auxiliary Service would not be impaired. By means of this amendment, they hoped to apply moral pressure against employers and Deputy Commanding Generals inclined to restrict these rights. Helfferich could not understand this. In his view either the amendment added to existing rights or it did not. In the first case, it could be interpreted as an effort to force Breitenbach to stop restricting the right of coalition for railroad workers. In the second case, it seemed to have no purpose at all and was best omitted. As if to prove that the Social Democrats had no intention of bringing up the railroad union question in this connection, the Socialist deputy, Becker, suggested that the amendment be dropped if Groener gave a verbal guarantee that already existing rights of assembly and coalition would not be abused. Unhappily, Groener seems to have been caught unawares, for he made an utterly meaningless statement which only increased the fears of many deputies: "Gentlemen, I take it as self-understood that the unions will support this bill without reservation and equally self-understood that the leaders of the workers will exercise that influence upon the workers which they must exercise upon the workers in the sense of this bill. That is their patriotic duty, and the War

[43] IISH, SPD Fraktionssitzung Protokoll, Nov. 30, 1916.

Office will work together with the worker leaders in this sense."[44]

The left wing deputies did not want a patriotic lecture on how they were to behave themselves. They wanted a guarantee that the employers and Deputy Commanding Generals would behave themselves and an assurance that the Law of Siege would not be abused any more. Helfferich had recently announced that a reform of the Law of Siege was being undertaken. The War Minister was to be appointed Commander of the Home Army, and he would have the right to hear complaints concerning the administration of the Law of Siege and to force the Deputy Commanding Generals to correct abuses. The left wing deputies, however, did not trust Stein, the government, or the employers. They would have had even better reason to distrust Stein if they had known that he was opposed to restrictions on the powers of the Deputy Commanding Generals.[45] Even without such evidence, the Progressive deputy Müller-Meiningen realized that faith was not enough when dealing with the military authorities:

> There you have it! You are now reaping the mistrust you have sown. I am confident that General Groener has the power and the good will to take the gentlemen [i.e., the employers] by the tuft. He certainly has the good will, as he now indicates by nodding his head. But many times we do not know today who will still be in power tomorrow, and we cannot make a law on the basis of two such friendly eyes which gaze upon the world so naïvely. (laughter and interjections from the left) Yes, he can bump into a stone [*Stein*]. I don't want to go into the matter any further.[46]

In the rather circular discussion which followed, Helfferich

[44] Reichstag Debates, Nov. 30, 1916, 308, p. 2234.

[45] Stein opposed limitations of the powers of the Deputy Commanding Generals in a note to the Prussian Cabinet of Nov. 14, 1916, but his view was rejected and he was appointed Commander of the Home Army on Dec. 8, BA, P 135/11652, Bl. 208.

[46] Reichstag Debates, Nov. 30, 1916, 308, p. 2235.

managed to annoy even the National Liberal deputies by continuously bringing up the railroad question. This, clearly, was not the issue, and the amendment was passed.

The Social Democrats also won the battle over what was to be regarded as an "important reason" for job changing when the majority of the Reichstag accepted, as the third section of Paragraph 9 of the bill, the statement that "A suitable improvement of working conditions in the Auxiliary Service shall be a particularly good reason."[47] Helfferich's reiterated request that equal emphasis be given to the purposes of the bill went unheeded. It should be pointed out, however, that the Social Democrats made an important concession when they accepted the word "suitable." Deputy Bauer defended this concession against strong attacks from Dittmann and other Minority Socialists in the most patriotic terms:

> My dear Dittmann, there are naturally also cases in which jobs are changed for completely incomprehensible reasons, and therefore one must be understanding enough in our present condition of need . . . to say: in this state of need we want to place some restriction upon ourselves; we want to do what we can, to relieve this need and to give our brothers the means of defense. (lively applause) If we want to do that, then we must also make certain concessions and accept this or that; one cannot always say: no restrictions! A certain voluntary limitation has been accepted here by the organizations in Berlin, and, in my view, the sensible workers must also undertake such a voluntary restriction today. (very true!)[48]

The Social Democrats were willing to compromise on other issues also. Thus they accepted a verbal declaration from Groener to the effect that he would try to follow their suggestions in the appointment of labor representatives to the

[47] See Appendix for the text of the law.
[48] Reichstag Debates, Nov. 30, 1916, 308, p. 2247.

committees and refrained from trying to force him to do so by law. Although they had originally demanded that workers committees be made obligatory for all factories employing over twenty persons, they now settled for a compromise figure of fifty. They were successful in forcing the government to accept the establishment of conciliation agencies in agriculture, but they were unsuccessful in getting the system of workers committees and conciliation agencies extended to the state railroad systems. Finally, the Socialists suffered a defeat in their efforts to have the bill officially expire on July 7, 1917, unless its continuation was approved by the Reichstag. This would have given them an opportunity to review the bill and make desirable changes and would have acted as a further check on the way the government implemented the bill. At the same time, the government's desire to leave the expiration of the bill to the discretion of the Bundesrat was also frustrated. Under the compromise that was worked out, the Bundesrat had the right to terminate the bill at any time, but the bill was to lapse automatically one month after the conclusion of peace.

Despite these compromises, it had been a good day for the Social Democrats. The Prussian Cabinet discussed the bill for the last time on December 1, and it would have been hard to find a sadder group of men.[49] Helfferich gave vent to the general disgust over the way things had turned out when he remarked, "One can almost say that the Social Democrats, Poles, Alsatians, and union secretaries have made the bill." It was difficult for the ministers to be angry at the left wing parties since one could expect little else from them, but they were furious at the Conservatives and National Liberals. The former had, in many cases, shown their lack of interest in the bill by staying home, and they had thus deprived the government of sorely needed support. The latter, under Stresemann's leadership, had fought "in a most agitatory way" for measures

[49] For the discussion of and quotations from this meeting, see BA, P 135/1810, Bl. 104e.

opposed by the government. As if his behaviour had not been bad enough, Stresemann was now yielding to the one union secretary in his party, Ickler, the head of a railroad workers union. Ickler, with his party's support, was preparing to bring in an amendment calling for the introduction of workers committees and conciliation agencies into the state railroad systems. Helfferich pointed out that this amendment was certain to be accepted if the National Liberals brought it in, and then "the limits of the bearable will have been reached." He hoped, however, to persuade them to withdraw the amendment.

The ministers were completely dissatisfied with the provisions that had been added to the bill. Sydow argued that the right of the workers to demand a leaving certificate en masse if the employers refused to abide by the decisions of the conciliation agencies amounted to nothing less than an "organized strike." Lentze indicated that Paragraph 9 rendered the bill "illusory" since it vitiated the effort to control the free movement of labor. The ministers debated the advisability of making an interpretative declaration concerning Paragraph 9 in the final meeting of the Reichstag, but Bethmann vetoed this proposal: "Experience dictates that we be careful with such declarations concerning the interpretation of the bill, because one can thereby easily achieve the opposite of what one intends and call forth Reichstag decisions that will make impossible the more valid construction and implementation of the bill which otherwise always remains possible for the government."

As always, Breitenbach and Schorlemer complained bitterly about the workers committees and conciliation agencies. Breitenbach was very worried. The private firms were not dependent upon state legislatures for the approval of their budgets, and they might be able to get rid of the workers committees and conciliation agencies after the war. Once introduced into the state railroad systems, however, they were there to stay. The civil ministers were unanimously agreed that the bill would prejudice the social order in peacetime. They received no comfort from General von Stein's remark that a "strong government would once again be mistress of her decisions and would not be hampered by the present bill." Stein did not know what he was talking about, and Bethmann felt that the time had come to enlighten him: ". . . the government after the conclusion of peace will need the agreement of the Reichstag in so many important matters, namely in the area of administration of the Imperial finances, that a situation of constraint will thereby be created. It is therefore very questionable whether successful resistance can be made to the Reichstag's efforts to maintain the concessions presently being fought for." Bethmann did recognize a bright side to the generally dismal picture. The New Orientation would undoubtedly include many of the concessions contained in the bill. The bill might thus serve as a natural transition to the New Orientation. Bitter conflicts might thereby be avoided. In any case, Bethmann told the ministers, they would have to accept the bill despite its unpleasant features. He had just received another telegram from the Emperor demanding its speedy passage. The ministers agreed that the government did not really have a choice.

On the same day the Social Democratic Party also decided to accept the bill. This step was taken over the objections of twenty-one of the forty-nine Reichstag leaders present at the meeting. The minority represented the radical wing of the party, which had not gone over to the Minority Socialists. While recognizing the improvements that had been introduced into the bill, they felt compelled to reject compulsory labor and restrictions on the free movement of labor for reasons of principle. Under party discipline, however, they were obligated to vote for the bill. At the same time the Socialist deputies decided to keep this decision a secret for as long as possible for tactical reasons.[50]

[50] IISH, SPD Fraktionssitzung Protokoll, Dec. 1, 1916.

Their reticence finds its explanation in the fact that they were planning to revive the demand for the introduction of conciliation bureaus and workers committees into the state railway systems. Helfferich had persuaded Stresemann to force Ickler to withdraw his amendment. At the same time he had persuaded Breitenbach to make a slight concession. A system of workers committees already existed for approximately four fifths of the railroad workers. These committees, however, unlike those being established under the bill, could not force management to discuss their petitions and complaints and were organized in an undemocratic manner. Breitenbach was willing to undertake a reform of the workers committees along the lines laid down in the bill. He refused, however, to introduce conciliation agencies into the railroad system. In his view the latter institutions could not possibly be conversant with the great variety of local circumstances affecting working conditions and wages throughout the system. They would be independent of the railroad authorities and yet be in a position to impose decisions upon the authorities at variance with a proper and expert management of the railroads. On the basis of Breitenbach's slight concession, however, the National Liberals dropped their amendment and in its place brought in a resolution asking the Bundesrat to do everything possible to introduce workers committees and conciliation agencies into the railroad systems.[51]

Unfortunately for the government, the Social Democrats had seen the National Liberal amendment before it was withdrawn, and they now decided to present it themselves. The Socialists had informed Helfferich of their intention on the evening of December 1. While stating his objections, Helfferich had in no way indicated that he would make a capital

[51] For Helfferich's negotiations with the National Liberals, see Lerchenfeld to Hertling, Dec. 4, 1916, BHStA, Abt. II, MA 1, Nr. 958. Helfferich related his discussion with Breitenbach to the Reichstag, Reichstag Debates, Dec. 2, 1916, 308, pp. 2312-2313. For the National Iiberal resolution, *ibid.*, 320, Anlage 562, p. 1075.

question of the amendment.[52] Thus, at the beginning of the third and final reading of the bill on December 2, Legien declared that his party agreed to the bill in principle, but asked that the government not make its acceptance of the bill difficult by refusing to accept the amendment. He concluded his speech with a final attack upon Helfferich:

> We assume that the present President of the War Office will alleviate many of the faults of the bill. . . . We hope that we will find the same understanding from the War Office . . . that we have previously found at the section of the War Ministry charged with the regulation of labor questions. We do not wish to have the spirit . . . of the State Secretary of the Interior find expression in the implementation of the bill (lively agreement from the Social Democrats), that spirit which sought to hinder the smallest improvement of the bill. Should that spirit become decisive, then, gentlemen, let the bill rest upon yourselves! (Very Good! from the Social Democrats). Then you will not get the needed forces in motion; then, in place of the active collaboration, you will set loose the passive resistance of the workers. (Lively applause from the Social Democrats)[53]

Helfferich, however, was to have the last word on one question. In his view, the Social Democratic amendment ran counter to the purposes of the bill and, "Therefore I must now, as much as it pains me, say that if the amendment as it is here presented is accepted, then the bill is truly endangered. (Hear! Hear! from the Social Democrats) I have not previously used this word, but on this point, unfortunately, I must."[54] These words, uttered with such solemnity, did not

[52] Breitenbach and Helfferich were prepared to resign if the amendment was accepted, Lerchenfeld to Hertling, Dec. 4, 1916, BHStA, Abt. II, MA 1, Nr. 958. See also Ebert's remarks, Reichstag Debates, Dec. 2, 1916, 308, p. 2322. For the Socialist amendment, Reichstag Debates, 320, Anlage 571, p. 1077.

[53] Reichstag Debates, Dec. 2, 1916, 308, pp. 2287-2288.

[54] *Ibid.*, p. 2313.

fail to have their intended effect. The Centrist labor leader Giesberts and Ickler now formally opposed the amendment. Progressive deputies planning to support the amendment wavered in their decision. The confusion and tension were heightened by the fact that, when the President of the Reichstag asked the deputies to indicate their approval or disapproval of the amendment, no clear majority could be ascertained. This necessitated a roll call vote. Finally, the amendment was defeated by one vote, 139-138.[55]

Helfferich had angered the Reichstag greatly by his obvious indication that the Bundesrat would veto the bill because of this amendment. He now angered it even more when, in answer to an attack from Ledebour, he remarked that he had never used the word "unacceptable" with regard to the amendment. Ledebour then proceeded to chide the Reichstag for having permitted itself to be "bluffed" by Helfferich. The latter replied with unbelievable casuistry: "Deputy Ledebour has accused me of bluffing. Nothing was further from my intention. Please, examine the situation! The Federated Governments have not yet taken a position. I did not say "unacceptable," and I could not say it; I could only express the way in which I was obligated to regard the situation and that is what I did."[56] Ebert was more furious than anyone else. Why had not Helfferich been honest the previous evening when the Socialists first informed him that they were going to present the amendment? "Had the State Secretary then given the declaration concerning the paragraphs which he gave today," Ebert remarked, "then, I believe, we could have been spared this agitated discussion."[57] The Social Democrats were too committed to the bill to let it fail over this issue, but

[55] *Ibid.*, p. 2314. On the effect of Helfferich's statement, see Lerchenfeld to Hertling, Dec. 4, 1916, BHStA, Abt. II, MA 1, Nr. 958.

[56] Reichstag Debates, Dec. 2, 1916, p. 2323.

[57] *Ibid.*, p. 2322. Helfferich blamed the entire episode on Groener, who "unconcerned by everything else, had permitted his willingness to give in to show through during the discussions." Lerchenfeld to Hertling, Dec. 4, 1916, BHStA, Abt. II, MA 1, Nr. 958.

if Helfferich had been less devious, he could have spared them so embarrassing an episode. All in all, it was a rather sour conclusion to what was supposed to be a great demonstration of national unity.

At the end of the third reading, the Auxiliary Service bill, which now contained twenty paragraphs, was passed by a vote of 235 to 19. The dissenting votes were those of the Minority Socialists. Eight Social Democrats broke party discipline and abstained. On December 4 the Bundesrat approved the bill, and on the following day the Emperor signed it.[58]

Measured in the simplest political and social terms, the Auxiliary Service Law was an important step in the direction of parliamentarization and of the integration of the German workers into the state through the recognition of their organizations. The Reichstag had refused to accept the government draft of the bill by acclamation and thereby give it the plebiscital character desired by the OHL and the government. The informal collaboration of the Socialist, Center, and Progressive parties in redrafting the bill and in compelling the government to make concessions demonstrated the potential power of the nascent coalition which was to be formally constituted in July 1917. The isolation of the Conservatives was intensified by the National Liberal surrender to the will of the Reichstag majority. At the same time the creation of a Reichstag committee to oversee the implementation of the bill was symptomatic of the breakdown of the exclusive executive prerogatives of the Bundesrat. Finally, the Auxiliary Service Law was a decisive turning point in German social history because the government had been compelled to recognize the unions and their right to equality with the employers.

These achievements, however, were made under the worst possible circumstances. The Auxiliary Service Law was the *reductio ad absurdum* of German interest politics and ultimately reflected the collective anxieties and ambitions of those

[58] Reichstag Debates, Dec. 2, 1916, 308, pp. 2328-2330. See also IISH, SPD Fraktionssitzung Protokoll, Dec. 2, 1916.

responsible for the formulation and passage of the law. The government, whose authority was threatened by the OHL, the interest groups, and the Reichstag, sought to make the bill as innocuous as possible by watering down its compulsory features. Fear of the centralizing tendencies of the bill drove the Bundesrat in the same direction. The Reichstag majority, acting out of a combination of distrust of the government and a desire to increase its own power, further diminished the potential efficacy of the bill. The Reichstag had proved as incapable of integrating the class interests which dominated German politics as the government. It failed to persist in its demand for the control of profits and was thus compelled to provide for the uncontrolled rise of wages. Paragraph 9 reflected the paralysis of both the government and the Reichstag. Ostensibly designed to reduce labor turnover, it actually encouraged the workers to change jobs for higher wages. The German workers were not only being integrated into German society, they were also being integrated into the chaotic political system upon which it rested. The union leaders were now being invited to become as irresponsible as their industrialist counterparts. The latter, in their quest for profits, had determined the nature of the Hindenburg Program. The former, in their quest for power and recognition, had determined the nature of the Auxiliary Service Law.

It is rather surprising that at no time between the presentation of the bill to the Budget Committee on November 23 and the final passage of the bill on December 2 did the OHL say anything about what was happening. Two explanations may be suggested for its silence. First, its members had placed their faith in Groener. Even the industrialists recognized this. Groener was supposed to be a "very understanding man," and the industrialists brought their objections to him.[59] Groener, therefore, had a certain independence and, as we have seen, he was not quite the "understanding man" that the

[59] VdESI meeting, Nov. 16, 1916, BA, R 131/149.

industrialists thought he was. The second and more basic reason for the OHL's silence is that there was no way in which it could restore its control of the situation. It had been cheap and easy to insist that the Reichstag pass the bill. The OHL was completely ignorant of political conditions at home and knew very little about the social and economic problems that dominated the thinking of the deputies. The members had brushed the warnings of the government aside with a soldierly disdain for political reality. The price that the OHL paid for its ignorance was the Auxiliary Service Law. Hindenburg congratulated Bethmann on the passage of the bill.[60] He should have congratulated Legien.

[60] Hindenburg to Bethmann, Dec. 3, 1916, DZA Potsdam, Kriegsakten 1, Bd. 10.

PART THREE

The War Office under the Leadership of General Groener

V

The War Office and the Problems of Production and Organization, December 1916-August 1917

On August 16, 1917, General Groener was removed from the leadership of the War Office. A month earlier, on July 13, 1917, Bethmann Hollweg had lost his position as Chancellor of the Empire. They were dismissed for similar reasons, and they both were victims of the OHL. It is the purpose of this and the following two chapters to analyze the economic and social origins of the great internal crisis of the summer of 1917. The famous Reichstag Peace Resolution and the intensified demand for a reform of the Prussian suffrage system were the most important manifestations of this crisis, but they were not its underlying causes. Groener and Bethmann were the OHL's scapegoats for the transportation and coal crises, the failure of the Hindenburg Program, the inadequacies of the War Office, the continued mismanagement of the food supply, the failure of the Auxiliary Service Law, the inflation, and the series of strikes which had exhibited themselves during the previous months. All these problems were interrelated, but, roughly speaking, it is possible to demarcate two broad areas of difficulty. First, there were the economic and organizational problems. Second, there were those problems which were of a more specifically social and political nature. It is with the first group of problems that the present chapter is concerned.

1. The Transportation and Coal Crises

The negotiations and debates over the Auxiliary Service bill had run their course in a spirited disregard of an increasingly grave transportation crisis. Only once did anyone question the assumption that the labor shortage was the only serious barrier to the fulfillment of the Hindenburg Program and thus come to the conclusion that there was no good reason for all the haste. In the Prussian Cabinet meeting of November 10, Sydow remarked

> that the presently existing great shortage of railroad cars hinders the practical implementation of the measures [i.e., the Auxiliary Service bill]. This shortage is hindering the production of coal and, with it, the increased production of munitions. Similarly, it will render difficult the transport of workers from one place to another. He [Sydow] is confident that this bad state of affairs will be overcome, but believes that, in view of this difficulty, the bringing in of the bill does not have to be so rushed that sufficient time does not remain for the negotiations with the employers and workers which he has proposed.[1]

Breitenbach admitted that there was a transport problem, but he expected that it would be eased by the end of November or the beginning of December. In reality, the transportation problem was going to get much worse, and when the bill was finally passed on December 2, the War Office was in no position to make much use of it.

The tasks imposed upon the German railway authorities by the war were extremely difficult.[2] The distances to be covered had increased enormously because of the need to supply the various fronts with troops and equipment, and to transfer them from front to front in accordance with military demands. The sudden entry of Rumania into the war in August 1916 added considerably to the kilometric distances to be covered. At the same time the domestic demands for railroad transport were much greater than ever before. Before the war much of the coal, iron ore, and food used by Germany had been

[1] BA, P 135/1810, Bl. 1.

[2] Basic studies of the wartime transportation situation are Adolph Sarter, *Die deutschen Eisenbahnen im Kriege*, Stuttgart, Berlin, Leipzig, 1930, and Prof. Weyrauch's report to the War Office, Jan. 1917, Nachlass Groener, 197.

imported from abroad and then sent into the interior by river and canal from the North Sea and Baltic ports. Now the burden of transporting coal from the Ruhr and Silesia, iron ore from occupied France, and food from eastern Germany fell almost exclusively on the railroads. Lastly, there was the difficult problem of providing for personal travel, particularly of troops on leave from the front.

Until the fall of 1916 the railroads had managed to meet this variety of demands, and this was no mean accomplishment. The railroad authorities were perpetually subjected to arbitrary changes in schedules. Under the War Production Law of 1873, the head of the Field Railways and the various line commanders in Germany who acted as his agents had the right to demand that priority be given to military transport. Thus every great battle at one of the fronts was something of a trauma for the railroad authorities in that it required them to supply extra rolling stock and to rearrange their schedules. Nevertheless, the railroads had managed to function well despite great shortages of manpower and the progressive deterioration of equipment.

The railroad authorities had borne these hardships silently, perhaps too silently, for their problems were not given the slightest consideration when the Hindenburg Program was established. Evidently Bauer, Ludendorff, and the industrialists simply assumed that the railroad systems would meet whatever demands were imposed upon them. Breitenbach was never consulted, and no discussions were held with the railroad authorities of the non-Prussian states. This was most unfortunate because the program, which required the building of numerous factories and the expansion of many of those already existing, necessitated the laying down of new tracks and a sudden concentration of transport either in entirely new areas or in areas in which transport facilities were overworked. Furthermore, the geographical distribution of the plants serving the war effort was irrational from a transportation standpoint. Most of the steel blocks manufactured in the Ruhr had to be sent to Berlin for transformation into ammunition and then sent back to the Ruhr again to be filled with powder. If the munitions factories had been located in the West, the transportation problem would have been much simplified. Unhappily, the owners of these factories wanted to be as close to the procurement agencies as possible and had, therefore, set up their plants in Berlin. The enormously increased demand for ammunition and for the construction of new factories under the Hindenburg Program were thus certain to bring about a breakdown of the transportation system.

The first signs that something was amiss appeared in late September 1916, when the transport of coal from the mines to the factories of the Ruhr became irregular. By mid-October, this was causing severe disturbances of production in some of the more important Rhenish war plants. The malady then spread, first to Central Germany, then to Berlin, and finally to Silesia. Freight stations could no longer hold the trains destined for them, and the stations were so jammed with cars that there were long delays in unloading. The longer the delays, the less railroad schedules bore any relationship to reality. In many cases schedules ceased to exist and trains ran "wild." Men and machinery worked overtime, the former not getting enough food, the latter not getting enough care. Yet less was delivered than ever before. This miserable situation was made even worse in January and February 1917 when a hard freeze made use of waterways impossible and intensified the difficulties of the railroads. Even some of the more important nitrates factories had to shut down because they did not have enough coal. The civil population, already suffering from the infamous "turnip winter," had to be cold as well as hungry.

Thus Germany once again faced a serious raw materials problem. Initially it was believed that there was enough coal, but this coal was not reaching the factories. If the distribution of coal was not organized, Germany's war industry would collapse. The first attempt to solve this problem was taken at the instigation of the General War Department in October

1916. On October 21 an Advisory Council was attached to the Railroad Office in Essen. This Council, composed of representatives of the coal-producing organizations, the most important industrial consumers of coal, and the Field Railways Service, had the task of hearing complaints concerning unsatisfactory coal deliveries and making sure that the most important war plants were given priority in deliveries. The competence of the Council was limited to the Ruhr. Complaints from other areas were passed on to the Central Railroad Office in Berlin.

This initial organizational effort was hardly adequate to solve what was increasingly a national problem, and at the end of November the newly created War Office went a step further. A Coal Adjustment Bureau (*Kohlenausgleichstelle*) was set up in the KRA under the direction of Dr. Kruse, a member of the Rhenish-Westphalian Coal Syndicate. The Bureau was composed of members of the coal-producing organizations, the Ministry of Commerce, and the War Office. An Advisory Council of coal producers was attached to the Bureau. In the first meeting of the Advisory Council on December 6, Koeth was careful to stress the point that the KRA did not intend either to ration coal or to interfere in the organization and functioning of the Coal Syndicate and the great coal merchant firms. Instead, the object was to secure the cooperation of the coal producers and merchants in the fulfillment of the production goals of the War Office and, at the same time, to make the War Office the only government agency competent in matters of coal supply.[3]

Yet conflicts of competence could scarcely be avoided, for so long as the root of the difficulty seemed to lie in the transportation situation and the control of internal German transport lay completely in the hands of the civil authorities, the possibilities of bureaucratic confusion and contradictory orders emanating from different agencies were very great indeed.

3 "Tätigkeitsbericht des Kohlenausgleichs Berlin," March 1917, BHStA, Abt. IV, MK, K Mob 12, Bd. V, Bl. zu 117, and report on Advisory Council meeting of Dec. 6, 1916, *ibid.*, Bd. I, Bl. zu 44a.

During December 1916 and the early months of 1917, considerable sentiment was expressed in the press and elsewhere for the management of the railroads by the War Office. This idea was stoutly resisted by Breitenbach, who warned that the sudden transferal of the management of the railroads from one authority to another was an invitation to chaos. It is highly probable that Groener and many of the other leaders in the War Office were inclined to take over the railroads. While head of the Field Railways Service, Groener had come to the conclusion that much greater military control of the railroads was desirable in both war and peace. Furthermore, the War Office was in continuous conflict with Breitenbach and his subordinates. Breitenbach, however, had the support of the Chancellor. Bethmann regarded the War Office's attacks on Breitenbach as yet another example of the effort to "militarize the entire life of the state."[4]

Since the War Office could not run the railroads, it had to content itself with an effort to collaborate with the civil authorities and to exert as much influence as possible through its personal representatives. In order to effectuate closer cooperation with the civil authorities, the head of the Field Railways appointed a commissar to the civilian transportation agencies and, in addition, established a special Section for War Economy Transport. The latter had the task of helping the civil authorities to organize transport in accordance with priority lists sent out by the War Office.[5] A massive and complex organizational pattern was developed in which repre-

[4] Bethmann to the Chief of the Civil Cabinet, Valentini, Dec. 31, 1916, in Rudolf von Valentini, *Kaiser und Kabinettschef. Nach eigenen Aufzeichnungen und dem Briefwechsel des Wirklichen Geheimen Rats Rudolf von Valentini, dargestellt von Bernhard Schwertfeger*, Oldenburg, 1931, p. 245. For Groener's attitude, see his *Lebenserinnerungen*, p. 269. On the public demands for military management of the railroads, see Prussian Landtag debates, March 10, 1917, V, pp. 5034-5039, and Sarter, *Eisenbahnen*, pp. 56-57, 123-124, 139-143. Sarter argues that military management of the railroads might have put an end to the steel industry's failure to produce railroad tracks, which yielded a lower profit than army contracts.

[5] *Mitteilungen des Kriegsamts*, Jan. 21, 1917.

sentatives of the War Office, the Field Railways Service, and the Ministry of Public Works were attached to each other's organizations.

The most important practical difficulty impeding the mastery of the transportation crisis was that of getting railroad cars unloaded quickly. Here the War Office could be of considerable assistance. The Deputy Commanding Generals were instructed to command that railroad cars be unloaded within fixed periods. Whenever this was not done, the generals were ordered to seize the cars and send the material, usually coal, to firms that would unload more rapidly. At the suggestion of Wichard von Moellendorff, special "flying unloading commandos," composed of workers from shut-down factories, were organized.[6] Furthermore, an effort was made to get WUMBA to revise contracts in such a way as to insure more rational use of the railroad network and to break industrialist resistance to the use of the slower waterways in the transport of goods. Finally, higher priority was given to the manufacture of tracks, rolling stock, and locomotives, and more labor was exempted to insure speedy repairs.

These measures were to have a mitigating effect upon problems that continued to exist until the end of the war. In January and February 1917, however, the most radical measures were required. The situation was so chaotic at this time that all additional traffic had to be stopped from January 24 to January 31 and from February 1 to February 5 so that the tie-ups could be cleared without interference. The most important cause of this regrettable situation, in addition to the freeze, was the "seizure by every imaginable authority of goods in transit."[7] Many of the local military and civilian agencies were convinced that no problems were worse than their own, and they simply raided the trains passing through their districts. Also, the coal producers were not demonstrating the "disci-

6 Report of Dec. 12, 1916, BA, Nachlass Moellendorff, Nr. 51a.

7 "Tätigkeitsbericht," March 1917, BHStA, Abt. IV, MK, K Mob 12, Bd. V, Bl. zu 117.

pline" expected of them. Instead, they were showing partiality toward their best customers.[8] The Coal Distribution Bureau seemed incapable of getting out from under the twelve hundred to sixteen hundred daily complaints it received. Unflattering comparisons with the organization of the food supply were being made, and the idea of appointing a "coal dictator" was gaining ground. On February 7 Wichard von Moellendorff proposed that the Bundesrat appoint a coal commissar to regulate the coal supply throughout the country.[9]

This idea was favored by the OHL, but it was treated with considerable skepticism by the civil authorities and the coal producers. Sydow feared that any new organizational measure would simply add to the existing chaos, and the coal barons were opposed to any interference with their control of the coal market. On February 15, however, Ludendorff won Stinnes over to the idea. Stinnes felt that the entire problem could be solved if nonessential factories were ruthlessly shut down, and he undoubtedly welcomed the prospect of having someone with the power to cut off the coal supply of such firms. If the commissar had complete power, Stinnes optimistically told Ludendorff, "the matter could be put in order in three or four weeks."[10] Once the OHL had Stinnes' approval, they forced the government to appoint an Imperial Coal Commissar. The Bundesrat gave its approval on February 24, and Privy Mine Councilor Fuchs was given the new post. To insure coordination between the Commissar and the War Office, the Commissariat was attached to the War Office, and the Coal Distribution Bureau was taken out of the KRA and placed under Fuchs' authority. The Coal Commissar, however, was responsible to the Chancellor, not to Groener.

[8] *Ibid.* and report of the Bavarian representative to the War Office, Captain Müller, Jan. 16, 1917, *ibid.*, K Mob 14, Bd. I, Bl. 101.

[9] Moellendorff to Haber, Feb. 7, 1916, BA, Nachlass Moellendorff, Nr. 51a. It is very likely that Haber once again communicated a Moellendorff proposal to the OHL through Colonel Bauer.

[10] Ludendorff to Groener, Feb. 16, 1917, Groener, *Lebenserinnerungen*, p. 359. For Sydow's attitude, see his note to the Interior Office of Feb. 1917, PrGStA, Rep. 120, Bd. 73.

Instead of matters now being "put in order," the disorder was intensified during March and April. The War Office had opposed the appointment of Fuchs and favored the appointment of his more energetic and competent subordinate, Privy Mine Councilor Stutz, instead. The civilian bureaucrats, however, felt that Stutz did not have enough seniority. From the very start, therefore, the foundation for collaboration between the War Office and Fuchs was quite shaky. Unfortunately, Fuchs was incompetent. He lacked ideas, energy, and self-confidence. When in the course of an angry exchange Stinnes advised Fuchs to "go home," the latter could only reply "that he himself was convinced that his organization was not viable, but he had not placed himself in this job."[11] Since, as Fuchs himself admitted, he spent nearly all of his time receiving petitioners, it is no wonder that he was never able to accomplish anything.

This was particularly unfortunate because the leading members of the War Office were in conflict as to how to solve the coal crisis. Koeth wanted a centralized solution, Groener a decentralized solution. In Koeth's view, the most important consideration was that there was not enough coal to go around. He therefore suggested that a survey of the need for coal be conducted and that the coal then be distributed on the basis of this survey. The specific allocation of coal among the various factories would thus be regulated from Berlin. Groener, while willing to have the general distribution of coal regulated from Berlin, felt that only the local authorities could accurately determine the specific allocation of coal. Moellendorff agreed with Groener. He wanted to set up "local coal bureaus" in the War Office bureaus. These would be composed of local industrialists and officials, whose task it would be to report local needs to the Coal Commissar in Berlin and then distribute the coal received through him. In late February the War Office, without waiting to hear what Fuchs would have to say,

[11] Captain Müller's reports of April 28, 1917, BHStA, Abt. IV, MK, K Mob 12, Bd. V, Bl. 201a, and May 5, *ibid.*, Bd. VI, Bl. 21a.

decided to act upon the decentralized solution supported by Groener. Fuchs, having no ideas of his own, accepted this *fait accompli.*[12]

Despite the easing of the transportation crisis in March and April and despite the institution of local coal bureaus, the problem became worse than ever before. On April 14 Ludendorff informed Fuchs of the large number of complaints he had received from industrialists and inquired as to what was going wrong. Since the transport problem had ceased to be serious, he remarked, there seemed to be no excuse for the continued difficulties with the coal supply. Fuchs' reply must have come as quite a shock: "In general, disturbances in the coal supply of the war industry cannot presently be avoided because, despite sufficient rolling stock, production is insufficient, the shipment from Westphalia being only two thirds of the peacetime amount."[13] The transport crisis during the winter had obscured the fact that Germany was no longer producing enough coal to meet her requirements. There had been sent 32,000 railroad cars to the Ruhr coal mines, but only 22,000 of them could be filled. In fact, the railroad authorities were beginning to worry about finding enough coal to keep the locomotives running![14]

In establishing the Hindenburg Program, the OHL had paid no more attention to the coal supply than it had to the transport problem. At the very beginning of the war, the army had made the mistake of drafting large numbers of miners. This situation was corrected to some extent by exemptions, but the mines were always short of manpower. As a result, equipment had deteriorated, shafts had run dry, and productivity had dropped. The bad food situation had also had an adverse

12 Captain Müller's reports of Feb. 28, 1917, *ibid.*, Bd. II, Bl. 61, and April 28, *ibid.*, Bd. V, Bl. 201a; War Office directive, March 24, *ibid.*, Bd. III, Bl. 234; meeting of Feb. 10, *ibid.*, K Mob 14, Bd. II, Bl. 144a-zu 144a.

13 Ludendorff to Fuchs, April 14, 1917, and Fuchs to Ludendorff, April 20, 1917, Ludendorff, *Urkunden*, pp. 178-179.

14 Captain Müller's report of April 28, 1917, BHStA, Abt. IV, MK, K Mob 12, Bd. V, Bl. 201a.

effect on production. Until the Hindenburg Program was launched, production had kept up with demand. This no longer was the case. The coal problem therefore was not merely a manifestation of the transportation crisis, and it could not simply be solved by efficient distribution. It was, above all, a matter of production. On May 10 the OHL was forced to agree to a War Office request for the return of 40,000 miners from the front.[15]

The realization that there was going to be a permanent coal shortage necessarily threw the weight of official opinion in favor of Koeth's centralized coal distribution program. Everyone was heartily sick of the organizational confusion. Too many agencies, particularly local ones, had executive authority. Complaints about the high-handed tactics of the War Office bureaus and procurement agencies were universal. The continuous surrender of the Coal Commissar to their demands had produced a situation of veritable anarchy. There was general agreement on the need for a central survey of coal needs and the establishment of a strict system of priorities. The OHL wanted the introduction of rationing, as did Fuchs. Nevertheless, it was decided not to take this step. The chief opposition to rationing came from Stinnes, who argued that more labor and the shutting down of nonessential factories would solve the problem. He warned against setting up yet another large organization, which he felt could only waste manpower and time and create further confusion. While recognizing that Stinnes' arguments reflected the special interests of the Coal Syndicate, which did not want the control of distribution taken out of its hands, both Groener and Fuchs were forced to agree with Stinnes' more objective arguments. Finally, there was general agreement that the situation was now too serious for Fuchs' mediocre talents. At the beginning of June, Fuchs was replaced by Privy Mine Councilor Stutz.[16]

15 Ludendorff to Groener, May 10, 1917, Ludendorff, *Urkunden*, pp. 179-180.

16 Captain Müller's reports, May 5, 1917, BHStA, Abt. IV, MK, K Mob

There were no miracles between June and August 1917, but only a practical acceptance of reality—even by Stinnes. Throughout May he had remained an optimist and had argued that all that was needed was more miners. At the beginning of June it was clear that the return of miners from the front would take longer than expected and that there would be a coal deficit for a long time to come. Later in the month the OHL agreed to surrender another 10,000 men. Yet a great increase in production could not be expected. The army could never surrender enough men to improve the quality of production. In fact, Groener was constantly reiterating that "we should be happy if production doesn't sink."[17] So, too, the organizational chaos was gradually cleared up, and more satisfactory collaboration between the military and civil authorities was established.

This was largely due to Koeth, whose KRA was given complete charge of the War Office's collaboration with the civil authorities concerning coal questions. In a meeting on August 15 he laid down the line to the War Office officials and particularly to the representatives of the procurement agencies:

> We must not come together here to complain and criticize, but rather to make do with the supply which is at our disposal and which is too short in every respect. From the very outset I want to make clear that I do not want, under any circumstances, to set up a new system, but rather to work with what is at hand, to supplement it with what we have learned by practice, and to bring everything into a system so that in time we can stop the daily interference with one bureau in order to stop up a hole in another.[18]

12, Bd. VI, Bl. 21a and, May 24, *ibid.*, Bd. VII, Bl. 133a; report of the Bavarian Bundesrat delegate, Dr. Huber, May 21, *ibid.*, Bd. VI, Bl. 135; Groener to Ludendorff, May 22, and Ludendorff to Groener May 10, Ludendorff, *Urkunden*, pp. 180-182.

[17] Captain Müller's report, July 22, 1917, BHStA, Abt. IV, MK, K Mob 13, Bd. III, and report of Generaldirektor Klaiber, June 20, 1917, *ibid.*, K Mob 12, Bd. IX, Bl. zu 83.

[18] Captain Müller's report, Aug. 15, 1917, *ibid.*, K Mob 12, Bd. X, Bl. 135a.

Having thus set the tone, he went on to demand that the procurement agencies always consider the coal supply when giving contracts. The armaments industry was no longer to be given first consideration. All authorities, including the OHL, were agreed that the miseries of the previous winter could not be repeated. The civil population had to have sufficient coal for heating purposes. The OHL was convinced that strikes and coal riots would harm production more than the losses that might be incurred through limitations on industry's coal supply. Also, the railroads had to be given priority over war industry. The procurement agencies were to accept these limitations and cease to act like "complaining wives." There was to be no more running to the Coal Commissar, either by the procurement agencies or by the War Office bureaus, with special requests. Only the KRA was to have direct contact with the Commissar, and all wishes and complaints were to be submitted to the Commissar through the KRA. The KRA would evaluate these requests before presenting them. The Coal Commissar, however, had the ultimate authority in the procurement and distribution of coal, and Koeth warned against further military interference with his work.

The War Office and OHL received warm applause from the public for their role in handling the coal problem. The *Correspondenzblatt* was particularly enthused over the OHL's willingness to give first consideration to the needs of the civil population. The OHL's decision to free miners from the front was given great praise. At the same time the civil authorities were accused of standing by and doing nothing.[19] This blind faith in the wonders of military intervention was hardly justified. The War Office had been just as confused as Fuchs. In reality, order was not restored until the military authorities stopped interfering with the work of the Coal Commissar. The OHL released miners from the front and decided to give priority to the civilian population's coal needs because it had no other choice. Finally, and most important, the OHL's muni-

[19] *Correspondenzblatt*, July 14, 1917.

tions program was largely responsible for the intensity of transportation and coal crises.

2. *The Failure of the Hindenburg Program*

The Hindenburg Program could not fare well under such circumstances. With the exception of the Weapons and Munitions Procurement Agency (WUMBA), the War Ministry had always been dubious of the program. In October 1916 the General War Department had gone so far as to write a memorandum stating its point of view, but this memorandum was never sent to the OHL. The most open opposition came from Koeth, who felt that it was impossible to produce enough steel to meet the demands of the program and who feared that the program would cause chaos. Koeth was so strongly opposed to the program that Groener, shortly after the establishment of the War Office, planned to dismiss him. It took a frantic last minute appeal from Rathenau and the Krupp director, Eberhard von Bodenhausen, to convince Groener that Koeth was indispensable.[20]

Some industrialists were skeptical. At the beginning of December 1916 Rathenau estimated that 60 percent of the program could be fulfilled by the summer of 1917. He believed, however, that this would give Germany superiority over her enemies and thus continued to favor the program. Much less sanguine was Privy Councilor Kirdorf of the Rhenish-Westphalian Coal Syndicate, who at the beginning of December warned that there would not be enough coal. Kirdorf was something of a maverick, however, and the vast majority of the industrialists, including the other great coal baron, Hugo Stinnes, remained as optimistic as ever.[21]

It is difficult to tell exactly when Groener became thoroughly convinced that the program was impossible. He had expressed

[20] Wrisberg, *Wehr und Waffen*, pp. 285-288; Spiero, *Schicksal*, p. 269.

[21] Rathenau, *Politische Briefe*, pp. 61, 170, and meeting in the Coal Commissar's office, May 2, 1917, BHStA, Abt. IV, MK, K Mob 12, Bd. VI, Bl. 21a.

his doubts to Helfferich and Breitenbach in October, but his refusal to join forces with Koeth demonstrates that he intended to take his stand for fulfillment of the program. He maintained his optimism throughout December despite the fact that production was declining. Thus he told the Reichstag committee on December 20 that fears concerning the proper supply of the army in the spring were "exaggerated" and that powder production would increase rapidly during the following months.[22] Most important, WUMBA was ordered to make its plans on the basis of the program, although it was generally recognized that only 60 percent of the program could be achieved by April. On January 8, in accordance with Groener's instructions, Moellendorff developed a plan of operations. This plan assumed that the program could be fully achieved by October 1917. First there would be a quick increase in production during the first months of 1917 as a result of the full utilization of already existent plant facilities. There would then be a slower rate of increase until the new factories under construction were ready to begin operation. Once this had occurred, there would be great increases of production and the full program would be achieved.[23]

Yet Groener certainly must have had his doubts because he ordered WUMBA to inform him the moment it felt that the program was no longer capable of realization. On January 23 Moellendorff felt that the time had come to enlighten Groener and the OHL. In a report to Coupette, Moellendorff pointed out that contrary to expectations, the transport crisis had not eased and that as a result production continued to decline. He was now firmly convinced that "Germany can never achieve the full Hindenburg Program." Furthermore, the program, with its "new constructions, disturbances, rivalries, and the like, would endanger the achievement of attainable goals": "Every

[22] Dr. Huber's report on the meeting of Dec. 20, 1916, BHStA, Abt. IV, MK, K Mob 11a, Bl. 9a. Also, Groener's "Bemerkungen zu dem Kapital 'Hilfsdienstgesetz und Hindenburg Programm' . . . von Karl Helfferich," Nachlass Groener, 192-I.

[23] Memorandum of Jan. 8, 1917, BA, Nachlass Moellendorff, Nr. 51a.

self-deception today presents a fatal danger for the country. . . . I am not for the giving up of all plans, but for clear-sighted program development [*Planmässigkeit*] instead of short-sighted plan making [*Planmacherei*]."[24] In his view, nothing further could be learned from "waiting and observing." He concluded that the time had come for the creation of a more realistic program.

Once Moellendorff had joined Koeth in opposition to the program, Groener was prepared to present the OHL with the facts. The OHL, however, was passionately attached to the program. Thus, on January 26 Ludendorff sent Groener a personal letter complaining about the unsatisfactory state of production and stressing the dangers this would create during the forthcoming campaign. The decline in production, in Ludendorff's view, was due neither to the raw materials shortage nor to the shortage of manpower, but rather to the transport problem. Yet on the basis of complaints he had received from industrialists, he could not help concluding that there were "*other reasons*" for the production delays. He demanded that the War Office work more quickly and supply the factories with the materials they needed. This rather unconstructive letter is a good example of the way the OHL blamed organizations and individuals for problems which had their origins in the economic facts of life.[25]

The War Office's pleas for a relaxation of the OHL's production demands did elicit some concessions from the OHL. In a meeting with Colonel Bauer on February 3, Koeth requested that the 14,000-ton powder program be dropped and that an effort be made to maximize the production of those factories already in existence. Insofar as the construction of new plants was concerned, Koeth suggested that they concentrate on plants which would be capable of beginning operation in the spring. Bauer agreed to these suggestions. At this time he made the interesting revelation that the OHL had never been fully

[24] Memorandum of Jan. 23, 1917, *ibid.*, Nr. 51.
[25] Ludendorff to Groener, Jan. 26, 1917, Nachlass Groener, 192-I.

convinced that the 14,000-ton powder program could be realized and that the program had been approved only because the industrialists indicated that it was possible. On February 6 Ludendorff ordered the cessation of work on all factories which could not be concluded before May 1917. The construction of nitrate factories, because of their paramount importance, was not included in this order. Ludendorff was careful to emphasize, however, that this cutback was to remain in effect only so long as the transportation situation continued to be serious.[26]

The conflict between the War Office and the OHL remained unsettled. Furthermore, there was some disagreement within the War Office itself. Koeth and the KRA argued that further increases in production were very unlikely. Moellendorff, representing WUMBA, felt that a gradual increase was possible if a carefully thought out program was developed. He proposed that nitrates production be emphasized and that all other production and construction work be treated as secondary. At the same time, production possibilities were to be statistically determined and practical measures were to be undertaken to relieve the transport crisis and to shut down nonessential factories.[27]

But Ludendorff was given to cruder solutions. On February 16 he sent Groener another letter in which he again transmitted the complaints he had received from various industrialists about over-organization in the War Office, the failure of its members to accept responsibility, and the uncertainty of the industrialists as to where they were supposed to turn. The industrialists felt that "there is much deliberation, but too little decision and command. The deliberations absorb precious time without helping."[28] Ludendorff was rather shy about associating himself with these complaints and claimed

[26] On the meeting of Feb. 3, see Cron, *Eisenwirtschaft*, p. 35; for Ludendorff's orders of Feb. 6, 1917, see BHStA, Abt. IV, MK, K Mob 10a, Bd. I, Bl. 63a, 75-76.

[27] Memorandum of Feb. 12, 1917, BA, Nachlass Moellendorff, Nr. 51.

[28] Groener, *Lebenserinnerungen*, pp. 357-358.

that he was simply bringing them to Groener's attention. The criticism was obvious, however, and Groener was undoubtedly quite irritated. Since there was not enough coal to go around, it had to be sparingly distributed, and this required a large organization. Furthermore, "As far as the lack of commands were concerned, the complaints came from just those gentlemen who were the first to try to evade the orders of the War Office."[29]

January and February 1917 were terrible months from the standpoint of production. In February, 1,187,000 tons of steel were produced, 225,000 tons less than in August 1916 and 252,000 less than anticipated under the Hindenburg Program. Although 7,500 tons of powder were supposed to be produced at this time, only 6,400 tons production was actually achieved. This low production was one of the chief reasons for the OHL's decision to conduct a strategic retreat in the West. The object of this retreat was to shorten the German lines and give the army a good defensive position behind the strongly fortified Siegfried Line. Ludendorff could not take the offensive in the West because munitions production, as he sarcastically remarked, "belied every description." The strategic retreat to the Siegfried Line was brilliantly executed in March 1917 and was duly hailed in the press as a great military success.[30]

The munitions problem also played an important role in Ludendorff's support for unrestricted submarine warfare, which was decided upon against the Chancellor's opposition on January 9, 1917, and formally introduced on February 1. Although Ludendorff was unquestionably encouraged by the navy's promise that the measure would bring England to her knees in five months, his arguments for unrestricted submarine warfare placed less emphasis on the navy's exaggerated expectations than on the desperate position of his army in the West

[29] *Ibid.*, p. 358.

[30] Report of the Bavarian military representative at Supreme Headquarters, March 12, 1917, BHStA, Abt. IV, MK, III a XV 39. For the statistics, see *ibid.*, K Mob 6, Bd. I, Bl. 152, and Reichsarchiv, *Weltkrieg*, XII, p. 23n.

and the unreliability of Germany's allies. Thus, when Bethmann suggested that unrestricted submarine warfare might even lengthen the war, Ludendorff replied by stressing the relief it would bring to the army, which was suffering from a shortage of munitions and which had to be spared a "second Battle of the Somme."[31]

It is important to note that Ludendorff's advisers were by no means of one mind concerning the submarine question. Where Colonel Bauer and the head of the Political Section, Colonel von Bartenwerffer, were convinced that it would bring total victory, the head of the Operations Section, Major Wetzell, and the head of the Balkan Section, Lieutenant-Colonel Ritter Mertz von Quirnheim, were very skeptical. The last-named officers opposed a purely defensive strategy on land and believed that the forces in the West would have opportunities to take the offensive. In rejecting this viewpoint, Ludendorff demonstrated that his decision to press for unrestricted submarine warfare was motivated not only by an excessive confidence in Germany's chances at sea, but also by a deep and possibly unjustifiable pessimism concerning the available possibilities on land. Indeed, it is very likely that the latter consideration was paramount, as Ludendorff indicated after the war: "While [the OHL] clung to a pure defense against the mighty armaments of the enemy on land, . . . it went over to a decision-seeking attack at sea, not, to be sure, as a means of directly achieving a decision of arms, but rather of achieving a decision which initially lay in the economic realm."[32] Just as

[31] Meeting between the OHL and Bethmann at Pless, Jan. 9, 1917, in Ludendorff, *Urkunden*, p. 323. See also his letter to Max von Baden of Oct. 16, 1918, *ibid.*, p. 345.

[32] Reichsarchiv, *Weltkrieg*, XII, pp. 1-3. There can be no question about the fact that Ludendorff had desired to begin unrestricted submarine warfare at the first available opportunity and had indicated this fact almost immediately after taking office, and, needless to say, he was strongly driven in this direction by right wing political and economic interest groups. The importance of the munitions situation in bringing Ludendorff to his final decision and the conflicts within the General Staff, however, do not receive enough stress in May's *World War and American Isolation*, pp. 387ff. This aspect of the problem receives more attention in Fischer, *Griff nach der Weltmacht*, p. 382.

the Hindenburg Program was designed to make Germany catch up with the superior production of her enemies, so the even greater gamble of unrestricted submarine warfare was designed to rectify the same imbalance by crippling the enemy's economic capabilities.

After March there was a gradual increase in production. In April 8,000 tons of powder were produced and 9,200 tons were produced in July. The OHL's goal of 12,000 tons production by May was thus frustrated. Naturally, the OHL expressed continuous dissatisfaction throughout March and April, while the War Office continued the attempt to bring the OHL to reason. Koeth was at the forefront of this effort: "We [the War Office] must give the Supreme Command a clear picture that, in view of the existing transport crisis and the shortage of coal, iron, and cement resulting from it, we are not in a position to achieve the goal which we have set for ourselves."[33] The coal crisis forced the OHL to act more moderately in practice if not in theory. On May 10 Ludendorff permitted Groener to cut back factory construction and certain types of weapons production. At the same time, however, he maintained the Hindenburg Program as the ultimate goal. By now this demand was almost comic, and the War Office simply went ahead and developed a program of its own in which "the wishes of the OHL are brought into consonance with production possibilities."[34]

What was really being achieved, ironically, was the War Ministry's old program of increasing powder production in a step-by-step fashion. The essence of the Hindenburg Program had been the radical increase of production by spring, and this had not been achieved. What the Hindenburg Program had done was to drain the army of an additional million men, to trigger a major transportation crisis, and to intensify the

[33] Captain Müller's report of March 19, 1917, BHStA, Abt. IV, MK, K Mob 10a, Bd. I, Bl. 128; for the statistics, see *ibid.*, K Mob 1, Bd. I, Bl. 90, and Reichsarchiv, *Weltkrieg*, XII, p. 24.

[34] Notation of May 25, 1917, BA, Nachlass Moellendorff, Nr. 59 and Ludendorff to Groener, May 10, 1917, BA, Nachlass Bauer, Nr. 14.

nascent coal shortage. Informed contemporaries were well aware of the havoc that had been wrought. In July Groener looked back on the transport crisis of the previous winter with thankfulness because it had acted as a "natural brake" on the Hindenburg Program.[35] Most telling is a comment made by Helfferich to the Bavarian Ambassador, Count Lerchenfeld, in June 1917:

> The program was decreed by the military without examining whether or not it could be carried out. Today there are everywhere half-finished and finished factories that cannot produce because there is no coal and because there are no workers available. Coal and iron were expended for these constructions, and the result is that munitions production would be greater today if no monster program had been set up but rather production had been demanded according to the capacity of those factories already existing.[36]

3. *The Shutting Down and Consolidation of Industries*

At the time of the debates concerning the Auxiliary Service bill, both the government and the Reichstag assumed that the shutting down and consolidation of industries would be undertaken for the purpose of securing labor. This assumption was false. The major reason for the shutting down and consolidation of industries during the last two years of the war was the need to save transport and coal. It cannot be said, however, that Groener had deliberately misled the Reichstag. On December 11, 1916, he set up a Standing Committee on Consolidations (SAZ) to advise him on "the curtailing or shutting down of factories in the sense of the Auxiliary Service Law."[37] The SAZ was placed under the chairmanship of Dr. Sorge and

[35] Statement by Groener before the Württemberg Cabinet, July 30, 1917, HStASt, E, 130, V, X^a, Bd. III, Bl. 1144. For a comparison of 1917 production with the old War Ministry program, see Reichsarchiv, *Weltkrieg*, XII, pp. 24-25.

[36] Lerchenfeld to Hertling, June 15, 1917, BHStA, Abt. II, MA 1, Nr. 958.

[37] *Ibid.*, Abt. IV, MK, K Mob 11a, Bd. I, Bl. 13.

was composed of representatives of the civil and military authorities and representatives of the German Industry War Committee, the chambers of commerce, and the organizations of craftsmen. As the wording of Groener's order demonstrates, he was convinced that the work of the SAZ would be directly related to the Auxiliary Service Law.

The leading members of the KRA and WUMBA realized from the beginning that the problem was of an entirely different nature from that previously supposed. One of the results of the government's "stretching policies" was, for example, that the cotton industry was producing at 7 percent of capacity. This constituted a waste of raw materials, as the leaders of the industry themselves recognized, and they approached the KRA concerning the need to consolidate their industry. Discussions were held on December 7-9, and a consolidation agreement was made in which there were provisions for the compensation of those factories to be shut down. This compensation was to be paid from the profits of the firms permitted to continue operation, a procedure that was to be followed in the consolidation of other industries. Thus the KRA had acted before the SAZ was even established.[38]

Koeth defended his action by pointing out that consolidations would have been necessary even without the Auxiliary Service Law because of the raw materials and transport shortages. The representative of the Labor Department on the SAZ, Dr. Oppenheimer, objected to Koeth's procedure. Such hasty consolidations were certain to create unemployment. Still thinking in terms of Groener's promises to the Reichstag, Oppenheimer demanded that no consolidations be undertaken before plans for the relocation of the workers to be affected had been made. Moellendorff, siding with Koeth, explained that there was not enough time to make such plans. In his view,

[38] Oberbürgermeister Peppel, "Die Durchführung von Zusammenlegungen (Stillegungen) in der Industrie während des Krieges 1914-1918. Darstellung und Beurteilung 1. Teil." (1937), Records of Headquarters German Armed Forces, Microcopy No. T-77, Roll 343, Wi/IF 5.2184 (hereinafter cited as Peppel study).

immediate action was necessary and the unemployed workers could be used to unload railroad cars. This conflict within the War Office was reflected in the completely contradictory statement Groener made to the Reichstag committee on December 20. He told the deputies that the original intention to make an early start in the consolidation of industries could not be carried out because, for the moment, there was no labor shortage. In fact, workers in essential plants were being laid off because of the coal shortages. But Groener also stated that consolidations were necessary in order to alleviate the transportation and coal shortages.[39]

Evidently the committee did not grasp the import of Groener's words, for no one pursued the matter. In an SAZ meeting on the same day, however, the War Office's legal expert, Dr. Eugen Schiffer, gave more careful consideration to what the Reichstag committee had momentarily overlooked. Two agencies were now involved in the shutting down of plants: the SAZ and the determination committees. The SAZ was going to have to shut down plants, not only because they were not essential but also because they were unfavorably located from the standpoint of transportation or because they utilized raw materials inefficiently. Thus the SAZ could even decide to shut down plants having war contracts. The determination committees were, by law, independent juridical bodies. Strictly speaking, they could decide to keep a plant open simply because it had war contracts. The determination committees could thus be used as a means of setting aside the decisions of the SAZ. As Schiffer pointed out at an SAZ meeting on December 30, 1916:

> The Auxiliary Service Law says nothing about shut downs, etc. In this connection it has only one means at its disposal: the calling up of those liable to Auxiliary Service. Every factory can protect itself against this measure by employing

[39] Report of Dec. 18, 1916, BA, Nachlass Moellendorff, Nr. 51a, and report on the meeting of Dec. 20, BHStA, Abt. IV, MK, K Mob 11a, Bd. I, Bl. 90.

> women and youth. *It cannot protect* itself against a refusal of raw material and contracts. These measures, which lie in the hands of the War Office, will have the effect of a shut-down. Since, however, individual measures will in certain circumstances depend on the action of the committees created by the Auxiliary Service Law, different decisions are always possible.[40]

Koeth was forced to admit that this danger was very real, because "in the deliberations on the Auxiliary Service Law only the labor question was considered." A decision was made to "enlighten" the determination committees concerning the necessity of acting in collaboration with the SAZ. On January 6 a directive was sent out warning the determination committees not to pass judgments in cases of firms belonging to an industry which was being considered for consolidation, "since, in certain circumstances, even factories in the Auxiliary Service will have to be shut down if there is a superfluity of such factories."[41]

No less confusing was the related question of what rights, if any, the Reichstag committee was now to have in this area. Since the shut downs handled by the SAZ seemed to have little or nothing to do with the Auxiliary Service Law, it was possible to argue that the committee did not need to be consulted. The question was of great importance because the committee was flooded with petitions from firms which felt threatened by the SAZ. The National Liberal and Progressive Party deputies on the committee treated these petitions with great sympathy because of the economic and local interests they had been sent to the Reichstag to protect. The Social Democrats feared the unemployment that the shut downs would bring. On January 23 the representative of the Secretary of Justice to the SAZ, Dr. Trendelenburg, presented a memorandum to the SAZ which demonstrated, with unimpeachable legal logic, that the Reichstag committee had not a word to say about measures

[40] SAZ meeting, Dec. 20, 1916, BHStA, Abt. IV, MK, K Mob 8, Bd. I, Bl. 21.

[41] Directive, Jan. 6, 1917, *Ibid.*, K Mob 14, Bd. I, Bl. 66.

taken to shut down plants because of the raw materials problem. Such measures were based on the deliberations of the SAZ and the voluntary agreement of the war committee for the industry involved. They were only indirectly concerned with the labor problem and hence had nothing to do with the Auxiliary Service Law.[42]

On January 26 Groener sought, in vain, to convince the Reichstag Committee of the correctness of this argument.[43] One deputy sarcastically replied that if the determination committees had nothing to do with shut downs, "then we can quietly go home, for the shut downs are the most important consequence of the law." The committee demanded to be heard on the "great economic questions," and a resolution was passed requiring that the committee be consulted before the War Office took measures to consolidate an industry. It cannot be said that the reasoning of the committee was particularly cogent. Legien, for example, argued that "There is, to be sure, nothing in the law on consolidations, yet these are the most important aspects of the law. . . . Raw material is not available in sufficient quantities, and, as a consequence, an arbitrary distribution of this raw material is an evasion of the law." In reality, the deliberations on the bill had been conducted on a completely false basis, and the law simply did not take into account the new situation that had arisen. The important thing, from the point of view of the deputies, was that major economic interests were at stake. They were uninterested in legal arguments. Deputy Gothein warned that "if we are going to be denied . . . a voice in the most important economic questions, then we will simply let things go as they are going and refuse any responsibility." Groener could hardly ignore the threat implicit in this statement. On January 20 he told the SAZ that "one must distinguish between the juridical and practical viewpoints. With the former we will never get on with the committee, because it always has the opportunity to

42 Memorandum of Jan. 23, 1917, BA, Nachlass Moellendorff, Nr. 60.

43 For the material on and quotations from this meeting, see BHStA, Abt. IV, MK, K Mob 14, Bd. I, Bl. 103.

bring its complaints into the Plenum, where debates of a very undesirable nature would develop."[44]

Indeed, the last thing the War Office wanted was a public debate on the procedure that had recently been used to consolidate the cotton industry. The cotton industry firms represented in the German Industry War Committee were by no means representative of the entire industry. They only represented the larger firms in fact, and the arrangements they made reflected this. One can therefore well understand the anger of the Reichstag committee: "The great ones of the industry come together and don't forget about themselves; the little ones have to be put to the sword; one forgets about them."[45] Groener admitted in private that the War Committee had "hacked away"[46] in the matter of the cotton industry, and he did not appreciate the embarrassing position into which he had been thrust by the KRA's independent action. He ordered new negotiations to take place in which all the interested parties received ample representation. At the same time he demanded that a procedure be developed which was less open to criticism. By late February such a procedure had been devised. Any civil or military agency or any industrial group could propose a consolidation. All such proposals were to be sent to the chairman of the SAZ. After examining them, the SAZ would pass them on to Groener, who was to give written approval for the introduction of negotiations within the industry concerned. The German Industry War Committee, with the possible inclusion of representatives of other industrialist organizations, would then draw up the agreement. The SAZ was to evaluate these proposals and then submit them to Groener for final approval. Needless to say, this was a rather long procedure.[47]

Yet little else could be done if fairness was sought in a

[44] SAZ meeting, Jan. 30, 1917, *ibid.*, K Mob 8, Bd. I, Bl. 37.

[45] Reichstag committee meeting, Feb. 9, 1917, *ibid.*, K Mob 14, Bd. I, Bl. 161.

[46] SAZ meeting, Jan. 30, 1917, *ibid.*, K Mob 8, Bd. I, Bl. 37.

[47] Directive of Feb. 21, 1917, *ibid.*, Bl. 59, zu 59.

situation in which so many interests were at stake. Moellendorff felt that the root of the problem lay in the absence of any organ which truly represented the various economic interests. The German Industry War Committee, which represented only the two largest industrialist groups, was insufficient. He thus hearkened back to an old idea of Bismarck's and wanted to establish a "people's economic council" in which all interests would receive equal representation. Such a council, Moellendorff argued, would settle economic questions on a fair basis and would be far less particularistic than the Reichstag. He recommended that the wartime situation be used to create such a body, which would then continue to function in peacetime. Moellendorff's idea was strongly seconded by the right wing Social Democrat, Dr. August Müller, who represented the War Food Office on the SAZ. Using rather strange language for a Social Democrat, Müller remarked: "In my view, it is of the greatest importance for the future of the German Fatherland that such matters not be settled in a parliamentary fashion. It is understandable that every member of the Reichstag represents the interests of his district; 397 electoral districts therefore come into competition. It is therefore necessary that Parliament be excluded from such decisions."[48]

Moellendorff submitted concrete proposals to the SAZ on February 10. He suggested that a "high economic war council" be established. It would contain five representatives each from industry, trade, agriculture, the craftsmen, and the workers. In this way the organization of the interest groups with which the state had to deal would be more unified and simplified. Groener and the SAZ showed considerable enthusiasm for Moellendorff's idea, but the government tabled the whole question. Quite aside from the practical problems involved in the sudden reorganization of the economic interests and the satisfactory adjustment of their differences which would have been required by the proposal, the government was undoubtedly fearful of challenging the Reichstag and, quite possibly,

[48] SAZ meeting, Jan. 30, 1917, *ibid.*, Bl. 37.

unwilling to let the control of socioeconomic affairs slide even further outside of its grasp. The whole episode, however, is another interesting illustration of Moellendorff's effort to use the war and the army's control of the war economy to implement his corporatist programs.[49]

The SAZ, although it played an important role in the consolidation of various branches of the textile industry and certain luxury industries, was not a very successful organization. To be sure, this was not completely the SAZ's fault. As Sichler pointed out, its efforts were continuously being sabotaged by the procurement agencies. Thus when the SAZ hoped to shut down 120 firms out of 240 in a particular industry by the end of March, it suddenly was presented with the horrendous report that the procurement agencies could not do without the production of the firms scheduled to shut down until the summer, and that they would require production from 150 of the industry's firms for an indefinite period of time. Much worse, however, was the way in which the owners of firms scheduled to be shut down managed to take advantage of the disunity and lack of coordination among the procurement agencies. If one procurement agency cut off their contracts, they proceeded to secure contracts from another. Once they had a new contract, they could prove to the determination committees that their firms were important to the war effort. The determination committees, despite the injunctions of the War Office, usually decided in favor of the firms. Similarly, the procurement agencies could then be counted upon to support the firms in their demands for coal and labor.[50]

An equally important defect, however, and one for which the SAZ was more directly responsible, was the great uncertainty as to the principles upon which their actions were to

[49] SAZ meeting, Feb. 23, 1917, and Moellendorff memorandum of Feb. 10, *ibid.*, K Mob 14, Bd. II, Bl. 144, zu 144a. See also Peppel study.

[50] For Sichler's report of March 24, 1917, see BA, Nachlass Moellendorff, Nr. 60. Groener described the situation in an angry directive to the War Office bureaus of July 18, BHStA, Abt. IV, MK, K Mob 8, Bd. I, Bl. 122.

be based. Moellendorff was one of the most influential members of the SAZ and, as an "idea man" with an axe to grind, he was always attempting to use the war emergency as a means of realizing his long-range programs. Many other members of the SAZ also had the postwar period in mind when making decisions. They thought of shutdowns and consolidations as a means of rationalizing the German economy and thus improving Germany's competitive position on the world markets. Koeth was completely opposed to this tendency: "War economy does not mean to run the economy in wartime in such a way as to create the least economic damage. War economy means much more to run it in such a way that one wins the war."[51]

A decision to carry out the shutting down and consolidation of industries on pure war economy principles seemed unavoidable once the permanent nature of the coal shortage became evident. One of the most important practical results of the coal crisis was a gradual replacement of the SAZ by the Coal Commissar. To be sure, the Coal Commissar did not have the right to shut down factories, but his right to deny a firm its coal supply was tantamount to the same thing. The actions taken by the Coal Commissar, however, did not have the planned and organized character of those taken by the SAZ, and this produced considerable friction between the two agencies. By the early summer of 1917 the shutting down and consolidation of industries, like the distribution of coal, presented a very disorderly picture.[52]

This disorder served to intensify the panic that was developing over the anticipated shortage of 25 to 30 percent of the coal Germany required. It coincided with a great shortage of reserves for the army. It became clear that not only nonessential, but also essential factories would have to be shut down if the civil population and the railroads were to be properly supplied with coal during the coming winter. In Groener's view, the time had come for a "Concentration of

[51] Peppel study. [52] *Ibid.*

Forces." This was the slogan of the summer of 1917, and what it meant was an abandonment of all long-term social and economic considerations to the necessities of war. It was, above all, an attack on the claims of the non-Prussian states to equitable treatment in the assignment of war contracts and to special consideration in the shutting down of nonessential plants. Groener expressed the new principle in very blunt language: "It would be desirable to do everything equitably. That is not possible. It is false to hold blindly to the principle of equity. It would be extraordinarily desirable to have the individual federal states called upon to perform and profit in accordance with their resources, abilities, and other special conditions. But that is not always in conformity with the Concentration of Forces."[53]

The federal states, as can well be imagined, feared the new policy, a fear intensified by the sudden and arbitrary withdrawal of contracts from some of their industries. The Bavarian government felt that the new policy would set back Bavaria's industrial development fifty years. Throughout late July and early August, Groener and Sorge traveled from ministry to ministry in South Germany in an attempt to secure agreement to the Concentration of Forces. This did not prove easy. The South German cabinets regarded the Concentration of Forces as an expression of Stinnes' desire to concentrate German industry in Prussia. Groener and Sorge returned to Berlin convinced that they could accomplish more by cooperating with the South German states and paying some heed to their interests than by ruthlessly neglecting them.[54]

Groener was removed from office at a time when the prob-

[53] Statement at a meeting of July 20, 1917, with the heads of the procurement agencies, *ibid.*

[54] For Groener's meeting with the Württemberg Cabinet on July 30, 1917, see HStASt, E, 130, V, X^{a}, Bd. III, Bl. 1144; for Bavaria's objections, see BHStA, Abt. IV, MK, K Mob 13, Bd. III. After returning from South Germany, Groener ordered the War Office Bureaus to consult with the states before taking any action to shut down plants, see the report of the Bavarian representative to WUMBA, Major Weigel, Sept. 4, 1917, BHStA, Abt. IV, MK, K Mob 8, Bd. I, Bl. 36.

lem was still very much unclarified. Everyone agreed that the SAZ had failed, but no one was sure as to what was supposed to take its place. In practical terms, however, the new combination of the KRA and the Coal Commissar was proving increasingly decisive in the shutting down of plants. As has been noted earlier in this chapter, the procurement agencies were denied access to the Coal Commissar in August. The control of the coal supply was now completely concentrated in the hands of the KRA and the Coal Commissar and, with it, albeit unofficially, the power to shut down plants. For the moment, therefore, Koeth's principles of war economy seemed to be triumphant.

4. The War Office and the Food Problem

During the winter of 1916-1917, the German people ate turnips instead of potatoes. The food problem was at its worst, and the high hopes once placed in the KEA had evaporated. The OHL from the very beginning recognized the dire necessity of adequately feeding the industrial workers. On this issue the army, industrialists, and unions were in agreement. The first OHL intervention in the food problem took place on September 27, 1916, when Hindenburg sent a letter to Bethmann emphasizing the necessity of properly feeding the workers. Hindenburg was particularly critical of the failure of the local authorities, the peasants, and the agrarian leaders to understand how important this was, and he laid great stress on the need for voluntary cooperation:

> The task of agriculture is not only to be seen in the continuous increase of production, but also in the greatest possible *voluntary* surrender of its products, particularly fats, to the consumers. Experience has shown that little will be accomplished by state compulsion, but I can count on success from a large-scale, organized propaganda by the agrarian leaders in favor of the feeding of the industrial workers.[55]

[55] DZA Potsdam, Kriegsakten 1, Bd. 9, Bl. 54.

However well-intentioned these words, their initial effect was most unfortunate. To begin the propaganda campaign, Bethmann published the Hindenburg letter, but the agrarian leaders proceeded to interpret the letter as an attack upon the compulsory system. Batocki, whose efforts were being sabotaged by the passive resistance of the farmers, was quite alarmed. He feared that the peasants and farmers would now use Hindenburg's words as a justification for their violations of the KEA's orders. To prevent this, an "interview" with the Field Marshal was arranged. In this interview Hindenburg expressed his "astonishment" at the misinterpretation of his letter and defended the use of compulsion as a last resort.[56]

What the public really wanted from the army, however, was deeds. Great things were expected of the War Office, and the War Office did, indeed, make a valuable contribution to the mitigation of the food problem. The interesting thing, however, is that this contribution was not made in the areas of distribution and prices, but rather in the area of production. In fact, the War Office's intervention in food questions was most successful where it did not involve interference in matters already being regulated by the KEA. Batocki wanted help from the War Office. The officials in the agricultural districts were horribly overworked. Many had actually died from the strain. Their tasks were twofold. First, they were responsible for carrying out the KEA's orders concerning the sequestration and distribution of food. Second, they were responsible for the promotion of agricultural production in their districts. Batocki did not want independent military intervention in matters of sequestration and distribution because this would lead to a duplication of the KEA's work. He and Schorlemer did want War Office help in the procurement of labor, horses, and machinery. The army already controlled these essential elements

[56] Batocki to Bethmann, Nov. 16, 1916; Helfferich to Bethmann, Nov. 19, 1916; Hindenburg to Bethmann, Nov. 19, 1916, *ibid.*, Bd. 10, Bl. 110-113, 117-118, 120-121. Interestingly enough, it was Director von Braun of the KEA who had solicited Hindenburg's intervention, Lerchenfeld to Hertling, Oct. 17 and 22, 1916, BHStA, Abt. II, MA 1, Nr. 958.

A Magic Trick

eemed Public. You see here a pig. ase, come closer so that you may con-ce yourselves that it is a true living .

Now I place a simple box over it, made of cardboard, with no double bottom, with no gimmicks; please, see for yourselves.

w, I write a magic formula on the :, tap on it with my magic wand,

lift the box—the pig has disappeared!

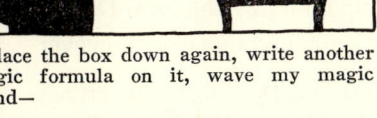

lace the box down again, write another gic formula on it, wave my magic nd—

and the pig is there again!

st Magic Formula: Maximum price 1.80 rks per pound

Second Magic Formula: Maximum price 6.50 marks per pound

of agricultural production and, if it would now help to organize their use during the planting and harvest seasons, production would improve, and at the same time the work load of the local officials would be cut down.[57]

On December 22 Groener responded to Batocki's request by proposing the establishment of war economy bureaus (*Kriegswirtschaftsämter*) in each of the army corps districts and war economy agencies (*Kriegswirtschaftsstellen*) in the district of each prefect (*Landrat*). The chief task of these institutions would be to organize the procurement of men, horses, machinery, and artificial fertilizer for the farmers in their districts. The war economy agencies were to be subordinate to the war economy bureaus and, under Groener's plan, both institutions were to be directed by military chairmen and staffed by local officials and prominent farmers. The officers in charge of the bureaus and agencies would have direct access to the Deputy Commanding Generals and thus be capable of getting speedy action on their requests for labor.

Batocki was not completely satisfied with Groener's scheme. The army corps districts did not coincide geographically with the provinces, and he did not want the provincial authorities brushed aside. He felt also that the local prefects, who bore the ultimate responsibility for production in their districts, had to have a decisive voice in the operation of the war economy agencies. Lastly, the distribution of fertilizer was being handled by the KEA, and Batocki did not want the War Office to become involved in this matter. Groener was willing to revise his proposal in accordance with the changes suggested by Batocki. Thus, war economy bureaus were set up in each province instead of in each army corps district. They were placed under military chairmen appointed by the local Deputy Commanding Generals. The war economy agencies, however,

[57] Batocki to the Federated Governments, Dec. 19, 1916, PrGStA, Rep B 30 I, Bd. 34. For further correspondence and discussion concerning this problem, see the Prussian Cabinet meeting, Jan. 3, 1917, BA, P 135/1784, Bl. 105.

were placed under the chairmanship of the prefects. Groener also agreed not to interfere in the fertilizer question. The new institutions, which were formally established on January 8, 1917, worked well. The war economy agencies ascertained the needs of the farmers in their districts before each planting or harvest and reported them to the Deputy Commanding Generals, who in turn would provide the necessary manpower, horses, and machinery. When the need for manpower was particularly pressing, troops would be exempted or put on leave, and special commandos composed of garrison troops would be sent into the countryside. The bureaus and agencies directed the allocation and utilization of these productive resources.

Groener was on very good terms with Batocki, and he stoutly resisted demands from both the producers and the consumers that he participate in the regulation of distribution and prices. The agrarian leaders wanted Groener to intervene in price questions, but he refused. He was equally negative in responding to union demands that the War Office replace the civil authorities in the management of the food supply and reminded them that "his office is so overburdened that it would be unthinkable to add the carrying out of the food regulations to its duties."[58] Groener could not evade all involvement in problems of sequestration and distribution, however. The farmers did not always tell the truth when asked to declare their stores. Indeed, they lied so much in the early spring of 1917 that Batocki had to ask for military help to conduct searches for hidden food stores. Also, under the order establishing the War Office, it was made responsible for the supply of special meat and fat premiums to "hard working" and "hardest working" industrial laborers. Here the intervention of the War Office was not very salutary. The actual decision as to who was to get these premiums lay in the hands of the War Office bureaus. Unhappily, they did not coordinate their policies. As a result the categories of workers

[58] Reported in *Correspondenzblatt,* March 24, 1917. See also his remarks at a meeting with the agrarian leaders on Feb. 28, HStASt, E, 130, V, X^{a}.1, Bd. II, Bl. 473.

entitled to premiums varied from district to district, as did the size of the premiums. This produced unrest among the workers and irritation on the part of the civil authorities.[59]

After mid-February, the conflict between the War Office and the civil authorities concerning food premiums was transformed into a conflict of a more fundamental nature. The quarrel was precipitated by the appointment of Undersecretary Michaelis as Prussian Food Commissar. One of the chief causes of the disorderly management of the food supply was the confusion in the Prussian administration. The ministries of Commerce, Finance, Agriculture, and Interior were all involved. The worst problem, however, was that Schorlemer undermined the efforts of the other ministers to force the farmers and prefects to conform to the KEA's regulations. Batocki's solution was to turn the KEA into an Imperial food office and place an Imperial State Secretary at its head who, at one and the same time, would control the food supply for the entire Empire and be able to command the local Prussian officials. The Prussian Cabinet, however, was not yet prepared to accept complete centralization. The Cabinet was also unwilling to establish a special Prussian Food Office on the model of the KEA because this might be interpreted as an "expression of Prussian particularism."[60] Michaelis proposed a compromise solution under which the Cabinet would appoint a Commissar to manage the Prussian food supply and issue orders to the officials in its name. If any of the ministers disagreed with his actions, they could appeal to the entire Cabinet. In making this proposal, Michaelis was quite frank about his desire to place the Agricultural Minister in a secondary position. In his view, it was high time that the "one-sided" defense of agrarian interests ended and that the enforcement of the KEA's measures "be placed in the *hands of one agency*, which, *unhindered*

[59] Batocki to Groener, March 21, 1917, MF, Marine Archiv, Nr. 4682, Bd. I; on the food premium problem, see the continuous series of complaints made by the civil officials in charge of the Ruhr food supply, StADü, Reg. Düsseldorf, N. 15073.

[60] Loebell to Bethmann, Feb. 1, 1917, BA, P 135/1784, Bl. 179.

by political considerations, is in the position to act wholly from the standpoint of the necessities of war."[61] Despite Schorlemer's loud objections, Michaelis' proposal was accepted, and he was appointed Commissar.

Michaelis now had virtually complete control over the Prussian civil agencies participating in the management of the food problem. Next he sought control over the military agencies as well. He went directly to Ludendorff and asked that the War Office make him its deputy in all food questions. In this way he would have more direct influence over the Deputy Commanding Generals, the War Office bureaus, and the war economy bureaus. Also, he would have some influence over the military authorities in the non-Prussian states. Although Ludendorff was inclined to support Michaelis' idea, Groener refused to give Michaelis such a powerful position within the War Office. He assured Michaelis that he was aware of the absolute necessity of close collaboration between the Commissariat and the War Office. To promote this, Groener appointed a special liaison officer to speed up communication between himself and Michaelis, and he promised to collaborate with Michaelis in the issuance of orders to the military authorities.[62]

Despite this expression of good will, Michaelis remained dissatisfied. He was particularly intent upon putting an end to the purchase of food on the black market by industrial firms. Some Deputy Commanding Generals banned such practices, while others did not. When they did forbid use of the black market, they did so in different ways and confusion arose from the multiplicity of orders. Michaelis demanded a "unified action on the part of *all* the Deputy Commanding Generals."[63]

[61] Memorandum by Schorlemer of Feb. 1917, *ibid.*, Bl. 149-157. See also Michaelis, *Staat und Volk*, pp. 290-291, and Skalweit, *Kriegsernährungswirtschaft*, pp. 184-187.

[62] Ludendorff to Groener, Feb. 16, 1917, Groener, *Lebenserinnerungen*, p. 359, and Groener to Michaelis, Feb. 19, 1917, BHStA, Abt. IV, MK, K Mob 6, Bd. I, Bl. 172.

[63] Quoted in War Office directive, April 17, 1917, MF, Marine Archiv,

In his view, no special local conditions justified use of the black market. Despite the fact that the War Office officially supported Michaelis' view, many Deputy Commanding Generals continued their lack of cooperation. Michaelis was also particularly critical of the way the War Office bureaus managed the distribution of food premiums for industrial workers. The root of both the black market and the food premium problems lay in the willingness of the military authorities to use any means to pacify the workers. The complaint of the Government President in Münster, Count von Merveldt, exemplified the difficulties that were thus being created for the civil authorities:

> It is very much to be regretted that the equal provision of food for the industrial population, toward which I and the responsible agencies have been striving, is being continuously disturbed by the way in which individual firms and mines get food in an underhand manner and distribute it to their workers. . . . Unfortunately, the attitude of certain factories is presently even receiving official support through the so-called Evaluation Bureau in Düsseldorf, which, apparently at the behest of the War Office, gives food to certain needy factories without first consulting the responsible agencies.[64]

Michaelis could not neglect such reports, and they necessarily made him even more critical of the War Office's role in the food problem. In this respect, there is much to be said for his viewpoint. As the chief opponent of Schorlemer, he can hardly be accused of disregarding the needs of the industrial workers. Throughout the war, Michaelis had fought for administrative unity in the management of the food supply. The War Office was doing fine work in the promotion of agricultural production, but its work in the area of food distribution, along with

Nr. 4682/III/15/24a, Bd. I. On July 13 Groener had to send out yet another directive to the Deputy Commanding Generals on this subject, BHStA, Abt. IV, MK, I Mob 4c, Bl. 80.

[64] Merveldt to General von Gayl, April 25, 1917, StAMü, Reg. Mü., Bd. 1307 I.

that of the Deputy Commanding Generals, was only serving to intensify the confusion.

5. *Organizational Problems and Competing Bureaucracies*

The examination of the War Office's role in the transportation, coal, and food problems has demonstrated that the War Office, however helpful its activities may have been in certain instances, contributed to the organizational confusion that already existed. This was to be expected. It would have been a miracle if the sudden establishment of so massive an organization in the midst of war did not cause difficulties. The older members of the War Ministry were not happy with the War Office. General von Wrisberg felt that the entire apparatus was too enormous, and he did not think it was necessary. In his view a new department for economic planning would have sufficed. Koeth was extremely critical of the War Office:

> Hastily built up under the pressure of events and by people who had previously little or no concern with the problems, . . . the War Office is a structure composed of very heterogeneous elements. To an organization which properly contains those elements which have to organize raw materials and manpower matters, one has added . . . great and hastily organized procurement agencies which, however, by no means encompass all the procurement in the area of weapons and munitions. To this was added a Technical Staff which has many parallel duties with the above mentioned three agencies.[65]

The coexistence of staffs and departments within the War Office was the subject of universal complaint. The members of the staffs were very energetic individuals, and in many cases Groener preferred to listen to them rather than to the department heads. The latter, however, unlike the members of the staffs, were directly responsible for the success of the War Office's work. Unbelievable confusion was created when both

[65] Meeting of May 5, 1917, BA, Nachlass Mentzel, Nr. 6.

the Chiefs of Staff and the department heads sent out directives on the same subjects without prior consultation. At one point the flood of directives issued by the War Office became so great that Groener had to ban the sending of all but the most important directives for a period of two weeks. Koeth was unquestionably correct when he remarked that "one cannot organize an administrative authority like a regiment."[66]

Groener was a man of great rectitude and moral courage, and he was relatively free of personal ambition. Unhappily, however, he was so blinded by his desire to rectify the "omissions" of the past and had so great a distaste for the bureaucratism of the civil authorities and the War Ministry that he neglected the principles of sound administration and created a bureaucracy of his own. Groener sought to "inoculate" his subordinates with the principle, "don't write too much, don't talk too much, but deal practically and risk a mistake rather than procrastinate."[67] This was a dangerous principle to carry into the overorganized German administrative apparatus. Furthermore, Groener was so intent upon using the War Office to correct the deficiencies of the previously established military and civilian agencies that he turned it into an administrative monstrosity and thus contributed to the overorganization. Moellendorff, who was an ardent supporter of military intervention in civil affairs, had to confess that the organization of the War Office left much to be desired: "At the beginning of the war, no authority was more careful about the establishment of new agencies than the army. . . . Today the army goes beyond even the Imperial offices in that the growth of its organization stands in laughable disproportion to the results."[68]

[66] Meeting of June 14, 1917, *ibid.* On the conflict between staffs and departments, see Spiero, *Schicksal*, p. 269, and Sichler and Tiburtius, *Arbeiterfrage*, p. 41. For the ban on directives, see BHStA, Abt. IV, MK, K Mob 6, Bd. I, Bl. 152.

[67] Groener at meeting on Feb. 18, 1917, HStASt, E, 130, V, X^a.1, Bd. II, Bl. 473.

[68] "Mentekel für heutige Militärführung," March 1, 1917, BA, Nachlass Moellendorff, Nr. 8.

It is very ironic that Michaelis felt entitled to accuse the great antibureaucrat, Groener, of having become "too bureaucratic of late."[69]

Groener had always disliked the Law of Siege and the power it gave to the Deputy Commanding Generals. He was thus particularly anxious to make the War Office bureaus as powerful and as independent as possible. One could not get rid of the Deputy Commanding Generals, however, and the effort to clarify the relations between the generals and the War Office bureaus produced a very unaesthetic administrative ballet.

When first established in December 1916, the War Office bureaus were instructed to report on economic conditions in their districts and to transmit the War Office's directives to the factories and Deputy Commanding Generals. Strictly speaking, all executive authority continued to reside in the Deputy Commanding Generals. Yet the War Office bureaus were not placed under the Deputy Commanding Generals, but rather "attached" to them. The chairmen of the bureaus received their orders from the War Office, and the officers serving in the bureaus, who were usually taken from the staffs of the Deputy Commanding Generals, now received their orders from the chairmen. The Deputy Commanding Generals, therefore, were now placed in the anomalous position of having the "power of command" in their districts but not having command over the War Office bureaus. Even more confusing, however, was the fact that the War Office bureaus, although officially having no executive functions, were assigned the tasks of procuring labor for industry and watching over industrial production. Did this mean that the Deputy Commanding Generals no longer had executive authority in all matters of exemptions and local production, or did it simply mean that the War Office bureaus were to assist and advise them concerning these matters? No one seemed to know.[70]

[69] Report of Kraft von Delmensingen, Bavarian representative at the headquarters of Crown Prince Rupprecht, on a discussion with Michaelis, Sept. 4, 1917, BHStA, Abt. II, MA 1, Nr. 945.

[70] For Groener's dislike of the Law of Siege, see his *Lebenserin-*

By January 1917 there was veritable chaos. The War Office departments, when sending out directives, simply evaded making any statement as to who was to implement them. General von Stein and General Groener were fighting over the problem, and, until they made up their minds, it is difficult to see what else the department heads could have done. Stein, like his predecessor, Wild von Hohenborn, objected to Groener's efforts to limit the authority of the Deputy Commanding Generals. Stein objected all the more, however, because he had been made Commander of the Home Army and was thus in charge of the Deputy Commanding Generals. He was unhappy about sharing this authority with Groener and was particularly adamant when it came to defending the prerogatives of his subordinates. Furthermore, although reserves and exemptions were handled by the Labor Department of the War Office, the function of organizing new military formations belonged to the General War Department of the War Ministry. The latter needed the cooperation of the Deputy Commanding Generals in the fulfillment of its task, and it opposed any diminution of their ultimate authority in manpower questions. The conflict between the Deputy Commanding Generals and the War Office bureaus was thus a reflection of the conflict between the War Ministry and the War Office.[71]

Finally, Groener and Stein reached a compromise. With much regret, Groener agreed to give the Deputy Commanding Generals the ultimate right to decide on all exemptions. The functions of the War Office bureaus in this area were limited to receiving exemption requests, rendering an opinion as to whether they were justified, and carrying out the final decisions of the Deputy Commanding Generals. Also, on February 9

---

nerungen, pp. 353-354. For the directive on the War Office bureaus, see *Mitteilungen des Kriegsamts*, Dec. 20, 1916.

[71] Report of Captain Müller, Feb. 1, 1917, BHStA, Abt. IV, MK, K Mob 14, Bd. I, Bl. 155. Wild von Hohenborn found the reports of the conflict between Stein and Groener "very droll." See his letter to his wife of Jan. 3, 1917, BA, Nachlass Wild von Hohenborn, Nr. 4.

Groener placed the bureaus under the authority of the Deputy Commanding Generals, and the officers serving in the bureaus were now subject to the disciplinary authority of the Deputy Commanding Generals. The bureaus continued to be organs of the War Office in all matters pertaining to the Auxiliary Service Law, the care and training of female labor, the surveillance of production, and the representation of the War Office in matters of transportation and coal supply. In matters of raw materials, exemptions, imports and exports, and food supply, they were to act as organs of the Deputy Commanding Generals. This was an extraordinarily puzzling arrangement, for the bureaus were now organs of both the Deputy Commanding Generals and the War Office. It would have made some sense if the Deputy Commanding Generals were uninvolved in those activities in which the bureaus served as organs of the War Office and if the War Office were uninvolved in those activities in which the bureaus served as organs of the Deputy Commanding Generals. But in reality the Deputy Commanding Generals and the War Office were involved in both types of activity, and the new regulation would have been no less unclear if it had been sent out in the form of a riddle.[72]

Despite the fact that the order of February 9 indicated an increased subordination of the War Office bureaus to the Deputy Commanding Generals, Groener insisted on interpreting the order as an effort to transform the bureaus into organs "capable of positive and practical collaboration."[73] He had a hard time convincing his department heads of the importance of the War Office bureaus, however. WUMBA and the KRA tended to neglect them and to deal directly with local firms and civil agencies. Groener demanded that the bureaus be treated as the representatives of the War Office and that they be consulted, kept informed, and utilized. In April he

[72] For the directive of Feb. 9, 1917, see BHStA, Abt. IV, MK, K Mob 6, Bd. II, Bl. zu 10. See also Captain Müller's report of Jan. 16, *ibid.*, K Mob 14, Bd. I, Bl. 101.

[73] *Ibid.*, K Mob 6, Bd. II, Bl. zu 10.

angrily warned his subordinates that the continued neglect of the bureaus "must damage the position of the War Office . . . in the eyes of industry."[74] Two months after making this demand, however, Groener had to reiterate it. At the same time the functions of the Deputy Commanding Generals and the War Office bureaus continued to be confused. On July 5 Groener had to order his subordinates "to check exactly whether a directive is to be sent to the Deputy Commanding General or to the War Office bureau."[75] In a final excursion into the realm of administrative metaphysics, he once again "clarified" the relationship between the Deputy Commanding Generals and the bureaus in a directive of July 6. The bureaus were now to be regarded as "organs of the War Ministry (War Office) for work on the war economy problems in the territories of the Deputy Commanding Generals."[76] In all other respects, however, this directive was a repetition of the directive of February 9.

Duplication of labor could hardly be avoided under such conditions. Industry was plagued by similar statistical surveys emanating from the War Office in Berlin, the War Office bureaus, and the Deputy Commanding Generals. At one moment, the War Office bureaus would act arbitrarily concerning raw material and coal supply problems; at another the bureaus would suddenly be cast aside, and the Deputy Commanding Generals would take it upon themselves to regulate these questions. Even the General Government in Belgium was subjected to an organizational nightmare. Despite the fact that the General Government had developed its own economic organization and that this organization had functioned fairly well, Groener insisted upon setting up a War Office bureau in Brussels. Originally it was supposed to serve as an information agency without executive power, but in hardly any time at all it began to encroach upon the powers of the General

[74] Directive of April 26, 1917, *ibid.*, Bl. 38a.
[75] Notation of July 5, 1917, BA, Nachlass Moellendorff, Nr. 59.
[76] Directive of July 6, 1917, BHStA, Abt. IV, MK, 11b, Bd. 6.

Government. The results were competency quarrels, duplication of work, and a fruitless expenditure of time. Little wonder that Koeth yearned for the return of General von Wandel![77]

Groener also ran into difficulties with the civil authorities. His relations with Helfferich were never pleasant, and they became worse. Groener's effort to set up special agencies to manage the production of chemical fertilizer and to fight plant diseases led to a vitriolic exchange between the two men. The civil authorities had already established such agencies, and Helfferich regarded the establishment of parallel agencies as a waste of time and effort. He warned Groener that he would "speak out decisively against every new organization for which there is no compelling necessity." Groener replied by asking Helfferich not to subject "the desire of the War Office for fresh and decisive action" to "the most painful consideration of every authority that is even slightly involved." The conclusion of a note sent by Helfferich to Groener on April 11, 1917, illustrates the complete deadlock between the two men:

> If Your Excellency concludes by generally pointing out that you, as Chief of the War Office, must reserve the right to take those measures which you consider necessary for the fulfillment of those tasks for which His Majesty the Emperor has made you responsible, then let me permit myself to emphasize, in reply, that I, on my side, must reserve the right, on the basis of the position given to me by His Majesty as Chief of the Imperial Office of the Interior, to set forth those viewpoints which, in protection of the economic interests placed in my charge, I feel obligated to see given consideration.[78]

[77] Directive of March 25, 1917, *ibid.*, K Mob 8, Bd. I, Bl. zu 129; directive of March 17, *ibid.*, K Mob 6, Bd. I, Bl. 223; notation of March 1, BA, Nachlass Moellendorff, Nr. 59; undated memorandum of the General Government of Belgium, HStASt, E, 130, V, X^{a}.1, Bd. II, Bl. 496; Rathenau, *Briefe*, I, p. 267.

[78] Helfferich to Groener, March 1 and April 11, 1917, BA, P 135/1784, Bl. 168-169.

Helfferich's hostility to the War Office is quite understandable given the fact that the economic functions of the War Office represented an incursion into realms formerly managed by the Interior Office. Undoubtedly, his irritation would have been lessened if the OHL was not also trying his patience to the limit. On April 3, 1917, the OHL sent a letter to the Chancellor making it clear that the General Staff did not want the Interior Office to reassert its position even after the war was over. In the OHL's view, the demobilization and the transitional period following the war (*Übergangswirtschaft*) would require strong state control of the economy. The release of men from the army and the war industry had to be organized in such a way as to avoid unemployment and promote the revival of the damaged sectors of the economy. This, according to the OHL, was the only way in which Germany could regain her position on the world market and achieve greater autonomy in agricultural production. The allocation of raw materials and manpower would have to be controlled, and it would be necessary to continue restrictions on the free movement of labor. At the same time, the possibility of a renewal of the war always had to be taken into account, and it would thus be necessary to keep the needs of the war economy in mind during the demobilization. Unified leadership would be necessary, and in the opinion of the OHL no agency had more experience with manpower and raw materials allocation than the War Office. It would be a mistake to place "leadership in the hands of a new authority, which must first gather together all previous experience and then have to find a new means of its own." The OHL proposed, therefore, that the War Office be placed in charge of the demobilization and transitional economy in order to insure unified direction and mitigate "political and parliamentary as well as social hindrances."[79]

The reaction of Bethmann and Helfferich to this letter can well be imagined. On April 17 Bethmann turned down the

[79] Hindenburg to Bethmann, April 3, 1917, DZA Potsdam, Kriegsakten 1, Bd. 11, Bl. 129-132.

OHL's proposal. He pointed out that it was unconstitutional and that the War Office had no experience whatever in the management of a peacetime economy. He assured the OHL that Helfferich would work closely with the army on the military aspects of the demobilization.[80] The OHL, however, persisted, and its second letter of May 5 was most revealing of its true intentions. What was really wanted was the subordination of the entire economy to the preparations for a future war:

> We will, in the future *peacetime period*, have to give a *military* agency the task of preparing the economic mobilization. . . . Only the . . . War Office has a general view of all these areas. If the War Office is therefore the only agency which can lead a future economic mobilization, then it must also direct the economic demobilization, for the latter, in each of its phases, bears the imprint of the future mobilization.
>
> A future enemy must never again find us in the state of economic unpreparedness we were in at the beginning of this war.[81]

Since the Interior Office was not directly concerned with the armaments industry, it was not, according to the OHL, capable of directing the postwar economy. At most it could only serve as a subsidiary agency. On June 6 Bethmann, in a reply actually penned by Helfferich, firmly refused to consider the OHL's proposal. The social and economic problems of a normal peacetime economy would have to be made paramount in the postwar period, and the Interior Office could not possibly give them their due if it were relegated to a completely secondary position.[82]

Helfferich's passionate resistance to the War Office's interference in matters as minor as the production of chemical fertilizer and the prevention of plant diseases may thus be regarded as a reflection of his fear that the War Office would

80 Bethmann to Hindenburg, April 17, 1917, *ibid.*, Bl. 149-151a.

81 Hindenburg to Bethmann, May 5, 1917, *ibid.*, Bl. 203-204.

82 Helfferich to Bethmann, May 24, 1917, *ibid.*, Bl. 219 and Bethmann to Helfferich, June 6, 1917, *ibid.*, Bl. 250.

eventually interfere in all questions for an unrestricted period of time. This is not to say that Groener completely shared the militaristic fantasies of Ludendorff and Bauer. Groener certainly expected the War Office to become a permanent institution charged with the preparation of future mobilizations. He also expected it to play an important part in the demobilization, but he understood that it would not be needed to direct the economy once "we have finally succeeded in returning to an actual peacetime economy."[83] Yet Groener, by constantly attacking the War Ministry and the civil authorities, demonstrated that he shared the OHL's belief that the old administrative agencies had to be made subordinate in wartime. On the one hand, he complained that the OHL was always interfering with his work and demanding reorganization. On the other, he continuously reshuffled bureaus and agencies and interfered in other spheres of authority. Like Moellendorff, he believed that only the army could straighten things out and at the same time was forced to admit the defects of the military apparatus. In becoming an administrator, he unwittingly became a bureaucrat. The trouble with the War Office was not, as Groener thought, that it was a part of the War Ministry. The real problem was that it was a completely alien body suddenly imposed upon a network of administrative agencies incapable of assimilating it.

[83] Report of Captain Müller, Jan. 1, 1917, BHStA, Abt. IV, MK, Bd. I, Bl. 101.

VI

The War Office and the Social Problem
1. The Failure of the Auxiliary Service Law and the First Major Strikes

1. The Labor Problem

THE manpower shortage was Germany's most serious problem during the First World War. The Hindenburg Program, which was designed to compensate for Germany's inferiority in manpower by creating superiority in the weapons of war, could be no more than a partial solution. The OHL was aware of this fact. The decision to surrender large numbers of skilled workers and to abstain from drafting large numbers of others was made under the assumption that these workers would eventually be sent to the front. The OHL counted upon the Auxiliary Service Law to provide substitutes for the exempted workers and assumed that the industrialists would do their share to relieve the army's manpower by training and utilizing other types of labor.

In the winter of 1916-1917 the OHL released 125,000 skilled workers from the front. The industrialists noted with pleasure that the battle against the War Ministry had been won and that their wishes had been "substantially fulfilled." Once started, however, the demand for exemptions never seemed to stop. From the end of September 1916 to mid-July 1917 the number of exempted workers rose from 1,200,000 to 1,900,000, and it was shortly to reach 2,000,000. Half of these exempted workers were "liable to field duty" (k.v.). As a result, battalion strength dropped from 750 to 713 men in the West and from 800 to 780 men in the East.[1]

[1] Report of the Northwest Group of the VdESI, Feb. 8, 1917, BA, R 13I/31 and Reichsarchiv, *Weltkrieg*, XIII, pp. 24-27.

In January 1917 the War Office warned the industrialists that they could not expect to keep all their exempted workers permanently and would have to begin to surrender them in the spring. To this, the industrialists replied that "if the largest segment of the workers does not remain longer than that, then the Hindenburg Program cannot be fulfilled."[2] By March 12, however, Ludendorff felt compelled to put an end to the practice of releasing men considered indispensable at the front. The OHL went a step further in late April and demanded that 10 percent of the exempted k.v. workers be drafted into the army by fall. The implementation of this order became all the more pressing when the army was forced to relinquish thousands of coal miners during May and June. Industry thought Ludendorff's request to be quite "reasonable."[3]

Generally speaking, however, industry was not very reasonable. Instead of collaborating with the War Office's efforts to substitute unskilled labor for the exempted workers, many industrialists refused to employ such labor. Indeed, at the beginning, they dismissed their female employees as soon as they received the skilled workers they had requested. The industrialists were very reluctant to encourage the employment of female labor by establishing suitable working and housing conditions. Threats by the War Office to deny release requests or remove released workers were not always successful. Industrialist appeals to Colonel Bauer usually brought good results. Also, some of the War Office bureaus seemed more interested in helping the industrialists to get labor than in helping the army to get troops. The War Office's periodical efforts to "comb out" industry were thus undertaken in the face of serious obstacles. Only rarely did the limited success of these "comb outs" directly benefit the army. Usually the exempted

[2] WUMBA Advisory Council meetings, Dec. 10, 1916, and Jan. 6, 1917, BHStA, Abt. IV, MK, K Mob 1, Bd. I, Bl. zu 39a, and K Mob 14, Bd. II, Bl. 7.

[3] Ludendorff to Groener, March 12, 1917, MF, Marine Archiv, Nr. 6447, Bd. I, Bl. 377-378; *Mitteilungen des Kriegsamt*, April 27, 1917; VdESI meeting of June 21, 1917, BA, R 13I/151.

workers who were combed out had to be sent to other factories where they were needed.[4]

The high hopes which the OHL had placed in the Auxiliary Service Law were sadly disappointed. As planned, Groener began by asking those liable to Auxiliary Service to volunteer for duty. The War Office was particularly anxious to find civilian substitutes for soldiers who were doing desk work, serving in depots, and guarding bridges. The various military agencies at home and in the occupied territories were thus instructed to announce their needs in the hope that these would be voluntarily satisfied. Groener expected to place 200,000 civilian personnel in the military agencies by the end of April. At the end of February, however, only 60,000 persons had reported for duty, and the majority of these were women. It thus became clear that the voluntary method was inadequate and that the draft committees would have to be used.[5]

On March 1, 1917, the Bundesrat, at the request of the War Office and with the approval of the Reichstag committee, issued regulations concerning the implementation of Paragraph 7 of the Auxiliary Service Law. Under these regulations, persons liable to Auxiliary Service were required to register with the communal authorities. From this requirement, however, were excluded not only those serving in the armed forces, but also those serving in the war industry, agriculture, every form of government and church work, the medical professions, public transport, and all other types of work designated as important to the war effort by the state authorities. The Bundesrat regulations did not, therefore, create a system of national registration which was entirely free of loopholes.[6]

The results of the Bundesrat order of March 1 were pathetic.

[4] *Mitteilungen des Kriegsamt*, Dec. 29, 1916, and July 26, 1917; Groener, *Lebenserinnerungen*, p. 356; BHStA, Abt. IV, MK, K Mob 7, Bd. II, Bl. 131a and 158.

[5] War Office directives of Dec. 8, 16, and 19, 1916, BHStA, Abt. IV, MK, K Mob 14, Bd. I, Bl. 43, zu 32 and 44. For the statistics, see *ibid.*, Bd. II, Bl. 51, and Bd. I, Bl. 150b.

[6] Bundesrat order, March 1, and Groener directive of March 9, 1917, *ibid.*, K Mob 20, Bd. I, Bl. 19.

At the end of May, 118,000 civilians were employed in military agencies, but only 36,000 of these were men liable to Auxiliary Service. There were 75,000 women and 4,000 were youths and old men. There were still 260,000 troops at home and in the occupied territories who had to be replaced by civilian personnel. On June 11 Colonel Marquard, the head of the Labor Office, summoned a meeting of the draft committee chairmen to discuss the situation. They were all disgusted with the law. In their opinion, it could almost say that "it was not written for Auxiliary Service but against Auxiliary Service." It was generally recognized that those who usually had to be drafted into the Auxiliary Service were the well-to-do. Members of the lower classes could hardly afford to remain idle. There were numerous means, however, by which prosperous individuals could evade Auxiliary Service. They could, for example, claim that the types of war work to which the draft committees wanted to assign them were unsuitable in the light of their previous occupations. Paragraph 8 of the law provided that consideration was to be given to such claims "wherever possible." The most important barrier to the effective implementation of the law, however, was that not everyone was registered. It was quite easy for wealthy or prominent individuals to escape registration with or assignment by the draft committees by becoming honorary members of war charity organizations and war corporations. The draft committee chairmen were thus happy to hear that the War Office was drawing up another order for the Bundesrat designed to eliminate exemptions from the registration requirement.

AUXILIARY SERVICE

As a result of nasty rumors that the undersigned is allegedly unemployed, he is taking the liberty of giving the Royal War Ministry a precise description of his daily routine in the service of the Fatherland up to now.

The undersigned property owner, Benno Hingerl, must do the following *every day*:

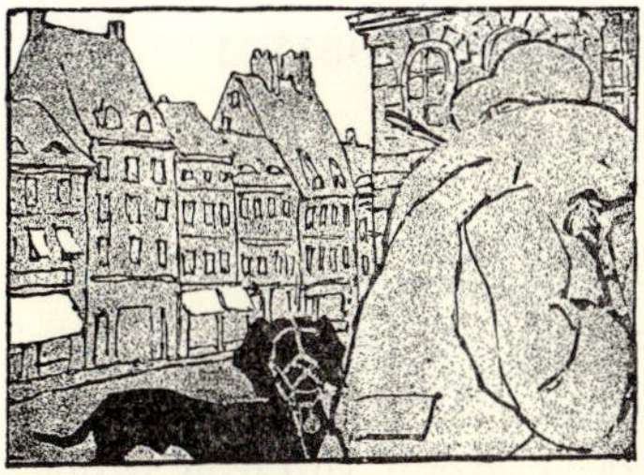

8 to 10: Walk the dog for purposes of evacuation, etc., in accordance with the police regulation that dogs should not be let out alone.

10 to 11: Discuss the affairs of the various tenants with the concierge and the possibilities of raising their rents.

11 to 1: Discuss town affairs with like-minded or otherwise-minded colleagues. Discuss the various decisions of the Town Council.

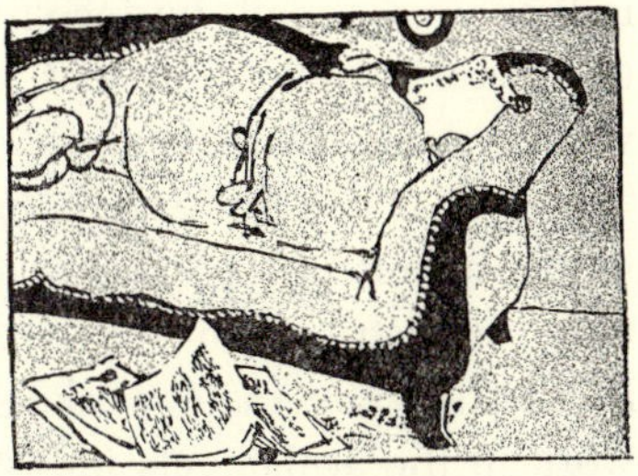

1 to 3: Rest, recuperation, and rejuvenation of energies.

3 to 6: Take measures to promote the local playing card industry.

6 to 8: Take a stand on the price ceilings and various food questions.

8 to 12: Discuss the situation on all fronts.

This should certainly give you another picture of my alleged unemployment!!

Prosperous persons seeking to evade the law also expected that the draft committee chairmen would show the proper *noblesse oblige.* The chairman in Stettin, who had been a lawyer in that city before the war, reported that he was not expected to make difficulties for his acquaintances and clients. "They are very patriotic," he noted, "but only so far as it does not involve their own skin."[7]

Needless to say, the War Office did not expect to employ millionaires, small businessmen, and retired landowners in the factories. The most that it could hope for from such individuals was that they would replace troops doing desk work. The War Office did expect, however, that the law would provide a means of forcing workers from shut down and consolidated industries into war work. Here, too, it was disappointed as most of the male workers subject to the law had taken work in the armaments industries before the law was passed. The vast majority of those affected by the shutdowns and consolidations were women, youths, and old men.[8]

In reality the most important reservoir of labor available to Germany was female labor. The utilization of this type of labor, however, was complicated by the need to provide proper working conditions, decent housing, and care for the children. Because of these difficulties and the excess of supply over demand, women had not been made subject to the provisions of the law. Nevertheless, the War Office wanted to do everything possible to promote the use of female labor. Captain Richard Merton, who was Groener's most important staff adviser on social questions, was placed in charge of the mobilization of female labor, and the noted social worker, Dr. Marie-Elisabeth Lüders, was appointed head of the Female Labor Section of the War Office. Well-educated women with experience in social work were placed in the War Office bureaus to direct the procurement of female labor. On January 29, 1917,

[7] The discussion and quotations are based on the protocol of the meeting, *ibid.*, K Mob 14, Bd. IV, Bl. 81.

[8] See Peppel study.

the various women's organizations were united into a National Committee for Womens' War Work. The War Office and the National Committee cooperated in establishing special labor exchanges, issuing propaganda, and conducting welfare programs.[9]

By the summer of 1917 a shortage of female labor had developed in some areas, but the employment of more women was not without its difficulties. Not only was it hard to provide for their social needs, but it was also hard to keep them on their jobs for any length of time. The latter problem was particularly serious in agriculture because women were easily enticed into going to the cities to take better paid work. The high female turnover rate in industry was usually the result of overwork, poor conditions, and the constant competition for workers among the employers. The War Office sought to combat these tendencies by a combination of propaganda and compulsion. Posters, slide lectures, and films were used to persuade women to stay on the farms or return to them. At the same time, the Deputy Commanding Generals were instructed to ban flight from the land if they feared that the food production of their districts might be endangered. Lastly, since early January the War Office was giving serious thought to the possibility of extending the leaving certificate system to employed women. The problem here, however, was that this would create an unfair discrimination between employed and unemployed women. Furthermore, the overworked female workers would not necessarily have been unhappy about being forced to take a two week vacation because they left their jobs without a leaving certificate.[10]

[9] The best studies of female labor during the war are Marie-Elisabeth Lüders, *Das unbekannte Heer. Frauen kämpfen für Deutschland, 1914-1918*, Berlin, 1936, and Charlotte Lorenz, *Die gewerbliche Frauenarbeit während des Krieges*, Stuttgart, Berlin, and Leipzig, 1928. See also Merton, *Erinnernswertes aus meinem Leben*, pp. 23-24.

[10] On the forcible prevention of flight from the land, see General von Stein's directive of April 18, 1917, BHStA, Abt. IV, MK, K Mob 7, Bd. I, Bl. 224. On the idea of extending the leaving certificate system to women, see *ibid.*, K Mob 17, Bd. I, Bl. zu 62; Bd. II, Bl. 193; Bd. III, Bl. 103.

For all the difficulties involved, the effort to increase the labor supply by the use of female labor was the most successful of the War Office's labor procurement operations. It is rather significant that those measures taken to increase the labor supply which may be directly attributed to the OHL were least successful. The Auxiliary Service Law produced little by way of additional labor. Most of the unemployed Belgians who had been forced to come to Germany turned out to be physically unfit, and in June 1917 the OHL dropped this program and permitted all Belgians who wished to return home to do so. The establishment of an independent Kingdom of Poland, which was supposed to induce the Poles to fight and work for the German cause, was an utter fiasco. It can thus be seen that the OHL had made some very serious miscalculations.[11]

2. *The Dilemmas of Paragraph 9*

The chief charge that is to be leveled against the Auxiliary Service Law, however, is not that it was ineffectual but that it was actually harmful. Nothing did more to upset the labor market and to promote turnover than Paragraph 9 of the law, under which the arbitration committees were obligated to give the leaving certificate to workers who claimed they could attain a "suitable improvement" of their wages and working conditions. The union leaders were well aware of the dangers of Paragraph 9, and in December 1916 when regulations for the implementation of this paragraph were being drawn up, some of the union leaders were willing to help the government to "interpret" the paragraph in a sense more favorable to the purposes of the law. Bauer, of the General Commission, informed the union representative to the War Office, Schlicke, that he would be willing to have the regulations state that only a "considerable" (*erhebliche*) improvement of wages was to be regarded as a satisfactory reason for permitting a worker to

[11] On the foreign worker problem, see the War Office discussion of June 18, 1917, *ibid.*, K Mob 7, Bd. II, Bl. 131a; Sichler and Tiburtius, *Arbeiterfrage*, pp. 41-43; Fischer, *Griff nach der Weltmacht*, p. 301.

change his place of employment. In Schlicke's view, even this concession was not enough because "it lacks any reference to the necessities of the Auxiliary Service." In other words, Schlicke was now prepared to introduce a clause into the regulations that would compensate the government for the Reichstag's unwillingness to state formally that the purposes of the law as well as the possibility of improving wages were to be taken into account in the decisions of the arbitration committees. Colonel Marquard and his legal adviser, Dr. Oppenheimer, were more than anxious to seize the opportunity Schlicke was giving them. Helfferich, however, feared that Schlicke's colleagues would not be quite so patriotic and wished "to avoid the impression that a change in the law is being carried out through the regulations."[12]

Helfferich was unquestionably correct in feeling that a new interpretation of Paragraph 9 would not be accepted by the Reichstag, as correct as he was when he first predicted that the paragraph would encourage job changing. During the first quarter of 1917 there was veritable chaos on the labor market. The workers seized every available opportunity to find better paid work. This was particularly the case with exempted workers, who also wanted to find employment near their homes. Many employers took advantage of the law to steal workers by offering them higher wages or more food. Furthermore, the War Office bureaus and government agencies were not above engaging in such practices themselves. Things were practically as bad as they had been when the wartime labor shortage had first developed.[13]

The War Office placed most of the blame for the sudden increase of turnover on the employers. In an appeal to the employers and employees on January 21, Groener declared that it was impossible to reproach the workers for wanting

[12] For these discussions, which took place between Dec. 16 and Dec. 28, 1916, see BHStA, Abt. IV, MK, K Mob 14, Bd. I, Bl. 110.

[13] See Groener's statement to the Reichstag committee of Jan. 19, 1917, and his directives of Jan. 15 and Feb. 3, *ibid.*, Bl. zu 117, 46 and 103.

to get higher wages and find work nearer their homes. It was therefore necessary for the employers to do everything possible to encourage the workers to stay on their jobs voluntarily. The employers were advised to pay satisfactory wages and to give special premiums for double household expenses even though the government was also paying such premiums. The employers also were told to put an end to their irresponsible efforts to bribe the workers into changing jobs. But Groener had a few serious words to say to the exempted workers as well. He reassured them of their right to appeal to the arbitration committees, but warned them that their military obligation took priority over their work in the factories. Consequently, the continued exemption of a worker could lose all justification if he found employment unrelated to the type of work for which he had been specifically exempted.[14]

This implicit threat to the exempted workers was soon to be realized. The factories producing submarines were particularly dependent upon skilled workers specifically exempted for this type of work. Wages in this industry were lower than wages in the munitions industry, and Paragraph 9 created a very dangerous situation, a situation made all the more serious because of the high hopes the OHL had placed in unrestricted submarine warfare. What, for example, was a firm to do when the arbitration committee gave leaving certificates to thirty of its skilled workers, twenty-one of whom had been especially exempted for its factory? It was possible to advise the firm to raise its wages, but it was impossible to force it to do so. At the same time, vital military interests were being threatened. A similar situation existed in the state railways. Wages in the munitions factories were much higher than wages in the railroad repair workshops. The transport crisis could never be overcome if the skilled workers especially exempted for the repair of locomotives disappeared into the munitions factories.[15]

[14] *Mitteilungen des Kriegsamt,* Jan. 21, 1917.

[15] See the note of the Weser firm to the Submarine Inspection Service, Jan. 31, 1917, MF, Marine Archiv, Nr. 6447, Bd. I, Bl. 262-267, and the

On February 2, 1917, Groener issued a decree which modified the War Office's policy of giving workers liable to military service all the benefits of the Auxiliary Service Law:

> When military considerations made it necessary to exempt a person liable to military service *for very definite purposes connected with the conduct of the national defense or the war at sea*, then this is to be stated in the exemption order. If the person liable to military service leaves such a position, then the basis for his exemption immediately disappears. He is therefore at the disposal of the military authorities for immediate drafting into the army.[16]

Following this general pronouncement, the decree went on to apply this principle to all workers who had been exempted for the submarine building industry.

In the Reichstag committee meeting of February 9, 1917, Deputies Bauer and Ebert raised strong objections to the decree. Bauer pointed out that his party had refrained from introducing a clause specifically guaranteeing the rights of the exempted workers to the benefits of the law because Groener had given a verbal declaration to this effect. In his view, the decree of February 2 stood in "direct contradiction" to Groener's promise. Groener defended his action by pointing out that he had already demonstrated his good faith by his appeal to the employers and workers of January 21, an appeal which had received high praise from the unions despite the fact that it had indicated the priority of military service over Auxiliary Service. In his view, the decree of February 2 was simply an expression of this principle. Most important, however, was that "our battle readiness at land and sea does not suffer because of theoretical considerations."[17] The other depu-

discussion in the War Office on Jan. 22, 1917, BHStA, Abt. IV, MK, K Mob 12a, Bd. I, Bl. 80a.

16 PrGStA, Rep. B 30 I, Nr. 34.

17 For the report of the meeting, see BHStA, Abt. IV, MK, K Mob 14, Bd. I, Bl. 161.

ties were more sympathetic to Groener's argument and pointed out that there was nothing in the decree which prevented exempted shipyard workers from changing jobs *within* their industry.

In a decree of February 12 which extended the limitations on the free movement of exempted workers to the state railways, Groener seized this point and, at the same time, reaffirmed his basic position. The decree specifically stated that workers affected by this decree and that of February 2 could request the leaving certificate in order to work at another plant within the "specific occupational sector" to which they had been assigned. Having made this concession, Groener then asserted the right of the War Office to extend the type of restrictions contained in these decrees to other occupational sectors and asked the Deputy Commanding Generals to inform him of cases where they considered this to be desirable.[18]

Unfortunately for Groener, General von Vietinghoff, the Deputy Commanding General in Stettin, and the industrialists running the shipyards could always be counted upon to justify the worst fears of the union leaders. No sooner had Groener's decree of February 2 appeared than Vietinghoff issued an order asking that he be informed about cases of high turnover in industries other than the shipbuilding industry. In such cases he intended to extend the order of February 2 to cover those factories as well. Obviously, Vietinghoff did not feel that it was necessary to consult the War Office first. In a similar expression of this tendency to stretch the application of Groener's decree arbitrarily, the Vulcan shipbuilding firm informed its officials that every employee of the firm could now be drafted for seeking work elsewhere. Also, evidence was mounting that the shipyard owners had made a secret agreement not to hire employees who had received leaving certificates from the arbitration committees and that the employers were once again threatening workers who displeased them "with the trenches." The unions brought these facts to

[18] Decree of Feb. 12, 1917, *ibid.*, Bd. III, Bl. zu 18.

Groener's attention in a note of February 28 and demanded that his decrees be repealed.[19]

Groener replied on March 24 with a long defense of his decrees. He pointed out that the OHL had made a great sacrifice in permitting so many exemptions and that it was impossible to permit men who had been exempted for a specific purpose to take work that could be done just as easily by other workers. He informed the unions that Vietinghoff's illegal decree had been changed, assured them that the War Office would act against secret agreements among the employers if their existence could be demonstrated, and declared that the War Office opposed the threat of the trenches.[20]

Although the unions officially expressed satisfaction with Groener's reply, they knew that the War Office did not have sufficient power to prevent abuses of the decrees. In a meeting of the special committee of union leaders which met periodically to advise the War Office, Schlicke complained about the way the shipyard owners were dismissing workers they didn't like in order to have them drafted into the army. Marquard admitted that such practices were very unfair, but he pointed out that "if the employers are compelled to employ particular workers, then that would be the beginning of a military dictatorship." He asked that "all theoretical and juridical considerations be put aside" because "special consideration has to be shown for all matters concerned with the construction of U-boats." Marquard went so far in showing "special consideration" for this industry that he permitted a ban on job changing within the industry if such job changing might harm production.[21]

Needless to say, the union leaders responded most negatively when Marquard informed them, on June 22, that the decree of February 2 might have to be extended to exempted

[19] Reprinted in the *Correspondenzblatt,* March 23, 1917.

[20] *Ibid.,* April 28, 1917.

[21] For the meeting of April 5, 1917, see BHStA, Abt. IV, MK, K Mob 14, Bd. III, Bl. zu 18. See also Marquard to State Secretary of the Navy Capelle, April 23, 1917, *ibid.,* K Mob 11, Bd. I, Bl. 53-zu 53.

coal miners. The OHL had released thousands of miners from the front in order to alleviate the coal production crisis, but many of them seemed to have wandered off to seek higher pay and easier work in the munitions industry. The union leaders felt that the War Office had not presented satisfactory evidence for this contention, and argued that an extension of the decree to the mining industry would ruin the miners' morale and encourage the mineowners to make black-listing agreements. From this discussion Marquard concluded that the "worker representatives are unanimously opposed to the extension of the decree of February 2, 1917, to the miners so long as its necessity is not demonstrated."[22]

He had thus shrewdly left the way open for an extension of the decree, and on July 23, 1917, after it had been demonstrated that 3,000 miners out of a group of 25,000 recently released from the front had found work in other industries, the exempted miners were placed under the decree of February 2. On August 10 the decree was extended to the airplane industry. Finally, on August 14 the decree was extended to all workers who had been specifically exempted for an occupational sector having to do with the national defense or the war at sea.[23]

The extension of the restrictions on the free movement of exempted workers, and particularly the decree of August 14, undoubtedly reflected the growing strength of industrialist attacks on Paragraph 9 of the Auxiliary Service Law. It would be wrong, however, to see these decrees as a surrender of the War Office to the demands of heavy industry. It was, after all, ridiculous for the OHL to release workers for specific industries and then stand idly by while they drifted elsewhere. The unions themselves recognized this. Their petition of February 28 had not been directed so much against the decree of Febru-

[22] Meeting of June 22, 1917, *ibid.*, K Mob 12, Bd. IX, Bl. 138.

[23] On the loss of miners to the munitions industry, see *ibid.*, Bd. XI, Bl. 8. For the decrees of July 23 and Aug. 10, see *Mitteilungen des Kriegsamt*, Aug. 7 and 10, 1917. For the decree of Aug. 14, see PrGStA, Rep. B 30 I, Nr. 34.

ary 2 as against its abuses. Similarly, their objections to the placing of restrictions on the exempted miners were based upon the dangerous effect this would have on morale rather than upon the illegality or lack of moral justification for the procedure.

It must not be forgotten that the vast majority of the exempted workers had not been officially exempted for a specific industry and were thus unaffected by these decrees. The same holds true for all male workers not liable to military service. The basic problems raised by Paragraph 9 continued to plague the economy, although the turnover rate decreased in the spring of 1917. Workers continued to seek higher paying jobs. This had an extremely inflationary effect when coupled as it was with high employer profits. Many employers went so far as to hire employees even though they did not have a leaving certificate. Also, some workers could afford to stay out of work for two weeks in order to take a new job despite the fact that they did not receive a leaving certificate. Initially, the War Office sought to control the competition among employers by banning newspaper advertisements for workers which promised higher wages and large food premiums. It was soon discovered, however, that this was harmful to attempts to win workers for particularly important factories, and the ban had to be lifted.[24]

The unions did not wish to encourage excessive turnover any more than the War Office did. From the very beginning they sought to discourage demands for leaving certificates:

> It is an old union principle to oppose job changing even in peacetime and, instead, to concentrate upon reforming factory conditions in accordance with the wishes and interests of the workers. . . .
>
> The unions and their members shall, therefore, seek to avoid job changing as much as possible. The leaving cer-

[24] On employer abuses of the system, see *Mitteilungen des Kriegsamt*, July 5, 1917. On the problem of censoring advertisements for workers, see BHStA, Abt. IV, MK, K Mob 7, Bd. I, Bl. 83, and Bd. IV, Bl. 34a.

> tificate is not the means of attaining justified wishes, but rather the . . . committees. What is there attained by way of improving working conditions benefits all the workers, while the leaving certificate may eventually only bring an advantage to the individual. Where it is not necessary, therefore, not the leaving certificate but the remedy of justified complaints should be sought. That lies in the general interest of the workers and collides in no way with the purposes of the law.[25]

The unions had much to gain from the Auxiliary Service Law. They were thus as interested as the War Office in keeping Paragraph 9 from getting out of hand. The collaboration of the unions with the War Office is explained by this fact, and the extraordinary opposition of the industrialists to Paragraph 9 and to the law itself must be seen in terms of the general social policy of the War Office and the greatly increased strength of the unions as a result of the law.

3. *The War Office and the Unions*

That Groener intended to work hand in hand with the unions was obvious from the attitude he had taken during the debates on the Auxiliary Service bill. The bond established between the unions and the War Office during the Reichstag debates was cemented in a gigantic trade union congress held on December 12, 1916, in Berlin. The congress was unique in German trade union history because all the trade union groups, exclusive of the yellow unions, were represented and because it was addressed by high government officials. Its purpose was to unite the workers and their organizations behind the Auxiliary Service Law. The assembled delegates did not place much stock in Helfferich's speech. He could not erase the memory of their recent struggle with high-sounding phrases. Groener's words, however, received a warm response from the delegates:

[25] *Correspondenzblatt*, Jan. 27, 1917.

> I have already come to know many of your representatives during the debates on the law, and I was happy to make their acquaintance, and I am particularly happy to be able to spend today with you. I may certainly assume that we will deal with each other with the greatest mutual confidence and that, one month after the conclusion of peace when the Auxiliary Service Law expires, we will shake hands with one another and say: we have done things quite sensibly (Agreement); and then we will be able to create, out of our common labor during the war, the hope and expectation that also in the coming peace much that is divisive will be set aside and that a noble seed has sprung forth for the development of the German people out of our common war work. (Lively applause)[26]

Nothing attests more to the sincerity of Groener's words than the instructions he gave to the War Office bureaus chairmen on the day following the trade union congress. They were told to obey the letter of the law and avoid putting unwarranted pressure upon the workers. The confidence of the workers in the rectitude of the military authorities was not to be endangered in any way. He pointed out that "the majority of the Reichstag takes the view that the unions are the legitimate organs of the workers. *The military authorities must, under all circumstances, accept this.*"[27] In practical terms this meant that the union nominations for the worker representatives on the Auxiliary Service Law committees were to be heeded.

Groener's social policy, therefore, was a continuation of the policy previously conducted by the War Ministry. Although the direct influence of Sichler and Tiburtius was not as great as it had been before, Groener was on excellent terms with them. His chief adviser on economic and social policy was Captain Richard Merton, who had previously served as Groener's adjutant in the War Food Office. Merton was the son

[26] *Soziale Praxis*, Dec. 21, 1916.

[27] Meeting of Dec. 13, 1916, HStASt, KM, Abt. f. allg. Armee- u. f. pers. Angelegenheiten, Bd. 1272, Bl. 101-106.

of the Frankfurt Metal Corporation head, Dr. Wilhelm Merton, who had been an important supporter of the Society for Social Reform. Richard Merton shared his father's progressive views and was on very good terms with Sichler and Tiburtius. Wichard von Moellendorff also had an important influence on Groener. Moellendorff shared the political and social convictions of Merton, Sichler, and Tiburtius, and he had close contacts with the right wing Social Democrats, August Müller, Rudolf Wissel, Max Cohen, and Julius Kaliski, who published the *Sozialistische Monatshefte.* The chief opponents of the social policies of the above mentioned individuals were General Coupette and Colonel Marquard. The former was by no means indifferent to social questions, as indicated by his support for worker vacations, but he was impatient whenever social considerations stood in the way of the need to satisfy industry's manpower needs speedily. Marquard, in contrast to Coupette, had very little patience with social questions. He was convinced that the best means of improving morale was to act with "more ruthlessness in the implementation of the regulations."[28]

One of Groener's most difficult tasks was getting the employers to permit the election of workers committees in their factories as required under the law. In the Düsseldorf area, for example, 922 factories were supposed to establish workers committees. Yet in May there were 254 and in August there were 144 factories which still had not complied with this provision of the law.[29] There could be no debate about the fact that the employers were obligated to set up these committees, but there was plenty of debate about the question of whether or not the law required the holding of new elections for those factories which had established committees before the law was passed. The older workers committees had not

[28] Sichler and Tiburtius, *Arbeiterfrage*, p. 40; Bowen, *Corporative State*, p. 187; *Soziale Praxis*, Dec. 21, 1916, and Jan. 25, 1917. Most of the information on the attitudes of these individuals comes from Senator Tiburtius' letter to the author of Nov. 19, 1962.

[29] StADü, Reg. Dü., Nr. 33556.

been elected by proportional representation as stipulated by the law. Furthermore, most of them were of prewar origin and no longer represented the majority of the workers. The Auxiliary Service Law did not specifically state that new elections were necessary, although this certainly was the implication of Paragraph 11. Paragraph 15 of the law was particularly confusing because it gave the military authorities the power to issue the regulations governing the election of workers committees in the state armaments factories. Workers committees already existed in these factories, and Coupette did not want to hold new elections. The Reichstag committee, however, insisted that the War Office "show a good example and not entrench itself behind dubious interpretations of the law." Finally, Groener forced Coupette to relent, and by August 1917 the workers committees in the factories run by the army had been completely reconstituted.[30]

Groener was thus willing to promote new elections. This willingness was not shared by the civil authorities in the various states, however, and it was they who were responsible for issuing the regulations concerning workers committee elections. Although the civil authorities were quite insistent that committees be established insofar as they did not already exist, they were equally insistent that the law did not require the holding of new elections. In June the Reichstag committee passed a resolution demanding that the Bundesrat issue general orders regulating the elections and requiring new elections where workers committees had been set up in a manner at variance with the Auxiliary Service Law. The Bundesrat discussed this resolution on July 6, but the delegates were incapable of warming up to it. Undersecretary of the Interior Richter rejected the Reichstag committee's contention that new elections were required by the law and added that "one should

[30] Reichstag committee meeting, Feb. 16, 1917, BHStA, Abt. IV, MK, K Mob 14, Bd. I, Bl. 161. For Groener's pressure on WUMBA, see Moellendorff's notations, Feb.-July 1917, BA, Nachlass Moellendorff, Nr. 59.

not only consider the wishes of the workers, but must also pay heed to the morale of the employers."[31]

Thus Groener received very little cooperation from the civil authorities on the workers committee question. In May, when he wanted the Bundesrat to issue an order requiring that the committees be set up by a specific date, Helfferich rejected the use of extreme pressure on the employers. In the same month Groener got into trouble for issuing an order permitting the workers committees in the army's factories to elect their own chairmen. It was customary for a management representative to serve as chairman in the committees that had been established in the state owned railways and mines and, needless to say, Breitenbach and Sydow were furious at Groener. Groener's action is a good example of his practice of going beyond his sphere of competence, but it is also a good example of his liberal attitude.[32]

The differences between Groener and the civil authorities concerning social questions, however, should not be exaggerated. Groener's basic policy of using the unions to pacify the workers had been the policy of the government and the War Ministry since the beginning of the war. If Groener carried this policy further than his predecessors, it was largely because of the serious internal situation in 1917 and the fact that the Auxiliary Service Law could not be implemented without the cooperation of the unions. Groener encouraged the use of the workers committees to help in the distribution of food premiums within the factories, and he urged the local authorities to invite union representatives to take part in the management of the food supply. Union leaders were exempted in order to increase the ability of the unions to direct and control the

[31] Report by Dr. Schäffer, July 6, 1917, HStASt, E, 130, V, Xa.29, Bl. 140.

[32] Prussian Cabinet meeting, May 1, 1917, and complaints of Breitenbach and Sydow, Aug. 8, 1917, BA, P 135/1811, Bl. 97-98. At one point Groener came into open conflict with Undersecretary Richter at a Reichstag committee meeting of Feb. 16, 1917, BHStA, Abt. IV, MK, K Mob 14, Bd. I, Bl. 161.

workers. Finally, union meetings to enlighten the workers were encouraged. On January 17, 1917, General von Stein issued an order to the Deputy Commanding Generals calling for a loosening of the restrictions on union meetings. The War Ministry believed that it was necessary to provide a "safety valve . . . to release the pent-up dissatisfaction:"

> An unhindered use of meetings is desired in many cases so that reliable leaders can have the opportunity to discover the complaints and wishes of the workers and to pacify and enlighten them. The union leaders have demonstrated themselves to be almost completely reliable in this connection. The workers, taken as a whole, have also shown understanding for the needs of the time and receptivity to reasonable influences. After the acceptance of the amended version of the Association Law, the unions can no longer be regarded as political associations insofar as their activity limits itself within the bounds of the revised law.[33]

This policy, coupled with the provisions of the Auxiliary Service Law, was bound to strengthen the unions. Union representatives now sat on the determination, draft, and arbitration committees scattered throughout the country. They participated in the work of the authorities on the food problem. They were elected to the ever-increasing number of workers committees. With the approval of the government, they were both permitted and encouraged to present themselves and their views to the workers, and it need hardly be said that the workers were impressed by the newly acquired influence of the unions. The decline in Free Trade Union membership which had marked the first two years of the war was at an end, and membership rose from 967,000 in 1916 to 1,107,000 in 1917.[34]

[33] BHStA, Abt. IV, MK, XIV c III 17, Bd. II, Bl. 58. See also Wrisberg, *Heer und Heimat*, p. 93.

[34] Bry, *Wages in Germany*, p. 32.

4. War Office Conflicts with Industry and the OHL

The "social partnership" (*Arbeitsgemeinschaft*) established between the War Office and the trade unions did not please the leaders of heavy industry. From the very beginning they refused to enter into such a partnership with the unions. In an editorial of January 7, 1917, the *Arbeitgeberzeitung* remarked:

> We also wish with all our hearts for a united, powerful social partnership for our people, but we understand this social partnership to be . . . a partnership for work, one which does not conceal behind it the impossible principles of general equality and the rule of the many, but which gives to each his own (*Jedem das Seine*), which puts everyone in his place, the one to lead, the other to follow, a partnership in which all the members willingly fall in line and in which the general good alone is decisive![35]

All of the employers did not support these sentiments. The quarrel between the "old" National Liberals led by Deputies Hirsch and Beumer and the "new" National Liberals led by Stresemann and List reflected this. List, for example, referred to the former group as "neither liberal nor social, but rather the spiritual relatives of the Prussian Junkers."[36] Heavy industry, however, dominated war production and had the ear of the OHL. Furthermore, the big industrialists could defend their position by pointing, with some justification, to the power politics of the trade unions, the inadequacies of the Auxiliary Service Law, and above all to the increasing number of strikes.

The industrialists were particularly incensed over the way in which the three major union groups had combined to ruin the yellow unions. Indeed, if there was anything that bound the Free, Christian, and Hirsch-Duncker unions together, it was their loathing for the various yellow unions. They would not sit at the same conference table with the yellow unions,

[35] *Arbeitgeberzeitung*, Jan. 1, 1917.

[36] List to Stresemann, April 6, 1917, Nachlass Stresemann, Nr. 6898, frame H134986.

and they refused to recognize them as legitimate worker organizations. This attitude is quite understandable, for the yellow unions were heavily subsidized by industry and their leaders were little more than lackeys. Thus, the "fighting" unions were not willing to sit on the Auxiliary Service Law committees with yellow union members unless the latter were serving as employer representatives. The Free, Christian, and Hirsch-Duncker unions collaborated in forming a single list of suggested representatives for the Auxiliary Service Law committees. In this way they hoped to exclude the yellow unions from participation and insure that the trade unions would represent both the organized and the unorganized workers on the committees.[37]

The yellow union problem was the subject of hot debate in the Reichstag committee. The left insisted that the War Office refuse to name yellow union representatives to the Auxiliary Service Law committees. Groener refused to discriminate against the yellow unions, but it must be said that he did precious little to bolster their position. He ordered that yellow union members be permitted to request that yellow union representatives serve as nonstanding members of arbitration committees hearing their cases. Needless to say, it was not very likely that many workers would take advantage of this dubious privilege. This was all the more the case because yellow union support was declining rapidly. At Krupp, for example, yellow union candidates received only 4,193 out of 43,110 votes in the workers committee elections. Yet Krupp was supposed to be one of the great yellow union strongholds.[38]

Neither the yellow union leaders nor their industrialist bosses found this situation acceptable, and they appealed to the OHL. In January and February Ludendorff brought their complaints to the attention of the government. One of Luden-

[37] For the union tactics, see the Düsseldorf police report of Dec. 29, 1916, StaDü, Reg. Dü., Nr. 15076.

[38] Reichstag committee meeting, Jan. 19, 1917, BHStA, Abt. IV, MK, K Mob 14, Bd. I, Bl. 117, and *Mitteilungen des Kriegsamt*, Feb. 9, 1917. On the Krupp elections, see the BBS Report of March 21, 1917.

dorff's appeals was sent to the chief of the Civil Cabinet, Valentini. Valentini was very conservative, but he was also a realist. He found the "cry of pain" of the yellow unions understandable, but he felt that "in this case, a small interest has been made subsidiary to a great goal by the War Office." The important thing, according to Valentini, was to win "the *voluntary* collaboration of the great organizations (Social Democratic and Christian unions)."[39] When Ludendorff brought Krupp's complaints to the attention of Undersecretary Wahnschaffe, the latter penned a long reply of a similar nature on February 28. While recognizing the value of the yellow unions and assuring Ludendorff that the government wanted to be impartial, Wahnschaffe pointed out that the yellow unions had only a half million members at the beginning of the war, while the fighting unions had three and a half million members. It was thus utterly futile to depend on the yellow unions, and it was absolutely necessary to have the support of the fighting unions:

> In general, the War Office has recognized, and in my view with complete justification, that the war cannot be won without the good will of the German workers. But no one in the world has nearly the influence upon the great mass of the industrial workers as do the union leaders. Nothing can be accomplished without these leaders or against them. Their influence rests upon their decades long work for the improvement of the position of the workers, work which has won them the complete confidence of their membership. Until now we have succeeded in holding the unions . . . to the policy of August 4, 1914. How we can hold out if this were to be otherwise cannot be seen.[40]

The situation of the yellow unions did not improve during the ensuing months. Yellow union leaders expressed their de-

[39] Valentini to Ludendorff, Jan. 30, 1917, in Valentini, *Kabinettschef*, p. 220.

[40] Institut für Marxismus-Leninismus, *Dokumente und Materialien*, I, pp. 558-561.

jection to the OHL by pointing out that their workers lacked the enthusiasm to celebrate the Emperor's birthday or to contribute to war bond drives because of the way the government was treating them. Industrialist representatives in the Reichstag attacked the "unfair" way in which these unions were treated. In June 1917 Colonel Bauer's good friend, the Secretary of the Catholic Worker Associations, Dr. Fleischer, reported that only two of this particular nonstriking union's members were standing representatives on the arbitration committees and only eight had been appointed nonstanding representatives. He demanded that the government show the yellow unions more consideration. On June 30 Groener made his final concession to the yellow unions. Now workers could request that both the standing and the nonstanding labor representatives on the arbitration committee be yellow union members. In short, yellow union members were now given the right to stew completely in their own juice if they so desired.[41]

Paragraph 9 of the Auxiliary Service Law was extremely aggravating to the employers. Here, as has been demonstrated, the complaints of the industrialists were not completely unjustified. Thus, at a meeting on January 26, Borsig, who had always recognized the necessity of arbitration committees where there were restrictions upon the free movement of labor, and Rieppel, who was an ardent supporter of these institutions, complained that Paragraph 9 was creating high turnover and encouraging an excessively rapid increase of wages. It was their fellow industrialist, Dr. Sorge, who replied for the War Office. Sorge recognized that the complaints were justified, but he pointed out that it was necessary to operate within the framework of the law and that all thought of what wages and

[41] See the yellow union complaint passed on to Bauer on April 20, 1917, BA, Nachlass Bauer, Nr. 11, and Reichstag Debates, March 3, 1917, 309, pp. 2475-2476. The Bauer papers are filled with letters from Fleischer. For the latter's remarks, see *Stenographischer Bericht über den 18. Delegiertentag des katholischen Arbeitervereine Deutschlands am 24. Juni 1917 in den Concordia-Festsalen in Berlin*, Berlin, 1917, pp. 15-16. For Groener's order of June 30, 1917, see BHStA, Abt. IV, MK, K Mob 11a, Bd. III, Bl. zu 89.

social relations would be like after the war had to be set aside. He concluded with the hope "that the influence of the unions will demonstrate itself to be stronger and better."[42]

Had the Auxiliary Service Law functioned under relatively peaceful internal conditions, however, industrialist opposition to the law would hardly have been able to become as universal and effective as it did. From January to March 1917 there were serious strikes in the Ruhr, Berlin, and elsewhere. The strikes in the Ruhr, some of which were so serious that military intervention was necessary, were largely the result of the inadequate food supply and the inequities of the food premium system. The workers usually demanded that they receive more food from the government or, if this was not possible, that they receive higher wages so that they could buy more food on the black market. In a number of instances, particularly at Krupp and in the Rhenish metal industry, the strikes were dominated by demands for higher wages from the very start. The strikes in the Ruhr coal mines were caused not only by inadequate food and low wages, but also by temporary unemployment as a result of the transport crisis and General von Gayl's practice of providing the mine owners with blank orders for the redrafting of unruly workers. These strikes were settled by the mediation of the War Office, General von Gayl, the civil authorities, and the trade unions. The settlements were usually based upon promises of more food and higher wages.[43]

The strikes involving the highly paid Berlin munitions factory workers were of a somewhat different nature. The food problem certainly played a role. In one case a firm actually supported the strike in order to force the government to provide more food. The desire to increase wages and lower hours, however, was the major motive of the Berlin strikers, and the

[42] BHStA, Abt. IV, MK, K Mob 14, Bd. II, Bl. 7.

[43] On these strikes, see the ZMG Reports of Feb. 17 and March 16, 1917, and the documents in Leo Stern, ed., *Die Auswirkungen der Grossen Sozialistischen Oktoberrevolution auf Deutschland*, 4 vols., Berlin, 1959 (hereinafter cited as *AGSOD*), II, pp. 377-381. See also Merton, *Erinnernswertes aus meinem Leben*, pp. 26-27.

strike succeeded. The Berlin Metalworkers Union leaders did not officially support the strike, but they did support the demands that had been raised.[44]

These strikes, the wage increases which followed them, and the high turnover created by Paragraph 9 of the Auxiliary Service Law drove the employers to action. On February 28 members of the Association of German Employer Organizations met to discuss the situation. There was general agreement that the surrender they had made to the wage demands raised during the recent strikes would only incite more unrest. While recognizing the importance of the food situation in precipitating the strikes, they attributed the strikes themselves to union and radical agitators. Above all, they were disgusted with the Auxiliary Service Law, which had only created new difficulties. They were certain that "because of this no one can desire to have the law remain in its present form." The law had deprived them of their previous control over the exempted workers, and the arbitration committee chairmen were being too easily influenced by the worker representatives. Many of the workers could afford to "bum around" (*bummeln*) for two weeks if they were refused the leaving certificate by the arbitration committees.[45]

On March 23 the association sent a series of proposals to General Groener. After pointing out that the industrialists had no objections to the law as it was first presented to the Reichstag by the government but only to the law as it had finally emerged, the employers went on to demand a long series of changes with regard to Paragraph 9. First, they wanted an official interpretation that would permit job changing only in those cases where the employee was not receiving a wage conformable to the prevailing wage rate in his part of the country. This was designed to prevent workers from leaving low wage districts for high wage districts. Second, they de-

[44] *Ibid.*

[45] For the protocol, which is falsely dated 1918, see BA, Nachlass Bauer, Nr. 14.

manded that exempted workers be denied the privileges of the Auxiliary Service Law and thus be denied the right to change jobs. Groener was reminded that the law said nothing about the rights of the exempted workers. Evidently the industrialists did not feel that he was obligated to fulfill his verbal promise to the Reichstag. Third, they demanded that workers who left their jobs without a leaving certificate be denied the right to employment for four instead of two weeks. Even the best paid workers would find it hard to "bum around" for four weeks. Fourth, they requested that the arbitration committees deal with individual cases only and not with the complaints of whole groups of workers. Thus, workers would be denied the privilege of collectively requesting the leaving certificate if the employers refused to accept the decisions of the conciliation bureaus. Lastly, the employers demanded that the deliberations of the arbitration committees be kept secret because newspaper coverage of their hearings usually involved mention of wage statistics and thus caused dissatisfaction among the workers. The War Office, however, was unprepared either to annul the Auxiliary Service Law, as desired by some employers, or to limit, at this time, the rights it gave to the workers in the manner suggested in the above discussed petition. As Dr. Sorge told the industrialists, the first solution was impossible, while the second presented "extraordinary difficulties."[46]

Some of the industrialists, however, preferred to send their demands to persons other than the Chief of the War Office and to make their demands truly extreme. Dr. von Gontardt, the director of the German Weapons and Munitions Factories in Berlin, proposed relatively simple solutions to the problems raised by the strikes and the Auxiliary Service Law. On March 1 he asked General von Kessel, the High Commander in the Mark, to place the workers under military surveillance, punish every refusal to work with imprisonment, set minimum hours

[46] For the petition, see BHStA, Abt. IV, MK, K Mob 19, Bd. II, Bl. zu 54, and for Sorge's comment, see *ibid.*, K Mob 12a, Bd. II, Bl. 48a.

and maximum wages, and ban all job changing. Gontardt was certain that this would end the "arbitrariness of the workers" and warned that he would have "to refuse all responsibility for the nonfulfillment of his obligations regarding munitions deliveries" if the suggested measures were not taken.[47]

On the same day, Gontardt sent a letter to Ludendorff to which he appended his note to Kessel. He reminded Ludendorff that he had done everything possible to fulfill the request the former had made in October 1916 for a great increase in machine gun production. The progress he had been making was now being threatened by the work of "systematic agitators." The Auxiliary Service Law, in his view, benefited the workers but did nothing for the employers, and conditions in Berlin had become worse since the law was passed. He concluded that "the half-measures of the government in this regard are absolutely insupportable and are leading to a catastrophe."[48]

Ludendorff was quick to seize upon this letter and a similar letter he had received from Krupp to send forth a tirade to the War Minister and the Chancellor on March 9. He warned that the situation at home was bound to have an "unhealthy influence upon the morale of the army." The continuous increase of wages was creating bitterness among the troops. It was "ironic" that soldiers who risked their lives received a few pennies a day while some skilled workers were earning more than high officials and field grade officers. Similarly, it was unjust that soldiers working in army bureaus should have to labor side by side with civilians who were earning many times more than they were. Strikes, initially caused by food shortages, were quickly being turned into wage movements. The employers had to give in to maintain production, and "the workers, driven on by conscienceless agitators, know this and use it more and more." The "unhappy wording" of the Auxil-

[47] DZA Potsdam, Kriegsakten 1, Bd. II, Bl. 103.

[48] *Ibid.*, Bl. 102. Gontardt did not, of course, mention that the extraordinary price he had demanded for the machine guns had caused Coupette and Count Roedern to support placing provisions for the control of profits in the law.

iary Service Law was largely responsible for this state of affairs. Instead of stressing obligation toward the Fatherland, the law "has become a means of fighting for so-called worker rights." In Ludendorff's opinion, the fact that the same workers who had gone out on strike were ready to die for their country when called into the army demonstrated that they were being "seduced." The workers needed to be enlightened, and "We must not leave the 'enlightenment' to wicked elements." Since the Auxiliary Service Law was creating so much difficulty, he suggested that more use be made of the Law of Siege to deal with agitators. He warned that "we are creating circumstances that we will only be able to overcome through the most convulsive shocks to the state."[49]

Ludendorff's note was built upon a foundation of half-truths and was almost completely lacking in constructive content. It was true that the inadequate family allotments and the discrepancy between military pay and the wages of the workers was causing bitterness in the army, but it was also true that the workers, unlike the troops, had to pay the entire cost of their own food and housing. Agitation had made some contribution to the recent strike movement, but there was also plenty to agitate about. Ludendorff found it quite simple to suggest repressive measures and declare that the government was "creating" a disastrous situation, but when it came to making constructive suggestions as to how a change of system was supposed to be brought about, he suddenly declared that "to go into the social and financial side of the question is not my office."[50]

Helfferich was given the task of replying to Ludendorff. He began by blaming the strikes on the serious food situation and went on to remind the OHL, undoubtedly not without some personal satisfaction, of the warnings he had given the OHL before presenting the Auxiliary Service Law to the Reichstag.

[49] *Ibid.*, Bl. 89. Reprinted in Ludendorff, *Urkunden*, pp. 136-137.

[50] *Ibid.* On the serious effects of the wage situation on the morale of the troops, see Sichler and Tiburtius, *Arbeiterfrage*, p. 38.

Father and Son

Empty.

Let them see who will make their ammunition!

His dire predictions had been fulfilled, but this did not mean that the mistake could be corrected:

> I would . . . regard it to be an even greater mistake to try *now*, in accordance with the wishes of certain employers from heavy industry, to annul the law or to set aside or limit the rights given to the workers under the law. The consequences would be disastrous. The well-meaning leaders of the workers would, even if they themselves wanted to renounce resistance, completely lose control of their people. The Auxiliary Service Law is there, and we must work with it and try to mitigate the worst aspects, like Paragraph 9, in collaboration with the representatives of the interests of the workers.[51]

Furthermore, Helfferich insisted that the union leaders were needed to enlighten the workers and that their help could not be bought without sacrifices, sacrifices "which the employers must also bear." The most important of these sacrifices was the "renunciation of embittering and provocative compulsory measures."

Ludendorff was completely dissatisfied, and on March 27 he sent a note to the Chief of the Military Cabinet, General von Lyncker, which was filled with impotent rage. In his view the worker question was much more serious than claimed and the enlightenment program had failed. Enlightenment was the job of the government. It was wrong to give this task to the unions and to a "certain press," i.e., the Social Democratic press. This was like "having the fox keep the geese."[52]

Groener did not share the views of the OHL and the industrialists. During the strikes in the Ruhr, he had sent Merton and Schlicke to investigate the situation and to negotiate with the trade union leaders. Merton had negotiated with the latter

[51] DZA Potsdam, Kriegsakten 1, Bd. II, Bl. 104. The draft of this note is dated March 13, 1917.

[52] The note to Lyncker was incited by General von Stein's support of Helfferich's views in a letter to Ludendorff of March 14. The two notes are reprinted in Ludendorff, *Urkinden*, pp. 87-89.

in a local inn in Essen. Shortly afterward, Alfred Hugenberg, who had been a member of the board of directors of Merton's father's firm, called on him. Hugenberg informed Merton that heavy industry had been "dealt a serious blow." He did not understand how Merton could permit himself to negotiate at an inn with union leaders while wearing the uniform of a Prussian officer. Merton did not think much of Hugenberg's attitude. He reminded Hugenberg that the War Ministry had long followed a policy of collaborating with the union leaders and that a union leader, Alexander Schlicke, held a responsible position in the War Office. In a directive of March 26, 1917, Groener carried this policy further by instructing the War Office bureaus to play a mediatory role in strikes. They were to listen to both sides and act with the greatest possible tact. He warned against a harsh attitude toward the strikers. This would only increase their bitterness. Finally, he ordered that the War Office be informed of all strikes and their causes so that it could take speedy action, particularly where food was the major problem.[53]

5. *The April Strikes*

In the spring and summer of 1917, Bethmann Hollweg's and Groener's policy of working with the trade unions was severely tested. At the same time the ability of the trade union and Social Democratic Party leaders to control the workers was greatly strained by the growing influence of the leftist opposition, the discontent of the workers, and the dilatory policies of the government. In April 1917, the opponents of the policy of August 4, 1914, organized the Independent Social Democratic Party. Although unanimously opposed to the policy of August 4, 1914, the new party was composed of very heterogeneous elements who were able to agree on little else. Recognizing the weakness of the party and the dangers involved in provoking the government excessively, the leaders refused to

[53] Merton, *Erinnernswertes aus meinem Leben*, pp. 27-28, and BHStA, Abt. IV, MK, IcIa15^{b}, Bd. I, Bl. 76a.

support a general strike or immediate revolutionary action. Instead, they tried to win the workers back to the traditional policy of noncollaboration with the state and middle-class parties. The Independents' program did not satisfy the smaller group within the new party which was gathered around Rosa Luxemburg and Karl Liebknecht and known as the Spartacists. This group supported the mass strike and had immediate revolutionary goals. The growth of German radicalism received considerable inspiration from the February Revolution in Russia, where the workers had played a very important role. The Majority Socialists, therefore, had serious competition for the loyalty of the war-weary and hungry masses of workers, and they were very alarmed when they learned that the government was planning to cut the bread ration on April 15.[54]

The decision to cut the bread ration was made in order to insure that the supply would last until the next harvest. Such a finale to the miserable turnip winter of 1916-1917, however, was certain to create bitterness and unrest. The food situation was largely responsible for the intensified Social Democratic insistence on political reform during the late winter of 1917. Events in Russia increased the demands for such reform, but as the Bureau for Social Policy pointed out in a report to the War Ministry of March 31, "*The deeper cause driving the representatives of the wish for immediate reform is their concern about how the anticipated difficulties with the food supply will affect the mood of the masses.* The Majority Socialists consider it absolutely necessary to give *rights* at the moment when little bread can be given."[55]

It was, therefore, highly appropriate for the president of the War Food Office, Batocki, to have taken the initiative in promoting suffrage reform. In a letter to Bethmann of April 1, he proposed that the Emperor issue an Easter decree solemnly declaring his intention to reform the Prussian suffrage. On

[54] On the various Socialist groups, see Rosenberg, *Birth of the German Republic*, pp. 117-122.

[55] BBS Report, March 31, 1917.

April 4, Valentini, at Bethmann's request, persuaded the Emperor to follow Batocki's suggestion and promise the introduction of direct, universal, and equal suffrage in Prussia. Bethmann knew that he would encounter much resistance from the OHL and the conservative members of the Prussian Cabinet. Nevertheless, he insisted that "vague assurances" would no longer suffice and that the step was necessary for the "support of the monarchy." He warned against creating the impression of weakness by adopting reform measures after the anticipated disturbances over the cutting of the bread ration. But Valentini was unable to persuade Ludendorff, who felt that the only thing necessary was a "strong government" and who warned that a proclamation supporting equal suffrage would "depress worthwhile elements" and have a bad effect on the army.[56]

Because of the opposition of the OHL and of the conservative members of the Prussian Cabinet, who were led by Loebell and Schorlemer, Bethmann was forced to retreat. He had also wanted the Emperor to promise suffrage reform during the war, but he now dropped this idea as he did the plan to have the Emperor promise equal suffrage. He proposed instead that the Emperor promise to set aside the class suffrage. This negative formulation was designed to leave the way open for Loebell's pet project, the introduction of a plural voting system. Despite these concessions on Bethmann's part, General von Stein still found it necessary to stress the OHL's warning that the proposed decree would have a bad effect on the army's morale. Bethmann, who suspected that the Emperor had changed his mind about his original proposal because of Ludendorff, retorted that he knew very well that the older, higher ranking officers were opposed to suffrage reform and went on to remark that

> He has the impression that these gentlemen at the front do not and cannot rightly evaluate political life as it has devel-

[56] Westarp, *Konservative Politik*, p. 264, and Görlitz, *Regierte der Kaiser?*, p. 271.

oped here during the war. Our officers . . . politicize now more than ever. They prefer to read the conservative newspapers and those directed against his [Bethmann's] policy. Among the men and the lower officers, on the other hand, there is a more democratic orientation and they read the left-oriented press. . . . One often believes at General Headquarters that the statesmen at home are subject to an unjustifiable nervousness; but one does not have enough contact with political life there to be able to judge the present situation. He feels obligated not to keep silent about the seriousness of the situation here. If one wants to go on the old way without any consideration for what's going on in the world, then one will come to disaster.[57]

On April 7, 1917, Emperor Wilhelm issued an Easter decree promising reform after the war and declaring that "there is no more room" for the class suffrage system. He also promised a reform of the Prussian House of Lords and asked the Cabinet to prepare the necessary legislation.

At no time, however, was anyone under the illusion that the proclamation of the intention to reform the suffrage would completely palliate the ire of the workers over the cutting of the bread ration on April 15. On the basis of the information received from the union leaders, from agents, and from the illegal leaflets being distributed by radical groups, it was clear that there were going to be strikes and demonstrations on Monday, April 16. Both the War Office and the government sought to lessen the intensity and duration of these untoward events. Groener negotiated an agreement with Helfferich under which 20 percent of Germany's food imports would be earmarked for the "hard working" workers. Helfferich was particularly nervous about the impending disturbances, and he conveyed his nervousness to Bethmann. In an effort to secure the support of the union leaders, the government negotiated with them on April 13. The union leaders were asked to oppose

[57] Protocol of the Prussian Cabinet meeting of April 6, 1917, *AGSOD*, II, pp. 417-419.

the strike and do what they could to control it. Although the willingness of the unions to act in this sense could not be questioned, the government remained worried because "by all evidence, the influence of the union leaders upon the working masses is no longer an unconditional one."[58]

The two most important centers of the wave of mass demonstration strikes that took place in Germany on April 16 and the following days were Berlin and Leipzig. In both cases the strikes were relatively spontaneous outbursts by the workers in response to the food situation. Agitation on the part of radical local union leaders and inflammatory leaflets, however, had done much to excite them. In Berlin the government sought to deal a serious blow to the strike leadership by arresting the radical shop steward leader, Richard Müller, on April 13. This act, however, served only to irritate the workers more. Rather than let the strike get out of hand, the Metalworkers Union leaders in Berlin, Cohen and Severing, decided to assume leadership of the strike. Cohen was particularly anxious to give the strike a completely nonpolitical character. On April 16, 217,000 workers struck in Berlin, and gigantic, but nonviolent, demonstrations were held throughout the city. Under union guidance, an eleven-man strike committee negotiated with Food Commissar Michaelis and General von Kessel. Kessel promised to release Richard Müller and guaranteed that the exempted workers who were participating in the strike would not be drafted back into the army. Michaelis assured the strikers that the workers would receive the stipulated food rations in full measure and on time and promised to increase the meat ration in compensation for the diminution of the bread ration. Also, an advisory council representing the workers was appointed to assist the mayor of Berlin on food questions. As a result of these successful negotiations, the majority

[58] Schoen to Hertling, April 13-14, 1917, BHStA, Abt. II, MA 1, Nr. 918, and Schleehauf to Weizsäcker, April 13-14, 1917, HStASt, E, 73, 12i.

of the workers decided to return to work at a general meeting held on April 17.[59]

Had the strike ended on this note, the government and the trade union leaders would have had good cause to congratulate themselves. The demonstration strikes over the food supply, however, gave the Independent Socialists and the extreme radicals a welcomed opportunity to play upon the discontent of the workers over the length of the war and the slow progress of political reform. In Leipzig the strike had a political character from the very beginning. The striking workers there demanded, in addition to a satisfactory supply of food and coal, a government declaration stating its readiness to conclude a nonannexationist peace, annulment of the Law of Siege and the Auxiliary Service Law, an end to all restrictions on the press and meetings, the liberation of political prisoners, and the introduction of universal and equal suffrage throughout the Empire. A delegation composed of one representative of the Independent Socialist Party and two representatives of the Metalworkers Union was appointed to present these demands to the Chancellor. At the same time, the Leipzig workers called on all the other workers in Germany to join them and proposed that, as in Russia, a workers council be established to represent the interests of the proletariat.

The government, however, refused to receive the Leipzig delegation until the strike was ended. Despite the fact that the strikers had resolved not to work again until their demands were met, they ended the strike on April 18 because the employers had promised to cut the working week to fifty-two hours and to raise wages. The termination of the strike on this basis demonstrates that the majority of the Leipzig workers were much more interested in the economic than in the political side of the strike. When the strike was ended, Wahnschaffe met the delegation from Leipzig and informed them that the government would not negotiate concerning political ques-

[59] Opel, *Deutsche Metallarbeiterverband*, pp. 59-60. See also Schoen's reports to Hertling, April 16-17, 1917, BHStA, Abt. II, MA 1, Nr. 918.

tions. Groener told the delegation that he was astonished over their dissatisfaction with the Auxiliary Service Law.[60]

The political aspects of the Leipzig strike affected developments in Berlin. After April 18 the political side of the strike in Berlin became apparent. Many of the workers did not return to work and workers who had not previously laid down their tools now did so. The demands of those who continued to strike after April 18 were identical with those raised in Leipzig. The Independent Socialist deputies Adolf Hoffmann, Ledebour, and Dittmann agitated for the Leipzig program at worker meetings. At this point General von Kessel decided to act vigorously against the strike. The rights of assembly in Berlin were severely restricted and some of the most dangerous of the agitators were drafted into the army. On April 19 the Martinickenfelde and Wittenau branches of the German Weapons and Munitions Factories were militarized because the demands for higher wages there had produced no agreement and political agitation of the workers was rampant. These factories were occupied by a company of soldiers under the command of Colonel von Feldmann of the Technical Institute of the Infantry. He commanded the workers to return to work by April 21, to refrain from agitation, and to maintain production rates. Violators of these orders were threatened with fines and imprisonment. Furthermore, all strikers liable to military service who did not return to work were automatically drafted into the army as of April 21. They would then be forced to work for soldiers' pay and be subject to military discipline. These various measures had the desired effect, and by April 23 the strike was over.[61]

These strikes, combined with a resolution the Socialists had brought into the Reichstag calling for a peace without annexations and indemnities, served to infuriate the OHL. It blamed everything on the "weak hand in Berlin," and was very worried

[60] Opel, *Deutsche Metallarbeiterverband*, pp. 60-61; *AGSOD*, II, pp. 475-477.

[61] On the militarization of the factories, see *AGSOD*, II, pp. 453-459.

about the effect that the events at home would have on the troops fighting on the Ainse. The more ruthless elements at Headquarters thought that the time had come to send a division to Berlin and "put a few hundred screamers against the wall." As the Bavarian observer at General Headquarters noted, Ludendorff's chief advisers on internal affairs, Colonel Bauer and the Chief of Army Intelligence, Colonel Nicolai, "are very excited and do not look too rosily into the future, as the ground at home seems to be tottering."[62]

The government did not want military assistance from Hindenburg, but it did want the latter's moral support. It was thought that an appeal by Hindenburg to the strikers would work wonders, and on April 19 Hindenburg sent a letter to Groener designed for publication. In his letter Hindenburg, while recognizing the food situation as the major cause of the strike, declared that even the smallest strike was "an irresponsible weakening of our powers of defense and appears to me as an unpardonable sin against the army and particularly against the men in the trenches who must bleed because of it." He demanded that the workers be enlightened in this sense. Groener had this letter published and also sent it to the unions with a personal reminder that the "Auxiliary Service Law has not only brought rights but also duties to the workers." He demanded that the unions give him their complete and unreserved cooperation.[63]

Groener's attitude toward the April strikes is of exceptional importance for an understanding of both the man and his policies. He did not take the original intention of the workers to strike on April 16 "very tragically." He was sympathetic to the depression the workers felt when, after the long turnip winter, they were suddenly confronted with a cut in the bread ration just at the moment "when they could breathe again." Groener knew that they were discontented over the nonfulfill-

[62] Report of April 23, 1917, BHStA, Abt. IV, MK, III a XV 39.

[63] The Hindenburg and Groener letters are reprinted in *Schulthess' Europäischer Geschichtskalender*, Bd. 32, pp. 422-423. On the background of the Hindenburg letter, see *AGSOD*, II, pp. 457-458.

ment of so many of the government's promises concerning the food supply, and he recognized that "the ground was ripe for mass suggestion." For this reason he had warned against harsh measures "because I was of the view that it would be well to open up the valve somewhat this time and let this mood blow away." The workers had been quite "reasonable" on the 16th, and when the unions seemed to have ended the strike on the following day, Groener was quite ready to forget the whole affair. On April 18, however, the strikes lost their "agreeableness" (*Gemütlichkeit*) for Groener. The political demands raised in Leipzig and Berlin infuriated him, and he had no intention of putting up with this kind of behavior.[64]

Groener was in fact so ardently in favor of calling up large numbers of the striking workers that the government and the industrialists had to calm him down. Groener was convinced, for example, that the workers at the Weapons and Munitions Factories were so corrupted by the Independent Socialists that the only thing to do was to exchange the exempted workers there for more reliable ones. He would have liked to break the back of the strike by letting the workers stay out of work until they ran out of money, but the military situation did not permit this. These factories were exceptionally important for the war effort, and, as Groener pointed out, the fact that "the military contracts have been excessively centralized instead of decentralized is revenging itself here."[65]

The government feared that the calling up of exempted workers, particularly after the government had promised to abstain from such measures, would lead to great bitterness. Bethmann was completely opposed to this aspect of Groener's policy.[66] Amusingly enough, however, the industrialists, who were always demanding ruthlessness, suddenly backed down when Groener demonstrated this quality. As a disciplinary measure and as a first installment on his redrafting program, Groener wanted to call up 4,000 strikers on April 20, and he

64 Statement by Groener, Budget Committee Debates, April 26, 1917.
65 War Ministry meeting, April 21, 1917, *AGSOD*, II, pp. 460-461.
66 Varnbüler to Weizsäcker, April 21, 1917, HStASt, E, 73, 12i.

sent officers to various firms whose workers were striking to ask for the names of the most undisciplined workers. The employers refused to cooperate and insisted that "one should not intervene so sharply." When Dr. Sorge reproached them for their anxiety a few days later, one employer explained that they did not want to help their competitors by giving up workers. Another emphasized that they could not maintain production if their workers were called up. Dr. Sorge criticized this "everyone for himself" attitude, and one of the industrialists, demonstrating more honesty than his fellows, admitted that they had been quite frightened by the strike. Sorge was thus reflecting the general policy of the War Office when he told the industrialists that "one believed for a long time that one could get by with conciliatory tactics. Now, however, we intend, although with the greatest circumspection, to act firmly."[67]

Groener also took the occasion of the strikes to attempt to clarify the relationship between the War Office and the Deputy Commanding Generals and between the Auxiliary Service Law and the Law of Siege. The Deputy Commanding General in Kiel had drafted a group of striking workers and then revoked his order. He blamed the War Office for the latter decision. Groener knew nothing of the case, but he did know that many of the generals felt that the War Office's policy had been too lenient. Thus on April 25 Groener informed the Deputy Commanding Generals that he did not approve of the revocation of the order drafting the workers because it undermined military authority, "whose unconditional maintenance is more necessary now than ever before." Once strong measures were decided on, it was absolutely necessary "never to give in!" He advised against the drafting of individual workers and suggested that those caught agitating be tried for treason. He did recommend, however, that young, unruly exempted workers be exchanged for older and more stable

[67] Meeting of April 21, 1917, BHStA, Abt. IV, MK, IcIa15^b, Bd. I, Bl. 93.

men. Groener insisted that a clear distinction be made between the Auxiliary Service Law and the Law of Siege. The former law was the War Office's business, and the Deputy Commanding Generals "would do well to concern themselves as little as possible with the Auxiliary Service Law." Strikers placed themselves outside of that law. The Law of Siege had priority over the Auxiliary Service Law because the former was the "guardian of the internal and external security of the Empire." Groener warned that "no measures should be taken which may be interpreted as a sign of weakness on the part of the military authorities with respect to the workers." And he reminded them that "measures which harm the production of weapons and munitions for a long time cannot be tolerated any more than long strikes, as we have no real reserves of matériel."[68]

As implied in the last sentence, Groener did not want the Deputy Commanding Generals to go overboard in using the Law of Siege. Indeed, one gets the impression that Groener was desperately trying to keep the Deputy Commanding Generals under his thumb while at the same time giving them enough leeway to maintain internal security. The strikes had presented a horrendous problem for Groener. He was most angry at the Independent Socialists because they had ruined his attempt to treat the April 16 strike lightly. He was equally angry at the industrialists for their efforts to sabotage the Auxiliary Service Law. He was also disgruntled over the failure of the unions and the Social Democrats to speak out energetically against the strikes. Groener was walking a tightrope which was being frayed at both ends. Each time the Independent Socialists or the industrialists stirred things up, Groener's ability to continue his policy of working with the unions and treating all sides fairly was endangered. The OHL and the Deputy Commanding Generals were looking for an excuse to employ repressive measures, and only Groener barred the way. If his policy was to succeed, Groener had to suppress the Independent Socialists and compel the indus-

[68] Directive of April 25, 1917, *ibid.*, K Mob 7, Bd. II, Bl. 21.

trialists to accept his policy. Above all, however, he had to have the unstinting support of the Social Democrats and the trade union leaders, for they were the key to the salvation of his policy. If they failed him, then he could no longer control either the industrialists or the workers.

On April 26 he met with the Deputy Commanding Generals to discuss the right of assembly. He advised them to make a sharp distinction between the Majority Social Democrats, on the one hand, and the Independent Socialists and Spartacists, on the other. It was necessary to collaborate with the former and permit them to hold meetings but, at the same time, to make sure that they "fulfill their promises and try to enlighten and pacify their people." Every effort was to be made to isolate the Independent Socialists and to act ruthlessly against those caught inciting strikes. He made special mention of Deputy Dittmann, who was known to have spoken at meetings in the factories that had to be militarized and who Groener considered "one of the most dangerous and skilled agitators." He insisted, however, that the workers be given a responsible role in food distribution, both within the government agencies and within the factories. Above all, he demanded that the Deputy Commanding Generals be fair:

> It is equally important that the employers finally become more reasonable. He [Groener] is going to act ruthlessly against those employers who persist in their antiquated views and do not want to see that things are completely different today than they were twenty years ago. If the agitators on the one side are to be taken into custody, then the same must hold true for those on the other side. It is necessary that the Deputy Commanding Generals stand completely above the workers and employers and do not allow themselves to be influenced in any direction.[69]

On the same day Groener expressed himself in a similar fashion before the Reichstag Budget Committee. He was most

[69] Meeting of April 26, 1917, *ibid.*, IcIa15^b, Bd. I, Bl. zu 110.

sympathetic in his discussion of the food situation that had created the strike of April 16-17, but he violently attacked the agitation that had led to the continuation of the strike. He informed the deputies that he was planning to issue a declaration on the following day banning strikes and promised that he would handle agitators with the greatest severity. The workers were to use the institutions created by the Auxiliary Service Law to express their wishes. But in his conclusion, and to the warm applause of the left wing deputies, he stated that he would act just as ruthlessly against those seeking to limit the rights of the workers as he would act against strike agitators:

> For there can be no doubt that the War Office stands on completely neutral ground. What is right for the one is right for the other. I will, therefore, also act against those agitators who try to agitate against the Auxiliary Service Law, and, from this place, I send out a warm, but final appeal to the employers to accept those rights that have been given to the workers and to collaborate in the loyal fulfillment of the Auxiliary Service Law.[70]

After hearing these words, the left wing deputies were truly astonished when they read Groener's proclamation of April 27. The overexcited Groener seems to have been convinced that only the sharpest military tone would prove truly effective in convincing the workers of their duty. He reminded the workers of Hindenburg's letter and demanded to know "Who dares to defy Hindenburg's call?" and "Who dares not to work when Hindenburg commands?" Most offensive, however, were the lines, "A cur is he who strikes so long as our armies stand before the enemy. I hereby order that all high-minded workers in the factories . . . enlighten their comrades about what the time and the future of the Fatherland demands from us all: work and again work until the victorious end of the war."[71]

[70] Reichstag Budget Committee, April 26, 1917.

[71] Reprinted in Institut für Marxismus-Leninismus, *Dokemente und Materialien*, I, p. 629. See also Groener, *Lebenserinnerungen*, p. 363.

If the workers read Hindenburg's letter, then they would know that the "worst enemies are hidden in our midst—they are the faint-hearted and the even worse ones, those who agitate for strikes. He who listens to their words is a coward."

The combination of Groener's "final appeal" to the employers and his "cur decree," as it was called, exposed him to much criticism from both sides. The conservative press praised the latter but expressed astonishment over the former, while the left wing press did the reverse. In general, the Socialists were more willing to forgive Groener. It was not often, after all, that they heard "final appeals" to the employers. The Socialist *Vorwärts* went so far as to suggest that Groener was not the real author of the "cur decree," and that it had been written by reactionary advisers.[72] Groener had made a bad mistake in sending forth his proclamation, however, and he was subjected to strong criticism from the left in both the Budget Committee and the Reichstag. The union leaders were very annoyed. As it was, they were continuously being attacked for being agents of the government. Now, in their enlightenment work, they would always be reminded of Groener's "I hereby order." Deputy Wels declared that the union leaders would henceforth be suspected of being "government commissars or agents of General Groener"[73] every time they opposed strikes. In a somewhat more humorous tone, Deputy Schöpflin suggested that Groener had let his Swabian bluntness run away with him and asked that he refrain from making such "temperamental" declarations in the future. Groener's "Attention! Eyes right!" tone was fine for the barracks, but could not be employed against free German workers. Schöpflin was also very critical of Groener's adherence to the "Hindenburg cult" and remarked that "it has become customary among us now to bring in Field Marshal von Hindenburg for every possible and impossible purpose."[74] Outside of the Reichstag there were

[72] *Vorwärts*, April 28, 1917, in Nachlass Groener, 194.
[73] Reichstag Budget Committee, April 27, 1917.
[74] Reichstag Debates, May 4, 1917, 309, pp. 3057-3058.

more conservative criticisms of the way Groener had used Hindenburg's name. Count Hertling pointed out that the Hindenburg cult was becoming "dangerous to the monarchical principle." He, too, felt that Groener's tone was unfortunate and not reflective of his usual common sense. Hertling came to the conclusion that Groener "must have learned such phrases in Berlin."[75]

Despite these criticisms, Groener felt that his proclamation had a good effect, and he defended it with all his might. He was most aggressive in answering Independent Socialist criticisms and blamed the political side of the strike on Independent Socialist and Entente propaganda.[76] Yet, as always, he coupled his attack on the radical agitators with an attack on the more antisocial of the employers. He was quick to point out that his harshest measures, particularly the militarization of factories, had been meant to benefit the workers as well as to discipline them. Indeed, Groener felt that these factories had to be militarized because of the failure of management to handle the workers properly. It is interesting to note that the employers were far from happy about the militarization and warned against endangering the authority of the employers by too frequent use of such methods.[77]

Above all, however, Groener defended his proclamation as the best means of stiffening the backs of those workers who wanted to resist the "terrorism" of the agitators in the factories. While recognizing the value of union proclamations against strikes, he warned the unions against "deceiving themselves." In the factories and on the local level, the union people did not always resist agitator terrorism: "Take care that your people

[75] Möser to Weizsäcker, May 3, 1917, HStASt, E, 73, 12i. See also Crown Prince Rupprecht's comments, *Kriegstagebuch*, II, pp. 152-153, 203.

[76] See his exchanges with Deputy Cohn, Reichstag Debates, May 5, 1917, 309, p. 3102, and with Deputy Dittmann, Reichstag committee meeting, April 23, 1917, BHStA, Abt. IV, MK, K Mob 7, Bd. II, Bl. 84.

[77] Reichstag Budget Committee, April 27, 1917; *AGSOD*, II, p. 461; notation on a meeting between Colonel Bauer and Borsig on April 29, BA, Nachlass Bauer, Nr. 11.

actually follow your instructions. Your people must also show their colors and not only calm down the workers, weakly react to terrorism, and try to bring things into order again after a few days by means of small sedatives. The unions must continually show their colors . . . and must openly and honestly say: Children, you must not strike!"[78]

[78] Reichstag Budget Committee, April 27, 1917.

VII

The War Office and the Social Problem
2. The Great Crisis and the Dismissal of Groener, May–August 1917

1. The Intensification of Social Conflict

NOT the least important of Groener's reasons for taking such a strong stand against the political strikes of April 1917 was his desire to prevent a recurrence of the strikes on May Day. Despite the continuous rumors that there were going to be strikes on that day, it came and went peacefully. The General Commission had done its share to prevent strikes by sending an urgent warning to the union functionaries on April 23:

> Germany is not Russia. The revolutionary games of the Independents and the Spartacists endanger the German labor movement, especially our union organization and the defensive strength of the country. We have succeeded until now in holding the responsible authorities back from the use of sharp measures. If the Independents succeed again in unleashing wild political strikes, then such measures will be unavoidable. The laming of all union activity and the serious damaging of our union organization will be the consequence while, on the other side, the political successes desired by the Independents will not be gained. It is much more to be feared that reaction will get the upper hand and that the certain prospect of political reform will be endangered.[1]

Equally important, however, was Groener's decision to speak personally to the Independent leader Haase. He warned Haase that he would employ troops to quell May Day demonstrations and asked Haase to give his word of honor that he would use

[1] Reprinted in *AGSOD*, II, pp. 467-469.

his influence to prevent a strike on May Day. Haase complied with Groener's request, but asked that this be kept a secret "because he was somewhat worried about his supporters."[2]

As Haase feared the more radical members of his party, so the Majority Socialists feared Haase and his friends. At the same time, there was considerable confusion within the ranks of the Social Democratic leaders. Groener's demand that they "show their colors" was not unjustified. They were by no means united in their attitude toward the strikes. At a meeting of the Socialist leaders on April 19,[3] Carl Severing was very critical of the absence of a clear policy. He pointed out that the party and the General Commission should have conferred before the strikes to decide on a common course of action. He recognized that the unions were opposed to "wild" strikes, but the union petitions concerning the food situation created a very different impression: "I must say that the last petitions of the unions to various agencies . . . necessarily created the impression that they were threatening with strikes and that the unions would then tolerate those strikes."

Deputy Robert Schmidt, speaking for the General Commission, pointed out that the unions felt incapable of doing anything about the strikes because of the spontaneous action of the workers. In fact the unions feared that their overt opposition would make the strikes more intense. Personally, he had nothing against a brief demonstration strike. The unions had often warned that the workers would not put up with the mismanagement of the food supply forever, and "what use are such threats when they are not permitted to be realized at the right time?" Nevertheless, the proposed strikes were very dangerous. The unions did not have the workers

[2] Groener, *Lebenserinnerungen*, pp. 363-364. Later Groener was much criticized by conservative elements in the army and industry for his willingness to discuss such matters with an Independent Socialist leader.

[3] For the quotations from and discussion of this meeting which follow, see SPD Archiv, *Protokolle der gemeinsamen Sitzung des Parteiausschusses und der Reichstagsfraktion*, April 19, 1917 (an unpublished manuscript), pp. 51ff.

A strike is not merely a work stoppage. Whoever strikes now works for the enemy.

under control, and the employers stood to benefit by them. He had reliable information that the employers wanted strikes as an excuse to attack the Auxiliary Service Law. Finally, he feared that the strikes would raise the Entente's morale and thus prolong the war.

Deputy Paul Löbe was of an entirely different opinion. However deplorable the fact that the strikes were incited by the Independent Socialists, they represented the "healthy idea that the people should make its own voice heard at this time." The important thing was to keep the strikes from getting completely out of control. Indeed, Löbe was willing to go quite far in using the strike weapon:

> And I do not shy away from saying that even strikes in the munitions factories do not worry me. The capitalistic governments have much more to lose in this war than we do, and, therefore, I know that they will give way to these strikes and give us reforms more quickly than they are now apparently willing to. . . . We have arrived at a period when we can and must bully something out of our opponents. . . . The Independent Socialists are never more pleased than when they can say: "that is the Social Democratic tactic—doing nothing to make the suffrage reform come sooner!" (very true!)

August Müller, speaking for the Executive Committee of the party, objected to Löbe's remarks. He warned that certain elements were just looking for an excuse to militarize the factories and declared that the party could neither approve of nor make concessions to the strike supporters. Thus there were serious differences within the Majority Socialist camp concerning the strike question. No one, including Löbe, advocated an abandonment of the policy of August 4, 1914, but there was considerable confusion as to the tactics to be employed.

Within the trade union movement there were sharp disagreements over both principles and tactics, for the Independents and Majority Socialists were forced to fight their battles within the framework of the old union organizations. Nowhere was this more the case than in the Metalworkers Union. As a member of the War Office and as a propagandist for the Auxiliary Service Law, Schlicke was the living embodiment of the policy of August 4. In Berlin, Leipzig, and other important industrial centers, however, there were strong union groups opposed to Schlicke's policies and extremely critical of the Auxiliary Service Law. Led by the Frankfurt Independent Socialist and union leader, Robert Dissmann, these groups argued that Schlicke had sold out the workers by supporting the law. They demanded that Schlicke give up his position in the War Office and redirect union policy along the lines of the class struggle. Schlicke sought to defend his policies in a series of articles explaining the law to the workers and describing its benefits. Finally, he summoned a Metalworkers Union Congress for June 27-30 in order to strengthen his position and receive a vote of confidence.[4]

Schlicke did receive his vote of confidence but, in the process, had to permit a public display of the deep cleavages within his organization. The debate over the Auxiliary Service Law was particularly ferocious. Schlicke admitted that the law was a "compulsory law," but stressed that "a few drops of social oil have come into this compulsory law which tend to weaken its compulsory nature." He asked whether it would have been better if the Deputy Commanding Generals had instituted compulsion under the Law of Siege, and replied

> No. From the practical standpoint the union leaders must say to themselves: If there is a possibility of avoiding a greater evil, then we must accept the smaller one. . . . The Auxiliary Service Law is there, and we cannot discuss it away. Shall we not, therefore, seize the opportunity to

[4] For Schlicke's articles, see *Metallarbeiter-Zeitung*, May 12, May 19, June 2, and June 9, 1917. For the discussion and quotations which follow, see *Die dreizehnte . . . Generalversammlung des Deutschen Metallarbeiterverbandes . . . vom 27. bis 30. Juni 1917 . . .*, pp. 53ff.

> utilize the few rights which the law has given us and attempt to have them applied in the sense desired by the workers.

In answer to criticisms that his position in the War Office was very weak compared to that of Dr. Sorge, Schlicke pointed out that he never intended to do more than represent the interests of labor there and that it was completely wrong to compare his position to that of a Minister without Portfolio or an Undersecretary of State.

Dissmann rejected these arguments. In his view the Auxiliary Service Law was an exceptional law against the workers and its provisions for the protection of the workers were of very dubious value: "When a free man is made a slave, it is a small consolation for him or, truer yet, no consolation at all, when he is told that provisions have been made with regard to the whip of the overseer so that it will not be brought down upon him too hard or too powerfully." Dissmann laughed at Schlicke's fear of what the government would have done if the unions had refused to support the law. There were limits to the power of the government, and it "knows very well that the workers are indispensable for the continuation of the war." Finally, he attacked Schlicke for minimizing his position in the War Office after its importance had been stressed by the trade union press. Schlicke's remarks demonstrated that his appointment was nothing more than a "sedative" for the workers.

The debate over the April strikes was equally vituperative. In Schlicke's opinion April 16 was "not exactly a glorious page in the history of our union." He objected particularly to the use of the strike for political purposes. Another union leader from Berlin, Kanow, irritatedly remarked that the workers at the Berlin Weapons and Munitions Factories had been lost to the union thanks to the agitation of the Independent Socialists and that some of the best union members had been drafted into the army. Here, indeed, was the real issue. Schlicke and his followers regarded the radicals as impractical dreamers who knew nothing of the real problems of trade union organization and who were willing to sacrifice the organization for theoretical and impractical purposes. The right wing trade union functionaries felt that it was ridiculous to "agitate before machine guns" and "swim in the policy of the future." The Dresden leader, Albert Schwarz, reminded Dissmann of the difficulties involved in awakening the workers to their own needs:

> I want to establish here that most of the wage movements receive very little response from the workers initially. (very true!) It is uncommonly difficult for us to get members to come to meetings. The meetings are almost always poorly attended. (everywhere!) We must make the greatest efforts in order to make our comrades aware of their old wage and working conditions. (very true!) We must enlighten them. We must tell them what they are to do and have done.

Viewed from this practical vantage point, the Auxiliary Service Law was a blessing. The Duisburg leader, Heinrich Kremers, confessed that he had once been an opponent of the law. He could not believe that Thyssen, Stinnes, and Krupp would permit the establishment of effective workers committees. Yet such committees had been set up, and General von Gayl had given them protection by forbidding the recall of workers committee members into the army.

> When the comrades saw this, they once again had confidence in their organizations, and I can, in the name of a large number of comrades, declare that the influence of the unions is so great today that we can protect our members against the arbitrariness of the employers. In Duisburg we have a hundred new members a week. Old comrades come out of the sulking corners into which they had withdrawn because of the brawl in the party. I therefore look upon the Auxiliary Service Law with somewhat different eyes today.

The statements of Schwarz and Kremers demonstrate what the union leaders really were out to accomplish and show why they were so angry at the Independent Socialists for making their lives so complicated. On the one hand, the trade unionists were promoting large scale and very successful wage movements among the workers. The institutions established under the Auxiliary Service Law were used for the fulfillment of these demands. On the other hand, they were gaining new members as a result of this policy and extending their sway into areas of the country where they had previously been powerless.

Although strikes and labor unrest before April usually involved demands for wage increases, this tendency became particularly marked during and after the April strikes. The War Office noted that, despite union claims that the workers cared more about a satisfactory food supply than about higher wages, the workers now seemed to be placing the latter above the former. One explanation for this phenomenon was that the workers had lost all confidence in the food supply administration and were turning to the black market. Equally significant, however, was the fact that the workers were demanding increases in their base pay rather than special wartime cost of living increases. Industry's policy, of course, was to keep base pay static, "for there is reason to fear that otherwise it will not be very easy to return to reasonable wage rates when the war ends and the cost of living decreases."[5] Lastly, the high profits of the industrialists incited the workers and their organizations to demand higher wages. Indeed, the unions continuously brought the high profits of the industrialists to the attention of the workers in meetings.

On June 2 the Association of German Employer Organizations sent a note to Groener concerning the wage problem. While forced to admit that the high turnover rate of the

[5] Northwest Group of the VdESI to its members, Feb. 8, 1917, BA, R 13I/31. On the growth of wage movements and the trade union propaganda for them, see the ZMG Reports, May-July, 1917.

winter months had abated, they pointed out that unrest among the workers now took the form of demands for wage increases. These demands were made through the workers committees and the conciliation agencies. The employers felt powerless to resist such collective wage demands. Thus in Berlin cases involving groups ranging from 190 to 1900 workers were being heard by the conciliation agencies. In each case the workers threatened to demand leaving certificates from the arbitration committees if the employers did not accept the awards of the conciliation agencies. The wages demanded were, in the view of the employers, "unhealthy and unjustified." The industrialists reminded Groener that these wages could only encourage black marketeering and endanger industry's ability to readjust to normal peacetime conditions. In contrast to the ambitious program for the reform of Paragraph 9 which they had presented on March 27, however, the industrialists now limited themselves to a single request. They wished the War Office to ban all newspaper reports on wage negotiations conducted in the conciliation agencies and arbitration committees.[6]

This petition was discussed in the War Office on June 25. There was agreement that the specific request made by the industrialists was justified because the publication of wage statistics did disturb the workers. Dr. Oppenheimer, of the Labor Office, suggested that Schlicke be asked to cooperate. Schlicke was sympathetic to Oppenheimer's arguments, for at the Metalworkers Congress on June 30, Schlicke told the delegates that "exact figures on wage increases are, in themselves, not only superfluous, but also misleading and are best avoided."[7] Schlicke's concession to Oppenheimer was in line with the union policy of opposing excessive turnover and *unorganized* wage demands.

Groener's attitude toward the wage question was rather

[6] BHStA, Abt. IV, MK, K Mob 19, Bd. II, Bl. zu 54.

[7] For the War Office discussion, see *ibid.*, K Mob 7d, Bd. II, Bl. 61. For Schlicke's standpoint, see *ibid.*, Bl. 20, and *Die dreizehnte . . . Generalversammlung des Deutschen Metallarbeiterverbandes . . . vom 27. bis 30. Juni 1917 . . .*, p. 142.

complicated. From the very beginning he opposed the notion that every increase in wages justified the granting of a leaving certificate. Similarly, he supported an interpretation of the law made by his two legal advisers, Dr. Schiffer and Dr. Junck, that the purposes of the law were to be considered in granting the leaving certificate.[8] The interpretation, however, represented the opinion of the War Office and was not legally binding upon the arbitration committee chairmen. In fact, their practices varied considerably, and one of the worst aspects of the law was the lack of uniformity in the decisions of the committees. Groener sought to mitigate this problem by sending commissars to advise the committees. In one case, however, a committee chairman actually refused to permit a commissar to take part in the deliberations. Groener insisted upon his right to send commissars, but assured the arbitration committee chairmen that there would be no interference with their independent decision-making powers.[9]

Generally speaking, Groener continued the War Ministry's policy of demanding strict neutrality on the wage question. In a directive of July 5, 1917, he instructed the War Office bureaus not to take a definite position on specific wage demands when mediating disputes. Five days after issuing this directive, however, he instructed a War Office bureau to support a wage increase and, when asked how this could be brought into consonance with his directive of July 5, replied that the latter did not exclude advising the employers to raise wages when they were clearly inadequate.[10]

[8] Dr. Schiffer, it will be remembered, was the Reichstag deputy who fought hardest for the inclusion of this type of clause in the Reichstag discussion of the law. For his interpretation, see *Der Deutsche Metallarbeiterverband im Jahre 1917. Jahr- und Handbuch für Verbandsmitglieder*, Stuttgart, 1918, p. 26.

[9] See Groener's directives of Jan. 3 and June 19, 1917, BHStA, Abt. IV, MK, K Mob 11a, Bd. I, Bl. zu 27, and K Mob 19, Bd. II, Bl. 189.

[10] For the directive of July 5, 1917, see *ibid.*, K Mob 6, Bd. II, Bl. 92. On the contradictory attitude of the War Office, see Peter Quante, "Lohnpolitik und Lohnentwicklung im Kriege," *Zeitschrift des Preussischen Statistischen Landesamts*, 59, 1919, p. 327.

Groener supported and recognized collective wage agreements in the hope that, insofar as they existed, they would serve to stabilize wages, but he also supported the necessity of increasing the wages stipulated in these agreements if they became insufficient due to the increased cost of living. In short, he was pragmatic about the wage question because of its complex nature and because of high employer profits. Thus, when an employer complained to Groener about wage movements in his industry, Groener replied along these lines:

> I have made the observation that industry has gone chasing after war profits in an unheard-of manner, and that this mad profit-making [*Kriegsgewinnerei*] . . . leads to jealousy on the other side. I wonder . . . whether you know that the War Office has had to stop a company from making a profit of thirty-five million; whether you know that a German employer permits four women who work for him to sleep in a barrack in one bed that is also full of lice and that a German employer takes workers from a colleague by offering them higher wages and then considers himself entitled to indemnification by the state in establishing his prices.[11]

The industrialists were shocked to learn the extent of Groener's critical attitude, and they were at a loss as to whom to turn. To their irritation over the "insane" wage demands of the workers was added their anxiety over the extension of union power and the disturbances thereby created. The situation in Upper Silesia was particularly serious. Before the war only a very small percentage of the workers there were unionized, and this percentage had decreased during the first part of the war. After the passage of the Auxiliary Service Law, the Social Democratic Metalworkers and Coal Miners unions sent organizers into the area. The work of these organizers is well described by one of the Metalworkers Union's district leaders:

[11] Reported by Dr. ter Mer at the VdESI meeting of June 21, 1917, BA, R 131/151.

> After the Auxiliary Service Law went into effect, the workers were enlightened in meetings, conferences, and discussions concerning the meaning of the law and its provisions. The workers were especially instructed to the effect that the workers committees would be much more important than they had been before and that the economic interests of the workers could be defended by use of the arbitration committees. In Upper Silesia the introduction of workers committees means the recognition of the workers as a co-determining factor in economic life.[12]

As a result of these efforts membership in the Metalworkers Union rose from 4,900 at the end of 1916 to 12,448 at the end of 1917, an increase of 154 percent. The successes of the Coal Miners Union were even greater.[13] When elections for the workers committees were held in May, they were accompanied by sporadic strikes. These strikes, which will be discussed in detail later, increased in number and duration during June and July. For the moment it is important to note that the disturbances in Silesia and the union organizing efforts there occurred at the same time.

Needless to say, the Upper Silesian industrialist leader, Hilger, regarded this situation as the fulfillment of the dire predictions he had made when the Auxiliary Service Law had first been discussed. At a meeting of the executive committee of the Association of German Iron and Steel Industrialists on June 21,[14] he angrily, almost hysterically, commented on the effects of the law. Previously, the Upper Silesian workers did not care a bit about workers committees. Now the elections and the union agitators were creating dissatisfaction among the workers. Once there were workers committees, "they had to have something to do." As a result there were "artificial demands" and strikes. The unions were holding meetings

[12] *Der Deutsche Metallarbeiterverband im Jahre 1917*, p. 195.

[13] *Ibid.* and *AGSOD*, II, pp. 723-724.

[14] For the quotations from and discussion of this meeting, see BA, R 13I/151.

"from morning to night." Thanks to the guarantee of the right of assembly stated in the law, nothing was being done to stop these meetings. Hilger detested this weak-kneed policy, which he characterized as

> reverence for King Mob, the fear of doing something because the great mass is involved. But one does not think that the employers are being shorn of their rights. We cannot bear a strike; we must simply give in in the interest of the Fatherland. We must agree to the most shameless wage demands. . . . If I were a Deputy Commanding General, I would say: "The devil take me! It will not do to have meetings, even concerning wage questions, in the Fatherland's direst hour. The rascals shall work and not hold meetings."

The Saar industrialist Dr. Schlenker pointed out that a similar situation had developed in his own area. There the Christian and Socialist unions, which had previously played a very minor role, had suddenly taken over. The yellow unions, which had been treated with "great affection" by the employers, were being ruined. He had discussed the question of restricting the right of assembly with the Deputy Commanding General. The latter, Schlenker confidentially told his colleagues, wanted to do something, but he felt powerless because of the instructions he had received from Berlin. The chairman of the meeting, Dr. Meyer, thereupon suggested that the time had come for the industrialists to gather together their material and send a petition concerning the dangers of the policy being pursued by the government. They were puzzled, however, as to where to send it. When Dr. Meyer suggested Groener, one of the industrialists remarked that "there you will find little response. Groener is usually very understanding, but when it comes to these problems he is very unreasonable." One solution to the problem was then found when someone cried out, "Above all, I would send it to the Field Marshal!" Thus, the employers were mobilizing against the unions, the Auxiliary Service Law, and, by implication, against Groener himself.

2. *The Army and the Great Crisis*

This mobilization of the employers was taking place at the onset of the most serious internal crisis since the beginning of the war. In late June the relative quiet that followed the April strikes gave way to unrest and disturbances. Serious strikes and food riots broke out in the Ruhr due to the food shortage and anger over the more satisfactory food situation of other areas, particularly Berlin. They were immediately combined with wage movements. At the same time, there was a notable increase of radical agitation for peace and political reform. To break the strikes, General von Gayl instituted extraordinary courts-martial, and heavy sentences were meted out to agitators. The most important strikes, however, were those in Upper Silesia. They were responsible for extremely serious losses of coal production, losses which amounted to a half million tons by July 14. It should be kept in mind that these strikes coincided with the coal crisis and the beginning of Groener's program for a Concentration of Forces. Such was the socioeconomic background of the great political crisis which took place at this time.[15]

In June even the optimism at General Headquarters seems to have evaporated. Previously, Bauer and Ludendorff were confident that the U-boats would bring England to her knees by August and that the annexationist program could be realized. They no longer placed complete faith in the submarines and showed some concern over America's entry into the war. The sloppy military performance of Germany's allies was an additional cause of anxiety.[16] The OHL even decided that the time had come to enlighten the Chancellor concerning the

[15] On the strikes in the Ruhr, see Captain Müller's report of July 5, 1917, BHStA, Abt. IV, MK, IcIa15^b, Bd. I, Bl. 133. For the production losses in Silesia, see *ibid.*, K Mob 12, Bd. XI, Bl. 8. On the Ruhr strikes, see also *AGSOD*, II, pp. 595-600. Finally, for the general deterioration of morale in the early summer of 1917, see the ZMG Report of July 1917.

[16] Report of Kraft von Delmensingen on his conversations with members of the General Staff, June 29, 1917, BHStA, Abt. II, MA 1, Nr. 945, Bl. 55-57.

seriousness of the situation. The peculiarity of this "enlightenment," however, was that it in no way conceded the necessity for a revision of Germany's annexationist program and the quest for a negotiated peace. On the contrary, the failure of the submarines was portrayed as a temporary setback and the responsibility for Germany's future success or failure was insidiously placed upon the shoulders of the homefront. Thus, in a note to Bethmann of June 19, Hindenburg pointed out that the belief the war would end by fall was "a great danger" and that it was time to enlighten the public about the "true situation." Instead of telling the truth, however, Hindenburg once again produced the old magic formula. He informed Bethmann that he was certain that the submarines would eventually drive the enemy to seek peace, but he could not say exactly when. The important thing, therefore, was to hold out and maintain confidence, for the enemy would continue to resist "so long as they can calculate that *the collapse of Germany and her allies will precede their own.* They hope to bring this collapse about . . . through food and raw materials shortages, through disunity, dissatisfaction and the victory of the radical Social Democrats."[17] Here, indeed, was the one magic formula of the OHL which was to work, the nascent stab-in-the-back legend.

At the same time, however, Colonel Bauer made the serious mistake of conveying some of the downcast mood at Headquarters to the powerful Centrist leader, Erzberger, during conversations they had on June 10 and 19. Bauer was counting on Erzberger to support the establishment of a "spiritual food office" to feed the country the right kind of propaganda. Erzberger, while keenly interested in becoming the head of such a propaganda agency, drew entirely different conclusions from the OHL concerning the deterioration of Germany's military situation. He felt that the government had to actively seek a peace of understanding and that the time had come for the Reichstag to play an important role in such an effort. Thus, at

[17] Hindenburg to Bethmann, June 19, 1917, *ibid.*, Nr. 975, Bl. 216-217.

the Budget Committee meeting of July 6, he triggered a major political crisis by launching a devastating attack on the navy's unrestricted submarine warfare program and calling for a Reichstag peace resolution.[18]

It is very unlikely that Germany could have escaped a severe internal crisis in July 1917 even if Erzberger had not made his sensational speech. The Social Democrats were already demanding a clear statement on war aims and suffrage reform. On July 3 Ebert announced that the mood of the workers was grim, as demonstrated by the strikes, and that a winter campaign had to be avoided. The people were tired of listening to promises of suffrage reform, and according to Ebert they would wait no longer. Deputy Hoch put the matter in much more brutal terms: "One is always speaking of revolution and whether there will be one. He can only say that Germany is already in the midst of a revolution."[19]

Bethmann was convinced that the failure to promise universal and equal suffrage in Prussia and to take steps leading to its immediate introduction had exacerbated this revolution, and his entire program for the management of the July crisis was centered about an effort to correct it. On July 9 the issue was debated by the highest officials of the Empire at a Royal Crown Council. Bethmann pointed out that Loebell's plan to devise a plural suffrage system would represent a monstrous injustice because it would benefit war profiteers. It was impossible to give those "with shot-off limbs and those . . . with the Iron Cross First Class a suffrage inferior . . . to that of those who . . . have understood how to make big war profits."[20] Most important, however, was the immediate depression of the workers. The promise that the war would be over by August could not be fulfilled. The food and coal supplies were insufficient. There were serious strikes in Silesia and elsewhere, and "if such movements become widely spread and are fought

[18] Klaus Epstein, *Matthias Erzberger and the Dilemma of German Democracy*, Princeton, 1959, pp. 186-187.

[19] Reichstag Budget Committee Debates, July 3, 1917.

[20] For these excerpts from the protocol, see *AGSOD*, II, pp. 589-593.

by the army with machine guns, then the consequences will be catastrophic." Something had to be done to pacify the workers, "for otherwise the people and the monarchy will collapse." Bethmann was supported by the majority of those present, but he was opposed by a vociferous minority which included Loebell, Trott zu Solz, Schorlemer, Stein, and Capelle. These men feared that equal suffrage would destroy the independence of the Prussian bureaucracy, depress the "best classes," and lead to further demands from the left.

The Emperor observed the discussion much as one would observe a tennis match. It reminded him of Frederick the Great's remark: "Heavens, the rascal is right, but the other one also!" Bethmann, however, was in a more somber frame of mind and offered his resignation when the Emperor tried to evade making a final decision. The Emperor refused to accept it, and on July 11 he signed an order commanding the Prussian Cabinet to prepare a bill providing for equal suffrage. It was to be submitted to the Landtag as soon as possible.[21]

Bethmann's victory was abortive, however, for his support in the Reichstag was collapsing thanks to the intrigues of Colonel Bauer, Stresemann, and Erzberger.[22] Stresemann had long supported the OHL's desire to get rid of Bethmann on the grounds that a stronger Chancellor was needed. Erzberger was angered by Bethmann's refusal to support his proposed Reichstag peace resolution. At the same time, he wanted National Liberal support for the Reichstag peace resolution, and he wanted that party's collaboration in the Interparty Committee of Social Democrats, Progressives, and Centrists which had just been established for the purpose of creating a strong Reichstag majority. Bauer, while opposed to the peace resolution and certainly uninterested in strengthening the Reichstag, was most anxious to turn the Reichstag against Bethmann.

[21] Varnbüler to Weizsäcker, July 10, 1917, HStASt, E, 73, 12i, and Fischer, *Griff nach der Weltmacht*, p. 516.

[22] For these intrigues and the general description of the fall of Bethmann below, see Epstein, *Erzberger*, pp. 193ff.

Furthermore, Bauer, Erzberger, and Stresemann shared the conviction that former Chancellor Bülow was the best man to replace Bethmann, a rather peculiar notion in the light of the Emperor's well-known antipathy to the man who had humiliated him during the *Daily Telegraph* Affair.

On July 9 Erzberger fulfilled his part of the vague bargain which had been reached when he persuaded the Center Party to come out in opposition to Bethmann. It was a fatal blow. Ludendorff, who had abstained from pressing the Chancellorship question so long as Bethmann had a Reichstag majority, now had an excuse to act. Armed with, of all things, parliamentary support, Ludendorff, Hindenburg, and General von Stein threatened to resign if Bethmann was not dismissed. The latter did not even put up a fight, and on July 13 he presented the much relieved Emperor with his resignation.

The OHL had thus succeeded in getting rid of Bethmann, but Wilhelm would not hear of Bülow's appointment as his successor. The Civil Cabinet Chief, Valentini, was compelled to engage in a mad hunt for a successor which terminated in the appointment of Michaelis. The new Chancellor was well liked at General Headquarters and, at the same time, had a good reputation in labor circles for his work on the food problem.[23]

It cannot be said that Ludendorff had not been warned before he agreed to this incredible choice. General Groener and the General Intendant of the Army, Eisenhart-Rothe, had both warned Ludendorff that Michaelis was a fine bureaucrat but not a statesman. Ludendorff admitted that Michaelis had not been his original choice, but declared that "he could do nothing more about the matter."[24] He had refused to recom-

[23] On the appointment of Michaelis, see Valentini, *Kabinettschef*, pp. 167-170, and Magnus Freiherr von Braun, *Von Ostpreussen bis Texas. Erlebnisse und zeitgeschichtliche Betrachtungen eines Ostdeutschen*, Stollhamm, 1955, pp. 113-116.

[24] E. von Eisenhart-Rothe, *Im Banne der Persönlichkeit. Aus dem Lebenserinnerungen*, Berlin, 1931, pp. 60-61, and Groener, *Lebenserinnerungen*, pp. 359-360.

mend the appointment of a general because he wanted "to avoid the impression of a dictatorship."[25]

This, however, was precisely the impression which had been created. One by one, Germany's chief agencies of political power had abdicated both responsibility and authority, and the result was an atmosphere that was as unclear as it was unclean. The Emperor and the civil authorities had revealed their impotence in the face of the OHL, and the Reichstag had permitted its great moment of self-assertion to be transformed into a demonstration of bankruptcy. To be sure, the OHL had suffered some setbacks. Bülow had not been appointed Chancellor. The government was now committed to the support of equal suffrage, and on July 19 the Reichstag had passed its peace resolution. Nevertheless, Michaelis was a staunch conservative. Ludendorff could be certain that the government would have a difficult time getting the suffrage bill passed by the Landtag. Finally, Michaelis' acceptance of the peace resolution "as I understand it" made any interpretation possible.

If the fall of Bethmann received almost universal applause from the officer corps, its end result was greeted with considerable reserve by politically sensitive officers in the army. There had been some officers on the General Staff who feared that Germany would have to accept a peace based on something less than her maximum war aims program. For reasons strikingly and ironically similar to those Bethmann had used when he espoused Hindenburg's appointment as Chief of the General Staff, these officers had wanted a high-ranking military officer appointed as Chancellor. Only a man who had the "blind confidence of the people" could persuade them to accept a negotiated peace.[26] This point of view reflected the more traditional attitude of the officer corps. It focused upon the danger of alienating the conservative political forces of

[25] Report of Kraft von Delmensingen on a discussion between Ludendorff and Crown Prince Rupprecht, July 11, 1917, BHStA, Abt. II, MA 1, Nr. 945, Bl. 59-61.

[26] Report of Kraft von Delmensingen, June 29, 1917, *ibid.*, Bl. 55-57.

the Empire and was, by implication, directed against internal political reform. The military leader of the government would have the prestige to win the right for a negotiated peace and have the strength to suppress the demands of the left.

Where the attention of these officers had been directed toward the problem of pacifying the conservatives, the attention of Groener and his followers had been directed toward the prevention of a revolution from the left. Groener had realized that the internal situation was extremely serious at the time of the April strikes, and he had become convinced that Germany could not count upon complete victory. Most important, if the war were lost, a revolution was certain to follow. In Groener's view, the time to prepare for this danger was during the war. Only in this way could one "steer" the "democratic wave" which the war had set loose.[27]

In addition to sending a flood of memoranda to high ranking personages, Groener had sought to win acceptance for his views through personal contact. In May, he had spoken to the Empress about the food shortage and its effect on the workers and their families. Though Empress Victoria, who was a well-meaning but very conservative *Hausfrau*, had been properly sympathetic, she could find no better solution to social problems than philanthropy. In June Groener had been invited to a dinner given by the Emperor and had hoped to use this occasion to enlighten the Emperor. Wilhelm, however, had turned the evasion of serious matters into an art, and Groener had been compelled to spend the evening listening to countless irrelevant stories. Having achieved nothing in this quarter, he turned to Bethmann and Valentini, warning them against the OHL's extreme war aims and stressing the danger of revolution. The Emperor had been informed of Groener's views by either Bethmann or Valentini. As a result, the Emperor's adju-

[27] Unless otherwise noted, this discussion of Groener's views and activities is taken from his accounts in the *Lebenserinnerungen*, pp. 366, 412, and at the 1925 "Dolchstoss" trial in Munich, reprinted in Hans Herzfeld, *Die deutsche Sozialdemokratie und die Auflösung der nationalen Einheitsfront im Weltkriege*, Leipzig, 1928, pp. 347ff.

tant, General von Plessen, whose major task in life seems to have been to protect the Emperor from reality, ordered Groener not to give the Emperor any more warnings. Finally, Groener had sought to enlighten Stinnes, but the latter was certain that "Ludendorff will win."

Groener had been convinced that the attempt "to feed the masses with ballots instead of meat and bread"[28] had to be made, and he had supported Bethmann on the suffrage question. At the same time, however, he had shared the widely held view that Bethmann was not strong enough to manage the internal situation. On the one hand, Bethmann had not been radical enough to push through the necessary reforms with the desired speed. Groener had been prepared to have the Emperor simply proclaim equal suffrage and abrogate the antiquated Law of Siege. On the other hand, Bethmann had not been strong enough to hold firm in the worst extremity. Groener had been opposed to the parliamentarization of the Empire. His eyes ever focused on English unity and efficiency, if not on English liberty, Groener would have liked to see a "Government of National Concentration" set up with Heydebrand at the head and Ebert in the regime. He had recognized, however, that it was "utopian" to believe that German Conservatives and Social Democrats could work together. He also seems to have thought that such a government might have been formed with Hindenburg as the *pro forma* head, the Progressive, Payer, as Vice-Chancellor and actual leader of the government, and Ludendorff as War Minister.[29]

It is difficult to find much merit in these weird combinations, but their significance should not be overlooked. The proposed Hindenburg-Payer-Ludendorff regime represented an effort to combine the three dominant political tendencies of the Empire

[28] Reported by Varnbüler to Weizsäcker, July 10, 1917, HStASt, E, 73, 12i.

[29] This program is somewhat similar to one espoused by Moellendorff in a letter to Nitrates Commissar Dr. Bueb on April 18, 1917, BA, Nachlass Moellendorff, Nr. 39.

during this final period of its history: plebiscital dictatorship, parliamentarism, and military dictatorship. Hindenburg was to be the charismatic "substitute Kaiser" that would satisfy the people's need for an irrational focus of loyalty. Payer would serve as a concession to the masses' growing demands for political liberty. Ludendorff was to represent the last resort of the disintegrating Empire, military force. Groener's longed-for Government of National Concentration or Cabinet of Personalities is of more practical significance. Here, one discovers the "revolution from above" of September-October 1918 in embryo, for in its initial stages the revolution from above was an effort to save the old regime through the establishment of a broad coalition government under precisely those disastrous circumstances which Groener feared.[30] Needless to say, a Heydebrand-Ebert coalition was as impossible in 1918 as it was in 1917, but the similarity between Groener's vision and the final effort to save the monarchy demonstrates that the latter was not completely lacking in antecedents. In 1917 Groener was thinking in terms of saving what could be saved of the monarchy's prerogatives by liberalizing the Empire in a pseudoparliamentary fashion.

The leaders of the German army, Hindenburg and Ludendorff, and their chief adviser, Colonel Bauer, however, had not yet abandoned their conviction that they could have total victory abroad and maintain the status quo at home. They did not understand, or did not want to understand, that their radical foreign policy was undermining their conservative internal policy, and that this was all the more the case because of their demand for the total mobilization of the nation. They refused to accept the political and social consequences of their own actions. The major source of contention between the OHL and Bethmann had not been foreign policy but internal policy. To be sure, the OHL had been irritated by Bethmann's op-

[30] For an analysis of the 1918 "revolution from above," see Wolfgang Sauer's forthcoming *Militär- und Zivilgewalt in der Revolution. Das Bündnis Groener-Ebert November-Dezember 1918.*

position to unrestricted submarine warfare and his sporadic verbal concessions to the supporters of a negotiated peace. In the last analysis, however, Bethmann had always succumbed to the wishes of the OHL on foreign policy. The OHL's attack against Bethmann was based on his failure to mobilize the country economically and psychologically and on his failure to maintain internal order.

This is demonstrated by a memorandum, "Remarks concerning the Imperial Chancellor," sent to Ludendorff by Colonel Bauer on March 6, 1917. In this memorandum, the criticism directed against Bethmann's foreign policy was limited to the charge that his vacillating policy had caused Germany to lose prestige among the neutral nations. Nearly all of Bauer's wrath was directed against the government's internal failures. The mismanagement of the food and coal supplies had compelled the army to intervene to maintain the health of the workers and the productivity of industry. The government, therefore, was responsible for the failure of the Hindenburg Program. Similarly, it was responsible for permitting the Reichstag to ruin the Auxiliary Service Law, and "the consequence is an unfortunate upward movement of wages and far-reaching demands for political rights." From this followed the demoralization of the middle classes, the industrialists, and the army, as well as the general corruption of the country:

> The careful observer cannot escape the fact that side by side with extraordinary and marvelous accomplishments of our industry and technology, German loyalty, morality, and sense of duty is declining monstrously. In every profession and group there is a search after gain, profiteering, pleasure-hunting, and waste. Hand in hand with this goes remarkable presumption, demands for rights, extension of the powers of parliament at the expense of the Throne, and a complete indifference to the burdens of those fighting the war. Instead of creating order by firm action and instruction, the government permits itself to be led and directed by *those*

> groups who even in peacetime had been recognized as a danger to the state and the monarchy.[31]

Bauer did not believe that it was necessary for the government to permit itself to be "terrorized by Jewish Progressivism and international comradeship." To reverse this tendency, however, "whole men and clear political minds" were needed.

That these were the reasons for the OHL's action against Bethmann is best illustrated by Hindenburg's memorandum to Michaelis of August 10, 1917. Although signed by Hindenburg, the August memorandum, in both content and language, was an unmistakable product of Bauer's pen. The OHL sought to explain why it had "been increasingly compelled to oppose the leadership of the Empire or exercise a certain pressure regarding its measures." As in the March memorandum, the catalogue of Bethmann's errors was most specific and most extensive in the area of internal policy. The failure to manage the food, transport, and coal problems was reiterated. Bethmann was once again blamed for the "extraordinarily harmful" Auxiliary Service Law, which had led to "profiteering, pleasure-seeking, and confusion of the concepts of right and duty." Hindenburg assured Michaelis that he had no desire to interfere with the work of the civil authorities. He had been compelled to do so by the inadequacies of the previous administration. He concluded with the hope that the new government would regulate those questions which the OHL held to be particularly important. Michaelis, in short, was being asked to take measures which, if successfully pushed through, would have made him the administrator of the Supreme Command's veiled dictatorship. Specifically, Hindenburg asked that the press be given greater direction, that the enlightenment program be intensified, and that the coal and food supplies be properly administered. Included among the demands was the "prevention of turnover in the war industry" and "the utilization of all available labor and replacement of those in the

[31] "Bemerkungen über dem Reichskanzler," March 6, 1917, BA, Nachlass Bauer, Nr. 16.

factories who are liable to military service." This required a "change and extension of the Auxiliary Service Law." Finally, the OHL demanded "measures against strikes."[32]

3. *The Attack upon Groener*

Groener had only six days left in office when the August memorandum was sent, and it is obvious that the OHL's charges against Bethmann were equally applicable to Groener. Groener was deeply involved in the problems of the food and coal supply, and he was a leading person in all matters pertaining to the Auxiliary Service Law and strikes. As we have seen, his policies were distinguishable from those of Bethmann only in that they were more radical. If Bethmann's departure was to mean a real change of system in the sense desired by the OHL, then there was not much place in the new order for a man of Groener's views. The crisis of the summer of 1917 was more than simply a conflict between the civil and the military authorities. The problem of responding to the revolutionary consequences of the war divided every segment of German society into moderate and radical camps, and this was as true of the army as it was of the civil government, the workers, and the industrialists.

Ludendorff had been dissatisfied with Groener's work for a long time, but there is no evidence that Ludendorff had any intention of dismissing him at the time of Bethmann's fall. It is not impossible that Ludendorff thought that Groener would adapt to the change of system. It also must be remembered that bringing Bethmann down had been a difficult operation and that Ludendorff may not have been prepared to embark upon another political enterprise immediately afterward. The evidence demonstrates that it was Groener's policy during July and August that provided the immediate grounds for his dismissal.

32 Reprinted in *Das Werk des Untersuchungsausschusses der Verfassunggebenden Nationalversammlung und des Deutschen Reichstags 1919 bis 1928. Vierte Reihe. Die Ursachen des deutschen Zusammenbruchs im Jahre 1918*, 12 vols., Berlin, 1919-1928 (hereinafter cited as *Ursachen*), II, pp. 39-41.

During these months, Groener came into conflict with the OHL, industry, General von Stein, and the Deputy Commanding Generals on the strike question. This was particularly the case with regard to Upper Silesia. The situation there was extremely complicated. The Silesian working class was an odd assortment of native Silesians, Poles, and Russian prisoners of war. Their wages and working conditions were poor in comparison to those of the workers and miners in the Ruhr. As mentioned earlier, the Silesian workers were hardly organized until 1917. The most powerful Silesian industrialists, Privy Councilors Hilger and Williger, went so far as to oppose yellow unions because "all worker organizations must turn against the employers."[33] The Deputy Commanding General in Breslau, General von Heinemann, and his chief adviser, Captain Nebelung, were veritable servants of the industrialists. The right of assembly was placed under more restrictions than elsewhere. Permission to hold "political" meetings had to be requested from eight to ten days before the meeting was held. Permission to hold worker meetings on food and wage questions had to be requested forty-eight hours in advance. During tense periods, permission to hold such meetings had to be requested eight days in advance. The unions, therefore, had good reason to complain that they were unable to act quickly to prevent strikes.[34]

The first outbreaks took place in May, when the workers committee elections were being held. Despite employer efforts to intimidate the workers into voting for those favored by the employers, the union candidates won a striking victory. Thus in one mine the union candidates defeated the list put up by the employers by a vote of 835 to 69. The unrest was intensified when some of the newly elected workers committee

[33] Hilger at the VdESI meeting, June 21, 1917, BA, R 13I/151.

[34] See Heinemann's remarks at the War Ministry meeting of April 25, 1917, BHStA, Abt. IV, MK, IcIa15b, Bd. I, Bl. zu 110. For Nebelung's views, see his remarks at a meeting with the industrialists on June 3 in *AGSOD*, II, pp. 533-541. Finally, see Deputy Schmidt's scathing criticism of these officers in Reichstag Debates, Oct. 10, 1917, 310, pp. 3858ff.

members were suddenly drafted into the army. At the same time the appearance of union organizers from the west, who busily set about informing the workers of their rights and who encouraged the workers to join unions, was bound to have an unsettling effect. If union agitation contributed to the unrest in Silesia, the union claim that the strikes were "wild" did not lack foundation. The food situation there was very serious, and the strikes were accompanied by street demonstrations, food riots, and plundering of food stores in which women and children, not workers, were the leading participants. Also, there were outside influences unconnected with the unions which agitated the workers. The strike in Warsaw over the German government's decision to cut the value of the ruble did much to stir up the Poles working in Silesia. Revolutionary developments in Russia added to the restiveness. Finally, the fact that the Imperial nitrates factories in the area were paying higher wages than the privately owned mines and factories was also an important source of discontent.[35]

The unions did not want a serious strike in the Silesian mines. They were as aware of the need to maintain coal production as were the military authorities. Thus when the strikes intensified, the Socialist Mine Union leader Huë was rushed to the scene to calm down the workers. At the same time the unions were equally anxious to use the strikes to organize the workers and force the employers to deal with the unions. They produced a leaflet for distribution among the workers which pointed out that "it is a mistake to begin a strike without making concrete demands and trying to negotiate."[36] The strikers were told to use the workers committees and informed that "where there are unsuitable representatives, this is the fault of the workers themselves, because they did not take the trouble to elect better ones during the elections." General von

[35] See the BBS Report of May 21, 1917, Groener's remarks to the Reichstag committee on July 14, BHStA, Abt. IV, K Mob 14, Bd. V, Bl. 13, and Hilger's remarks at the June 21 VdESI meeting, BA, R 131/151.

[36] This description and the quotations are taken from Deputy Schmidt's remarks, Reichstag Debates, Oct. 10, 1917, 310, pp. 3858-3859.

Heinemann, however, refused to permit the distribution of this leaflet because "the content is likely to create unrest among workers who think otherwise." Despite this setback, the unions persisted in their efforts "to bring order to this undisciplined mob of workers." The workers were demanding very high wage increases. The unions now sought to bring these demands down to a negotiable level and present a common series of wage demands for all the strikers. It is impossible to determine whether or not the unions had helped to create the high demands in order to then take credit for having moderated them, but this certainly might have been the case since the unions had encouraged the formulation of concrete demands. It is certain, however, that the unions wished to unify the demands of the strikers and make them reasonable. Again, General von Heinemann did not permit the union leaders to promote these goals at union meetings.

The great problem in the Silesian strikes thus became the union attempt to compel the mineowners to negotiate with union secretaries concerning these wage demands. Some of the mineowners were willing to negotiate with the unions. At a meeting of the Coal Commissar's Advisory Council on July 14, one of the Upper Silesian industrialists remarked that "one must act according to the individual case. Where there are unions, one should negotiate . . . and make some concessions."[37] Hilger and Williger did not agree. Hilger would not negotiate with union secretaries because "one cannot discuss the difficult problems in the mines with editors of Social Democratic newspapers or cheesemongers or cigar dealers."[38] These employers were prepared to discuss things with "real workers" only. Above all, they insisted that the workers use the institutions established by the Auxiliary Service Law, namely, the workers committees and the conciliation agencies. In other words, they would not engage in

[37] Report on a meeting of the Coal Commissar's Advisory Council, July 18, 1917, BHStA, Abt. IV, MK, K Mob 12, Bd. XI, Bl. 8.

[38] VdESI meeting, June 21, 1917, BA, R 13I/152.

collective bargaining. Finally, they demanded that the army act energetically and ban all meetings, draft agitators, and draft those unruly workers designated by the employers.[39]

In a formal sense, Hilger and Williger were absolutely correct. It was clear that the unions were using the Silesian situation to engage in a power struggle with the employers in order to force the latter to accept collective bargaining. The unions were doing the same thing in Cologne just at the time of the Silesian strikes. On July 6, 30,000 metalworkers went out on strike for a fifty-one hour week and a wage increase. The industrialists in Cologne, like those in Silesia, refused to negotiate with the unions and demanded that the workers use the conciliation agencies and arbitration committees. The unions replied that it would take three years to settle 30,000 cases by those means. In short, the unions were trying to demonstrate that the institutions created under the Auxiliary Service Law, however beneficial, were inadequate for the settlement of large-scale differences between the employers and the workers and that the time had come to accept collective bargaining.[40]

Groener and his subordinates in the War Office and War Office bureaus were fully aware of the fact that the unions were going beyond the Auxiliary Service Law in making this demand. The War Office bureau in Breslau frankly called the Silesian strike a "power test" (*Machtprobe*) by the unions. Yet the War Office bureau opposed the stand taken by the employers and characterized the views of certain of the industrialists, particularly Williger, as absolutely "fatal" to the restoration of order.[41] Groener agreed with this judgment. In fact he came out in open support of negotiations between the employers and the unions, although he recognized that he was

39 See Captain Müller's strike reports of July 6, 9, 18, 1917, BHStA, Abt. IV, MK, IcIa15^{b}, Bd. I, Bl. 13a, 115, 159.

40 *Metallarbeiter-Zeitung*, Sept. 1, 1917.

41 Müller's report of July 18, 1917, BHStA, Abt. IV, MK, IcIa15^{b}, Bd. I, Bl. 159.

powerless to compel the employers to negotiate. On July 14 he told the Reichstag Committee that

> He agreed that most of the strikes have been so-called wild strikes, whose origins are not easily determined. It would be very desirable to bring the employers and the union leaders to one conference table. There is also good reason to believe that this can happen. The idea that it is absolutely necessary for the employers and authorities to work together with the unions is becoming more pervasive. The War Office does not, however, have any powers enabling it to achieve this goal, and one must try to introduce it on a voluntary basis.[42]

Groener's patience with the union demands was not shared by General von Stein and the OHL. When the Silesian industrialists sent a telegram to Stein in early July demanding the banning of meetings and the drafting of unruly workers, Stein's marginal notation was, "It must be done."[43] At the same time Ludendorff sent a telegram to Stein asking that such measures be taken. On July 23 Ludendorff repeated this demand, and Stein issued an order to the Deputy Commanding Generals insisting that the strikes were due to radical agitation and calling upon them to act with "rigor, firmness, and decisiveness."[44] The Silesian strikes were ended in early August by a combination of military repression and loss of striker morale. The War Office and its Breslau bureau had thus suffered a defeat. Many of the other Deputy Commanding Generals shared the views of Stein and the OHL, and they disliked the mediátory activities of the War Office and War Office bureaus. As one of them pointed out, "It is necessary to set down who is actually responsible for the handling of strikes: the War Office bureau, which has been working inde-

[42] Reichstag committee meeting, July 14, 1917, *ibid.*, K Mob 14, Bd. V, Bl. 13.

[43] Müller report, July 9, 1917, *ibid.*, IcIa15^b, Bd. I, Bl. 115.

[44] *Ibid.*, July 23, 1917, Bl. 154.

pendently, or the Deputy Commanding General?"[45] The Deputy Commanding Generals were not unjustified in complaining about this dualism, but the dualism created difficulty here because of the lack of agreement between the War Office and the Deputy Commanding Generals.

In Groener's support of management-union negotiations, however, there was much more at stake than the immediate question of how the strikes should be handled. In taking this stand, Groener was, in effect, giving tacit approval to some of the long-range goals of the unions. On June 30 the trade unions had sent a petition to the Bundesrat and Reichstag entitled "Union Demands for the Transition from a Wartime to a Peacetime Economy." In this petition they asked that the workers committees, conciliation agencies, and arbitration committees be retained by the government after the conclusion of peace. Furthermore, they asked that worker chambers be established to represent worker interests and that the government promote "social partnerships" between the employer and employee organizations. They demanded also that the government encourage the creation of collective wage agreements and that such agreements be recognized in public law. With this petition, the unions formally opened their campaign to maintain their wartime achievements (*Errungenschaften*).[46]

The August 1917 memorandum of the Association of German Iron and Steel Industrialists, "Labor Policy and Labor Unrest in the War,"[47] was both a reply to the union petition and an attack upon the social policies of the War Office. The memorandum was sent to the Chancellor and the OHL, but not to Groener. The significance of this memorandum is not that it said anything startlingly new, but rather that it represented the most comprehensive statement of the complaints and fears

[45] War Ministry meeting, Aug. 13, 1917, *ibid.*, Bl. zu 228a.

[46] For the petition, see *ibid.*, K Mob 25, Bd. I, Bl. 38.

[47] "Arbeiterpolitik und Arbeiterunruhen im Kriege," *ibid.*, K Mob 19, Bd. II, Bl. zu 54, for the quotations and discussion below.

of heavy industry yet penned. It began with an historical survey of the association's struggle with the War Ministry over the war boards question. Thus the root of the evil lay in the establishment of the Berlin War Board. The latter served as a "school" for the union leaders, teaching them a "means of reviving their decade-long efforts to establish conciliation agencies and worker chambers with the prospect of success." At the same time it gave the unions, who had lost much of their membership during the war, a new lease on life. Despite all the warnings of the employers, the War Ministry persisted in giving the unions "undeserved compensations" for their collaboration with the war effort. The unions took advantage of this situation to create dissatisfaction among the workers. Despite the fact that the employers had spent a fortune establishing kitchens in their factories, distributing food at cheap prices, and providing family supports,

> It was, unfortunately, impossible for the employers to satisfy the workers completely. Their covetousness grew from month to month thanks to the influence of the unions and its press, an agitation which was accepted in silence by the authorities in the belief that intervention would only lead to a sharpening of the situation, and that one had to fulfill the wishes of the unions in order to keep the workers "in a good mood."

The Auxiliary Service Law was portrayed as the successful culmination of the union attempt to take advantage of the wartime situation to achieve political goals. The law was "whipped through" the Reichstag in ten days and bore all the marks of a "premature birth." It could only be characterized as "the greatest imaginable defeat which the government has had to suffer in a long time." The union leaders had then used the law to make themselves indispensable and to further their goals. There was now the danger that "Russian conditions" would be created for the peacetime economy. The unions were courting the favor of the workers by supporting "unhealthy and unjustified" wage demands. The policy was causing strikes, as demonstrated recently in the Ruhr and Silesia, and threatening Germany's ability to compete for foreign markets after the war.

The industrialists, however, were most concerned by the political dangers of the Auxiliary Service Law. They pointed to the recent trade union petition concerning the postwar economy and to the demands for equal suffrage in Prussia as examples of the trend toward "the complete democratization and republicanization of our monarchical German Empire." In their view it was ridiculous to make distinctions between a Schlicke and a Dissmann when the former, at the recent Metalworkers Congress in Cologne, had assured the union members that his union had not given up its old goals. "A determined and strong-willed policy" was necessary to save the Fatherland.

The industrialists then launched into an attack on the War Office. They objected to the independent mediatory activity of the War Office bureaus and to the use of union help to pacify strikers. The failure of the War Office to support and promote the yellow unions was the subject of particular criticism. The industrialists, however, did detect signs that the military authorities were recognizing the error of their ways. The use of harsher measures in dealing with strikes was a healthy sign. The industrialists were not happy about the militarization of factories and suggested that this be used only as a last resort. They looked with great favor, however, upon the banning of worker meetings.

"Labor Policy and Labor Unrest in the War" was the swan song of those employers who wished to maintain their position as absolute "masters of their own houses." The emphasis, therefore, was less on an immediate change of the Auxiliary Service Law, although this certainly was requested, than upon the undesirability of continuing the social provisions of the law in peacetime:

> Insofar as the question of the compulsory introduction of the workers and white collar workers committees and the conciliation agencies into the peacetime economy is concerned, we urgently request that such a step not be taken. The Auxiliary Service Law was meant only for the war, not for peace. The provisions have not worked in wartime. We cannot, therefore, expect them to promote a favorable industrial development in peacetime. Those employers who find the workers committees and conciliation agencies useful . . . are free to institute such measures. But he who thinks that he can get on with his workers without such agencies should not be disturbed in his practices.

Beneath these words one can detect a certain insecurity on the part of the authors of the memorandum. They knew that all the industrialists did not share their views. If Stinnes, for example, was convinced that recognition of the unions would lead to strikes in the Ruhr, there were other industrialists like the head of the lignite industry, Dr. Silverberg, who felt that "one accomplishes most in negotiations where the workers are organized. Industry must relearn and understand that it is best when the workers are strictly organized and thus stand under union discipline."[48] Indeed, how could the authors of the memorandum feel secure when they knew that Dr. Sorge, a man upon whom they had pinned so many hopes, was highly critical of the memorandum? Sorge, to be sure, was in agreement with the general position of heavy industry, but he could not withhold his criticisms of the many distortions contained in the memorandum. He did not agree that wages "in general" had kept pace with prices, nor did he agree that the industrialists "in general" had provided their workers with sufficient quantities of food. He knew of plenty of cases where industrialists were not giving the workers food at low prices. The unions, in Sorge's opinion, were not the only cause of the increase of prices and wages. Finally, Sorge could not agree

[48] Statement by Dr. Silverberg at a Coal Commissar's Advisory Council meeting, July 14, 1917, *ibid.*, K Mob 12, Bd. XI, Bl. 8.

that the Auxiliary Service Law had been such a great defeat for the government. Evidently Sorge was aware of the fact that it was the OHL that had rushed the law through despite the government's very serious reservations.[49]

If the more conservative industrialists could not count on the moderates in their own camp, they could count on the OHL. In May the OHL had received a report on the financial situation of the Empire, a report which demonstrated the growing costs of the war and its inflationary effects on the economy. On June 15 Hindenburg sent a note to the Chancellor which blamed the inflation on "the monstrous increase of worker wages." The Auxiliary Service Law was, in the OHL's opinion, largely responsible for the wage increases, and it demanded that something be done.[50]

The OHL's demands for a change of the law were motivated by two types of considerations. The first was the manpower shortage. The supply of reserves for the army was diminishing steadily, and the law, in its existing form, was not helping to solve the manpower problem. The second was the role played by the law in promoting turnover and wage movements. The War Office was fully aware of the inadequacies of the law, and Groener had instructed the Justice Division of the War Office to prepare a revised Auxiliary Service Law for presentation to the Reichstag in the fall. In fact a change of the Auxiliary Service Law was an integral part of Groener's Concentration of Forces program.

The draft of the proposed changes in the law demonstrates that Groener was prepared to go quite far in extending and altering the provisions of the law.[51] Groener's first object was

49 Sorge to the VdESI, Aug. 27, 1917, BA, R 131/370.

50 Reprinted in Ludendorff, *Urkunden*, pp. 138-139.

51 The draft and explanation of these changes is to be found in BHStA, Abt. IV, MK, K Mob 14, Bd. V, Bl. 52a. Although Capt. Müller did not send it to the Bavarian War Ministry until Oct. 10, 1917, there can be no question about the fact that it was a product of the Groener period. See the latter's remarks to the heads of the procurement agencies, July 20, 1917, BHStA, Abt. IV, MK, K Mob 13, Bd. III, and his comments to the Württemberg Cabinet, July 30, 1917, HStASt, E, 130, V, X[a], Bd. III, Bl. 1114.

to gain greater control over the workers in the factories. Since a large number of these were youths between fifteen and eighteen, this age group was now to fall under the provisions of the law. The significance of this becomes apparent from the very radical change the War Office wished to make with regard to the drafting of workers into the Auxiliary Service (Paragraph 7). It wanted to deprive those liable to Auxiliary Service of the unrestricted right to take any job they pleased within two weeks of being called up by the draft committees. In one case, a draft committee had requested two hundred persons to take a particular job without any success. These people found jobs of a more congenial nature. The War Office wanted to remedy this by the following clause: "The War Office can designate individual factories to be particularly important for the duration of the war or for a specific period. Those liable to Auxiliary Service can be assigned to work in such factories even if they are already serving in the Auxiliary Service." By combining this change with a projected Bundesrat regulation requiring all male civilians, including those previously exempted from the requirement, to register, the War Office hoped to make the law much more effective.

A second series of important changes in the law involved Paragraph 9. Here, four new clauses were to be added. First, a worker requesting a leaving certificate from the arbitration committee was to be required to state the specific factory in which he intended to work and was to take work only in that factory. In other words, the workers would continue to have the right to seek better paid work elsewhere, but they had to be specific about where they were going—"The mere possibility of an improvement anywhere, even in the same area, shall not suffice." Second, a clause was to be added giving the War Office the right to limit the free movement of specially exempted workers to specific occupational sectors. This, of course, was an *ex post facto* legalization of a method employed by the War Office since February 1917. Third, a loophole in the law was corrected. Previously, workers who left their jobs without awaiting the arbitration committee's decision had been able to receive compensation for time lost if the committee eventually decided in their favor. Now workers who did this were to automatically lose their cases and thus be compelled to bear the full costs of their involuntary two week vacation. Finally, a clause was inserted subjecting female workers between seventeen and sixty years of age to the provisions of Paragraph 9 of the law. It is to be noted that this did not mean that women were now being compelled to work, but only that those who did work would be forced to get a leaving certificate before changing jobs. In this way the War Office hoped to cut down the high turnover rate of female workers.

If these proposed changes in the law did not bespeak all the wishes of heavy industry and the OHL, they still represented a very significant effort to tighten the provisions of the law. Groener, therefore, was willing to satisfy the OHL's demands for a change of the law, and, indeed, he promoted this endeavor. He also agreed with the OHL and the industrialists that wages were, in many cases, too high and that the recurrent wage movements were dangerous to the economy. Unlike the OHL and the industrialists, however, Groener refused to shut his eyes to the fact that employer profits were playing an extremely important role in the situation, and that it was the spiraling of wages *and* profits that was producing the inflation.

4. *The Fall of Groener*

The Hindenburg Program had created an orgy of profit-making. Alfons Horten, the head of the Iron Section of the KRA, who had first discovered the outrageous profit the industrialists were making on Martin process steel, did not last long in office. Once the Hindenburg Program was launched, the investigation of Martin process steel prices was "temporarily" halted. Horten, however, proceeded to offend the iron and steel producers once again by proposing that various French and Belgian steel producing firms be reactivated in order to increase production for the Hindenburg Program. One of the chief war aims of the German industrialists was the ruin of these firms and the annexation of the Belgian and French mines. Horten's plan threatened this program, and the industrialists appealed to the OHL. In early 1917 the OHL ordered Horten's dismissal. He was replaced by Captain Burgers, a director of the Gelsenkirchener iron mining firm. At the same time Dr. Fischer, a banker who sat on the directing boards of no less than forty iron mining companies, was appointed Commissar of the Iron Section. He was a close friend of Stinnes and Peter Klöckner. The latter, who owned gigantic iron and steel works in the Ruhr, and whose brother was KRA representative to the Steel League (*Stahlbund*), was given a virtual monopoly of the scrap iron collected by the KRA. The other industrialists, however, were not neglected. It will be remembered that Horten had first discovered the excessive price of Martin process steel by comparing it with the price of Thomas process steel and noting the strange differential between the two prices. This disagreeable differential was eliminated now by two extraordinary Thomas process steel price increases, the first in April and the second in July. In August the price of Martin steel was also raised. Finally, since the profits on inferior grades of steel, e.g., the type used in the manufacture of barbed wire, were low in comparison to the profits on higher quality steel, the KRA raised these profits also. It was the only way to induce the industrialists to produce the steel needed for barbed wire.[52]

The Secretary of the Treasury, Count Roedern, seems to have lost all interest in controlling prices after the defeat of his effort to do so in November 1916. He now chose to rely completely on the war profits tax, and his motto became: "One should not cut the fat from the pigs during the feeding."[53] At the same time, Koeth was demonstrating some of the less admirable of his character traits. As Horten noted:

[52] Horten Memorandum, BA, Nachlass Mentzel, Nr. 8.
[53] Merton, *Erinnernswertes aus meinem Leben*, p. 37.

> Everyone who has anything to do with him knows that Lieutenant-Colonel Koeth is not only a smart and talented, but also a diplomatic man. One should not attempt to devaluate his services and his abilities, but he is smart enough not to overestimate his power. So far and no further! One may shut down textile factories without compunction. To demand their cost calculations is a sad necessity, and injustices often occur, but necessity knows no laws. Where so much blood is being sacrificed, income cannot be considered. But when it comes to iron and steel, no man who knows the way things are can demand of the leader of the KRA that he act against that Great Power. . . . A military command from above and one must go, must drop the work which he has enjoyed and in which he has felt the right to say that he has accomplished something. Above . . . Koeth stands Colonel Bauer, who is also a very clever man and who is always ready to take advice from the first men of industry.[54]

Horten was not being completely fair to Koeth. The latter was permitting the textile industry to make gigantic profits also. Since the great textile firms were being forced to pay compensation to the owners of shut-down factories, the KRA paid extremely high prices to the operating firms in order to make the compensation payments less burdensome. Thus both the owners of the firms who produced something and the owners of the firms who produced nothing derived great profit from the situation.[55]

This is not to say that the KRA was opposed to wage increases. The opposite was the case. On August 10, 1917, for example, Captain Braumann of the KRA acted as mediator between the employers and union representatives in a discussion of cost of living increases for the leather industry workers. There was no real dispute between labor and management. Everyone agreed that increases were necessary. In

[54] Horten Memorandum, BA, Nachlass Mentzel, Nr. 8.
[55] Peppel study, pp. 134-148, 157-159.

fact the union and employer representatives worked hand in hand. Thus it was the union leader who informed Captain Braumann that "the employers are not disinclined to agree to the demands of the workers, which they consider justified, but they cannot pay the wage premium out of their own pockets, since they have not yet received the compensation they requested for the last cost of living increase in the fall of 1916."[56] He also threatened that the workers would leave the leather industry and go to work in war factories if their pay were not raised. Both the unions and the employers were blackmailing the army. Since, as Captain Braumann pointed out, "the steadiness of the labor market is in everybody's interest," the army agreed to compensate the employers for the wage increase.

The best example of the way in which the army played midwife to inflation, however, is to be found in the coal mining industry. It was typical of the mineowners' attitude that Privy Councilor Williger, after blaming the Silesian strikes on the Auxiliary Service Law, agitators, and high wages in state-owned factories, concluded by placing the responsibility on "the root of the evil, namely, the low coal prices."[57] The mineowners were specialists in blackmailing the government into permitting price increases by threatening to refuse to give wage increases. If their refusal to meet wage demands which they themselves recognized to be justified caused strikes, these strikes also enabled them to secure military support for their price demands.

In the late summer of 1917 the Ruhr coal miners unions demanded a general wage increase. The mineowners immediately complained to General von Gayl that there would soon be a new series of appeals to the conciliation agencies and that the latter would agree to increases which some of the mineowners could not afford to pay. General von Gayl re-

[56] For the report of the negotiations, see BHStA, Abt. IV, MK, K Mob 7d, Bd. II, Bl. 101.

[57] *AGSOD*, II, p. 541.

sponded by pointing out that the union demands had to be met because of the increased cost of food and because high wages were being paid in the munitions factories. Furthermore, he emphasized that morale was particularly low because of the failure of the submarine campaign to end the war as quickly as had been anticipated. Gayl then went on to say,

> If it is not possible for the poorer mines to pay higher wages, then there must be an increase in coal prices or the state must help in some other way. I therefore suggest that the *Mineowners Association contact the Minister of Commerce and Industry*, who is being sent a copy of this letter, *as soon as possible*. I consider it essential that the general decision of . . . the Association . . . be reached within a week. The matter is too important . . . to be dragged out. The *coal question* is *decisive to the war effort*, and one would have to reproach oneself if severe consequences resulted from production losses due to wage disputes, particularly when the necessity of a certain increase must be recognized.[58]

In short, Gayl was encouraging the mineowners to demand a price increase and applying pressure on the Minister of Commerce to acquiesce in this demand. Just four months earlier, in May, Sydow had granted an increase in coal prices under similar circumstances, and now he had to do so again! Given the basic importance of coal to the entire economy, the effect of these coal price increases was the general increase of all prices. As a result, the wages of the miners ceased to be adequate almost at the very moment they were increased. It is to the credit of the Social Democratic Coal Miners Union that they openly fought this system which was so conducive to inflation. Even if there were a few mining companies which could not afford to pay the wage increases, the effect of each *general* price increase was to increase the already enormous profits of the mineowners who could afford to pay the higher

[58] General von Gayl to the Mineowners Association, Aug. 28, 1917, StAMü, Oberbergamt Dortmund B, 119, Nr. 225.

wages. Furthermore, it is not unreasonable to ask why the wealthier mining companies could not have been compelled to contribute some part of their large profits in order to help out their less opulent fellows. Finally, it should be noted that the Owners Association in the Ruhr, which was led by Hugenberg and Stinnes, was the chief ally of the agrarian leaders in fighting the food regulations. In March, for example, Hugenberg was crass enough to petition the KEA for an increase of potato prices on the grounds that the workers were making high wages and thus cared less about the cost of food than about its availability.[59]

The more far-sighted members of the War Office viewed this situation with growing alarm. As we know, Coupette and Moellendorff made an attempt to use the Auxiliary Service Law to control profits in November 1916. After the passage of the law, Coupette did not give up his efforts to persuade the industrialists to be reasonable. He warned them that "Germany's economic strength has definite limits" and that the only way to control wages was to keep profits at a moderate level.[60] In a memorandum written sometime in early 1917, Moellendorff expressed his disgust at "the unrestrained money-making and the dance around the golden calf . . . which has . . . gripped the entire people." Moellendorff was particularly concerned about the political and moral consequences of this situation:

> The desire to make more money has increased on all sides in just that measure as the desire to work has decreased. The symptoms of this are demonstrated in the increase of revolutionary tendencies on the one side and the increase of reactionary tendencies on the other. In both extreme camps

[59] For the price-wage increase of May, see Sydow's letter to the Mineowners Association, May 28, 1917, *ibid.*, 84, Nr. 131. For the Hugenberg letter to Batocki and the latter's very negative reply, see *Bergarbeiter-Zeitung*, April 7, 1917. For the union attacks on the price increases, see *ibid.*, Dec. 30, 1916, Sept. 1, 5, 22, 1917.

[60] WUMBA Advisory Council meeting, Dec. 10, 1916, BHStA, Abt. IV, MK, K Mob 1, Bd. I, Bl. zu 39a.

> one finds those elements most inimical to the state, and they are just those who have profited most from the economic boom created by the war.[61]

Groener was equally critical of the profit-making of the industrialists. His attitude toward this question, while certainly influenced by Coupette and Moellendorff, was most influenced by Captain Richard Merton. Merton continuously brought that matter to Groener's attention. In early July Groener decided that something had to be done, and he asked Merton to put his views on paper.

On July 12, 1917, Merton presented Groener with a "Memorandum on the Necessity of State Intervention to Regulate Profits and Wages."[62] Merton began by pointing out that the great productivity of German industry during the war was due only very slightly to "ethical motives, like a sense of sacrifice, love of Fatherland, and the like." In reality it was due "almost exclusively to the incentive of gain." As the war became longer, industry took advantage of the great demand for its products to make larger and larger profits. At the same time the workers took advantage of the competition between firms for manpower to secure higher wages. This was particularly the case in the munitions industry and in areas where there was a great need for skilled labor, such as Berlin: The result was a wage-price spiral:

> The workers know that their power has grown endlessly and the employers, especially the short-sighted ones or those who are to be regarded only as war industrialists and have no stake in the future development of the peacetime economy—and both together are the majority—can, to a great extent, protect themselves against the growing wage demands by raising the price of their products, and the state,

[61] BA, Nachlass Moellendorff, Nr. 41.

[62] The discussion and quotations are taken from the "Denkschrift über die Notwendigkeit eines staatlichen Eingriffs zur Regelung der Unternehmergewinne und Arbeiterlöhne," reprinted in Groener, *Lebenserinnerungen*, pp. 520-525.

which is the final purchaser, can do nothing else under the present circumstances than agree to the price which is demanded of it.

Merton then proceeded to examine the kind of contracts the industrialists were forcing upon the procurement agencies. He noted that a new type of contract was becoming increasingly prevalent, a contract in which the firms reserved the right to state the final price *after* delivery. The firms justified this type of contract with the claim that they could not be certain about how raw materials and labor costs would develop. At times a variation of this type of contract was employed. Here, an initial price was stated, but the procurement agencies obligated themselves to pay all additional cost increases incurred between the date of signature and the date of delivery. Since the profit was usually calculated on the basis of a fixed percentage of the costs, the industrialists were thus being relieved of all risk and encouraged to raise costs. Many industrialists and union leaders were beginning to realize the dangers of this situation. The union leaders, however, were showing a strong tendency to promote wage movements in order to win popularity and, above all, to keep "the workers from more dangerous things."

In Merton's view, however, the real source of these bizarre contracts was not the uncertainty about wages, but rather the uncertainty about the development of raw materials prices. Coal, iron, and steel prices formed the basis of the finished products industries' high cost calculations. The prices of these raw materials were very poorly controlled by the state, and the producers thus had a relatively free hand. Those industries producing finished products were forced to do business with the army on the basis of long-term contracts because the kind of work involved took a long time. The raw materials producers, however, insisted upon dealing with the finished products industries on the basis of short-term contracts. Raw materials costs could thereby be increased many times in the course of a manufacturer's efforts to fulfill a long-term army contract. Merton believed that the only solution to this problem was to demand that the raw materials producers supply the manufacturers of finished products with all the raw materials they needed to complete a given contract at one fixed price. In fact, Merton felt that there was no reason to permit any further increases in the prices of coal, iron, and steel. The profits of heavy industry were so high that it could well afford to increase wages without increasing prices.

Merton concluded the memorandum with a three point program. First, all future contracts, as well as all those concluded before a fixed date, were to be based on a fixed price stated at the time of signature. Second, the war profits tax was to be increased to the point where it would be impossible to make war profits. Finally, and most important, a law, modeled on the English Munitions Act, would be enacted which would give the Chancellor the right to seize and operate all factories in which the owners refused to accept the prices determined by the War Office or in which there were labor-management disputes which could not be peacefully settled. The War Office would implement this law. Such a law was, in Merton's opinion, indispensable for Germany's healthy economic development:

> The employers must become clear about the fact that wartime is not the time to make money, but rather that it is actually a time which demands and, where necessary, compels everyone to make sacrifices. At the same time, all members of the German economic community will be so trained by this compulsory system that they will be in the position to bear the much greater moral and material strains . . . necessary to make our Imperial finances and our entire economic life healthy again when the war is over.

To say that Merton represented the interests of the finished products industries and those firms which, like his Frankfurt Metals Corporation, had a great stake in low raw materials costs, is in no way to cast a reflection upon his motives in presenting his memorandum. In fighting the excess profits of heavy industry, Merton was really continuing the fight of the finished products industries against the antisocial economic policies of heavy industry. The battle over tariffs was thus continued in the battle over profits. Unhappily, however, few of the industrialists in Merton's camp were prepared to speak out against high war profits in such a forthright manner. In private, as Alfons Horten reported, many confessed shame over the profits they were making.[63] The power of the group led by Hugenberg, Stinnes, Duisberg, and Klöckner was too great and their stranglehold over raw materials was too strong, however, for many industrialists to be willing to defy them. The shame felt by those who recognized the evil was not strong enough to deter them from seizing the advantage which it brought. Furthermore, as Merton noted, the unions were far from angelic. Many union leaders were playing the dangerous game of encouraging wage demands to win adherents and keep the workers' minds away from political questions. At the same time they were beginning to fear that they would become the victims of endless wage demands and the prisoners of the policy which they had initially encouraged.

Groener was very impressed by the Merton memorandum, and he asked Merton to discuss it with Count Roedern. The latter, as noted earlier, was unwilling to stop "feeding the pigs." Groener, however, was convinced that something had to be done and that the effort to change the Auxiliary Service Law could succeed only if measures were taken to control profits. On July 25 he sent the memorandum to Chancellor Michaelis. In a covering letter he declared his complete agreement with Merton's views and pointed out that it was impossible to permit the situation described by Merton to continue into the fourth year of war without creating further "demoralization." A "new note" had to be brought into "our

[63] Horten Memorandum, BA, Nachlass Mentzel, Nr. 8.

economic conceptions," one which would perhaps "also be able to have a beneficial effect on our general internal political situation." Groener indicated that he intended to discuss the memorandum with representatives of labor and industry, but that he wanted to secure the government's opinion first.[64]

He never received a reply. After the war the memorandum was found in the archives with the notation "not to be pursued."[65] Michaelis had sent the memorandum to the Interior Office. Helfferich, who had fought against profit controls ever since entering the government and who disliked Groener, must have been very displeased by it. Indeed, Groener's days were now numbered, for to his many sins he had added that one which was most unpardonable: an attack on profits.

Groener had alienated many powerful people. He had been a friend of Ludendorff's for many years, but their relationship was now quite cool. Groener had disappointed Ludendorff by "not showing the expected energy and permitting the program to be so watered down by the left that it is hardly useful."[66] Colonel Bauer detested Groener's "democratic feelings."[67] Michaelis had come into conflict with Groener over the question of who should manage the food premiums. Helfferich disliked Groener's interference with his prerogatives and was jealous of his popularity with the Reichstag. General von Stein felt that Groener's right to issue orders to the Deputy Commanding Generals was detrimental to his authority as War Minister. Colonel Koeth resented Groener for diminishing his previous independence as head of the KRA and wanted a free hand in the shutting down and consolidation of industries. Undoubtedly, he also found much in the Merton memorandum that suggested a criticism of his own attitude toward heavy industry's profits. Finally, many of the Deputy Commanding

[64] Groener, *Lebenserinnerungen*, p. 521.

[65] Dorothea Groener-Geyer, *General Groener: Soldat und Staatsmann*, Frankfurt a.M., 1955, p. 63.

[66] Albrecht von Thaer, *Generalstabsdienst an der Front und in der OHL*, ed. Siegfried A. Kaehler, Göttingen, 1958, p. 200.

[67] Bauer, *Grosse Krieg*, p. 255.

Generals disagreed with Groener's "soft" policy and disliked the interference of the War Office bureaus.[68]

Groener's most important opponents, however, were the heavy industrialists. He could count on little support from the business community. Borsig and Rieppel were good friends of his, but they were representatives of the finished products industries. Although his relations with Stinnes were always correct, the gulf between their views could not be bridged. The August memorandum of the Association of German Iron and Steel Industrialists was a thinly disguised attack on Groener, and it certainly must have had some influence on the OHL and the Chancellor.[69]

It is extremely difficult to piece together the precise details of the intrigue that brought Groener down. An affair of this nature is not often the subject of extensive correspondence. Certain facts, however, do stand out clearly. The immediate cause of his dismissal was the Merton memorandum. The memorandum had been discussed with some of the industrialists before it was sent to Michaelis. Presumably, however, they were men likely to be friendly to the Groener-Merton cause and to reply, as did Rieppel, that "if we proceed in this manner, then the old enthusiasm of 1914 may take hold again."[70] Whatever the case, the hostile industrialists had good connections in Berlin, and news of the memorandum did leak out. Merton knew that trouble was brewing, and he warned Groener to take the initiative by bringing the matter before the Reichstag. He was certain to win great sympathy there, and and this public support might have protected him against his enemies. Groener, however, refused to play politics and reminded Merton that such a solution was impossible for an officer. Evidently the game which Ludendorff and Bauer had played to bring Bethmann down did not appeal to Groener.[71]

[68] Groener, *Lebenserinnerungen*, pp. 360-361.
[69] *Ibid.*, pp. 369-370.
[70] Herzfeld, *Sozialdemokratie*, pp. 364-365.
[71] Groener-Geyer, *Groener*, pp. 62-63.

At some point during the last week of July, the OHL definitely decided to get rid of Groener. For all their antipathy to the latter, Michaelis and Stein seemed to have resisted the OHL's demand, probably because they were afraid of public opinion. Ludendorff therefore decided to buy them off. On August 2 he sent a telegram to Michaelis and Stein asking "that the responsibility for the feeding of the workers, particularly with regard to their supply of meat and fat, be taken from the War Office and given to the agencies responsible for the feeding of the civil population."[72] Thus Ludendorff had resolved the old conflict between Groener and Michaelis concerning the question in the latter's favor. On August 13 General von Stein sent Michaelis the draft of a royal order which declared that "now that the guidelines for the activity of the War Office have been set down, all directives of a basic nature concerning the affairs of the War Office are to be issued by the War Minister."[73] On August 14 Michaelis countersigned this draft and sent it to the Emperor. Stein's object in presenting this draft to Michaelis was to place the War Office under his direct control and thus give himself real authority over that agency. Needless to say, he could not have taken this step without Ludendorff's consent. Ludendorff's concessions to Michaelis and Stein were then combined into one secret Royal Cabinet order which the Emperor signed on August 22, six days after Groener's dismissal.[74] Groener, of course, had never been consulted about these measures. They represented a severe diminution of his personal power, and he hardly could have accepted them. It should also be noted that the OHL was so anxious to get rid of Groener that they were willing to retreat from their old goal of giving the War Office as much power and independence from the War Ministry as possible.

The big question is, who drove Ludendorff to make a final

[72] The DZA Potsdam was kind enough to research this problem for the author. The quotation is taken from their letter to the author of May 17, 1961.

[73] *Ibid.*

[74] BHStA, Abt. IV, MK, K Mob 6, Bd. II, Bl. 17.

decision? It is very likely that Stinnes, Colonel Koeth, and Koeth's good friend, Peter Klöckner, were involved. It is certain, however, that Duisberg and Bauer played the most important roles. Both directly after Groener's dismissal and after the war, Duisberg denied this. In the light of the evidence, however, it is virtually impossible not to conclude that Duisberg was a liar. Two weeks before Groener was dismissed, Duisberg told Dr. Sorge that Groener was going to be given command of a division on the Western Front.[75] Most important, two days before Groener's dismissal, on August 14, Duisberg sent Bauer the copy of an invitation to a "confidential meeting of a small group of representatives of the various industries" on August 19 at the Düsseldorf Industry Club. In it, he promised that a representative of the OHL, i.e., Bauer, would attend. The opening lines of Duisberg's invitation read:

> The complaints and agitation over the one-sided burdening of the workers by the restrictions upon the free movement of labor in the Auxiliary Service Law do not cease. Measures designed to assault the employers by limiting profits are also being considered. Speed is therefore necessary to counter this and also to set aside the dangers which the Auxiliary Service Law has presented to the production needed for the successful carrying on of the war.[76]

It is obvious that Duisberg was cognizant of the Merton memorandum and that he took the initiative in mobilizing industry against the Merton program. Furthermore, it is clear that Duisberg had reached an agreement with Colonel Bauer before calling this meeting because Duisberg was certain that the OHL would send a representative. The two men had certainly been plotting for some time.

[75] Groener, *Lebenserinnerungen*, p. 556. For Duisberg's denials, see his correspondence with Maximillian Harden of Nov.-Dec. 1918, BA, Nachlass Harden, Nr. 31, and his letters to Groener of Aug. 27, 1917, and to the chairman of the Budget Committee, Fehrenbach, of Aug. 25, 1917, Nachlass Groener, 192-II.

[76] BA, Nachlass Bauer, Nr. 11, Bl. 161-162. The meeting will be discussed in the next chapter.

On August 15, the day after Duisberg's invitation was sent, Groener visited General Headquarters at the invitation of Ludendorff. Merton and Groener discussed the memorandum before the latter's departure. Merton was certain that the memorandum would be discussed with Groener at headquarters and feared that Groener was in serious trouble. During their one and a half hour meeting, however, Ludendorff discussed nothing but routine matters with Groener. Thus Groener returned to Berlin on August 16 in a cheerful mood. Merton was better informed. Captain Kurt von Schleicher, a protégé of Groener's serving on the General Staff, had telegraphed Merton the previous evening in order to warn him that Groener was going to be dismissed. Merton suggested, therefore, that Groener postpone his optimism until he read the mail on his desk. One can well imagine Groener's shock when he discovered that he had been relieved of his position as Chief of the War Office and appointed Commander of the 33rd Division.[77]

What most angered Groener was Ludendorff's dissimulation during their meeting on the previous day. Groener had frequently indicated to Ludendorff that he would rather be relieved of his post than remain in office without Ludendorff's confidence. There was no excuse for Ludendorff's lack of honesty and rudimentary decency on the 15th. On August 19 Ludendorff sent a telegram to Groener thanking him for his services as Chief of the War Office, with its "heavy and not always appreciated tasks,"[78] and extending best wishes to Groener for his future career. To Groener this telegram must have seemed like the worst hypocrisy, and that is precisely what it was. When Groener requested permission to employ Merton on his staff, permission was denied. Schleicher later told Merton that Ludendorff had remarked that "the marriage must be separated."[79]

[77] Groener-Geyer, *Groener*, p. 63. Schleicher had served under Groener in the Railroad Section of the General Staff.

[78] Ludendorff to Groener, Aug. 19, 1917, Nachlass Groener, 192-II.

[79] Merton, *Erinnernswertes aus meinem Leben*, pp. 38-39, and Groener-

If Ludendorff is to be condemned for his dissimulation, however, he must not be denied a certain innocence concerning the motives of those who had turned him against Groener and Merton. Strange as it may sound, Ludendorff seems to have known nothing about the Merton memorandum! During a Reichstag debate on the profits question in March 1918, the well-informed Erzberger inquired as to whether or not Groener had sent the government a memorandum proposing a reform of the war contracting system. A few weeks later, Groener's successor, General Scheüch, replied that he had been unable to find the alleged memorandum and that the Imperial Chancellery had informed him of its inability to find such a memorandum either. He promised to ask the OHL whether they knew anything about the matter.[80]

When Groener read this statement in the newspapers, he angrily called it a "pack of lies." Scheüch, however, was not lying. He had evidently not found the memorandum because he did ask Ludendorff if it existed. On April 18, 1918, Ludendorff sent a telegram to Groener, who was in Kiev at the time, inquiring as to "whether such a memorandum was actually written"! Groener immediately replied with an affirmative answer but admitted that he did not know where the memorandum was.[81]

How is one to interpret this strange exchange of telegrams? It is not impossible that Ludendorff was attempting to put on an honest front. This explanation, however, is not very plausible. There was no good reason for Scheüch and Ludendorff to make secret telegraphic inquiries about a memorandum of whose existence they were already aware. Furthermore, in no eventuality was the government or Ludendorff going to permit Scheüch to go before the Reichstag and proudly announce that

---

Geyer, *Groener*, pp. 63-64. Schleicher protected Merton from being sent to a particularly dangerous sector of the front.

[80] Budget Committee Debates, March 3, 1918, and Reichstag Debates, April 16, 1918, 311, p. 4599.

[81] For the documents, see Nachlass Groener, 192-II.

he had found the memorandum. The available circumstantial evidence indicates that Ludendorff was genuinely puzzled and that Colonel Bauer and Duisberg who, as has been demonstrated, knew about the memorandum, had made certain to keep its existence a secret from Ludendorff. As Groener himself admits, he had never sent a copy to the OHL. The memorandum was given to Michaelis who, in turn, sent it to Helfferich. The latter did such a fine job of burying it in the files that it was not found until after the war. Ludendorff did not discuss the memorandum with Groener on the day preceding the dismissal because Ludendorff did not know it existed. Ludendorff had listened to Bauer's attacks on Groener and Merton because, as he told his good friend Colonel Albrecht von Thaer, Groener had handled the strikes with insufficient vigor and had done nothing about the high wages of the workers.[82] This last charge could not have been made if Ludendorff had really been informed of Groener's policy.

What is most significant is that Groener felt so isolated from Ludendorff that he had not even thought of sending Ludendorff the memorandum or discussing it with him and that Ludendorff was so completely in Bauer's clutches and so isolated from more moderate influences in July 1917 that the existence of the memorandum was never brought to his attention. Indeed, it is interesting to speculate on what might have happened if Groener had discussed the Merton memorandum with Ludendorff. As shall be demonstrated, the time would come when Ludendorff could be moved to oppose excessive war profits, and this suggests that Groener might have outfoxed Bauer if he had presented a clear and forceful program. At the same time, it must be recognized that Bauer had the all-important advantage of constant access to Ludendorff. In any case, Groener had two trumps in his hand, the Reichstag and Ludendorff. In refusing either to appeal to the Reichstag or to present his case directly to Ludendorff, his fall became inevitable.

[82] Thaer, *Generalstabsdienst*, p. 200.

Needless to say, nearly everyone who had wallowed in the morass of greed and intrigue which underlay Groener's dismissal sought to deny his complicity in the affair. General von Stein was least disagreeable in this respect. He told Groener that the dismissal was the result of attacks by heavy industry, projected changes in the War Office, and plans to reintegrate the War Office into the War Ministry. Stein also spoke of Groener's "leftist tendencies, which are understandable in South Germany, but not possible in Prussia." Koeth assured Groener that he had not worked for his dismissal, but Groener regarded Koeth as a "Jesuit of the first order"! Similarly, the Chancellor informed Groener that he had no hand in the matter and was quite surprised to learn of the dismissal. Groener seems to have believed this lie. Duisberg also denied any involvement in the affair and even Colonel Bauer made a point of protesting his innocence![83]

The official explanation for Groener's dismissal was that his services were no longer needed now that the War Office had been firmly established and an effort was being made to limit its activities. No one believed this explanation. The unions and Socialists were well informed about the true causes of Groener's dismissal. It is not impossible that Groener had discussed the Merton memorandum with some of the left wing leaders, or that Merton had done so himself. Whatever the case, the reaction of the *Correspondenzblatt* typified the left wing and liberal reaction. In the view of that paper, the official explanation was an illustration of Talleyrand's saying that words are used to hide the truth. Groener had long been on heavy industry's "Index":

> Groener, from the first moment of his activity, wished to consider and deal with the workers as a partner entitled to equal rights in the productive process. But that was already a demonstration of partiality toward the workers in the eyes of the employers. . . . Yet he demonstrated more than once

[83] Groener, *Lebenserinnerungen*, pp. 556-558.

that he was no enemy of the employers. Not a syllable of any of his directives indicates partiality toward the workers. He wanted justice, a reasonable compensation, and provisioning of the workers and not only war profits for the employers. He never left any doubt that he took a very different view of war profits than most of the members of the Imperial Government, and that was a further reason for his being sent elsewhere.[84]

This was both a fair and an accurate appraisal of Groener's work. Groener is not above criticism. Like Bethmann, he shared too many of the OHL's proclivities. He collaborated with and contributed toward the attack on the War Ministry, and one might almost say that in suffering at the hands of the intriguers who brought about his downfall, he did penance for his own role in the dismissal of Wild von Hohenborn and the subordination of the War Ministry. Groener was as prone to interfere in matters which were none of his concern as were Ludendorff and Bauer, and he had too great a faith in the virtues of military intervention. Groener was, like Ludendorff and Bauer, a "political" soldier, but his politics were both more rational and less radical than theirs. This put him at a disadvantage, for his capacity for action was always limited by his fundamental conservatism. He was not the "South German democrat" his opponents believed him to be:

> I was brought up by my parents in a conservative world view, and I have maintained it my whole life, but it is true that my conservatism is different from that of the East Elbians and the profit-egoism of heavy industry. I always tried to understand their views, but I believed that I had to maintain my views. . . . The worker, to me, was a human being and citizen with equal rights; I did not thereby overlook the dangers of Social Democratic propaganda.[85]

[84] *Correspondenzblatt*, Aug. 25, 1917. See also the collection of press comments in Nachlass Groener, 192-II.

[85] Groener, *Lebenserinnerungen*, p. 373.

It is to Groener's great credit that he recognized the dangerous nature of the political and social situation and that he realized the need to end the war quickly and grant reforms. He belonged to that group of "conservative reformers whose hour," in the words of his friend Friedrich Meinecke, "had struck too late."[86] Groener sought to combine South German social egalitarianism with the Prussian tradition of reform from above, and his desire to grant substantive concessions to labor in the social sphere was designed to prevent the complete destruction of those authoritarian political and military traditions with which he identified himself. He was thus paving the way for the alliances of industry and labor and of the army and Social Democracy which were to determine the course of the Revolution. For the moment, however, he was forced to surrender the field to men like Privy Councilor Ziese, who defiantly informed the workers at his shipyard that "Bethmann and Groener have been driven out, and Scheidemann has nothing more to say."[87]

[86] Friedrich Meinecke, *Erinnerungen, 1901-1919*, Stuttgart, 1949, p. 169. On Groener's friendship with Meinecke and the conservative supporters of Bethmann in the so-called Mittwochgesellschaft, see Groener, *Lebenserinnerungen*, p. 14.

[87] *Metallarbeiter-Zeitung*, Nov. 24, 1917.

PART FOUR

The Failure of the Army

VIII

The Ludendorff "Dictatorship," August 1917–February 1918

DID Scheidemann have nothing more to say? Although the last two years of the war are traditionally regarded as a period of military dictatorship in which the OHL supplanted the Emperor as the ultimate source of authority in the Empire, the weakness and limitations of this "dictatorship" require greater emphasis and attention. This is particularly the case in the sphere of internal politics, where, as has been demonstrated, Ludendorff had suffered continuous frustration. Unlike the later totalitarian dictatorship of Hitler, whose mad imperialist adventure was preceded by a ruthless "coordination" (*Gleichschaltung*) of German society, the dictatorship of Ludendorff was dependent upon the acquiescence of an independent labor movement and of a military and civilian bureaucracy whose traditional modes of operation were unsuitable for the conduct of a total war. Furthermore, it is important to note that Ludendorff, in contrast to Hitler, was a victim of his advisers. He lacked independent judgment and the ability to play off the competing "demigods" at General Headquarters against one another. Like Bethmann Hollweg, Ludendorff tended to vacillate.

The dismissals of Bethmann and Groener were designed not only to insure the satisfactory implementation of the OHL's policies, but also to enable the OHL to retreat from its direct and very time-consuming political activities. The ability of the OHL to successfully dictate from afar through its memoranda, however, was rendered doubtful from the very beginning because of the personnel upon whom it was forced to depend. It must be remembered that Michaelis' name was not associated with any particular point of view at the time of his appointment. When he entered office, he publicly committed himself to support the introduction of equal suffrage in Prussia. He even had a certain popularity because of his excellent record as Prussian Food Commissar and his championship of consumer interests. Furthermore, the changes he made in the highest positions of the Prussian and Imperial administrations were not reactionary in character.[1] The Reichstag majority could take pleasure from the resignations of Loebell, Schorlemer, Lentze, and Trott zu Solz. Their opposition to the introduction of equal suffrage made their continuation in office impossible. The new ministers, Bill Arnold Drews (Interior), Paul von Eisenhart-Rothe (Agriculture), Oskar Hergt (Finance), and Friedrich Schmidt-Ott (Culture), were more moderate than their predecessors. The appointment of the right wing Centrist leader, Dr. Peter Spahn, as Justice Minister in place of Dr. Hans Beseler represented a concession to the Reichstag's demand that somebody from its ranks be taken into the government. Helfferich resigned his position as State Secretary of the Interior but continued on as Deputy Chancellor.

The Interior Office, as long desired by the Reichstag, was finally split up. A new Imperial Economic Office (*Reichswirtschaftsamt* [RWA]) was established to manage social questions and make preparations for the demobilization and peacetime economy. This constituted an important step toward a more centralized direction of the economic and social problems of the Empire. The man appointed to head the Economic Office, Dr. Rudolf Schwander, had previously served as Lord Mayor of Strasbourg and was known to be a man of liberal views. The more conservative Lord Mayor of Cologne, Dr. Wilhelm von Waldow, was appointed State Secretary of the Interior. The War Food Office (KEA) was now placed under the Interior Office, and Waldow was made President of the KEA and, at the same time, Prussian State Food Commissar. He was also given a seat on the Prussian Cabinet. Michaelis'

[1] On these changes, see *Schulthess' Geschichtskalender*, p. 744.

efforts to unite the KEA and the Prussian Commissariat had finally succeeded. Batocki's resignation, however, caused considerable alarm. He had won a respect and admiration rarely accorded to a Conservative by the left wing parties, and many believed that he had been thrown out of office because he had refused to raise potato prices and would not act like a "normal" Conservative. The anxiety caused by Batocki's departure, however, was somewhat allayed by the appointment of Dr. August Müller as Undersecretary of the Interior. This was the first time that a Social Democrat had been appointed to high office, and the fact that Müller's special area of activity was to be the food problem seemed to bode well.[2]

These changes, which were announced on August 5, could not, therefore, be regarded as definite indications of the triumph of reaction. The new regime represented an effort to maintain bureaucratic government and, at the same time, conciliate the Reichstag majority. Groener's dismissal on August 16, however, was clearly a concession to heavy industry, and the shock it created was very great. Groener's successor, General Heinrich Scheüch, was an Alsatian with a long record of service in the War Ministry, where he had been head of the General War Department at the outbreak of the war. Little was known of his views, and his sudden replacement of the popular Groener was hardly likely to be reassuring. Nevertheless, the mere fact that Scheüch was so closely associated with the old War Ministry bureaucracy suggests that he was not the kind of man who was likely to promote or support radical changes of policy.

1. *Attempts to Reform the Auxiliary Service Law*

Radical changes of policy were very much on Carl Duisberg's mind when he addressed the leading Rhenish-Westphalian industrialists at the Düsseldorf Industry Club on

[2] On Schwander, see the BBS Report of Aug. 21, 1917. On Batocki, see *Correspondenzblatt*, Sept. 1, 1917; *Zentralblatt*, Sept. 10, 1917; and Groener, *Lebenserinnerungen*, p. 371.

August 19. He had opposed the legal restriction of the free movement of labor even before the Auxiliary Service Law was passed. Like Stinnes and Hilger, he felt that it ruined willingness to work and served the interests of the unions.[3] Now, nine months after the law had gone into effect, Duisberg was convinced that all his fears had been realized. He claimed that the productivity of the exempted workers had dropped 40 percent, and that this was due, in part, to their efforts to drag out their work in order to avoid being recalled into the army. Duisberg placed the chief blame for the diminished productivity and morale of the workers, however, upon the Auxiliary Service Law. He would have liked to have the entire law annulled, but he definitely wanted Paragraph 9 eliminated.[4]

Duisberg pointed out that Paragraph 9 was regarded as a concession to the employers and was now being used as the justification for an attempt to limit profits. In order to prevent this, he deemed it necessary that the employers renounce the advantages of Paragraph 9. He did not think this would constitute a real sacrifice. The workers were changing their jobs anyway, thanks to the wording of the paragraph, and the enforced two weeks vacation placed no burden on higher paid workers who left their jobs without permission. He thought that little was to be gained from increasing the enforced vacation period to six weeks since "experience has demonstrated that work done under compulsion is of little value." He then proceeded to contradict this last statement by arguing that the annulment of Paragraph 9 was the only way to force exempted workers to stay on their jobs. Indeed, the chief charge against the paragraph was that, thanks to the promise made by Groener in the Reichstag, the exempted workers were able to use it to change jobs with impunity. Duisberg recognized that it was impossible to revoke Groener's promise with-

[3] See his remarks at the WUMBA advisory council meeting of Oct. 15, 1916, BA, Nachlass Moellendorff, Nr. 58.

[4] The discussion and quotations are based upon the protocol of the meeting in Nachlass Groener, 192-I.

out creating "disturbances," but "if the employers . . . find themselves prepared to give up the limitations on the free movement of labor, then the military authorities will have a free hand with the exempted workers and will be in the position to reintroduce the earlier method of dealing with them."

Between the lines of Duisberg's remarks, however, it is possible to detect the most important motive for his opposition to Paragraph 9. Duisberg knew that the unions had a great stake in this paragraph because it provided the basis for the activity of the arbitration committees and conciliation agencies. The latter institutions would atrophy without the restrictions placed on the free movement of labor. He thus sought to belittle the objections the unions would make against his proposal:

> One does not need to be frightened away from this measure out of fear of the power of the unions. The importance of the unions is very much overestimated. Between 1913 and 1915 the percentage of the German workers organized by the unions dropped from 37 percent to 14 percent, but it has risen again considerably during the war. The expectations which have been placed in the union leaders have been disappointed. Instead of maintaining peace among the workers, they have actually destroyed peace and order in the factories. The drop in work performance is due mainly to their agitation, not to poor nourishment or long hours, for the low productivity has remained even though the food supply is now satisfactory and working time has been regulated according to the wishes of the workers.

Needless to say, this was a rather contradictory statement, for it suggested that the power of the unions was very great indeed.

The industrialists present at the meeting, particularly the coal barons Hugenberg and Kirdorf, were in complete agreement with Duisberg. They also felt, however, that Paragraph 9 could not be dispensed with unless the exempted workers were compelled to stay on their jobs as they had been before the law was passed. Only the War Office representative, Dr. Lewinski, warned that union resistance was to be taken seriously. The industrialists were unclear as to how to proceed. Duisberg suggested three possibilities. Paragraph 9, in his view, could be annulled by the Reichstag, by the Bundesrat, or by a private agreement among the employers not to make use of its provisions. None of these procedures was particularly satisfactory. It would be very difficult to secure the Reichstag's agreement. The Bundesrat, Lewinski informed Duisberg, did not have the right simply to annul a paragraph of the law. Finally, it would be extremely difficult to get all the industrialists to agree to give the leaving certificate automatically to workers requesting permission to change their jobs. Colonel Bauer had the will to help the industrialists, but he was uncertain about the way to do so. He agreed that the "harmful features of the Auxiliary Service Law which affect the exempted workers must be set aside," but pointed out that this was the job of the War Ministry, not the OHL. He concluded, however, by indicating that there were "many possibilities at hand and he hopes that a solution will be found."

Five days later, on August 24, this "secret" meeting and Groener's dismissal were the subject of lively debate in the Reichstag Budget Committee.[5] Erzberger expressed great regret over Groener's departure and warned that his successor would be wise to continue Groener's policies and not give in to the demands of heavy industry. Scheidemann was much more demanding and specific in his discussion of the question. He pointed out that Groener "had won the confidence of the workers," and he demonstrated that he was extraordinarily well-informed about the reasons for Groener's dismissal. He knew that Groener had written a memorandum demanding that restrictions be placed upon profits if there were going to be any limitations of the rights provided by the Auxiliary

[5] The discussion and quotations which follow are based upon the protocol of the Budget Committee debate, Aug. 24, 1917.

Service Law. He also had information concerning the industrialists' meeting of August 19 and knew that Duisberg had played a role in Groener's dismissal. Finally, Scheidemann wanted to know why Ludendorff had said nothing about what was going to happen during his conversation with Groener on the day preceding the latter's dismissal.

General von Stein and Helfferich did not have an easy time answering these inquiries. Stein praised Groener's work, hinted that Groener was not really very happy in his job, claimed that he had never heard any complaints from heavy industry against Groener, and assured the deputies that the change in the leadership of the War Office would not mean a change of policy. Helfferich, while admitting what everyone knew, namely, that the industrialists did not like the Auxiliary Service Law, denied all knowledge of the Groener memorandum. Under further interpellation, Helfferich admitted that some consideration was being given to changes in the law, but truthfully insisted that preparations for these changes had been begun under Groener's administration. Much less truthfully, he assured the deputies that the changes being considered were not of a serious nature. He agreed with the deputies that it "would be a mistake if a change was made that was unfavorable to the workers." Only Count Westarp was satisfied by these explanations. Scheidemann thought that they were "worth nothing" and warned that "one should not play with fire. General Groener or, better said, Herr Duisberg, can very easily become the match which, once struck, can ignite monstrous explosions."

The OHL was immune to such warnings. On September 10 Hindenburg ("L") sent a long note to Michaelis, Stein, and Scheüch with demands which were in large part an unmistakable product of the industrialists' meeting of August 19.[6] The OHL declared that it would be necessary to call up large numbers of exempted workers by spring, but that it would be

[6] The discussion and quotations which follow are based upon the document in DZA Potsdam, Kriegsakten 1, Bd. 12, Bl. 11-13.

impossible to cut munitions production. Practical measures to solve the labor problem were thus necessary. Ludendorff's attitude toward an annulment of the Auxiliary Service Law was very ambivalent, and he left the decision as to whether or not this was advisable from the standpoint of internal politics to the government. He was certain, however, that "even an indication that the Bundesrat could be forced to annul the law would make the left wing parties tractable."

The OHL then went on to demand a long series of changes in the law, many of which were very similar to those planned by the War Office under Groener's regime. They wanted the Auxiliary Service obligation extended to youths between fifteen and seventeen years of age, and they insisted that the War Office and the determination committees be empowered to assign workers to the most essential war plants. Naturally, the OHL was most concerned about Paragraph 9. They demanded that the compulsory layoff period for those who changed jobs without a leaving certificate be lengthened. Furthermore, the OHL wanted the right to change jobs limited, for *all* workers, to the particular occupational sector in which they were employed. It also proposed a complete ban on job changing for particularly important war plants. The OHL was convinced that "the present equality of the exempted workers with those liable to Auxiliary Service is insupportable." The only solution was to assign each exempted worker to a specific factory and not to permit him to change jobs unless he had the permission of the local War Office bureau. The OHL also asked that something be done about the drop in productivity. Ludendorff, repeating Duisberg's argument, declared that this had been caused by the desire to evade recall into the army and not by the poor food supply.

In conclusion, the OHL warned that an extension of the ages of liability to military service could become necessary in order to replace k.v. personnel in the occupied territories with older men and youths. The OHL insisted that the situation was critical and that everything depended upon the home front: "If we act internally, then the army will bring the war to a good conclusion. The agencies responsible for the handling of the above-discussed questions thus bear an enormous responsibility. The Reichstag, the unions, etc., must also be left in no doubt about the fact that *they* also will be subject to the heaviest reproach if they procrastinate or refuse to cooperate." Thus, the responsibility for the fulfillment of the OHL's program was shifted elsewhere in the usual fashion, for it was not Hindenburg's "office to make further proposals as to how the above discussed matters are to be put into practice."

Very little of this program was fulfilled, and the expectations which the OHL had placed in the new military and civilian leadership were generally frustrated. Scheüch would not give the slightest consideration to the annulment of the Auxiliary Service Law. He noted that it was precisely because the law, as the OHL complained, had given so many advantages and rights to the workers that it was impossible to do away with it. Most interesting, however, is the fact that Scheüch, unlike Groener, was not even willing to bring an amended version of the law before the Reichstag. Scheüch felt that it was necessary "to avoid a discussion in the plenum of the Reichstag which could lead to debates and consequences which are militarily and politically undesirable." The Interior Office was at one with Scheüch in his opposition to the annulment or legislative amendment of the law.[7]

This is not to say that Scheüch did nothing to fulfill those of the OHL's demands which he considered capable of realization. Although he did not think that it was necessary to extend the powers of the determination committees, he was able to report that these committees, under his administration, were

[7] The Interior Office informed the industrialists that the law could not be changed for "political reasons." See the VdESI executive committee meeting, Sept. 24, 1917, BA, R 13I/152. On Dec. 19, 1917, Scheüch sent a long report to Undersecretary of State Radowitz concerning his efforts to fulfill the OHL's demands of Sept. 10. See DZA Potsdam, Kriegsakten 1, Bd. 12, Bl. 106-107.

no longer treating all war plants equally. They were distinguishing between more and less essential war plants and thus permitting the draft committees to remove workers from factories of the latter type. Scheüch was careful to mention, however, that the Reichstag committee had raised no objections to this practice.

Scheüch did succeed in establishing a much more effective system of national registration, but here he was only completing Groener's work. On November 13 the Bundesrat, with the approval of the Reichstag committee, issued regulations requiring that all persons liable to Auxiliary Service, with the exceptions of those serving in the armed forces and those exempted for work in the factories, register with the local authorities. The War Office representatives told the Bundesrat that universal national registration would not only make the law more effective, but would also be very useful if the army found it necessary to ask for an extension of the ages of liability to military service.[8]

This willingness to prepare for a possible extension of the Military Service Law did not mean that the War Office supported such a step. In October the OHL followed up its note of September 10 by demanding that the War Minister present the Reichstag with a bill extending the liability to military service to all males between fifteen and sixty. Although General von Stein was fully aware of the difficult reserves situation, he was no more convinced that the time had come for this radical step than Wild von Hohenborn and Bethmann Hollweg had been a year before: ". . . the War Minister takes the view that the taking of this measure, which will cut so deeply into the life of the German people, should be delayed until the last extremity. The presentation of a bill at the present time is regarded as neither necessary nor advisable."[9]

[8] For the regulations and the Bundesrat and Reichstag committee discussions, see BHStA, Abt. IV, MK, K Mob 14, Bd. V, Bl. 82, zu 90, 124, 152, and K Mob 11a, Bd. V, Bl. 12.

[9] Scheüch to Radowitz, Dec. 19, 1917, DZA Potsdam, Kriegsakten 1, Bd. 12, Bl. 106-107. For the OHL's request, see the report of Undersecretary Graevenitz, Oct. 24, 1917, *ibid.*, Bl. 14-15.

The War Office was much more receptive to the OHL's demand that the industrialists be prepared to surrender large numbers of exempted workers by spring. On September 26 Ludendorff ordered that military considerations be given priority in the evaluation of requests for exemptions, and on October 3 Marquard ordered that 30,000 exempted workers be returned to the front by December 31. In taking these steps, however, the OHL and the War Office were simply reverting to the old War Ministry policy of giving priority to the demands of the field army. The trouble was that the damage had already been done and was now well nigh irreparable. In January 1918 there were no fewer than 2.3 million exempted workers serving the war economy, 1.2 million of whom were k.v.[10]

The control of the free movement of these exempted workers was the most important demand raised by the OHL and the industrialists. Scheüch wanted to satisfy this demand, but he knew that it would be far from easy to escape the commitment made by Groener to give exempted workers all the benefits of Paragraph 9 of the Auxiliary Service Law. One thing was certain: this commitment could not be escaped without the permission of the trade union leaders. In late September Scheüch conducted secret negotiations with the union leaders at which an extraordinary agreement was concluded. The report on these negotiations is worth quoting in full:

> On September 24, 1917, a confidential discussion with the representatives of the workers and in the presence of Deputies Bauer and Legien took place under the chairmanship of the Chief of the War Office.
>
> The labor representatives showed insight and a willingness to make concessions, and a temporary agreement has been reached that workers shall be exempted for individual factories alone.
>
> If an exempted worker wishes to leave the factory to

[10] Reichsarchiv, *Weltkrieg*, XIV, p. 29n2. For the Ludendorff and Marquard directives, see MF, Marine Archiv, Nr. 7867.

> which he has been assigned, then he must turn to the arbitration committee. The latter is only to examine whether or not the working conditions [i.e., wages] are satisfactory. If they are not, then the responsible Deputy Commanding General will either try to persuade the employer involved to grant suitable conditions, or he will assign the exempted worker to another factory important to the war effort so long as important military reasons do not necessitate his recall into the army.
>
> If the employer resists the influence of the Deputy Commanding General, then he receives no replacement for the exempted worker.
>
> The regulation which is to be developed upon this basis shall be discussed in the Reichstag committee.
>
> If the position of the exempted workers is regulated according to this agreement, then [the War Office] will abstain from changing Paragraph 9 of the Auxiliary Service Law.[11]

The last line of this report suggests that Scheüch may have threatened to bring a bill changing Paragraph 9 before the Reichstag. This, however, was hardly a very significant threat since it was the army, not the union leaders, which had cause to fear the Reichstag. At the same time it is very likely that the union leaders did fear arbitrary actions on the part of the army and were seeking to prevent the "worst." Yet this scarcely suffices to explain the remarkable concessions they were willing to make.

What the agreement really reveals is the intense patriotism of the union leaders, their continued faith in the army, and their desire to control wages. By making this agreement, the union leaders were tacitly admitting that the previous arrangement did not serve military interests, and they were expressing their desire to serve those interests. Despite the dismissal of Groener and despite the very repressive tactics that, as shall

[11] Captain Müller's report of Nov. 22, 1917, BHStA, Abt. IV, MK, K Mob 14, Bd. V, Bl. 128.

be shown, the Deputy Commanding Generals were employing at this time, the unions were prepared to give the military authorities the right to determine the wages and working conditions of the exempted workers. Finally, between the lines of this agreement one can read the anxiety of the union leaders concerning the recurrent wage demands of the workers and their fear that they might become the prisoners of those wage demands.[12]

It was heavy industry which sabotaged the agreement reached between the union leaders and the War Office, as is demonstrated by the report on the negotiations conducted between Scheüch and the leaders of heavy industry on October 25:

> The representatives of heavy industry refused to engage in any discussion of the annulment of the free movement of exempted workers if it was to be bound up with the control and surveillance of wages by the Deputy Commanding Generals. In that case, they would prefer to leave things as they are.
>
> A representative of Bavarian industry demurred from this standpoint. If one refuses all discussion, then one compels the War Office to initiate changes in the law without consulting industry.
>
> General Scheüch confirmed this. If industry takes the view that it has no interest in a change if it is bound up with definite conditions, then the War Ministry takes the view that military interests demand a change. It is absolutely necessary that we acquire more influence over the exempted workers; if industry cannot bring forth compelling reasons against this, then it will be implemented without their approval.[13]

12 On union efforts to moderate wage demands at this time, see the BBS Report of Sept. 1, 1917.

13 Captain Müller's report of Oct. 27, 1917, BHStA, Abt. IV, MK, K Mob 14, Bd. V, Bl. 128. More meetings with the industrialists were planned, but the author has found no record of them.

The industrialists were thus as suspicious of the army as they were of the trade unions, and they intended to remain masters of their own houses at any price. Despite all their complaining about the exempted workers and all their protestations of patriotism, they preferred to set military interests aside—one might almost say stab the army in the back—rather than surrender their right to establish wage rates and working conditions without outside interference. Although he had threatened to act without the industrialists, Scheüch did not do so. In the face of industrialist resistance and the inability of the army to act without making some concessions to the unions, the effort to increase the army's control over the exempted workers failed. Scheüch, of course, might have tried to act on the basis of the agreement with the unions despite the industrialists' disapproval. Groener's fate, however, was undoubtedly quite fresh in his mind.

2. *Koeth's Triumph*

In dismissing Groener the OHL removed not only the one man who was willing to handle the social problem courageously and energetically, but also the most important supporter of the War Office. Stein's opposition to the War Office and the powers of its head was apparent throughout Groener's term in office. In fact, Stein had come to agree with the views of his predecessor, Wild von Hohenborn, with amazing rapidity. Scheüch, who had made his career in the War Ministry, was likely to share the Ministry's reserved attitude toward the War Office. Thus Scheüch's appointment was marked, as noted in the previous chapter, by the establishment of the War Minister's authority over the War Office and by the termination of the War Office's independent activity in the supplying of food to the industrial workers. The section of the War Office concerned with food problems was dissolved. The War Office bureaus were asked to continue to advise on the allocation of food premiums for industrial workers, but they were deprived of all executive authority. Within the War Office itself, Scheüch proceeded to diminish the importance of the staffs and restore the independence of the various departments. Generally speaking, these changes were improvements. They were sound from an administrative standpoint, and they relieved the overburdened War Office of tasks for which it was not suited.[14]

Officially, Scheüch also took the shutting down and consolidation of industries out of the hands of the War Office. He requested that this question be turned over to the new Imperial Economic Office (RWA) because the problems were too complex and too many interests were involved for it to be handled by a military agency. The government agreed and, on November 3, 1917, the Standing Committee on Consolidations (SAZ) was dissolved. This did not mean, however, that the War Office no longer had anything to do with this problem. Representatives of the War Office continued to take part in the deliberations concerning shutdowns and consolidations, and, most important, the War Office and the War Office bureaus were charged with implementing decisions reached by the RWA.[15] The real significance of the change, however, is not to be sought so much in Scheüch's efforts to cut down the responsibilities of the War Office as in Koeth's desire to have a free hand in implementing the Concentration of Forces.

It will be remembered that the federal states, particularly Bavaria, feared that the Concentration of Forces would mean the ruin of their industries. They recognized that Colonel Koeth and the leading persons in the KRA tended to take the view that the social and economic needs of the smaller states had to be made subsidiary to the demands of the war, and they feared that the KRA, in collaboration with the Coal Commissar, would arbitrarily deny coal to the South German factories. At the same time, they feared that they would cease

[14] For the various directives concerning the organization of the War Office, see *ibid.*, K Mob 6, Bd. III, Bl. 17 and 29. See also Wrisberg, *Wehr und Waffen*, pp. 142-143.

[15] See Scheüch's directives of Nov. 3, 1917, BHStA, Abt. IV, MK, K Mob 8, Bd. I, Bl. 139-140.

to receive a satisfactory number of war contracts. There was extraordinary bitterness in South Germany, a bitterness felt not only by the people, but also by those who were most highly placed. A typical expression of the Bavarian's suspicion of Prussia and heavy industry is to be found in one of Crown Prince Rupprecht's letters to Hertling:

> Bavaria will find it much more difficult to recuperate from the consequences of the war than North Germany because her industry is less developed. But her further development is also being made more difficult during the war because, on the pretext that she is not sufficiently capable of producing, she receives relatively fewer contracts from the central agencies. Heavy industry is now supreme in Germany. . . . Using the needs of war in the most ruthless fashion, the Berlin business people have managed, by the creation of all the central agencies set up in Berlin, to bring the entire internal economic life of Germany under their control and power, and the consequence will be that, after the war, the middle class, which already finds itself in dire distress, will disappear and a trustification worse than America's will set in. For Bavaria, where the middle class is rather numerous, this will be catastrophic. The members of this class, who were previously very monarchically minded, are now in part more antimonarchical than the Social Democrats because they blame the government for their misfortune.[16]

Groener understood these feelings, and however much he demanded that the states collaborate in the Concentration of Forces, he recognized that such collaboration could not be secured without some measure of concession on his part.

The Bavarian government was not blind to the need for quick action to meet the emergencies created by the coal crisis. Consequently, it accepted the necessity of centralized decision-making. It did insist, however, that it be consulted

[16] Rupprecht to Hertling, July 19, 1917, *ibid.*, Abt. II, MA 1, Nr. 975.

about these decisions so that it might prevent untoward actions. It demanded also the right to self-determination within the confines of its own territory. That is, on the basis of general guidelines set forth in Berlin, it was to have the final decision as to what factories were to be shut down in Bavaria. Bavaria was most vocal in making these demands, but Württemberg and Baden were also adamant about protecting their interests. Groener had accepted these principles. Almost immediately after Groener's dismissal, however, Koeth and the Coal Commissar, Stutz, began to violate them by cutting off the coal supply of individual Bavarian factories. The Bavarian government became as frightened over his dismissal as the Social Democrats.[17]

Koeth, in a meeting of September 10, stated his open opposition to maintaining the agreement Groener had reached with the South German states. The coal shortage had created too much of an emergency to permit consultations and division of the executory powers, and he had to be "in the position to make decisions from hour to hour if necessary." He felt that South Germany's acceptance of the KRA's right to control raw materials for the entire Empire at the beginning of the war had been a step in the right direction. He could not understand the sudden withdrawal of this support just at the moment when "everything is at stake."[18] The Bavarian representative to the War Office, Captain Müller, pointed out in reply that the states had not imagined that the war would last so long when they agreed to the establishment of the KRA. Many mistakes had been made since then, and the federal states could not permit Koeth to act without prior consultation.[19]

The root of the difficulty between the states and the KRA was that the immediate measures needed to handle coal shortages were continuously being confused with plans for the large-scale consolidation of industries. At a meeting on Sep-

[17] See the Bavarian War Minister Hellingrath's strong protest to Scheüch of Sept. 11, 1917, *ibid.*, Abt. IV, MK, K Mob 6, Bd. III, Bl. 5.
[18] Meeting of Sept. 10, 1917, *ibid.*, Bl. 166. [19] *Ibid.*

tember 13 Koeth and the Coal Commissar sought to clarify the matter. There was a shortage of twenty million tons of coal, and Stutz could not wait until the complicated negotiations leading to the consolidation of more industries had taken place. Some firms had to be deprived of coal immediately. The Coal Commissariat was compelled to act on the basis of priority lists drawn up by the KRA in collaboration with the OHL. Koeth pointed out that he was willing to discuss formal and long-term shutdowns and consolidations with representatives of the states. Shutdowns necessitated by immediate shortages, however, could not be handled in the same way. Scheüch concluded the discussion by declaring that the War Office and the Coal Commissar had to reserve the right to act without prior consultation, but he promised to keep the states informed through their liaison officers. On September 22 he issued instructions along these lines.[20]

This arrangement lasted throughout the rest of the war. Needless to say, it did not prove completely satisfactory from the Bavarian point of view. On a number of occasions the Bavarian government had to remind the War Office of its right to be heard and demand that the War Office not interfere with state prerogatives. The seriousness of Bavaria's plight, however, should not be overestimated. In fact, in comparison with the other South German states and in comparison with some of the northern areas of Germany, including Berlin, Bavaria was relatively well supplied with coal. The Bavarian representative to the War Office confessed that the blame for his state's economic problems could not be placed on Berlin alone. Bavarian industry had been too poorly developed before the war, and she would have been far more favorably located to receive coal transports if she had built up her waterways. He concluded that "one must view the situation objectively and not overlook one's own responsibility."[21]

[20] Meeting of Sept. 13, 1917, *ibid.*, Bl. zu 168 and directive of Sept. 22, *ibid.*, K Mob 8, Bd. I, Bl. 111.

[21] December 1918 memorandum of Captain Müller, *ibid.*, K Mob 6,

In the last analysis, Koeth, with his brutal insistence on the necessity of immediate action to meet immediate needs, was largely responsible for keeping the ill-effects of the transport and coal problems of the winter of 1917-1918 to a minimum. Even the OHL obeyed Koeth's injunctions. In December, when the problems were at their worst, Koeth and Stutz went to the OHL and demanded that production quotas be cut back temporarily. This effort was successful. Similarly, Koeth demanded that the industrialists stop complaining and accept reality. He made it clear that "all complaints and petitions which do not involve those factories most important to the war effort can only end in the wastepaper basket."[22] Koeth's methods were all the more necessary because the RWA was very dilatory in undertaking the formal shutdowns and consolidations which were now its responsibility. As Koeth recognized, the root of the problem lay in the fact that none of these measures had been prepared before the war. His arbitrary methods, therefore, were the only solution.

3. *The Uncertain Dictatorship*

The most important consequences of Groener's dismissal, however, are not to be found in the abortive efforts to change the Auxiliary Service Law, the diminution of the War Office's role, and the reassertion of Koeth's independence. Rather, they are to be found in the increased use of the Law of Siege and the restored independence of the Deputy Commanding Generals. After the April 1917 strikes, Groener had summoned the Deputy Commanding Generals to a meeting at which he advised them not to ban union meetings and to collaborate with the union leaders in the prevention of strikes. After the July-August strikes, however, it was General von Stein who called a meeting of the Deputy Commanding Generals, a meeting

Bd. IV, Bl. 128. For a statistical comparison of the coal supply of major German cities, see the Coal Commissar's report of Dec. 12, 1917, *ibid.*, K Mob 12, Bd. 11, Bl. 166.

[22] War Office meeting, Dec. 14, 1917, *ibid.*, K Mob 12, Bd. XIII, Bl. 13. See also the Peppel study.

conducted under the impress of the OHL's and industry's demand for a reversal of Groener's "soft" policy toward union meetings.

The meeting was held on August 13,[23] three days before Groener's dismissal, and thus provides another example of how the rug was pulled out from under Groener's feet during his last days in office. General von Stein opened the meeting by pointing out that two specific developments had led to the summoning of the conclave at this particular time. First, a revolutionary group had been discovered in the High Seas Fleet. Second, there was the threat of a general strike. Leaflets had been found calling for such a strike on August 15 or August 20. Consequently, preventive measures were necessary. Stein placed particular emphasis on the need for stricter control of worker meetings and more vigorous handling of exempted workers.

The War Ministry had not only received its information concerning the general strike plans from leaflets. The industrialists were extremely upset by the strike rumors and found the growing demands for shorter hours and higher wages unacceptable.[24] The role of the industrialists in driving the War Ministry to its decision to apply the Law of Siege more energetically becomes obvious from the remarks made by the Head of the General War Department, General von Wrisberg, who chaired the meeting. In Wrisberg's view, most of the strikes were started for completely "frivolous reasons." The complaints about the food supply were, in most cases, "unjustified." This is not to say that Wrisberg had completely abandoned all sympathy for the workers, a sympathy he certainly felt when he had been in charge of the labor question during the first two years of the war. When the complaints of the workers were justified, Wrisberg told the

[23] Unless otherwise indicated, the discussion of and quotations from this meeting are based upon the protocol, BHStA, Abt. IV, MK, IcIa15[b], Bd. I, Bl. zu 228[a].

[24] Meeting of the Northwest Group of the VdESI, Aug. 8, 1917, BA, R 13I/164.

Deputy Commanding Generals, then something was to be done so that the workers would feel entitled to say: "We have a military administration that is *just*, that helps us when our complaints do not lack an actual foundation." Wrisberg's big concern on this occasion, however, was not the workers' feelings, and he went on to remark, "But that should not lead to a continuous making of concessions, as has recently been the case. In the last analysis, that is a vicious circle! Right now we are having a loss of many hundreds of thousands of tons of coal because of partial strikes. It is impossible for things to go on this way any more, particularly in view of the revision of the wage scale in peacetime."

Wrisberg then turned to the practical measures needed to improve the situation. First on the list was a stricter attitude toward the right of assembly. If it was necessary, the Deputy Commanding Generals "should not be frightened away from banning all meetings." Then Wrisberg recommended the timely and judicious militarization of those factories where there was trouble so that the striking workers might be compelled to return to work. He laid particular emphasis on the desirability of redrafting exempted workers even if they "only seemed suspect" of being agitators. It was preferable to act "too early than too late." In short, the Deputy Commanding Generals were being given a free hand to employ the powers at their disposal, each "according to his own judgment and on his own responsibility" and with the assurance "of the active support of the Commander of the Home Army [the War Minister]."

Needless to say, the Deputy Commanding Generals were very pleased by the new instructions. General von Gayl, in the name of all the generals, thanked the War Minister and expressed "joy and satisfaction over the tone of the very definite guidelines." Freiherr von Vietinghoff's representative was overjoyed that "the Law of Siege is coming into full force again." General von Hepke, the general in Coblenz, took the opportunity to give vent to his antiunion feelings. He pointed out that wage demands could no longer be conceded because they were "so extraordinarily high" and that, in the end, the taxpayer would be the victim of these increases. In his view, "the union secretaries are a cancerous sore [*Krebsschaden*]." Only one of the assembled officers, the representative of the Deputy Commanding General in Karlsruhe, ventured to suggest that the food situation was really quite bad and that a more conciliatory attitude was desirable. It was obvious that most of the Deputy Commanding Generals greeted the opportunity to reverse Groener's policy.

Strange as it may seem, the Majority Socialist leaders had something to do with the instigation of the harsh measures over which they were shortly to complain so loudly. On August 9 the Secretary of the Navy, Capelle, had summoned Ebert to his office to inform him of the underground movement in the High Seas Fleet. Fifty sailors had been arrested and a large number of propaganda leaflets had been seized. Capelle claimed that the leaflets were the work of the Independent Socialists and some of the more radical Majority Socialists. Ebert denied this, but he condemned such "treasonous activity" and agreed with Capelle that "one must use every means to establish a front . . . against such stupidity." As if to demonstrate his own loyalty, Ebert then informed Capelle that "a big new propaganda campaign of the Haase group for a general work stoppage . . . is planned or already in progress."[25] Little wonder, therefore, that Wrisberg felt entitled to tell the Deputy Commanding Generals that "it is very noteworthy that the nationally minded Social Democrats strongly advise sharp intervention."

If Ebert had sought to direct the army's wrath against the Independent Socialists in order to keep it from falling upon the Majority Socialists and trade union leaders, then his effort backfired. The Deputy Commanding Generals were not given to subtle distinctions. The new policy of the War Ministry made itself felt almost immediately after the August 13 meet-

[25] Capelle to Michaelis, Aug. 9, 1917, *AGSOD*, II, pp. 646-650.

ing. On August 22 General von Gayl banned all efforts to persuade workers to change jobs. Although Gayl later excused his order by claiming that it was directed against the agents of companies trying to steal workers, the order was easily interpreted as an attack upon union secretaries who supported wage demands. Much less ambiguous were the orders issued by other Deputy Commanding Generals requiring that all meetings concerned with the Auxiliary Service Law and wages be reported at least eight days in advance, that the content of speeches be submitted for censorship, and that a police inspector be permitted to attend the meetings. Particularly shocking were the threats of two Deputy Commanding Generals to punish strikers with ten years imprisonment and even death. The measures of the Deputy Commanding Generals, therefore, were not merely directed against political meetings and political strikes, but also against meetings and strikes in which food problems, wages, and working conditions played the chief role. In conformity with this policy of giving the Deputy Commanding Generals a blank check, the War Office bureaus were ordered to follow the lines laid down by the Deputy Commanding Generals in their efforts to mediate labor disputes.[26]

This sudden increase of military repression was made all the more aggravating by the growth of annexationist and reactionary propaganda during this period, propaganda inspired and financed by the army and heavy industry. The Fatherland Party was founded on September 2. Although placed under the leadership of Admiral von Tirpitz, the party was really the creation of the OHL. Specifically, it was the brainstorm of the Chief of Military Intelligence, Lieutenant-Colonel Nicolai. Nicolai had gotten the idea from Major-General Magirus of the Württemberg War Ministry. In the spring of 1916 Magirus had expressed his concern over the morale problem to Colonel

[26] See the petition of the General Commission to General von Stein, Sept. 8, 1917, BHStA, Abt. IV, MK, XIV c III 17, Bd. II, 143[a], and the Scheüch directive of Oct. 4, 1917, *ibid.*, IcIa15[b], Bd. II, Bl. 14.

Nicolai and to the War Minister. In the course of a meeting he made the following proposal:

> In peacetime, each party prepares the entire people before each election through the press, through leaflets, and above all through the spoken word, in that even the smallest place is visited by suitable speakers. Why should we not be able to do in wartime what the parties do in peacetime? We need an enlightenment and arousing of the people, not in the sense of a particular party but in the sense of the patriotic idea of holding out to the last. An organization must be set up for this purpose now so that it will be at hand in time of need. At the head there must be a man who knows the soul of the people and understands how to win over others. At his side there must be an advisory council of men from many professions and parties bound together by a glowing love of the Fatherland and by the will to hold out. From this agency will come the slogans and guidelines that are to be spread among the people. The people, however, should not have the impression that they are dealing with an organization influenced by the state. For this reason the organization must be created with the greatest skill and caution. Mistakes can easily lead to the opposite of what is intended.[27]

The Fatherland Party was Nicolai and Ludendorff's distortion of Magirus' idea. They encouraged Tirpitz and his friends to organize a mass party of the right to fight the peace resolution and political reform. Although supposedly open to Germans of all political persuasions, the Fatherland Party was really a rallying point for bourgeois annexationists and extreme conservatives, and it was seen in this light by the left wing parties from the moment of its birth. By July 1918 it was to overtake the Social Democratic Party and have a peak membership of

[27] HStASt, Nachlass Magirus, Heft 45. Statement at a War Ministry meeting of June 9, 1916 and undated memorandum on the subject, presumably written in late 1917.

1,250,000. Its success demonstrated that a large segment of the German bourgeoisie could be organized into a mass movement in support of imperialism and militarism. At the same time, the role which the OHL played in the establishment of this party shows that the type of radical militarism which it espoused required the creation of new forms of mass political organization to support its programs.[28]

To counter the Fatherland Party, the moderate annexationists set up a People's League for Freedom and Fatherland on September 14. This group included leading members of the Society for Social Reform, the moderate conservatives associated with the *Preussische Jahrbücher*, and right wing labor leaders. Thus Friedrich Meinecke and Deputies Giesberts and Bauer all spoke at the first meeting. The League for Freedom and Fatherland, however, never achieved very great importance. The reason for this is very simple: fantastic sums of money and the propaganda machine of the army were behind the Fatherland Party. At the meeting summoned by Duisberg at the Düsseldorf Industry Club, for example, the industrialists decided to enlarge their expenditures in support of annexationist propaganda. For tactical reasons, the Association of German Iron and Steel Industrialists decided not to support the Fatherland Party publicly, but they also decided to give it their maximum moral and financial support.[29]

During this same period the OHL launched a program of "patriotic instruction" (*vaterländischer Unterricht*) for the troops. Although this instruction was supposed to be nonpolitical, it was really an attempt to indoctrinate the troops with the ideas of the Fatherland Party. In fact, the propaganda was so annexationist and conservative that some field commanders refused to support the program lest it harm morale.

[28] Fischer, *Griff nach der Weltmacht*, pp. 559-562. Hindenburg and Ludendorff publicly stated their agreement with the principles of the Fatherland Party. See *Schulthess' Geschichtskalender*, p. 782.

[29] On the People's League, see Richter, *Gewerkschaften*, pp. 130-131. For the industrialist support, see Nachlass Groener, 192-II, and BA, R 13I/152.

The OHL, therefore, did not limit itself to a policy of repression. It also sought to expand the conception of the army as the "school of the nation" to include the support of mass political movements and the introduction of a large-scale propaganda effort.[30]

The repressive measures employed against the trade unions and Social Democrats by the Deputy Commanding Generals were not often extended to the Fatherland Party. The union leaders were angered by this demonstration of partiality and were very concerned about the effects of the Deputy Commanding Generals' measures upon their work. As the Society for Social Reform warned the War Office:

> In leading union circles the restrictions that have been placed on the right of assembly in the districts of certain Deputy Commanding Generals are found extremely injurious to union activity. No union can live without meetings. The meeting is the central point of its spirit and chief instrument for the formation of will. Through them the mass of the organized workers determine the attitudes of the leaders, but the leaders also use them to drive on or control the masses. . . . If one takes away the possibility of holding meetings from the unions, then the masses return to a chaotic state and will, and, depending on their structure and local characteristics, either lapse into apathy or permit their natural radicalism to express itself through illegal means.[31]

In a petition to General von Stein of September 8, 1917, the General Commission threatened to stop trying to persuade the workers to support the war effort if the Deputy Commanding Generals continued their harsh practices. It regarded the restrictions recently placed on union meetings as a violation

[30] On the Patriotic Instruction program, see Reinhard Höhn, *Die Armee als Erziehungsschule der Nation. Das Ende einer Idee*, Bad Harzburg, 1963, pp. 518ff., and Walther Nicolai, *Nachrichtendienst, Presse und Volksstimmung im Weltkrieg*, Berlin, 1920, p. 113ff.

[31] BBS Report, Oct. 25, 1917.

of Paragraph 14 of the Auxiliary Service Law, which guaranteed that persons employed in the Auxiliary Service would not be denied the exercise of their rights of association and assembly. Stein replied on September 22 by pointing out that Paragraph 14 did not give those employed in the Auxiliary Service any special privileges, but only guaranteed that their rights would not be restricted any more than anyone else's. Stein insisted that the Deputy Commanding Generals had not changed their policies, and he simply brushed aside the charge that an antiunion policy was being followed. He did promise, however, that union meetings which were concerned with "economic questions" would not be hampered. Stein did, in fact, want a slight loosening of the reins at this point, for on September 25 he instructed the Deputy Commanding Generals not to impose excessive restrictions on meetings concerned with coal and food shortages. This new directive did not represent a change of heart on Stein's part. As he pointed out, a new war bond drive was being launched, and, most important, the Reichstag was scheduled to meet again shortly. It was thus inadvisable to be too rigorous at this time.[32]

It was, however, too late. The union leaders had secured a copy of the protocol of the meeting which had taken place in the War Ministry on August 13, and they were not entertained by the contents. In the course of a debate in the Budget Committee, Ebert suddenly inquired about the August 13 meeting and asked why the War Minister had permitted a Deputy Commanding General to call the union secretaries a "cancerous sore." Stein gave a very weak reply in which he defended the Deputy Commanding Generals and pointed out that the meeting was solely concerned with the prevention of "frivolous strikes."[33] The Social Democrats were not satisfied by this reply. In fact, they had already presented an interpellation to the Chancellor asking what he intended to do about the recent

[32] For this correspondence, see BHStA, Abt. IV, MK, XIV c III, Bd. II, Bl. 143a.

[33] Budget Committee Debates, Oct. 8, 1917.

decrees restricting the discussion of economic questions at union meetings and the favor being shown to Pan-German propaganda by the army.[34] On October 10 this interpellation was the subject of a full dress debate in the Reichstag. The debate was all the more vituperative because, on the preceding day, Michaelis had committed political suicide by accusing the Independent Socialists of having instigated the recent hunger strikes and revolutionary activities in the navy for which two sailors had been executed and many others sent to prison. Michaelis had no evidence for his charges, and the Social Democrats were bent upon bringing about an end to his very inglorious Chancellorship.[35]

The Social Democrats were not in a gentle mood when they discussed the Law of Siege of October 10.[36] Deputy Schmidt began the debate by pointing out that the right of assembly had been virtually annulled and that "arbitrariness and dictatorship" had taken its place. If this was the New Orientation, then "God save us from the New Orientation." In Schmidt's view, the protocol of the meeting of August 13 demonstrated that the War Ministry was encouraging the restrictive policies of the Deputy Commanding Generals, and he noted that the change in policy was coincident with Groener's downfall: "The social-political insight which had happily been present for a long time in the War Ministry has disappeared. We have set aside many inequities with the help of the unions. The War Minister may be a good soldier; a politician, as demonstrated by his attitude, he is not."

Stein's reply to this attack was a mixture of the carrot and the stick. He read his directive of September 25 asking that the restrictions on the right of assembly be made milder. But he pointed out that the harsher measures had been called forth by the Upper Silesian strikes and the threat of a general strike. He noted that things had become "quieter" since these

[34] Reichstag Debates, Anlage Nr. 1050, 322, p. 1787.

[35] *Ibid.*, Oct. 9, 1917, 310, pp. 3713ff.

[36] For the quotations from and discussion of this debate, see *ibid.*, Oct. 10, 1917, pp. 3858ff.

measures had been taken and hoped that they would not be necessary again. "But I make no bones about it, gentlemen, in telling you that if any kind of difficulty is made, if we are not met half way, if behavior is unfriendly or seems to be seeking other ends, then I will naturally be put into the position of having to implement the measures more sharply."

Despite the ruthless attitude assumed by Stein and the Deputy Commanding Generals, the union leaders were convinced that a visit to the OHL would do much to straighten things out. Legien believed that the war could only be ended "by planes and machine guns." He wanted to collaborate with the OHL and, at the same time, bring the trade unions some relief from the oppression of the Deputy Commanding Generals. The OHL was willing to speak with the union leaders, and in late September and mid-October they met separately with representatives of the various union organizations.[37]

On October 15 Ludendorff sent a report to General Scheüch concerning these meetings.[38] This report is exceptionally interesting because it demonstrates a willingness to compromise and meet the union demands half way. Ludendorff reported that the Free Trade Unions and Christian Union leaders had complained about the very negative attitude of the leaders of heavy industry toward negotiations with the unions. The Christian Unions leader, Stegerwald, was very anxious to set up "communal economic committees" composed of employer and worker representatives in each army corps district. These institutions would be directed by the Deputy Commanding Generals. Astonishingly enough, Ludendorff agreed with the union leaders. He thought that management-trade union collaboration would be necessary for the demobilization and transition to a peacetime economy. He also liked Stegerwald's idea because he thought that the communal economic com-

[37] Foreign Office report of Oct. 23, 1917, to the Prussian Minister of the Interior on a meeting with the union leaders on Oct. 5, 1917, *AGSOD*, II, pp. 745-746. On the meetings with the trade union leaders, see *Zentralblatt*, Oct. 22, 1917, and *Correspondenzblatt*, Oct. 20, 1917.

[38] Reprinted in Ludendorff, *Urkunden*, pp. 94-97.

mittees might provide a means of controlling the exempted workers. Ludendorff pointed out that this might solve the problem created by the refusal of the employers to permit the Deputy Commanding Generals to determine the wage rates of the exempted workers. Ludendorff admitted that a distinction had to be made between agitators and the more reliable labor leaders and remarked that "control of the orders of the Deputy Commanding Generals is, perhaps, indicated." His general impression was that "all representatives apparently have the good intention of striving to keep their workers peaceful and have them do their duty."

There were, to be sure, harsher comments. Ludendorff thought that the workers demonstrated very little understanding of how other classes were suffering from the food shortage. He warned the union leaders that the OHL would not put up with strikes "under any circumstances" and that strikers would be treated as traitors. Furthermore, he declared himself to be in complete agreement with the complaints of the yellow union leaders over the way the authorities had treated them. Yet there can be no question about the fact that Ludendorff's attitude at this time was by no means as negative as one would have been led to believe by the events leading to and following Groener's dismissal.

The major explanation for Ludendorff's "reasonable" attitude toward the union leaders is that he knew their help was going to be necessary during the demobilization and transitional economy. The industrialists themselves were beginning to recognize this. An illustration of the gradual modification of heavy industry's views is provided by the report of the steel industrialist Beuckenberg concerning a discussion with State Secretary Schwander in September:

> We assume that the social-political section of the Imperial Economic Office will wish to have representatives of the workers take part in the discussions. The State Secretary comprehended immediately and said: yes, he already

> thought of that, it is self-understood. I told him that insofar as I have discussed the matter with my colleagues, they are of the opinion that we would be willing . . . to negotiate concerning legislation with the participation of the workers under the chairmanship of the government.[39]

Beuckenberg's one condition was that the representatives of the yellow unions be brought into the negotiations and that the representatives of the "fighting" unions agree to this. Schwander, while admitting a certain justice to this demand, pointed out that the fighting unions had told Groener that they would not deal with the yellow unions. To this Beuckenberg replied that "now that there has been a reordering of affairs, I assume that he will want to undertake things with a strong hand, since he [Beuckenberg] has also agreed to the new ideas which will not be easy to get accepted." Given the previous attitude of heavy industry, Beuckenberg was making an important concession, and some of the other industrialists did raise objections. Beuckenberg, however, insisted that his willingness to discuss legislation with the union leaders did not mean that heavy industry would have to accept collective bargaining.

Of even greater significance, however, is the fact that in October 1917 the heavy industrialist leaders Stinnes, Kirdorf, and Hugenberg held secret conversations with the Free Trade Unions leaders Bauer, Schmidt, Leipart, and Schlicke in the Hotel Continental in Berlin. Very little is known about these conversations, and they did not lead to any immediate results. Although there is some evidence that war aims were discussed, the chief topic of conversation seems to have been the demobilization question. The most detailed explanation of the industrialists' motives was given by Stinnes' associate, General Director Vögler, after the war:

> It was not purely tactical considerations that compelled us to give up our position. It was a practical consideration in

39 VdESI meeting, Sept. 24, 1917, BA, R 13I/152.

> the first instance. When we assumed in 1917 that the end of the war would soon come, we became clear as to the monumental tasks involved in suddenly bringing 10 to 12 million people back into the factories in a relatively short period of time. We had a great fear that the War Office . . . would solve this problem bureaucratically. . . . We wanted to solve this enormous task in common with the workers and the first negotiations, which began in 1917, . . . were concerned above all with the problem of how to bring the 10 million human beings back to their places of work.[40]

Vögler's remark about the desire to avoid a "bureaucratic" management of the problem by the War Office demonstrates that the industrialists had more confidence in their ability to wrest concessions from the unions and in the ability of the unions to control the workers than they had in the ability of the government, and particularly the army, to control the potentially dangerous social situation that was anticipated.

Michaelis was also a proponent of collaboration with the trade unions. In the course of the government crisis in the latter part of October 1917, Michaelis' entire effort to remain in power was based on the assumption that he would receive trade union support if he agreed to cooperate with the unions in the development of social legislation. He pointed out that "this would in any case be necessary in the transition to a peacetime economy. The lowering of wages from their present abnormal heights will have to be accomplished by the introduction of arbitration courts and the extension of the competence of the unions. etc."[41] The OHL's positive attitude toward management-labor negotiations at this time, therefore, must be understood in the general context of the growing recognition of the part of even the most conservative elements that

[40] Quoted in Richter, *Gewerkschaften*, p. 159. On the same subject, see the RWA report of Nov. 23, 1917, concerning Stegerwald's meeting with the OHL, *AGSOD*, II, pp. 772-774, and Hans von Raumer, "Unternehmer und Gewerkschaften in der Weimarer Zeit," *Deutsche Rundschau*, 80, May 1954, p. 428.

[41] Varnbüler to Weizsäcker, Oct. 13, 1917, HStASt, E, 73, 12i.

union participation in the postwar reorganization of the economy was both necessary and desirable.

This, however, was not the only reason for Ludendorff's softer line. Not all of Ludendorff's advisers were as reactionary as Colonels Bauer, Nicolai, and the head of the Political Section of the General Staff, Bartenwerffer. Captains Geyer and Harbou, who were members of Colonel Bauer's section, were convinced that concessions had to be made to the left. The head of the Operations Section, Major Wetzel, and the head of the Balkan Section, Lieutenant-Colonel Mertz von Quirnheim, did not share the extreme views of Ludendorff's dominant political advisers.[42] Furthermore, Ludendorff was subject to the influence of Stresemann, who was in constant contact with the OHL and who sought to exert a moderating influence. Despite Bauer's personal views and Hugenberg's efforts to get the OHL to pay more heed to the right wing National Liberal leader, Hirsch, Bauer placed a great deal of confidence in Stresemann. If Bauer did not go so far as to support Stresemann's internal political program, their friendship still provided the latter with a means of bringing the ideas of the more moderate industrialists to the attention of Ludendorff.[43]

Furthermore, Ludendorff's desire to interfere in internal politics was far from constant. He was fearfully overworked, and he had greeted Michaelis' appointment as an opportunity to withdraw from his preoccupation with domestic concerns.[44] The collapse of Michaelis' Chancellorship in October 1917 found the OHL in a state of veritable paralysis. Michaelis' downfall was completely the work of the Reichstag and the appointment of his successor, the aged Minister-President of Bavaria, Count von Hertling, was made with the approval of

[42] On Geyer and Harbou, see Bauer, *Grosse Krieg*, pp. 33-34. On Wetzel and Mertz, see Reichsarchiv, *Weltkrieg*, XII, pp. 2-3.

[43] See Hugenberg's letter to Bauer of Aug. 12, 1917, and Bauer's letter to Duisberg of Dec. 25, 1917, BA, Nachlass Bauer, Nr. 11.

[44] See Kraft von Delmensingen's report of Sept. 4, 1917, BHStA, Abt. II, MA 1, Nr. 975, Bl. 81-85.

the Reichstag. Thus for the first time in the history of the Empire, the Reichstag had been consulted about the appointment of the Chancellor. Helfferich was replaced as Deputy Chancellor by the Progressive, Payer, and a National Liberal, Friedberg, was appointed Vice-President of the Prussian Cabinet. Also, Hertling, before taking office, committed himself to the immediate presentation of an equal suffrage bill to the Landtag and declared that he was prepared to dissolve the Landtag and hold new elections in wartime if the bill was turned down. Similarly, Hertling promised to introduce a worker chambers bill and annul Paragraph 153 of the Industrial Ordinance, which protected strikebreaking. In short, Hertling's appointment was coupled with major concessions to the Reichstag majority.[45]

Although Ludendorff was very displeased over the appointment of the Bavarian Catholic with whom he had quarreled during the previous spring, he refrained from interfering in the crisis for a variety of reasons. He had no candidates to offer but Bülow and Tirpitz, neither of whom would have been acceptable to either the Reichstag or the Emperor. Ludendorff also felt, along with Stresemann, that Hertling was too old to last long and that Bülow might then follow him. The OHL was made all the more susceptible to Stresemann's arguments by its fear of a strike. It was aware of Stresemann's policy of working with the Social Democrats in order to keep the workers behind the war effort and was most anxious to use Stresemann for this purpose during the crisis. Thus Bauer telegraphed Stresemann: "See to it . . . that the Social Democrats remain on the leash. We cannot bear even a strike of only eight days, since we are not overly supplied with ammunition because of the continued battle in Flanders." Ludendorff went so far as to tell Stresemann that he would not oppose the appointment of the Social Democrat, David, to a ministerial post if "peace could thereby be established."[46]

[45] On this crisis, see Valentini, *Kabinettschef*, pp. 173-184.

[46] Stresemann to Reichsrat von Buhl, Nov. 12, 1917, Nachlass Strese-

Hindenburg and Ludendorff were extraordinarily well-behaved during and immediately after the government crisis. In the course of a trip to Berlin in early November, they indicated, in the presence of Major Wetzel and Colonel Mertz von Quirnheim, that they had no objections to Hertling's appointment and were prepared to work with the new Chancellor. Wetzel then suggested to Mertz that it might be useful if the OHL sent a representative to Hertling to convey its friendly feeling and express regret over previous quarrels. When Mertz brought this proposal to Hindenburg, the latter gave his approval and sent Mertz to the Chancellor. Hertling was very pleased by what Mertz had to say, but he complained bitterly about "how disturbing and unfortunate Colonel Bauer's influence and activity are" and asked that something be done about it. Mertz then proceeded to enlighten Ludendorff about Bauer, and Ludendorff, who was obviously in one of his more "reasonable" moods, agreed to restrict Bauer's influence. Later events will demonstrate that Ludendorff did not follow Mertz' advice for very long, but the incident certainly worried Bauer, and the latter made considerable effort to ingratiate himself with Mertz.[47]

This oscillation between repression and concession was not limited to the OHL. It permeated the entire military bureaucracy at home. Scheüch, for example, did not diverge very sharply from the social policies carried on by the War Ministry and the War Office. He was on excellent terms with his chief adviser on social questions, Tiburtius, and he was sympathetic toward the policy suggestions of the Society for Social Reform. The War Office consequently continued to give official support to the reports of the Bureau for Social Policy, reports

---

mann, 6885, frames H133047-H133048. Also, see Matthias and Morsey, *Interfraktionelle Ausschuss*, pp. 476-478. On Hertling's earlier quarrels with the OHL, see the report of General von Hartz to the Bavarian War Ministry, Oct. 30, 1917, BHStA, Abt. IV, MK, III a XV 39.

[47] Report by General von Hartz, Nov. 8, 1917, BHStA, Abt. IV, MK, III a XV 39.

which were prounion in tone and highly critical of heavy industry and the Deputy Commanding Generals.[48]

It was not easy to follow in Groener's footsteps, and Scheüch had a difficult time breaking down the reserve with which the union leaders were treating him. In the winter of 1917-1918, however, Scheüch received strong support from the union leaders for the first time. This was due largely to the battle he waged to secure compensation for workers laid off as a result of coal and raw materials shortages. Scheüch feared that the layoffs would cause unrest among the workers, and he wanted the Bundesrat to pass a decree requiring the employers and the state to contribute to the compensation of the idle workers. After a hard struggle with Sydow and Breitenbach, who feared that the measure would set an unfortunate precedent for the peacetime economy, Scheüch had his way. The employers and unions reached an agreement in negotiations directed by Scheüch, and the Bundesrat passed a general regulation of the question on the basis of these negotiations in January 1918. The General Commission paid special tribute to Scheüch for his handling of this problem and, while giving high praise to Groener, remarked that it would be wrong not to ascribe good will to the new Chief of the War Office.[49]

4. The OHL and the Great Strikes

The position of the Chief of the War Office, however, was no longer as important as it had been in Groener's time, and

[48] Letter from Senator Tiburtius to the author of Nov. 19, 1962. Sichler left the War Ministry after Groener's fall to serve as General Director of the Skoda-Werke in Pilsen. The BBS Reports were written by Dr. Hans Carl Heyde of the Society for Social Reform. Heyde received much of his information from trade union leaders, particularly from Sassenbach and Heinemann of the General Commission. I am grateful to Dr. Eberhard Pikart for this information, which is based on an interview with the late Professor Heyde. For an example of the War Office's dissemination of the BBS Report defending the union point of view on the right of assembly, see the report of Nov. 15, 1917.

[49] On the compensation question, see BHStA, Abt. IV, MK, K Mob 7d, Bd. II, Bl. 119, 121; Bd. III, Bl. 107, zu 108, 120; K Mob 19, Bd. II, Bl. 118, 120. For the tribute to Scheüch, see *Correspondenzblatt*, May 11, 1918.

the good behavior of the OHL was short-lived. Germany was now living in a state of permanent internal crisis. The October Revolution in Russia, toward which Ludendorff had contributed by sending Lenin to that country, increased radical sentiment among the German masses. The food situation was worse than ever, and government controls had completely broken down. The unification of the government's food administration under Michaelis had come too late. Black marketeering had increased enormously, and the industrialists had lost all inhibitions about buying food for their workers on the black market. The entire situation was brought to the attention of the public in the most sensational manner when the Social Democratic *Vorwärts* published the memorandum of the Neukölln Municipal Council of December 3, 1917, on "The Breakdown of Waldow's System." In this memorandum, which was addressed to the KEA, the collapse of the food supply system was described in vivid detail. Industrial firms competed with the municipal authorities for food. Since the firms were willing to pay black market prices, the municipal authorities were forced to follow suit. Consequently, both the firms and the local authorities were deeply involved in illegal operations. The price ceilings had thus been reduced to meaninglessness. Also, certain communities and firms were more favored than others. Rhenish coal mining concerns, for example, were given preferential treatment by the farmers if they agreed to barter coal for food. The memorandum concluded with the astonishing threat that the town council was "disposed to pursue the illegal methods already adopted unless the War Food Office immediately provides a remedy."[50]

Food shortages and war weariness naturally affected the productivity of the workers. The industrialists were in the habit of attributing this lower productivity to excessively high wages, a rather curious charge since the industrialists themselves admitted the inadequacy of the food supply and were moving heaven and earth to supply their workers with food from the

[50] Translated in Lutz, *Fall of the German Empire*, II, pp. 177-186.

black market. The decreased productivity resulted in a demand for more exempted workers. This was particularly the case in the U-boat industry. The navy wanted to expand its production program in the late fall of 1917 and asked the OHL for more skilled workers. Ludendorff could not spare the men, however, and he demanded that productivity be increased instead. In a meeting with the naval leaders on December 4, 1917, Ludendorff and Bauer demonstrated that the relatively sympathetic attitude which the former had displayed in the October conferences with the union leaders had evaporated. Bauer was in the saddle again. He pointed out that a 10 percent increase of production could "easily" be achieved if "energetic means" were used, and he demanded that the "soft treatment" of the workers be terminated. Ludendorff added that the fear of strikes was a "slogan" behind which everybody was hiding, and he blamed the decreased productivity of the workers on the high wages they were receiving.[51]

The OHL's tone during the December meetings with the naval authorities was typical of its general swing toward the extreme conservative camp at the close of 1917. On the one hand, the military situation was looking brighter. An armistice was signed with the Soviet Government on December 15. Peace in the East thus seemed to be in the offing and, with it, the opportunity to receive the first installment on the war aims program and to free troops for a great final offensive in the West during the coming spring. On the other hand, the internal situation was getting worse. The government presented a bill for the introduction of equal suffrage to the Prussian Landtag on December 5. It was well known that the majority of the deputies were opposed to the government bill. The right wing deputies believed that a great German military victory would obviate the need for social and political reform.[52]

[51] For the meeting with the naval authorities, see MF, Marine Archiv, Nr. 7867. It is interesting to note that Scheüch did not share the OHL's view that the workers were holding back production. See Scheüch to Radowitz, Dec. 19, 1917, DZA Potsdam, Kriegsakten 1, Bd. 12, Bl. 106-107.

[52] Rosenberg, *Birth of the German Republic*, pp. 210-211.

The attitude of the OHL was of vital importance to the success of the conservative effort to block suffrage reform. As one of the chief conservative opponents of equal suffrage, the former Agricultural Minister Schorlemer, pointed out to Ludendorff, the right wing Centrists, who held the balance in the Landtag, were inclined to vote against the government bill. They had been told, however, that there would be great strikes if the bill were rejected and that the OHL was terrified at this prospect. Schorlemer considered it "unthinkable" that the Social Democrats would strike "in the decisive hour of this mighty war," and he wanted the OHL to disassociate itself from such rumors. Ludendorff replied to this appeal immediately: "The contention that the OHL has spoken for an acceptance of the bill out of fear that a refusal of the suffrage bill would lead to strikes is *not* based upon the truth. The OHL has taken no stand . . . on the suffrage question. We wish to remain outside of internal politics and not be drawn upon by either side."[53]

The OHL's "neutrality," however, could only be interpreted as support for the opponents of the suffrage reform. The Saar industrialist and Landtag Deputy, Carl Röchling, who was another leader of the opposition to the government bill, was in constant contact with the OHL during the Landtag debates. It was he who informed the OHL that the Prussian ministers Drews and Friedberg had spread the rumors about the OHL's fear of strike if the bill was voted down. In notes to Drews on November 26 and December 8, Ludendorff insisted that the government deny the veracity of these rumors. He contested the view that the government's policy had to be determined by fear of a general strike and pointed out that the workers and union leaders knew very well that a lost war would "impoverish" the German working class. Ludendorff denied that he had taken any stand on the suffrage question, but he made no effort to hide his true feelings: I am of the view that the

[53] Schorlemer to Ludendorff, Dec. 5, 1917, and Ludendorff to Schorlemer, Dec. 6, 1917, BA, Nachlass Bauer, Nr. 17.

war has not really given us any reason to democratize or parliamentarize; the situation within the democratically ruled enemy lands can in no way incite us to imitate them." Ludendorff held the surrender to the "spirit of the times" to be "extraordinarily dangerous" and did not think that there was any possibility of a general strike.[54]

Ludendorff's remarks demonstrate that he was in complete agreement with Röchling and, indeed, was repeating the arguments which Röchling had used in telephone conversations with Ludendorff and letters to Bauer:

> In my [Röchling's] view it is the task of the civil and military authorities to *prevent* munitions strikes as much as possible. This can be done, aside from the satisfactory provisioning of the workers, by making it clear to them that munitions strikes must necessarily bring about the loss of the war, and that the German worker will thereby be harmed the most. Anyone who calls upon the workers to engage in munitions strikes is guilty of high treason and must be placed before a court-martial. The democratic suffrage, even if one wanted to give it to babies, cannot change this. This train of thought must be hammered into the men again and again.[55]

Given the ability of Röchling and his friends to win the OHL over to these views, it is little wonder that the vacillating opponents of the suffrage reform regained their confidence. As a result, the bill was sent to a committee for lengthy reconsideration.

The OHL, however, was whistling in the dark. On December 13 the *Vorwärts* called upon the workers and soldiers to engage in "powerful demonstrations" for suffrage reform. The OHL's response to this editorial was a demand that *Vorwärts* be banned. Hertling was by no means insensitive to the dan-

[54] Ludendorff, *Urkunden*, pp. 290-293.

[55] Röchling to Bauer, Dec. 16, 1917, BA, Nachlass Bauer, Nr. 11.

gers of the editorial and noted that "the Russian model should not be underestimated." He refused, however, to ban the paper because he did not want to drive the Majority Socialists into the camp of the Independents.[56]

At the same time, the OHL was coming into sharp conflict with the government over the peace negotiations with the Russians. It is impossible to speak of Hertling's and Foreign Secretary Kühlmann's demands on the Russians as "moderate." Nevertheless, Hertling, Kühlmann, and the Chief of Staff of the Eastern Command, Major-General Max Hoffmann, were committing the cardinal sin of being less extreme than the OHL. Furthermore, their "moderation" had the Emperor's support. To counter this, the OHL launched a campaign to get rid of Kühlmann. Hertling, however, would not let Kühlmann go. But the OHL did secure one major triumph in forcing the Emperor to dismiss the Chief of the Civil Cabinet, Valentini. The latter was replaced by the archconservative Friedrich von Berg on January 16, 1918. Berg was a close friend of Hindenburg, and the OHL could count on him to win the Emperor over to their side. The Emperor was resentful over the way Ludendorff had forced him to change his most intimate adviser, but it did not take long before the Emperor had fallen completely under Berg's influence.[57]

The political tension reached its height in January 1918. On January 10 the Independent Socialists began disseminating a leaflet addressed to the workers. In this leaflet the Independents pointed out that the government had finally revealed its extreme annexationist aims in the negotiations at Brest-Litovsk and that, as a result, the peace negotiations were breaking down. The leaflet concluded by reminding the workers that they "had the last word" and that it was necessary to raise their voices for a peace without annexations and in-

[56] *AGSOD*, III, pp. 838-839, 908-909.

[57] Fischer, *Griff nach der Weltmacht*, pp. 621ff.; BA, Nachlass Berg, Nr. 331-332; reports of General von Hartz, Jan. 1-18, 1918, BHStA, Abt. IV, MK, III a XV 39.

demnities. The leaflet did not openly call for a political strike, but its inflammatory character cannot be denied.[58]

If the Majority Socialists were, officially at least, in agreement with the Independents on the peace question, their major emphasis was still on the suffrage problem. The attitude of the Prussian Landtag toward suffrage reform presented a tremendous danger to the Social Democrats because the entire policy was based on gaining internal reform as compensation for their support of the war effort. With the eyes of the masses riveted on the negotiations at Brest-Litovsk and the debates in the Landtag, and with the impending failure of their hopes in both those quarters, the Social Democrats had no choice but to take a more radical tone.[59]

The agitation of the workers was intensified by Russian revolutionary propaganda and particularly by the general strikes in Vienna and other industrial centers of the Austro-Hungarian Empire between January 14 and 21. The German military censors sought to prevent the news of the Austrian strike from leaking out. Their efforts backfired. On November 21 the *Vorwärts* was banned for reporting a speech by the Austrian Socialist leader, Victor Adler. The Social Democrats were particularly irritated by the ban because nothing had been done to punish the right wing papers which carried reports on the strike, and they hit back at the government in the Reichstag Budget Committee hearing on January 22. Scheidemann harshly declared that "the *Vorwärts* ban is having an agitating effect. The censors should be clear as to the fact that the situation in Germany now is just like that in Austria before the strike. . . . We are not threatening, but we warn you."[60]

The distinction between a threat and a warning in this case was purely semantic. Scheidemann would have been much more accurate if he had simply stated: "We are not threaten-

[58] The leaflet is reprinted in *AGSOD*, III, pp. 951-954.
[59] BBS Report, Jan. 21, 1918.
[60] Budget Committee Debates, Jan. 22, 1918.

ing that our party will launch a strike, but we are warning you that we are no longer in control of the masses, and we may have to join them if they do strike." The real question was not whether there was going to be a strike, but rather what kind of strike it was going to be. The Spartacists and the radical shop stewards in Berlin led by Richard Müller wanted the Independent Socialists to come out in favor of a mass strike. This demand was supported by the Independent deputies Ledebour and Hoffmann, but it was opposed by the party leaders because they feared that it would lead to the destruction of the party. The Independents called instead for a demonstration strike, and on January 28, 400,000 Berlin workers laid down their tools. In a meeting of the representatives of the strikers on this day, a seven-point program was drawn up: (1) peace without annexations, (2) sending of worker representatives to the peace negotiations, (3) improvement of the food supply, (4) termination of the Law of Siege, (5) no militarization of factories, (6) release of all political prisoners, and (7) democratization and suffrage reform. An eleven-man "Workers Council" was organized and placed under the chairmanship of Richard Müller. The strikers' representatives decided to invite the Independents and, despite considerable opposition, the Majority Socialists to send three members each to sit on the Workers Council.[61]

The General Commission and the Social Democratic Party felt "too weak" to prevent the strike, a strike which, as even Colonel Bauer admitted, they did not want.[62] Once the strike broke out, however, they felt compelled to join the Workers Council in order to gain control over the workers. The Social Democratic members of the Council, Ebert, Scheidemann, and Otto Braun, did not find the company of Haase, Ledebour, and Dittmann very congenial and they loathed having to work with revolutionary radicals like Müller. The Social Democrats

[61] Opel, *Deutsche Metallarbeiterverband*, pp. 70-72, and Rosenberg, *Birth of the German Republic*, pp. 211ff.

[62] Bauer to Major Müldner von Mülnheim, Feb. 10, 1918, BA, Nachlass Bauer, Nr. 12.

disliked working with the radicals all the more because Secretary of the Interior Wallraf was unwilling to receive a deputation of strikers but was willing to receive a deputation of union leaders so long as the latter were not involved in the strike. In short, the government would not discuss political questions and would not deal with the strikers.[63]

The Social Democrats wanted to accept Wallraf's offer, but the Independent Socialists and radicals insisted that the government deal with the Workers Council. The Majority Socialists now faced the alternative of staying on the council or leaving it. Bauer, of the General Commission, preferred the latter alternative. In his view the Social Democrats could now say that the Independents had ruined all chances of negotiating with the government thanks to their fanaticism and had thus ruined the strike's chances of success. Ebert disagreed with Bauer. In his opinion, an opinion shared by the majority of the party and union leaders, Bauer's method would have left the party open to the charge that it had betrayed the strike. If the Social Democrats remained loyal to the Workers Council and let the strike fail because of the stubborn refusal of the radicals to deal with the government on Wallraf's terms, then the Independents could be blamed for the failure.[64]

Ebert's policy was followed. The deadlock between the government and the Workers Council was resolved by military force. Workers' meetings were banned. Many of the big munitions factories were militarized. Large numbers of striking exempted workers were taken into the army and a "B-18" (Berlin-1918) was placed on their records to make sure that they were never exempted again. Dittmann, whom the army had long hoped to catch agitating, was arrested while addressing a workers' meeting and sentenced to five years' fortress imprisonment by a court-martial. By February 4 the strike was

[63] On Socialist policy, see *Internationale Korrespondenz*, Feb. 25, 1918, and IISH, SPD Fraktionssitzung Protokoll, Feb. 5, 1918. On Wallraf's policy, see the Prussian Cabinet protocol of Feb. 4, 1918, in BA, Nachlass Heinrichs, Nr. 24.

[64] IISH, SPD Fraktionssitzung Protokoll, Feb. 5, 1918.

broken. There could be no question about the fact that it had been a total failure.[65]

The strikes were not limited to Berlin. There were serious strikes in Kiel, Hamburg, Halle, and Magdeburg, all of which were put down by militarization of factories, extraordinary courts-martial, and calling up of exempted workers. In the Ruhr there were short coal miners' strikes. These were less political and more economic in character than those that were taking place elsewhere. They coincided with new union wage demands and were aggravated by union demands that the mineowners negotiate. When General von Gayl threatened to use military force and draft all strikers into the army, the strike collapsed. Gayl then summoned the union leaders to his office and bluntly told them that "the understandable wish of the unions to increase their power must not lead to the use of means that are not consonant with the common good." He rejected the lastest union demands as excessive, but informed the union leaders that some wage increases would be possible if the employers were permitted to keep more of their export profits. Gayl refused to discuss the question of union-management negotiations, a question which he demanded be set aside until after the war. Finally, he warned the union leaders that he would not give the workers any time to think things over in case there was another strike. From now on, he intended to act immediately and with every means at his disposal.[66]

Only in Bavaria and Cologne were the strikes treated in a milder manner. Minister-President von Dandl of Bavaria decided to deal with the strike leaders because the Majority Socialist leaders had the workers under control. He went so far as to thank the Social Democrats for ending the strike so quickly. In Cologne, Wallraf's successor, Mayor Konrad Adenauer, handled the strike there in a similar fashion. Both

[65] Opel, *Deutsche Metallarbeiterverband*, pp. 72-73. See also Captain Müller's reports on the strikes, BHStA, Abt. IV, MK, IcIa15^{b}, Bd. II, Bl. 67, 74-75.

[66] Report of Feb. 20, 1918, StAMü, Oberbergamt Dortmund B, Nr. 119, Bd. 226.

Dandl and Adenauer were praised by the left wing Reichstag deputies. To the OHL, however, Dandl's and Adenauer's methods were extremely irritating, for it was the OHL which had deliberately sought to stiffen the backs of the government and prevent the granting of any concessions to the strikers.[67]

In contrast to its attitude during the October crisis, the OHL was not worried about the production losses that might be incurred through resistance to strikes. The munitions supply was, for the moment, plentiful. Also, many factories were not operating at full capacity anyway because of the wintertime transportation and coal difficulties. Political considerations were now paramount. The OHL wanted no interference with the annexationist program in the east and no disturbances behind the lines during the forthcoming offensive in the west. Thus the OHL sent Bauer to Berlin at the beginning of the strike to inform the government that the OHL was prepared to bear production losses "because this damage will be less great than that incurred through concessions to the strikers' demands."[68] The OHL was enthralled with the results of the tough policy in Berlin. Immediately after the strike Colonel Bauer told Röchling once again to fight the "shameless lie" that the OHL supported suffrage reform out of fear of strikes. As the strike had demonstrated, the loss of production "is not as serious as it appears to anxious spirits."[69]

The OHL's pressure and the reassurance that it could stand production losses certainly helped the men in Berlin to take a firm stand. Indeed, the government was rather fearful of what the OHL would do if such a stand were not taken. As Wallraf pointed out to the Bavarian Ambassador, Count Lerchenfeld, an agreement with the strikers was impossible because it

[67] Reichstag Debates, Feb. 2, 1918, 311, p. 4168; Möser to Weizsäcker, Feb. 1, 1918, HStASt, E, 73, 12i; reports of General von Hartz, Feb. 4 and Feb. 22, 1918, BHStA, Abt. IV, MK, III a XV 39.

[68] Ludendorff, *Urkunden*, p. 99n, and Bauer, *Grosse Krieg*, pp. 182-183. See also Bauer to Duisberg, Dec. 25, 1917, BA, Nachlass Bauer, Nr. 11.

[69] Bauer to Röchling, Feb. 10, 1918, BA, Nachlass Bauer, Nr. 12.

would lead to a "military dictatorship."[70] It would be wrong, however, to overestimate the inducement necessary for the government to act in the sense desired by the OHL. Once the initial prompting on the part of the OHL and General Scheüch, who received particular praise from Bauer for his role in forcing the government to take a strong stand, had taken place, the civil authorities suppressed the strike with much enthusiasm.[71] Wallraf was convinced that it was necessary to "keep a cool head and remain firm," for "if one enters into negotiations and makes compromises, then things will rise over one's head and, even if there is an armistice now, things will flame up again in a few weeks." Many members of the government thought that the situation had been "clarified" by the strike. The "red specter" had turned out to be a "scarecrow" and it was possible now to count "on at least a few weeks of quiet" which could be used to present Trotsky with an "energetic ultimatum."[72]

The success of the OHL and the government in beating down the January strikes, however, owed much to the deep divisions among the strike leaders and to the nonrevolutionary attitude of the workers. The performance of the Social Democrats was particularly miserable. They feared the masses, hated the radicals, and in many cases were annexationists. The Independent Socialists were unwilling to do more than instigate demonstrations and vote against war credits. The Spartacists did not lack courage, but they had imposed upon themselves the impossible task of trying to revolutionize a working class that did not believe itself to be truly enslaved. The Berlin strikers were the best paid workers in Germany, and it is noteworthy that their demands for peace and reform did not

[70] Lerchenfeld to Dandl, Jan. 29, 1918, BHStA, Abt. II, MA 1, Nr. 921. The OHL prepared a division for possible use at home, see Kraft von Delmensingen's report of Feb. 4, 1918, *ibid.*, Nr. 945, Bl. 107.

[71] For Bauer's praise of Scheüch, see his letter to Major von Mülnheim, Feb. 10, 1918, BA, Nachlass Bauer, Nr. 12.

[72] Varnbüler to Weizsäcker, Jan. 30 and Feb. 3, 1918, HStASt, E, 73, 12i.

include demands for the socialization of industry or even the limitation of war profits.[73]

When the strike was settled, there was once again a parting of the ways between the OHL and the government. On February 17 Hindenburg sent a note to Hertling concerning strike problems. He pointed out that Bolshevik and enemy propaganda would continue to cause unrest among the workers and that a strike later in the year would be dangerous because production needs would be greater. Strikes, therefore, had to be prevented. The OHL considered it necessary for the government to make clear that strikes would be regarded as treason and punished as such. On this basis the government could demand that the unions and the Social Democrats "show their colors" and formally condemn strikes. If they refused, then they could be branded as traitors in the press and Reichstag. General von Stein, who received a copy of this letter, agreed completely with its recommendations. Freiherr von Stein, who had replaced the ailing Schwander as Secretary of the RWA in November 1917, disagreed: "Under present conditions, it does not seem desirable to me to take special measures in order to prevent a yet greater strike. Above all, I must strongly advise against a renewed discussion of this ticklish matter in public. This seems to me to be not only unnecessary, but actually harmful, because a disturbance of the workers can thereby really be created."[74] This was a complicated way of saying that the government did not want to press its luck. The fact of the matter was that the pressure of the masses and the discontent over the dragging of suffrage reform had forced the Social Democrats, even if only momentarily, to support a strike. The government could not back down from its promises of social reform, and it could not engage in too active a policy of repression.

Looking back upon the period between the dismissals of Bethmann and Groener and the suppression of the January

[73] Rosenberg, *Birth of the German Republic*, p. 212.
[74] *AGSOD*, III, pp. 1174-1176.

1918 strike, it becomes clear that Ludendorff could boast few positive achievements in his sporadic attempts to control internal affairs. The attempt to change Paragraph 9 of the Auxiliary Service Law had failed, largely because of the intransigence of Ludendorff's industrialist supporters. The OHL's most important positive demand thus remained unfulfilled. In a very indirect manner the OHL had strengthened the opponents of equal suffrage. The Fatherland Party and the OHL's propaganda efforts undoubtedly helped to rally large segments of the bourgeoisie for the annexationist-conservative cause, but they also increased the disaffection of the workers. The chief success of the OHL, however, was to be found in the increased use of repressive measures, a policy which culminated in the handling of the January 1918 strike. Even here, however, the triumph was far from unequivocal. War bond drives, Reichstag pressure, and, most important, munitions shortages had compelled the army to refrain from harsh measures or to fear their employment. One cannot escape the conclusion that the OHL forced the issue in early 1918 because the munitions supply permitted it to do so. As demonstrated above, it was far from sanguine about its capacity to act under less favorable circumstances.

In a very real sense, the dismissal of Groener had marked a retreat of the army from its potential role as a positive stabilizing institution in German society. Groener recognized that the key to controlling the revolutionary situation brought about by the war lay in the granting of substantive concessions to labor in the form of collective bargaining and equal suffrage and in the control of prices and wages. He thus carried the social policy of the Prussian War Ministry during the first two years of the war to its logical conclusion. After his fall the army and the industrialists pursued a purely opportunistic course. They recognized the need for union assistance in the demobilization, and they therefore sought to establish a limited agreement for this purpose. When frightened enough, Ludendorff was even willing to see a Social Democrat taken into the government. Neither the leaders of heavy industry nor the leaders of the army, however, were willing to create the basis for a permanent integration of the workers into the state. Their ultimate solution to the internal problem was imperialism, and, unlike Groener, they refused to face the contingency that their imperialist strivings might fail.

In the last analysis, the Ludendorff "dictatorship" in internal affairs was very shaky. If the civil authorities had decided to negotiate with the strikers in January 1918, Ludendorff would have been put to a real test. He could have sought to impose the military dictatorship which Wallraf feared. This, however, would have been a very dangerous endeavor in the midst of the war and his preparations for the great spring offensive. He might have been more successful in threatening, once again, to resign if a new Chancellor were not installed. Berg's growing influence over the Emperor might have broken down the barriers to a Bülow or Tirpitz Chancellorship. Such speculations, however, miss the true nature of the situation. The Hertling government was too conservative to drive the OHL to the last extremity just as it was too reformist to drive the Social Democrats to revolution. Similarly, the great mass of the German people, constantly fed with rosy reports from the front, had too much faith in the OHL and too much of a hankering after annexations to really ruin the war effort. The German worker's yearning for peace, unlike that of his Russian counterpart, was not a yearning for peace at any price. If the German workers had been truly revolutionary, the strike would not have been such a fiasco. The chief supporters of the Spartacists were youths, and it is difficult to tell whether these young people were juvenile delinquents or true revolutionaries.[75]

The Independent Socialists represented all that was best in

[75] The war was having a very bad effect on young people. Many sought factory work as a means of escaping parental discipline. The juvenile crime rate mounted fantastically, and it is very difficult to believe that all the young people who joined forces with the Spartacists were really inspired by Marxist ideas. The ZMG reports of 1917-1918 are filled with complaints on the "Verwilderung der Jugend."

See, Michel, all is well.

the German labor movement when they voted against the brutal Treaty of Brest-Litovsk, which was signed on March 3, 1918. The Social Democrats revealed their moral bankruptcy when they abstained.[76] The workers, however, did not cry out against the treaty. It did, after all, mean peace in the East; and the Treaty with the Ukraine was supposed to be a "bread peace" that would relieve the German food shortage. Whether this peace could really be imposed and whether the great offensive in the West would succeed were the real questions. Ludendorff's dictatorship in matters of foreign policy and his intermittent excursions into internal politics were tolerated because the great mass of the German people believed that he would win. To be sure, a man like Scheidemann could have a moment of doubt and ask, "If you let the negotiations in the East collapse and if the expectations in the West are disappointed, what then?" He did not wish, however, "to spin out these reservations any further."[77] The faith which the government and the people had placed in the OHL since August 1916 had not yet disappeared.

[76] Fischer, *Griff nach der Weltmacht*, p. 664.
[77] Budget Committee Debates, Jan. 24, 1918.

IX

Germany in the Concluding Months of the War: The Defeat and the Search for a Scapegoat

1. The Social Consequences of the War

THE period from March to July 1918 was one of relative calm within Germany. There were no serious strikes and no important political crises. Instead, the German people impatiently awaited a victory that was never to come. For the last time they were permitted to enjoy illusory military successes as Ludendorff launched five offensives designed to break through the Western Front. This was their only compensation for the economic deprivation, the social and moral disruption, and the political divisiveness that plagued German society.

The war had deprived the German people of sufficient quantities of the basic necessities of life. The food problem had arisen early in the war. The coal shortage developed in the winter of 1916-1917. Now, in the last year of the war, there were serious shortages of clothing and housing as well. The clothing supply had deteriorated sharply because of the shortage of raw materials and the use of inadequate "substitute" (*Ersatz*) products. Shoes were in particularly short supply. No less serious was the shortage of soap. Coal miners could not wash properly after work, and housewives were unable to keep clothing clean. Many German workers were now being forced to contend with lice. Finally, the flood of workers into the war production centers created a housing shortage and a rapid rise of rents.[1]

As usual, the management of these problems was hindered either by an excess of organization or by the absence of any

[1] On economic and social conditions during the last year of the war, see the ZMG reports.

organization at all. Thus factories requesting shoes for their workers had to apply to the local War Office bureau, the factory inspector, and the local clothing distribution agency. These agencies, in turn, had to apply to the central agencies in Berlin. Getting materials for the repair of shoes required an appeal to no fewer than ten different Berlin agencies. During the first eight months of 1918 the army and the civil authorities collaborated in supplying the workers with clothing and paying some of the extraordinarily high costs with government funds. At the beginning of August a more systematic approach was taken. "Clothing specialists" were set up in each of the War Office bureaus to evaluate and report on the clothing needs of their districts to the Imperial Clothing Agency. Orders were issued permitting the continued operation of textile and shoe factories scheduled to be shut down, and the needs of the workers were given priority over those of the army. Similarly, the War Office decided to release the raw materials needed for the construction of worker housing, and the Deputy Commanding Generals issued orders controlling rents. As in the case of the ceilings placed on food prices at the beginning of the war, the rent control orders of the Deputy Commanding Generals were not issued in any uniform manner. The handling of the clothing and housing problems, therefore, fell into much the same pattern that had already been exhibited in the management of the coal and food problems.[2]

It is a fitting commentary on the failure of the government's food supply system to note that it did not even have reliable statistics concerning the 1917 harvest upon which to base its economic plan for 1918. According to the Imperial Wheat Agency, there was going to be a shortage of 400,000 tons of wheat. Waldow feared that this estimate was too low. He believed that the workers' reaction to another reduction of the

[2] For directives and discussions concerning the clothing and housing problems, see BHStA, Abt. IV, MK, K Mob 6, Bd. III; Bd. IV, Bl. 78; K Mob 12, Bd. XIV, Bl. 188a; *Mitteilungen des Kriegsamt*, July 2, 1918; *Soziale Praxis*, Aug. 22, 1918.

bread ration might lead to a repetition of the April 1917 strikes. In March 1918 he decided to reduce the ration of the farmers instead. He hoped to save 140,000 tons of wheat by this means and thus tide things over until the arrival of shipments from the Ukraine and the coming of the new harvest.[3]

Unhappily for Waldow, the peace treaty concluded with the Ukraine turned out to be another one of the OHL's fiascos. Conditions in southern Russia were utterly chaotic. The puppet regime was incompetent and the peasants were uncooperative. As a result, the German government was compelled to censor optimistic reports concerning the possibility of getting substantial quantities of Ukrainian wheat in the near future.[4]

By late April Waldow became convinced that it would be necessary to reduce the bread ration of the industrial workers in June. The labor leaders were infuriated but helpless. Although they agreed to oppose strikes, they ruthlessly attacked the KEA. As one Social Democrat sarcastically remarked, "the black market has become the one really successful organization in our food supply system."[5]

This was true. The KEA was at war with the Deputy Commanding Generals, the industrialists, and the trade unions over the black market question. In February 1918 the KEA decided to act vigorously against firms supplying workers with food from the black market. It ordered that black market products purchased by the industrialists be seized and that the purchasers be punished if they persisted in their illegal practices. The KEA ordered that the sequestered food be turned over to special "industrial provision agencies" for distribution to the workers at low prices. In taking this last step, the KEA tacitly recognized that the workers needed this additional food and

[3] Schäffer to Weizsäcker, March 13, 1918, HStASt, E, 130, V, Xa. 1, Bd. II, Bl. 599, and *AGSOD* III, pp. 1252-1256.

[4] Groener, *Lebenserinnerungen*, pp. 385-401, and *AGSOD*, III, pp. 1352-1353.

[5] Reichstag Debates, July 6, 1918, 313, p. 5869. Also, see *AGSOD*, III, pp. 1305-1309.

could not live on the legal rations. Its object was to end the demoralization created by the ability of some firms to supply their workers with more food than others. The trouble was that there was no guarantee that the industrial provision agencies could continue to secure as much food by legal means as the industrialists had been able to secure from the black market.[6]

The industrialists raised strong protests against the KEA's procedure. Some went so far as to blame the KEA's order on the Social Democrats. They accused the latter of fighting the black market in order to deprive the workers of food and thus incite strikes. This charge was completely unfounded, and the unions were no less critical of the KEA's decision than were the industrialists. Although they admitted the desirability of putting an end to the black market, the unions continuously indicated that the abolition of the black market presented a "serious danger." In their view the measure had come "too late," and they warned that the KEA's venture was justifiable only if the workers continued to receive the additional food by legal means. Most decisive in sabotaging the KEA's measures, however, was the fact that the Deputy Commanding Generals joined with the industrialists and the unions in the fight for the black market. This bizarre defense of black marketeering by the army represents the best example of the degree to which the mismanagement of the food supply had led to a loss of respect for law on the part of those agencies most responsible for its strict enforcement.[7]

There was a strong movement to scrap the entire compulsory system. Many of the agrarian leaders had long sought such a solution, arguing that a return to the free market system

[6] See the KEA meeting of July 26, 1918, HStASt, E, 130, V, X^{a}. 1, Bd. II, Bl. 627-628.

[7] Waldow continued to have difficulty with the Deputy Commanding Generals as late as Sept. 1918. See his remarks at the Prussian Cabinet meeting, Sept. 27, 1918, BA, Nachlass Heinrichs, Nr. 28. For the Deputy Commanding Generals' attitude, see the ZMG reports and especially the April 1918 report. For the Socialist attitude, see *Internationale Korrespondenz*, Feb. 19, 1918.

and high prices would provide the needed incentive to the farmers and would ultimately benefit everyone. The General Intendant of the Army, Eisenhart Rothe, and the agrarian leader, Freiherr von Wangenheim, felt that the food supply could best be regulated by the joint efforts of forcibly established producer and consumer cooperatives. Ludendorff strongly supported this idea in a note to Waldow of December 13, 1917. He pointed out that the compulsory system was demoralizing the people and had to be done away with. The government and even some of the agrarian leaders, however, opposed a sudden change of system for both practical and political reasons. Whatever the defects of the compulsory system, there could be no question about the fact that a sudden change of system and an increase of prices would cause major unrest. As Merton had noted in his memorandum to Groener of May 1916, it was impossible to organize the food supply in defiance of the industrial workers.[8]

Yet it must be recognized that the food supply system was organized in defiance of the farmers and the peasantry and that this was certainly not conducive to their morale. The exaggerated importance of the industrial workers during the war created a new type of social injustice, and the sufferings of the workers, however real, must not be permitted to blind one to the extraordinary hardships suffered by other classes. The plight of the farmers was truly miserable. Their best horses had been sequestered by the army. They did not have sufficient labor, and the peace with Russia now threatened their most important source of prisoners of war. They had been forced to engage in massive pig slaughters, and they did not have enough fodder for the livestock that remained. They were encumbered by hundreds of regulations and victimized by periodic searches for hidden food stores. Their land was being ruined by overcultivation and the shortage of artificial fertilizer. In some cases farmers and peasants no longer had

[8] Ludendorff, *Urkunden*, p. 277; Eisenhart Rothe, *Im Banne der Persönlichkeit*, pp. 159-164; Ludendorff, *Kriegserinnerungen*, pp. 273-277.

enough to eat. Until March 1918 they were not even considered "hard working" laborers and were thus denied the food premiums given to the industrial workers. Although they were refused the right to charge the high prices they felt entitled to demand for their products, they were forced to pay extremely high prices for clothing and other manufactured goods. Little wonder that more and more peasants were saying: "I'm selling the whole business and going to the munitions factory where I will earn much money, will not have to come off so stupidly, and will have my peace."[9]

The farmers were also resentful in a political sense. As one Deputy Commanding General reported:

> The farmers view the far-reaching consideration shown to the Social Democratic workers with complete mistrust. As the most faithful . . . supporters of the government, the peasants have experienced the severe year-long struggle against the Social Democrats led by the prefect or mayor, and they are embittered that the Social Democrats are today in favor with the same government. . . . The important reasons for this moderate policy toward the Social Democrats . . . cannot be made clear to the peasants.[10]

At the same time, the peasants expressed their irritation at the government with the threat, "Next time, I'll vote red." They had, to be sure, uttered similar threats even before the war when they were annoyed at the government, but the frequency with which they now indicated that they wanted to vote against the government demonstrated how strongly they felt that they had been betrayed.

If the peasants' talk about "voting red" was not to be taken too seriously, the same cannot be said for the similar threats made by large segments of the so-called *Mittelstand.* The minor officials, small businessmen, and craftsmen were the people hardest hit by the war. The last mentioned two groups

[9] ZMG report, Sept. 15, 1918.
[10] *Ibid.,* June 15, 1917. See also the report of Dec. 15, 1917.

had to see their enterprises shut down in order to spare coal. The officials were overworked, underpaid, and underfed. Their cost of living increases were never adequate. They could not afford to buy on the black market, and unlike a goodly number of the workers, they did not always have relatives on the countryside from whom to get additional food. The plight of these groups cannot simply be viewed from the economic standpoint. The social side of their problem is equally important. One of the important distinctions between the minor officials and the workers was their clothing. Officials who were now forced to go about the cities on Sundays in old and worn *Beamtenkleider* were bound to feel resentful when they came face to face with workers in new clothing or in clothing in a better state of repair than their own. The "proletarization" of the middle class was becoming a catchword on everyone's tongue, and the danger of its radicalization was the cause of deep concern. The Deputy Commanding General in Frankfurt warned that

> all those living on fixed salaries are facing a change of social position; they are slipping from the level upon which they have stood and are approaching the level of those who find it necessary to live from hand to mouth. This social decline of the officialdom contains a not-to-be-underestimated danger to the state and society. Previously the officials could be counted among those who stood for the regulation of working conditions without great economic conflicts. The state and the communities must guard against letting the officials feel that they are being given up to the storms of economic developments without protection.[11]

The danger of proletarization and radicalization was most serious in the case of the *Angestellte*, the salaried white-collar employees serving in military agencies or in private industry. This was an extraordinarily variegated group which included clerks and typists at the lowest level and architects and engi-

[11] *Ibid.*, Oct. 15, 1917.

neers at the highest level. No group was more fearful of losing its status. As "mental workers" (*Kopfarbeiter*), this group insisted that it be treated differently from the manual workers and that due regard be given the fact that its members were better educated and engaged in more "dignified" and "cleaner" forms of labor. Although many of the white-collar workers were organized, the white-collar unions eschewed the strike and fought for minimum wages and recognition in a peaceful manner. The industrialists sought to utilize the white-collar workers' fear of identification with the proletariat to keep them unorganized and conservative. Thus the employers spoke of the white-collar workers as "the connecting link between the employers and the workers."[12]

It was impossible, however, to eat social status. During the war the salaries of the white-collar workers became increasingly inadequate. Although some of the employers tried to secure additional food for the white-collar workers through the black market, they were never given the special premiums granted to the manual workers. A great many white-collar workers were employed in army bureaus, and their conditions were even worse than those of their counterparts in private industry. The army was reluctant to pay these workers higher salaries than were paid in private industry because it did not want to create unrest and turnover in private industry. Although the white-collar union leaders continually pleaded with the War Office to accept minimum wage standards, the War Office refused to set such a precedent. The War Office was willing to discuss complaints with the representatives of the unions, but it was unwilling to offend the private employers. The situation was made all the more galling by the fact that the manual workers in the army-run factories were higher paid than those in private industry.[13]

[12] VdESI petition to Hertling and the OHL, Dec. 21, 1917, BA, R 13I/113.

[13] See the War Office meeting with the union representatives on June 22, 1917, BHStA, Abt. IV, MK, K Mob 12, Bd. IX, Bl. 138, and the union petitions of April 5 and June 8, 1917, *ibid.*, K Mob 14, Bd. III, Bl. 122, zu 210.

By 1918 the bitterness of the white-collar workers had reached a high point. They were extremely jealous of the favor shown to the manual workers. The latter had won higher wages, had forced many employers to deal with their unions, and had been increasingly successful in getting employers to sign collective wage agreements. In contrast, the white-collar unions had made no headway in their struggle for recognition and had received no acceptance of their demand for a minimum wage. Even well-paid technicians were bitter because, although they were supposed to be the superiors of the manual workers, their demands received little attention from the employers. The white-collar unions could no longer be silent about the dangers created by this situation: "The great need of the white-collar workers is demonstrated by the fact that the thought of striking is discussed in an ever more lively way in their ranks. This is the result of the failure of all their efforts to improve their condition. Until now the organizations have not approved of this idea; they are proud of the fact that they have until now chosen a path other than that chosen by the workers."[14]

The threat implicit in this statement became increasingly alarming to the employers. The white-collar unions had already associated themselves with the demands and programs of the Free, Christian, and Hirsch-Duncker unions. At a meeting of the white-collar unions in Duisburg in the spring of 1918, Deputy Huë was wildly cheered when he told the white-collar workers that the time had come to stop pleading with the employers and to use the unions to force through their demands.

The employers were all the more concerned by this situation because the evolution of modern industry had made the commercial and technical officialdom of the firms more important and more numerous than ever before. Some employers

[14] Statement by the Bavarian union leader Fedisch on Feb. 23, 1918, *ibid.*, K Mob 7d, Bd. IV, Bl. zu 67. Also, see *AGSOD*, III, pp. 1385-1386, and *Internationale Korrespondenz*, June 1 and Aug. 3, 1918.

sought to solve the problem by raising salaries, but Borsig pointed out this was a dangerous solution:

> If it were possible to relieve the situation and make things better again by raising salaries, then it would be wonderful. But I believe that we also have an obligation to see to it that salaries don't increase beyond all bounds during the war . . . because we will find it much harder . . . to be able to lower them for the officials than for the workers. If the officials today . . . demand that they earn at least as much as the best paid worker, . . . then this is comprehensible, but it is unrealizable. For the workers have understood how to drive wages upward at the present time, and it would be insane to want to raise the salaries of the officials in the same way, for in actuality one cannot easily lower the salary of an official. It would be regarded as an insult, as a sign of mistrust or dissatisfaction.[15]

The white-collar workers were thus trapped by their own demand for status. Placed as they were between the workers and the employers, they were too disorganized and conscious of their superior social position to strike and too vulnerable to indignity to accept the eventual wage reduction that would have been the price of significant wartime salary increases.

The last important group to be economically victimized by the war was the soldiers. Torn from their homes, their businesses, and their jobs, the troops bitterly resented the profit-making and "high wages" at home. Furthermore, they could not look forward to the end of the war with optimism. Peace would bring a cessation of danger and a termination to the nightmare of the trenches, but it would also bring new hardships. The process of readjustment to normal life was bound to be difficult, and the economic prospects were, at best, uncertain. Needless to say, the troops would regard a reduction of wages at the end of the war as a terrible injustice. They

[15] VdESI meeting, Sept. 2, 1918, BA, R 13I/155.

felt entitled to enjoy the benefits others had received while they were risking their lives for their country.[16]

Only two groups may be said to have derived any benefits from the war: the industrialists and the workers employed in the war industries. Their common support of black-marketeering was symptomatic of the special position they had assumed in the economy, but it was also symptomatic of the disruption created by the sudden promotion of two special interests at the expense of all others. The triumph of the industrialists and the industrial workers during the war was marked, on the one hand, by the increased economic strength of certain segments within each group and, on the other hand, by the growing power of their organizations.

The net earnings of German corporations rose from 1,656 million marks in 1912-1913 to 2,213 million marks in 1917-1918, and the average dividend rate rose from 8.7 percent to 10.1 percent during the same period. These statistics, however, include the earnings and dividends of those enterprises which had suffered during the war, e.g., the merchant marine, and they thus veil the real profits made by the industries producing directly for the war effort. During the 1912-1918 period, for example, net earnings in the metal manufacturing industries rose from 34 million to 111 million marks. Finally, capital stock was watered down to avoid high nominal dividends, and the dividend statistics do not do full justice to the actual profits that had been made.[17]

These increases of net earnings and dividends were not indications of economic health. Many of these profits had only paper value because of the inflationary condition of the economy. Much of the money was made on the sale of scarce raw materials. Shrewd entrepreneurs like Hugo Stinnes, Jacob Michael, and Friedrich Flick were clever enough to invest their money in enterprises that were to bring great profit after

16 Volkmann, *Der Marxismus und das deutsche Heer*, pp. 149-150, and Ludendorff, *Urkunden*, p. 142.

17 Leo Grebler and Wilhelm Winkler, *The Cost of the War to Germany and Austria-Hungary*, New Haven, 1940, p. 64.

the war. They used the inflationary situation during the war to strengthen their economic power just as they used the inflationary situation after the war to liquidate their costs. At the same time, heavy industry engaged in a program of vertical concentration. The iron and steel producers sought to assure themselves of satisfactory supplies of coal and iron by buying up the mines. Similarly, the heavy industrialists sought to take over the manufacturing industries in order to share in the high profits of the latter industries and to achieve greater freedom in the establishment of raw materials prices. One of the chief impulses to concentration came from the anticipation that German industry would face stiff competition in its efforts to regain its old markets after the war. Carl Duisberg had used this argument very effectively in persuading the leaders of the chemical industry to establish a pool (*Interessengemeinschaft*) in 1916, a pool which was to serve as the basis for the great I. G. Farben cartel. No less significant, however, was Duisberg's contention that only through such a concentration of resources could the chemical industrialists have sufficient capital and unity of direction to fight the unions and withstand long strikes.[18]

Added to this agglomeration of economic power was the growing tendency of the employers to pull together in an organizational sense. Uncertainty concerning the postwar economic situation was coupled with anxiety over government and trade union interference in the management of the economy. The desire to establish an effective means of industrial self-government and self-protection had led to the 1916 decision of the Central Association of German Industrialists and the League of German Industrialists to perpetuate their wartime collaboration. On February 16, 1918, the German Industrial Council (*Deutschen Industrierat*) was formally constituted. It was meant to serve as the successor to the German

[18] Wilhelm Treue, ed., "Carl Duisbergs Denkschrift von 1915 zur Gründung der 'Kleinen I. G.,'" *Tradition. Zeitschrift für Firmen-Geschichte und Unternehmer-Biographie*, 8, Oct. 1963, pp. 193-227.

Industry War Committee, and it was to become the predecessor of and model for the very powerful Reich Association of German Industry (*Reichsverband der deutschen Industrie*) of the Weimar period.[19]

What advantages, if any, did the workers receive from the war? The available wage statistics are of limited value. The wage structure of German industry demonstrated tremendous variety because wage rates and price structures varied from locality to locality. Furthermore, the evaluation of wages is extremely difficult because the predominance of the black market renders official prices very suspect. Finally, the wage statistics themselves are extremely deceptive since they do not take special food premiums or private food sources into account.[20]

Within the framework of these reservations, however, certain important generalizations can be made. With the advent of extensive rationing, the introduction of the Hindenburg Program, and the passage of the Auxiliary Service Law, there began an extremely rapid rise of wages. The pattern of these wage increases demonstrated two contradictory tendencies. On the one hand, there was a leveling of traditional wage differentials. Because of the shortage of male labor, the use of mass-production methods, and the need to protect low-paid workers from the consequences of monetary depreciation, skill, age, and, particularly, sex differentials tended to narrow. On the other hand, the war economy brought about a growing wage differential among industries. Between 1914 and 1918 the daily earnings of male workers in the war industries increased 152 percent, while those of female workers increased 186 percent. In the civilian industries the percentage increases

[19] On the Industrial Council, see *industriellen Spitzenverband*, pp. 83ff., Nachlass Stresemann, 6820, frames H122823-H122834; BA, Nachlass Sydow, pp. 430-432.

[20] For the discussion of the wage question below, see Waldemar Zimmermann, *Die Veränderungen der Einkommens und Lebensverhältnisse der deutschen Arbeiter durch den Krieg*, Stuttgart, Berlin, Leipzig, 1932, pp. 360-362, 366-367, and Bry, *Wages in Germany*, pp. 191-214.

were, respectively, 81 percent and 102 percent. It must also be remembered that the workers in the war industries received the lion's share of the food premiums given to the "hard working" and "hardest working" laborers. Some consideration must also be given to family as well as to individual earnings. The combined earnings of a husband, wife, and older children did enable a great many worker families to meet their needs and, at times, to improve their condition. Cases in which worker families, particularly in Berlin, bought expensive luxury goods or put money into banks and invested in war bonds were not unknown. Such examples of worker prosperity were most frequent among certain categories of highly specialized skilled workers whose wages had increased very sharply relative to those of their unskilled compatriots. Despite the general tendency toward a leveling of skill differentials, the continued existence of such differentials in exceptional cases coupled with the exaggerated differentials among industries promoted considerable stratification within the working class. The wage extremes were so great in certain instances that those earning low wages frequently referred to the highly skilled group of workers as "war profiteers."

Nevertheless, it was completely irresponsible of the employers to take advantage of the high wages of a small and elite group of workers to try to create the impression that the workers were now in a position to "light up their cigarettes or pipes with bank notes." The real wages of the majority of the workers declined during the war, while the real wages of a small percentage returned to their prewar level. Only a very select few exceeded their prewar real earnings. What is important is that the living standard of the workers approached that of the members of the middle class during the war. This, however, was due less to the improvement of wages than to the deterioration of the economic position of the middle class. In short, relative to the middle class and the farmers, the workers were doing well. This created the impression that the workers were being excessively paid and created resentment against them. Greater social justice was thus accompanied by serious social discontent among all classes of German society.

As the workers had strengthened their relative economic and social positions, so had they strengthened their political power. From the political standpoint the war had been a disaster for the employers and a blessing for the unions. The efforts of the former group to block social legislation were a total failure. At a Prussian Cabinet meeting on November 27, 1917, the Hertling government decided to prepare bills for the annulment of Paragraph 153 of the Industrial Ordinance and for the establishment of worker chambers. The plan to annul Paragraph 153 was a gesture of more symbolic than practical importance. There were other laws which provided, in an indirect way, for the punishment of those who attempted to prevent strikebreaking by means of threats, insults, or violence. Although Paragraph 153 gave the government a direct means of protecting those "willing to work," it was by no means indispensable for this purpose. Since the paragraph was clearly directed against the unions and since the unions had long sought its annulment, however, the government felt compelled to do away with it.[21]

The decision to present a worker chambers bill was the fulfillment of one of the most important positive demands of the unions. The government had presented such a bill in 1910, but it had failed over the question of the eligibility of trade union secretaries for election to the chambers. Now, because of the unions' support of the war effort, the government felt obliged to drop its objections to the election of union secretaries. Otherwise, it hoped to maintain the 1910 bill intact. Thus chambers would be set up for each major industry and be organized on the principle of parity between labor and management. They would have two basic functions. They would serve as legally constituted bodies through which the workers could protect their interests and influence legislation,

[21] Prussian Cabinet meeting, Nov. 27, 1917, BA, P 135/1254, Bl. 177-178, and RWA memorandum P 135/186, Bl. 16-18.

and they would provide an institution through which labor and management could settle their differences and regulate problems pertaining to the various industries.

The unions, however, had more ambitious plans with regard to the worker chambers. On December 3, 1917, the unions presented the government with a draft of a worker chambers bill in which they demonstrated their desire to use the bill as a means of maintaining the institutions created by the Auxiliary Service Law. The union draft provided for the establishment of workers committees in every factory employing over twenty persons and for the creation of conciliation agencies and mediation agencies. The unions also demanded that the chambers be set up on a territorial basis rather than on an industry-by-industry basis.[22]

Heavy industry objected to both the annulment of Paragraph 153 and the introduction of a worker chambers bill. In a meeting with State Secretary of the Economic Office, Freiherr von Stein, the industrialists warned against a repetition of the mistakes that had been made with the Auxiliary Service Law, insisted that the workers committees be denied the right to discuss wage questions, and bemoaned the proposed worker chambers law as the establishment of "war with the workers in permanency." The government was accused of destroying employer authority and "making the new bill out of fear of the masses and the gutter." Stein brushed aside these charges by pointing out that "the workers have gotten used to the arbitration committees," and that "it would be a threat to our economic life to set aside the institutions created during the war." Without them, "the radical organizations would gain the upper hand."[23]

If the industrialists fumed, it is important to recognize that they had by no means abandoned their own efforts to make an arrangement with the unions. Many of the employers were

[22] BA, P 135/186, Bl. 19-24.

[23] For the protocol of this meeting, which took place on Jan. 5, 1918, see BA, R 13I/371.

conscious of the fact that however much they may have gained from the war in terms of profits and increased economic power, their social policy had suffered a serious defeat. Although the October 1917 attempt of the heavy industrialist leaders to establish the basis for some form of collaboration between industry and unions for the demobilization through direct negotiations had come to nought, their efforts did not cease entirely. Another fruitless effort was made in December at the instigation of Undersecretary of the Interior August Müller. Despite the absence of concrete results, the door to further negotiations was by no means shut. In April 1918 Director Vögler declared: "Employers and workers have very similarly directed interests. For this reason they ought to get together and represent them in common. If they can only find themselves in agreement on the great economic questions, then perhaps they will have found the bridges which may lead to a mitigation of the social conflicts."[24] At the same time, however, the leaders of heavy industry were unwilling to pay for union collaboration in advance, and they opposed every form of social legislation which would bind their hands and commit them to surrendering more than was absolutely necessary.

In May 1918 the bills were presented to the Reichstag. The annulment of Paragraph 153 was easily passed over the objections of the right wing deputies. The worker chambers bill, however, caused considerable difficulty. The parallels between the conflict over this law and the conflict over the Auxiliary Service Law are interesting. Once again the unions were furious at the government for not paying heed to their proposals. The government had made no provision for workers committees in the bill, although it did promise to bring in a separate bill establishing compulsory workers committees. While providing for the establishment of mediation agencies within the chambers, the government bill did not require the employers to accept mediation. Most important, the government bill did not establish the chambers on a territorial basis

[24] Quoted in Varain, *Freie Gewerkschaften*, p. 115.

as desired by the unions. Although the government recognized that the territorial solution had the advantages of enabling the members to meet more quickly and of enabling them to deal with problems of a regional nature common to all industries, the government feared that the workers and employers from different industries would have few points of common concern and that the chambers would be turned into "political debating clubs."[25]

As in the case of the Auxiliary Service Law, the problem of the state railroad workers played a particularly important role in helping the government to come to a decision guaranteed to provoke left wing opposition. Breitenbach had very reluctantly agreed to the inclusion of the railroad workers within the law. In return, however, he insisted that a special clause prohibiting railroad strikes be included and demanded that the chambers be set up along "professional" rather than territorial lines. He did not want the railroad workers mixing with metal workers, coal miners, and other types of workers who might influence the railroad workers in ways that were undesirable from his standpoint. It was precisely the creation of such divisions among the members of the working class and the denial of rights to special categories of workers which the unions wished to avoid. Thus there were many points of conflict between the unions and the government. On May 2 the Reichstag turned the bill over to a special committee. By June there was a complete deadlock between the government and the committee because the majority of the committee members supported the territorial solution.[26]

The plenary debate on the bill was supposed to be resumed in September, but by then there were other questions of a more pressing and fateful nature occupying the minds of the deputies. Nevertheless it is safe to say that the government

[25] Prussian Cabinet protocols, Feb. 28 and March 9, 1918, and RWA note concerning the necessity of introducing a separate bill establishing compulsory workers committees, July 27, 1918, BA, P 135/186, Bl. 52-53, 84a. See also Reichstag Debates, May 1-2, 1918, 312, pp. 4838ff.

[26] IISH, SPD Fraktionssitzung Protokoll, June 13, 1918.

would have been forced to accept a compromise favorable to the union point of view. It desperately needed union support during the demobilization period, and it was anxious to get the worker chambers bill passed before the Auxiliary Service Law expired. Also, the South German states did not agree with the Prussian Cabinet's opposition to a territorial solution. Given this situation and given the pattern of wartime politics, it is hard to believe that the unions would have suffered a defeat. Heavy industry, which did not want any type of worker chambers bill, gave the government lukewarm support. The industrialists felt frustrated and powerless. In a fit of rage, Hilger placed the blame for the entire state of affairs on the army: "The union secretaries rule at the moment, . . . not we; we have been shut out. As is well known, these people have only become so important because we have a few social acrobats in the Berlin War Ministry who are using this war to carry through demands which could not be realized in peacetime."[27]

2. *Army and Society*

This charge, as has been demonstrated time and again in this study, was not unfounded. The policies followed by Wandel, Groener, and to a lesser extent by Scheüch had indeed been of tremendous assistance to the union cause. The presence of social reformers like Tiburtius and union leaders like Schlicke in the War Office had made conservatively minded persons fear for the very virtue of the army. As General von Vietinghoff reported: "The royally minded are fearful that through the entrance of civilians, even of persons of an antimonarchical and republican character, into advisory positions in the army, the old Prussian character of the royal army may be damaged or taken away."[28] In attacking the presence of "civilians" in the army, however, Vietinghoff was undoubtedly thinking of civilians of every class. The traditional disdain of the army for business and businessmen ap-

[27] VdESI meeting, Sept. 2, 1918, BA, R 13I/155.
[28] ZMG report, Jan. 15, 1917.

pears to have diminished in the course of the war. The continuous involvement of the military authorities in economic matters helped to break down old prejudices. In fact the hobnobbing of officers and businessmen was producing some very unpleasant results. As the Conservative Deputy Albrecht von Graefe noted in June 1918: "Another thing which I also consider most regrettable . . . is the going-over of officers from the War Ministry or similar agencies into private industry. I would hope that this would not happen, for it makes a painful impression and one should avoid bad appearances here. The gentlemen must at least remain at their posts until the war has ended."[29]

Neither the associations with trade unionists and social reformers nor the connections with industrialists, however, should be taken as an indication of the army's alliance with one side or the other. Both were the byproducts of the unexpected involvement of the army in social and economic affairs. Only on the war aims question was there considerable unanimity of opinion between the army and the industrialists. Otherwise the general and most pervasive aspect of the army's policy was the attempt to pacify both industry and labor. It courted these antagonistic social groups in order to use them, and it was this policy of expediency which was so disastrous. Blindly, without giving serious consideration to the implications of its actions, the army at once made concessions to the left under the fictitious claim that they were mere wartime measures and accepted high profits under the equally fictitious claim that costs did not matter in wartime. Unable to control labor and unwilling to control industry, the army had failed miserably in its efforts to fulfill the sociopolitical tasks that had been thrust upon it. The army's traditional claim that it was a disciplinary and educative force in German life was

[29] Reichstag Debates, June 12, 1918, 313, p. 5427. Groener was invited to join the board of directors of Autogen-Gasacululator A. G. in August 1917. He was promised a high income and informed that the firm expected to benefit from both his fame and from his expert knowledge of railroad questions. See Nachlass Groener, 192.

THE NEW SOCIETY

Come now, Herr Lieutenant, when you come to my "five o'clock," then kindly put on your monocle and the whole affair will have some style.

belied by its own actions. It began by participating in and encouraging a wage-price spiral, and it ended up by supporting black-marketeering.

The high profits were, indeed, creating one scandal after another. In December 1917 Alfons Horten presented Deputy Meyer-Kaufbeuren, the chairman of the Reichstag Commerce Committee, with a memorandum on his experiences in the KRA and the profits made on iron and steel by the industrialists. The KRA tried to answer Horten's charges in a memorandum of its own, but the latter was both contradictory and evasive. The KRA claimed that it had not permitted the industrialists to exceed their peacetime profit rate, but it also admitted that it had agreed to high prices and profits in order to provide the incentive necessary for production. At the same time, Horten's account of his efforts to investigate Martin process steel prices was not even discussed in the KRA's defense.[30]

Most sensational, however, was the Daimler case. It was well known that this Stuttgart motor manufacturing firm was making extraordinary profits, but the government had always argued that its exceptional services entitled it to rich rewards. When the firm demanded a new price increase at the end of 1917, however, the War Ministry balked and demanded the right to investigate Daimler's cost calculations. The firm refused, and, on February 12, 1918, it threatened to eliminate all overtime and night work, which it found unprofitable, unless the army granted the price increase. When the Ministry threatened to militarize the factory, the firm revoked its strike threat. At this point, however, the army decided to militarize the factory anyway because of Daimler's continued refusal to open its books.[31]

[30] In 1919 the matter was investigated by a special nonpartisan committee whose report substantiated Horten's charges. See BA, Nachlass Mentzel, Nr. 8.

[31] For the government's earlier defense of Daimler, see its statement before the Reichstag Committee for the Investigation of War Contracts on June 19, 1917, HStASt, Verwaltungs Abteilung B, Bd. 1360. On the Daimler case, see Reichstag Debates, March 20, 1918, 311, pp. 4498ff.

The army's efforts to act against the Daimler firm were hampered by the absence of satisfactory legal means. While the right of the army to use the Law of Siege to stop a firm from reducing production was unquestionable, the army's right to use this law to compel a firm to open its books was far from clear. In fact, the entire matter had to be taken before the courts. Thus in order to prevent future legal complications, the government decided to ask the Bundesrat to pass a decree permitting the surveillance and investigation of factories producing for the war effort. This was all the more necessary because the Daimler case caused profound public dissatisfaction and was the subject of furious debate in the Reichstag during March and April.

The Reichstag's anger was quite understandable. Hundreds of workers had been immediately called into the army for taking part in the January strikes, but the army had moved with unpardonable caution in dealing with an employer strike threat. Indeed, the War Ministry had been patient for months before taking action in the Daimler case. One Deputy noted that Paul von Gontardt, the General Director of the Weapons and Munitions Factories, was a member of Daimler's Board of Overseers and that Gontardt's brother was one of the Emperor's general-adjutants. This suggested one of the reasons for the army's slowness in dealing with the firm. The Socialist deputy Noske attacked the "orgy of capitalistic profit-making" that had been going on during the previous three years and suggested that the director of the Daimler firm was "ripe for jail."[32]

The decision of the army to act in the Daimler case reflected a growing awareness that the financial side of the war could no longer be treated with the customary neglect. There had, to be sure, always been elements in the army which recognized that very serious mistakes had been made. Late in the fall of 1917 the Labor Department of the War Office developed an economic mobilization plan for a future war which was

[32] Reichstag Debates, April 16, 1918, 311, pp. 4593, 4510-4512.

Two Types of Strikers

I also struck out of conviction . . . My conviction is that one has to make one hundred and fifty percent.

filled with criticism of contemporary military policies. As might be expected, the army was taken to task for its failure to have an economic mobilization plan. The war had demonstrated the need to train army officers in economic as well as in military matters, to prepare stocks of vital raw materials, and above all to insure that a sufficient labor force was left behind to produce the needed matériel and food. Although the Labor Department opposed government operation of war plants, it insisted that more stringent state controls were necessary. The maintenance of the free enterprise system in wartime could not be allowed to become a surrender to "egotistical wishes" and a "boundless expansion of private economic interests." On the contrary, it required that the state determine wages, profits, and prices. The Labor Department even went so far as to imply that if the employers could not be brought to agree through expectations of a fair profit and a low turnover rate, then the state could still count upon public opinion, "a not to be underestimated factor in wartime," to "enthusiastically greet such measures." Thus the Merton-Groener program was incorporated into the plans for a future war.[33]

Unfortunately, however, State Secretary of the Treasury Roedern did not think that the army could delay facing its financial responsibilities until the next war. In October 1917 he informed Scheüch that the financial situation of the Empire was so serious that "its further deterioration can only have the consequence of making the continuation of the war impossible."[34] This was not the first time Roedern had given such warnings, but the fact that he was once again thinking in terms of a "militarization" of the factories through state controls, as he had at the time of the Auxiliary Service Law, demonstrates that Roedern was reaching the end of his tether.

The OHL could no longer ignore Count Roedern's reports, particularly since they were confirmed by other high government leaders and by General Scheüch. In a note to the government of December 8, 1917, Ludendorff pointed out that the profits of the industrialists were "in the main, high beyond any justifiable measure."[35] He greeted all efforts to investigate cost calculations and praised the methods employed in England, where the government did have the power to set prices. Particularly remarkable was the statement that the lowering of profits and prices was the necessary "first step" in the direction of a serious effort to control and reduce wages. So, for the

[33] This mobilization plan was sent to the Bavarian War Ministry on Dec. 17, 1917, BHStA, Abt. IV, MK, K Mob 25, Bl. 113a.

[34] Meeting of Oct. 21, 1917, DZA Merseburg, Rep. 120, VII 1, Bd. 6, Bl. 53.

[35] Ludendorff, *Urkunden*, pp. 139-142.

first time the OHL had actually come out in opposition to high profits as well as high wages.

The significance of this belated recognition that profits were, indeed, a problem should not, however, be overestimated. Even after the war Colonel Bauer felt that "for Thyssen, Krupp, Duisberg, etc., money as money has no attraction. It plays a role for them only as a means of carrying through their ideas, which are directed toward entirely different purposes. They strive for an increase of their production, for the increase of power that comes with the increase of production, for expansion. Sitting on sacks of money is not the life goal of these strong ones."[36] One cannot help suspecting that if Ludendorff and Bauer were prepared to see any profits reduced, it certainly was not the profits of the "strong ones." Even more revealing is the fact that when concrete steps were finally taken to alleviate the financial situation, they were taken in the direction of reducing wages.

During the early months of 1918 the civilian and military authorities made a concerted effort to reduce the wages of the workers in the armaments factories. The chief instigator of this endeavor was the Minister of Public Works, Breitenbach. Unlike Roedern, who tended to support state control of prices, profits, and wages and who, in desperation, wanted to reduce officers' salaries in order to save money, Breitenbach consistently upheld the view that lower worker wages was the key to financial solvency. While alarmed over the high profits, Breitenbach felt that it was best to act against employers upon an individual basis. Above all, he wished to have the procurement agencies act more moderately and fight the slogan "money plays no role in wartime." When it came to the workers, however, Breitenbach was a proponent of more wholesale forms of action.[37]

Breitenbach's passionate concern with the wage question

[36] Bauer, *Grosse Krieg*, pp. 204-205.

[37] Breitenbach to State Secretary von Stein, March 12, 1918, MF, Marine Archiv, Nr. 4682/III/15/24, Bd. 4.

stemmed from his irritation over the demands of the railroad workers. Despite many wage increases, these workers were poorly paid in comparison to workers in private industry and very poorly paid in comparison to workers in the army's munitions and weapons factories. He was particularly incensed over the fact that the War Office had supported wage increases for the railroad workers and had thus permitted the unions to play off one government agency against another. Initially he insisted that this practice be terminated and that the army stop giving wage increases to its workers. When the railroad worker unions went over his head and appealed to the OHL, Breitenbach took advantage of the situation to win the OHL over to a program of reducing wages in the armaments industries. In his view this was the only way to stop the wage demands of the railroad workers.[38]

Breitenbach's proposal was quite consonant with the militaristic social policy of the OHL. Ludendorff and Bauer were enraged by Roedern's effort to reduce the salaries of active officer corps and thus "proletarianize" the "chief pillar" of the state. Roedern was accused of surrending to the antimilitarist "slogans" of Germany's "internal and external enemies." The OHL, however, not only wished to maintain the officer "estate," but also sought to give the old militarism a mass base. It was symptomatic of Ludendorff's thinking that he expressed great interest in the idea of a young Munich engineer and economic crank, Gottfried Feder, who suggested that every *Frontsoldat* be promised a personal war indemnity in order to win the troops over to large war aims and to strengthen the classes most economically endangered by the war. Although General von Stein rejected, for "ethical and financial reasons," the scheme of the man who was to write the Nazi Party program, the OHL's continuing interest in providing land for the settlement of returning soldiers and increasing the birth rate are

[38] Meeting of Oct. 21, 1917, DZA Merseburg, Rep. 120, VII 1, Bd. 6, Bl. 53; Ludendorff, *Urkunden*, pp. 139-142; speech by Deputy Leinert, Prussian Landtag Debates, March 11, 1918, 7, pp. 8376-8378.

indicative of the protofascist character of the OHL's thinking. Indeed, Ludendorff and Bauer, with their concern for the economic plight of the *Mittelstand* and the *Frontsoldat*, provide a bridge between the old conservative effort to rally the status-conscious lower middle class to their cause and the later fascist appeals to precisely the same groups for even more diabolical purposes. The victim of these policies, in each case, was the worker.[39]

The government and army's decision to embark upon a program of cutting wages before the end of the war was fraught with difficulties. In the view of the War Ministry the first step in cutting prices in the raw material industries was cutting wages, because the latter were held responsible for the high costs. It was impossible, however, for private industry to take the initiative in reducing wages without provoking strikes. The only solution, therefore, was to begin by cutting wages in the army's munitions factories. This was logical because the wages in these factories were higher than those in private industry and had, indeed, set the pace for the wage increase in private industry. The time had now come to reverse this process. Nevertheless, the timing of this wage reduction was of considerable importance. The Ministry was convinced that the workers, if properly enlightened concerning the financial situation, would agree to a decrease in wages. The important thing was that there be "a favorable political situation, e.g., after the introduction of universal and equal suffrage or when there is a favorable military situation at the front or a satisfactory food situation."[40]

In the end, however, the army did not wait for such ideal conditions. On March 1, 1918, General Coupette ordered a "revision" of the piece rates paid in the army-run factories. Coupette's directive expressly stated that this was necessitated

[39] On the conflict with Roedern, see Ludendorff, *Urkunden*, pp. 143-156. For the Feder proposal, see the report of the Bavarian representative to the OHL of July 6, 1917, BHStA, Abt. IV, MK, III a XV 39.

[40] An undated note from Captain Wehsig of WUMBA to Moellendorff, BA, Nachlass Moellendorff, Nr. 42.

by private industry's "disquiet" over the high wages being paid by the army. The Social Democrats did not wait long to respond to this measure. They were quite well informed about the plans of Breitenbach, the OHL, and the War Ministry. On March 11 Prussian Landtag deputy Leinert attacked the new policy in savage fashion. He accused Breitenbach of being the "most backward minister with regard to wage questions." The OHL was not spared either. Both the civil and the military authorities were accused of taking an "antilabor standpoint." They were only willing to grant high premiums to agriculture and high profits to industry. Leinert concluded by warning that the workers had "horns and teeth." Breitenbach sought to parry this attack by accusing Leinert of having a "limited" economic perspective and seeing "only the present and not the future." He reminded Leinert that, in peacetime, a third of Germany's labor force worked for export and that the exporting industries would be ruined by the high wartime wages. If anyone enjoyed this exchange between Leinert and Breitenbach, it was the Independent Socialist Adolf Hoffmann. He was pleased with Leinert's tone. It demonstrated that the Social Democrats were beginning to learn their lesson now that they were being told "the Moor had done his duty, the Moor can go." After four years of collaboration with the government, the Majority Socialists had finally discovered that "the workers are tired of being patient, of patiently letting themselves be exploited, of having their health ruined for all time."[41]

If Hoffmann was overemphasizing the significance of Leinert's speech, it was nonetheless true that the relatively good relations between the army and the unions had deteriorated. The unions were by no means satisfied with the way the Auxiliary Service Law was now being implemented. In their view, many of the arbitration committee and War Office bureau chairmen were "flesh and blood of the flesh and blood

[41] Zimmermann, *Einkommens und Lebensverhältnisse*, p. 409, and Prussian Landtag Debates, March 11, 1918, 7, pp. 8376-8378, 8389-8395.

of the employers." The chairman of the War Office bureau in Baden, for example, was an industrialist whose factory had not set up a workers committee for months after the Auxiliary Service Law was passed. The unions praised the work of many of the arbitration committees, but they criticized others for interpreting Paragraph 9 in a sense antithetical to the interests of the workers. It must be said, however, that the War Office was also disgusted by the varying practices of the arbitration committees. Some of the more liberal committee chairmen were supporting wage increases in large factories that were bound to create similar demands elsewhere. On March 11 Scheüch, pursuing a policy begun by Groener, asked the chairmen to request advice from War Office commissars in cases where a decision might have broad implications. To some extent, therefore, the unions and the War Office were pulling in different directions in their attempts to influence the arbitration committees.[42]

No less irritating to the unions was the powerlessness of the army with regard to the employers. Many employers refused to accept the awards of the conciliation agencies. Although this was their right and although the unions had previously rejected the idea of compelling either side to accept these decisions, some of the union leaders now supported compulsory arbitration. This was probably because it provided a useful means of keeping the workers in check and loyal to the demands formulated by the unions. The union leaders were particularly incensed over the refusal of some of the Ruhr coal mineowners even to participate in conciliation agency hearings if a union leader served as the advocate of the workers. In one case, an employer ostentatiously walked out of a hearing when the union advocate walked in. The law permitted the use of advocates, and both the War Office and the Commerce Ministry disapproved of the employers' attitude. Yet

[42] *Metallarbeiter-Zeitung*, March 23, 1918, and BBS reports of Feb. 27, March 15, April 15, and May 15, 1918. Scheüch directive of March 11, 1918, BHStA, Abt. IV, MK, K Mob 19, Bd. II, Bl. 145.

they were powerless to act. In a scathing speech, Deputy Huë remarked:

> This is the way one "calms" the workers! The organizations make the greatest effort to formulate a unified inexorbitant demand. They get the agreement of the workers; they appear together before the conciliation agency; and then the great mogul declares: "I will not negotiate if a representative of the unions takes part in the negotiations!" See, Herr Minister [Sydow], this is the way the workers are "calmed"; this is the way your injunctions are carried out, . . . and when the bitterness in the mining district is expressed, then one talks of "treason."[43]

A particularly exasperating instance of an employer attempt to sabotage the Auxiliary Service Law was the secret agreement concluded by the Berlin Association of Metal Industrialists on January 1, 1918, not to hire white-collar workers who had left their previous jobs without their employer's permission. In effect this was an agreement not to hire white-collar workers who had received leaving certificates from the arbitration committees. Similar agreements affecting manual workers or white-collar workers were concluded in other parts of the country. As might be expected, these agreements gave rise to furious interpellations in the Reichstag. On March 23 Scheüch issued a directive in which he declared that the secret employer agreements were a "violation of the spirit of the Auxiliary Service Law" and were having a "disturbing" effect on the workers. The military authorities were instructed to persuade the employers to annul the agreements or, where necessary, to use the Law of Siege to achieve the same end.[44]

The War Office sought to alleviate this situation, but the backlog of irritation and frustration had increased. Each time

[43] Prussian Landtag Debates, March 2, 1918, 7, pp. 8056-8058.

[44] A copy of the industrialist agreement is to be found in BA, P 135/1811, Bl. 207. For the Scheüch directive, see BHStA, Abt. IV, MK, K Mob 7, Bd. VI, Bl. 82.

one cause of complaint disappeared, another sprung up in its place. If there were some Deputy Commanding Generals who followed the War Office's policy and were sympathetic to the unions and willing to permit worker meetings, there were others, like the generals in Magdeburg, Breslau, Münster, and Coblenz, who listened to the advice of the industrialists serving as reserve officers on their staffs. Nearly every concession made to the unions was made on the basis of expediency, not principle, and to every union triumph was added the bitter memory of a hard struggle.[45]

Nothing was more frustrating, however, than the dreary spectacle in the Landtag, where the government desperately sought to fulfill the royal promise to introduce universal and equal suffrage, the opponents of the reform tenaciously blocked the government's efforts, and the OHL gave indirect support to the antigovernment camp. The committee of the Lower House appointed to reconsider the bill in the winter of 1917 produced a legislative monstrosity. It rejected equal suffrage and brought in a plural suffrage system that was a continuation of the three-class voting system in disguise. The government refused to accept the committee's bill and threatened to dissolve the Landtag. On May 2 the Landtag gave its reply: a 235-183 vote against equal suffrage. The opponents of equal suffrage had all along been heartened by the victories on the Western Front and the knowledge that the OHL had taken a strong stand against the dissolution of the Landtag.[46]

The official reason for the OHL's opposition to dissolution was that it would be dangerous and disturbing to hold new elections in the midst of the war. As usual, Ludendorff publicly proclaimed neutrality toward the suffrage question. This, of course, was nonsense. The OHL, and Bauer in particular, actively engaged in the fight against the government's bill through the Crown Prince and the Civil Cabinet Chief, Berg.

[45] See the comments of the union leaders at a meeting with Freiherr von Stein and General Scheüch, April 26, 1918, Institut für Marxismus-Leninismus, *Dokumente und Materialien*, II, pp. 143-149.

[46] Rosenberg, *Birth of the German Republic*, pp. 222-224.

On April 16 Bauer sent the Crown Prince a note attacking the government's claim that the Landtag had to be dissolved if equal suffrage was defeated. In Bauer's view it was fallacious to argue that the King's word required the passage of the bill. The King had kept his word by permitting the government to present the bill. If the Landtag defeated the bill, then the King was absolved of all further responsibility. There was no reason why "the monarchy should dig the grave of Prussia and Germany." Since Vice-Chancellor Payer and Interior Minister Drews were the most ardent supporters of dissolution, Bauer came to the conclusion that the time had come to get rid of this "Bethmannite inheritance." Indeed, it was one of the most "monstrous things in world history" that the government should think of holding elections at a time when a majority of voters were on the battlefield. Democracy was the road to Bolshevism, and "of what purpose are all these sacrifices now in order finally to end up being smothered by Judaism and proletarianism."[47]

At the beginning of May the Crown Prince telegraphed his father asking that the latter state his opposition to the dissolution of the Landtag and demanding that Ministers Drews and Friedberg be dismissed. At the same time, Civil Cabinet Chief von Berg informed Hindenburg that he had been working "in the sense desired by Your Excellency."[48] It must be said, however, that the OHL was more alarmed than necessary at this time. Hertling had no intention of asking for dissolution until every parliamentary means had been exhausted. He feared a dissolution of the Landtag because "although it is not to be doubted that new elections will bring a majority for suffrage reform, there also exists the concern that this method can be more effective than the government wishes and that the latter will have to deal with too radical instead of too conservative

[47] Bauer to Major Müldner von Mülnheim, April 16, 1918, BA, Nachlass Bauer, Nr. 12.

[48] Berg to Hindenburg, May 3, 1918, *ibid.*, Nr. 17. Also, Görlitz, *Regierte der Kaiser?*, pp. 373-374.

a Lower House."[49] The Prussian House of Lords still had to pass judgment on the Lower House's decision, and Hertling hoped to use the threat of dissolution to persuade the former to vote for equal suffrage.

The efforts of Germany's military leaders to fight the introduction of equal suffrage did not abate after the bill's defeat in the Lower House. On May 25 General von Stein issued an order banning all public meetings held in support of equal suffrage. No one was fooled as to the real purpose of this order. The Bavarian War Ministry subjected it to a ruthless analysis and criticism:

> The reason and purpose of the directive are not immediately apparent. But the noteworthy fact may be gathered from it that the highest Prussian military commander wants to use the powers given to him through the war to suppress efforts aimed at realizing a royal promise and carrying through a bill brought in by the Prussian Cabinet. If the order is supposed to push back the suffrage movement, then it hardly can be expected to have much success, for the demand for the introduction of general suffrage in Prussia has already sunk such deep roots in the people that it cannot be suppressed by such forceful means for any length of time.[50]

Indeed, the Bavarian War Ministry could only see harm in the order. It violated the government's promise to keep restrictions on meetings to a minimum; it belied the claim that there was no political censorship; it smacked of partiality; and it "gives a welcome means of agitation to those who maintain that the civil authorities are powerless in Germany and that the military party also rules exclusively internally."

When one looks at the internal situation in May and June of 1918, one wonders why there were no serious strikes. The effort to attain suffrage reform had not succeeded. The bread

[49] Lerchenfeld to Dandl, April 28, 1918, BHStA, Abt. II, MA 1, Nr. 922. On Hertling's conservative attitude, see also Freiherr Kerckerinck zur Borg to Colonel Bauer, May 27, 1917, BA, Nachlass Bauer, Nr. 17.

[50] BHStA, Abt. IV, MK, XIV Mob c III, Bd. 17, Bl. 28-29.

ration was being reduced. Wages in the army's factories had been cut in March, and they were cut again in May. The Worker Chambers bill presented by the government was unsatisfactory from the union viewpoint, yet the unions persisted in opposing strikes and the workers obeyed their injunctions. One reason for this certainly was the vivid memory of the way in which the January strikes had been suppressed. Much more important, however, was the fact that "the workers are of the view that now, when the decisive battle is being fought, they should not strike."[51] But by late June this reason was ceasing to be viable. The great offensives were not bringing the desired results. In fact, just as in June 1917 when Ludendorff had warned the government against premature hopes that the U-boats would bring the enemy to terms, so now he was informing the government that "we must . . . think about preparing our people in the sense that the war can last yet longer and that the greatest unity and decisiveness will be needed to bring it to a victorious end."[52]

3. *A Final Demand for Total Mobilization*

Ludendorff's false calculations in 1917 and 1918 had their origin in his inability to develop military programs based upon a realistic evaluation of Germany's resources. This last failing was the direct result of his incapacity to accept anything less than total victory. The great offensives of the spring of 1918 were undertaken in defiance of the opposition of some of the army's leading strategists and in complete disregard of the War Office's warning that Germany's supply of reserves would be exhausted by the spring of 1918. The ultimate effect of these offensives was to extend the German lines and drastically reduce the number of men available to hold those lines. Ludendorff's claim that the offensives were wearing the enemy down was ridiculous. Between March and July 1918 the

[51] Statement by Dr. August Müller, April 22, 1918, *AGSOD*, III, p. 1306.

[52] Ludendorff to the OHL's representative to the Chancellor, Colonel von Winterfeldt, June 19, 1918, BA, Nachlass Bauer, Nr. 17.

strength of the field army dropped from 5.1 million to 4.2 million men, while the Allied forces were supplemented by over 2 million fresh American troops. Ludendorff complained that he could have succeeded if he only had 200,000 more men. Even if this were true, however, it was impossible to justify the offensives by arguing that the men should have been there.[53]

Similarly, Germany was no match for her enemies in matériel. Germany's long-term productive capacity was simply inferior to those of her enemies in every respect and the Allies' increasingly massive employment of tanks and the OHL's failure to properly encourage the use and production of this weapon doomed the German cause. Ludendorff had never understood that his army's ability to hold back its numerically superior opponents depended almost entirely upon the efficacy of the machine gun. It was this—not the heavy artillery, which after a point simply further devastated what had been destroyed already—which gave a modicum of truth to Ludendorff's claim that machines could be substituted for men. Machine guns, however, were useless against tanks, and the introduction of the latter marked the end of Germany's temporary tactical advantage.[54]

By the fall of 1917 the production of machine guns and field artillery had surpassed the requirements of the Hindenburg Program. The very success of the Hindenburg Program, however, revealed its fatuity. The production quotas for light artillery and mine throwers had to be constantly reduced because there were not enough men at the front to use them. The monthly powder production quota of 12,000 tons was not attained until April 1918, but this did not adversely affect the munitions program. By 1918 powder production had ceased to be the basis for munitions production. Steel was now the basic problem, and it had become apparent that, because of labor, transport, and coal difficulties, Germany was incapable of

[53] See Hans Delbrück's famous criticism of the offensives in *Ursachen*, III, pp. 277ff. For the statistics, see Reichsarchiv, *Weltkrieg*, XIV, pp. 516-517. See also Thaer, *Generalstabschef*, p. 213.

[54] See Wolfgang Sauer's forthcoming *Das Bündnis Groener-Ebert*.

producing enough steel to justify more than a 10,000-ton powder program. Once again the War Ministry's munitions program was justified by events. The War Ministry's program had proved sufficient to meet even the enormous needs of the 1918 offensives and the defensive battles which followed. The Hindenburg Program had produced enormous waste. Money, raw materials, and labor had been expended on useless factories. Most important, the army had been deprived of the reserves it so desperately needed.[55]

The deleterious effect of the Hindenburg Program on the manpower supply, however, could no longer be remedied. By 1918 neither the machines nor the workers were operating at maximum efficiency. The exempted workers were now needed to maintain existing production levels. Ludendorff cut the production quotas on many items, but he insisted that general production levels be maintained and even increased. His situation was made all the more difficult because both industry and government had been so geared to the idea that the war was coming to an end that the former began to prepare for peacetime production while the latter began to reopen shut-down plants. Not only did Ludendorff feel that it was necessary to reverse this tendency, but he was also convinced that the time had come for a new and more massive mobilization of the war economy. The result, as in 1916, was a fierce struggle between the OHL on the one side and the War Ministry and government on the other.[56]

On June 18 the OHL sent a note to the Chancellor demanding the extension of the Military Service Law to all men between fifteen and sixty and the extension of the Auxiliary Service Law to women.[57] Hindenburg pointed out that it was

[55] Reichsarchiv, *Weltkrieg*, XIV, pp. 33-35; Schwarte, *Grosse Krieg*, VIII, pp. 129-134; production reports in BHStA, Abt. IV, MK, K Mob 1, Bd. I, Bl. 90-156; Cron, *Eisenwirtschaft*, pp. 78-80.

[56] On the attempts to go over to peacetime production, see BHStA, Abt. IV, MK, K Mob 12, Bd. XIII, Bl. 133.

[57] The discussion and quotations which follow are based on the text of the note in Ludendorff, *Urkunden*, pp. 107-109.

impossible to reduce production, but that it was absolutely necessary to secure more reserves. The productivity of the workers had declined because "the wages are so high that the necessities of life do not compel them to work or give them an incentive to earn more." The union leaders were accused of trying to keep production low in order to prevent the recall of the workers into the army. The official patriotism of the union leaders "should not blind us and should not prevent us from seeing behind their faces." Also, those vital industries paying lower wages were unable to compete for labor with those paying higher wages. The only solution, therefore, was to place all labor in the common service and free men for the front and for the essential factories by this means.

The situation, in the OHL's view, was analogous to that of the fall of 1916. At that time the Chancellor had turned down the OHL's proposal to extend the military service obligation and to employ compulsion against women. The government had produced instead the disastrous Auxiliary Service Law. The failure of the latter now compelled the OHL to revive its initial demands. The workers would be forced to raise their productivity, and they would be compelled to stay on their jobs. In contrast to 1916, however, the OHL now recognized that the wage and profit questions could no longer be neglected:

> I am fully conscious of the fact that such an extension of the obligations to military service and the Auxiliary Service will have far-reaching consequences for our entire war economy. It is not possible to leave the regulation of wages to the employers if the workers are tied to specific factories and if their productivity is maintained by state intervention. It will be necessary to place the wage question and, as a logical consequence, the profit question under state regulation. In the final result, a certain militarization of the armaments factories will thus be brought about, which is also desirable because in many factories the concern with the

later peacetime economy is becoming pervasive in a manner completely insupportable for our war economy.

The OHL had thus finally come to support Richard Merton's program. Indeed, it now even wanted Merton's services. During a trip to Berlin, Merton was approached by his good friend Professor Fritz Haber with a startling message from Colonel Bauer. The latter wanted to know if Merton was willing to join Bauer's staff! Merton indicated in reply that he "could not see why I should help to dish out the soup which Colonel Bauer has cooked up."[58]

Merton was quite wise in refusing to get entangled with Bauer at this point. Bauer's belated conversion to the Merton program and his invitation to Merton suggest that Bauer was seeking to protect himself at the last minute by associating himself with the ideas and person of one of his chief opponents. After the war Bauer made the false claim that the OHL had always sought to restrict profits.[59] As we know Ludendorff never mentioned the restriction of profits until December 1917, and it was only in June 1918 that the OHL finally declared itself in favor of a thoroughgoing system of control. Whatever the case, June 1918 was hardly the time to once again launch a complicated economic and social program.

On June 24 General von Stein sent a personal letter to Hindenburg arguing against the OHL's latest program. He pointed out that an extension of the Military Service Law would burden the nation's finances by requiring the government to pay, clothe, and support the new soldiers and their families. Most important, he saw little value in the OHL's program. Both the older and the younger men were already employed in positions where they were indispensable. Compulsion was not needed for women, as they were employed in large numbers already. The sudden shifting about of workers entailed by the program would disturb production. Although Stein was very careful to disassociate himself from any politi-

[58] Merton, *Erinnernswertes aus meinem Leben*, pp. 44-45.
[59] Bauer, *Grosse Krieg*, p. 159.

cal objections that might be raised to the OHL's proposals, he actually revealed tremendous pessimism concerning their political chances:

> The political situation does not influence me. It is self-understandable that a presentation of the idea will lead to the greatest disquiet in the country, . . . and finally we will get another monster like the Auxiliary Service Law. One result would please me, the dissolution of the Reichstag over the question, but I do not believe in this possibility because a ruthless and very strong man would be necessary. Also, I doubt whether the external and internal impression created by such a step would be bearable.[60]

In Stein's view it was best to avoid any kind of reorganization. Since his experiences with the Auxiliary Service Law and the War Office, "I have defended myself against every new transformation and have always chosen to add to and extend what already exists."

At a meeting between Bauer and the government leaders, Stein's arguments were strongly supported by the civilian leaders and General Scheüch. They were particularly horrified at the prospect of having to bring a new bill before the Reichstag. The Reichstag was scheduled to adjourn for a few months, and the government had no desire to ruin this happy prospect. It had been having a hard time with the deputies, and it feared that the presentation of the OHL's proposals would lead, as in 1916, to an orgy of "cattle trading" in which suffrage reform and other reforms would be demanded. Scheüch reminded those present that the unions had agreed to the binding of exempted workers to specific factories "if a guarantee is given against the power of the employers. This cannot be accomplished. If one wants to introduce military control, then the workers are agreed, but not the employers, who do not want

[60] Handwritten note from Stein to Hindenburg, June 24, 1918, BA, Nachlass Bauer, Nr. 18. Bauer filled this note with angry marginal comments.

to obey the military authorities."[61] Colonel Bauer did not reply to this comment. He did not say, for example, that the industrialists would now have to do their duty like everyone else, and this raises serious questions about the OHL's sincerity when it came to the control of profits or the establishment of a truly equitable economic mobilization program. Colonel Bauer stated in the end that the political side of the question was a matter for the government to decide, but that the army had to have its reserves. Since the government, like the army, was incapable of surmounting the barriers of a political society which it was unable to control but which, because of its conservative proclivities, it was unwilling to transform, nothing could be accomplished.

Once again the Ludendorff dictatorship had reached its limit. Only in the realm of foreign policy was its influence supreme, and here only because of the faith placed in the promises of victory. The left wing parties accused him of being a dictator, as did later historians, but Ludendorff was never really willing to make full use of his potential power. Colonel Bauer had long sought to promote truly radical changes. In February 1918 he actually wanted to get rid of the Emperor and replace him by Crown Prince Wilhelm. The latter was strongly influenced by Bauer on political questions, but the unruly young man could not bring himself to overthrow his father. Ludendorff opposed this solution, as he opposed Bauer's continuous demands that Hertling be removed and that Stein and Scheüch be replaced by more "energetic soldiers."[62] Bauer was very partial to the establishment of a real Ludendorff dictatorship, and he was not alone in holding this view. General Eisenhart Rothe and the Chief of Staff to the Second Quartermaster General, Colonel Albrecht von Thaer, also tried to persuade Ludendorff to take the helm. The latter gives a colorful and revealing portrayal of Ludendorff's reaction:

[61] Meeting of July 1, 1918, Ludendorff, *Urkunden*, pp. 110-116.
[62] Bauer, *Grosse Krieg*, p. 187.

> During my latest report to Ludendorff on June 26, he repeated that, in his view, the Emperor would appoint neither Bülow nor Tirpitz as Chancellor. I took a chance and said that the only one to come in question, in my estimation, was His Excellency himself. "No, oh, no; *no thought of it*! Completely aside from the fact that His Majesty would never consider it, I am the totally wrong person. Cobbler, stick to your last! As a soldier, I will succeed. How shall I go before parliament as Chancellor?" Upon that, I said only one word: "Dictatorship—only solution! It's high time!" "Completely out of the question! Don't talk to me about such things! It will also never be considered; His Majesty would never do it!"[63]

The temptation may have been there, but not the self-confidence or the willingness to take the ultimate responsibility.

Ludendorff was powerful enough to force Hertling to dismiss Foreign Secretary Kühlmann for making a Reichstag address on June 24 indicating that the war could no longer be won by military means alone, but Ludendorff abstained from attacking Hertling because the OHL "needed him to avoid parliamentary crises."[64] Hindenburg and Ludendorff did not feel that they could afford to risk serious internal difficulties when the military situation was so critical. After the war was won, they would be free to act. As Hindenburg told the Duke of Braunschweig at the height of the great offensives: "Internal politics cannot continue on as before. After the war it will be necessary to show the Reichstag who is the master of the house. The Duke interpreted these remarks of the Field Marshal to mean that Hindenburg will eventually promote the establishment of a military dictatorship after the war."[65]

Not the least important cause for Ludendorff's lack of confidence in the early summer of 1918 was the darkening military

[63] Thaer, *Generalstabsdienst*, p. 211; Eisenhart Rothe, *Im Banne der Persönlichkeit*, pp. 159-162.

[64] Lerchenfeld to Dandl, July 10, 1918, BHStA, Abt. II, MA 1, Nr. 923.

[65] Report of Kraft von Delmensingen, *ibid.*, Nr. 945, Bl. 145-146.

situation. On July 15 he launched his final offensive, and it failed miserably. Three days later the Allies launched the successful counterattack that was to mark the beginning of the end for Germany. Ludendorff was badly shaken, and he sought the advice of General Fritz von Lossberg, one of the army's leading strategists. Lossberg advised the cessation of all offensive operations, the withdrawal of forces to the Siegfried Line, and the building up of strong defensive zones further to the rear. This would insure an orderly retreat, save equipment, shorten the German lines, and give the troops a sorely needed rest. Ludendorff agreed that Lossberg's proposals were unimpeachable from a military standpoint. Nevertheless he turned them down "out of regard for the impression upon the enemy, upon our army, and upon the homefront." When Lossberg reproached him for giving primacy to political considerations at such a time, Ludendorff, visibly shaken, went to Hindenburg and offered his resignation. Hindenburg refused to accept it. Lossberg, however, now lost confidence in Ludendorff, who seemed incapable of making a "thoroughgoing decision."[66] Finally on August 8 the decision was made for him when the British broke through the German lines. For the first time German divisions fled before the enemy. This "black day of the German army" compelled Ludendorff to assume the defensive.

Colonel Bauer had also lost confidence in Ludendorff and was now busy informing General von Stein and other leaders in Berlin that Ludendorff was no longer meeting the demands of his position and that it was time for a change.[67] For the third time in the history of the war, Bauer was intriguing against his military superior. If Bauer was plotting against Ludendorff in secret, however, he had by no means ceased giving the latter "advice." This was particularly the case when it came to the encouragement of Ludendorff's resentments.

[66] Fritz von Lossberg, *Meine Tätigkeit im Weltkriege, 1914-1918*, Berlin, 1939, pp. 345-347.

[67] Eisenhart Rothe, *Im Banne der Persönlichkeit*, p. 111.

When Interior Minister Drews sent a note warning against a lowering of wages because rumors concerning such plans were causing unrest among the workers, Ludendorff replied that the German workers were "too reasonable and too patriotic" to ruin the war effort and declared that the disproportion between the pay of the troops and that of the workers was a "screaming injustice." Ten days later Bauer wrote yet another note for Ludendorff to send to the government, this one demanding an increase of soldiers' pay. Ludendorff did not send it, but its conclusion is a good example of the kind of influence Bauer was exerting: "In conclusion, I must once again emphasize that the above is perhaps one of the most serious questions that now exists. The war is not yet won. We will win it if the homeland no longer stabs the army in the back (*dem Heer in den Rücken fällt*) and if the army, by receiving that to which it is entitled, can maintain trust and confidence."[68]

This shifting of the responsibility is the *Leitmotif* of Bauer's writings at the termination of the war. Thus, at a meeting of the Düsseldorf Industry Club on July 20, Bauer again indicated that the people at home were to blame for everything: "War Ministry does nothing thoroughgoing; neither does Chancellor; we have a continuous danger at our backs." In a letter to the yellow union leader, Dr. Fleischer, this theme was coupled with a complete exoneration of the OHL.

> The results of the faintheartedness at home and the internal disunity are, unfortunately, also evident at the front. This is no wonder; on the contrary, it is remarkable that the discipline and willingness to sacrifice has held up in the army for so long. The OHL did not have a direct influence on the direction of internal politics and the maintenance and improvement of morale and the will to hold out, and the OHL cannot therefore be made responsible. It is also not valid to say that we should have assumed such an influence. I

[68] The notes are dated July 2 and July 12, 1918, BA, Nachlass Bauer, Nr. 14.

cannot go into the reasons, but it was simply impossible. The attempt would have brought more harm than use.[69]

In the last months of the war, therefore, the stab-in-the-back idea was being given very concrete expression. What had been implicit in the OHL's notes to the government, the constant combination of concrete demands with the claim that "to go into the details is not my function," was now being turned into the claim that others, not the OHL, were responsible for Germany's plight.

4. *"Stab in the Back" and "Revolution from Above"*

If the stab-in-the-back idea itself was a legend, the series of accusations of which it was constituted were not always completely false. It was precisely this fact that made it so potent and effective. The German wartime governments were woefully inadequate, and their machinery was slow moving, ponderous, and bureaucratic. But most important was the absence of adequate leadership. In its most critical period the German Empire could produce nothing better than the vacillating Bethmann Hollweg, the incompetent Michaelis, the superannuated Hertling, and, finally, the insipid Max von Baden. The OHL thus had good cause to complain bitterly that Germany lacked men like Lloyd George, Clemenceau, and Wilson. If the complaints concerning the civil leaders were justified, however, it cannot be said that the OHL had anything better to offer. Neither Bülow nor Tirpitz was a model of political sagacity. Indeed, they both had contributed mightily to the diplomatic morass that eventually brought about the war. Germany did lack the kind of political leader needed to maintain internal discipline and, it may be added, to put the army in its place. This, however, was one of the direct results of the Bismarckian political legacy that the OHL fought so ardently to maintain.

[69] The sketchy handwritten notes on the meeting of July 20 and the letter to Fleischer of Sept. 3, 1918, are to be found in *ibid.*, Nr. 13.

If the OHL blamed the civil authorities at home, it by no means spared the military authorities there. As the Bavarian liaison officer at General Headquarters reported, "The War Ministry will be made responsible for the failure on the Western Front because it did not implement the Auxiliary Service Law with the necessary sharpness and thus permitted too few men to be placed at the army's disposal."[70] The unedifying conflict between the OHL and the War Ministry reflects very poorly upon Germany's military organization. For all the criticisms that may be leveled against the Ministry, there can be not the slightest question about the fact that its opposition to the Hindenburg Program, War Office, and Auxiliary Service Law were based upon sound and realistic judgments.

The OHL's chief scapegoats were, of course, the left wing parties and the union leaders, who were accused of using the wartime situation to achieve old social and political objectives. The strikes and the unrest among the workers were blamed on the manner in which the unions pursued this policy. It would be a complete falsification to deny all validity to these charges. As has been demonstrated, the union leaders did seek to use the wartime situation to increase their power, did engage in agitation, and did not always act as innocent bystanders in the development of strikes. In the balance, however, the union leaders gave the OHL the greatest possible support. The partiality of the OHL and government toward the industrialists was largely responsible for the mounting wage demands during the last two years of the war. If the government had been willing to control profits, Paragraph 9 of the Auxiliary Service Law would never have been passed in so harmful a form. Also, if the employers had been willing to permit the Deputy Commanding Generals to regulate wages or if the army had forced the employers to accept this, the union leaders would have readily accepted greater restriction on the free movement of the exempted workers. There can be no greater testimony

[70] Report of Oct. 10, 1918, BHStA, Abt. IV, MK, III a XV 39.

to the justification of most of the workers' wage demands and the fundamental loyalty of the union leaders than Colonel Bauer's own words:

> The black market is destroying our entire moral and economic life. We are possibly facing serious strikes, all of which are indirectly the result of the black market, for the ration is insufficient and the men must get their food elsewhere. That is possible through the black market, but the prices are monstrous—for example, 30 marks for a pound of butter in the industrial district. As a consequence, the workers demand—and from their standpoint, with a certain justification—a wage increase. The union leaders are completely reasonable. They also regard the high wages as a terrible danger, but they are powerless.[71]

It was absurd to expect the union leaders to control the masses if the government's incompetence continually made this impossible, and it was equally absurd to ask the unions to control the masses if they were not to be granted the necessary power.

The supporters of the stab-in-the-back idea were also engaging in a falsehood when they claimed that it was the home front that had destroyed the morale of the army and that it was the home front that let the army down at the end of the war. The monthly reports of the Deputy Commanding Generals demonstrate this in rich detail. In the reports for March and April they were able to report good morale due to the successes at the front. Morale was also good in May, although there was some concern over the pause in offensive operations. By June, however, the people had become acclimated to the idea that there had to be some delay between offensives. They expected "more powerful blows, . . . hoping that it will be possible to beat the enemy before winter." Throughout the period from March to June, therefore, the morale at home was relatively good despite the cutting of the bread ration and the

[71] Bauer to Colonel von Haeften, Aug. 26, 1918, BA, Nachlass Haeften, Nr. 13.

suffrage reform problem. Only the Kühlmann speech at the end of June darkened the picture slightly and created anxiety concerning the future military prospects.[72]

The military disaster in July accelerated the destruction of the home front's morale:

> The joyous—partially exaggerated—hopes which were attached to the renewal of our offensive . . . have been strongly shaken by the enemy counterattack and the withdrawal on our front. While the great mass of the people, because of the successes during the spring, have become accustomed to counting on the ending of the war this year, the prospect of another war winter has created a certain dullness and indifference in many people, and the economic cares and privations have come to the forefront again more than before.[73]

The Deputy Commanding Generals were forced to admit that "the morale has never been so bad as in the last few weeks." It is important to note that this depression was coincident with the prospect of an improved food supply due to the proximity of the harvest. There can be no better demonstration of the fact that the morale at home was ultimately determined by the military rather than the economic situation. So long as the military prospects seemed favorable and there were grounds for faith in the OHL, the workers accepted the cutting of the bread ration without serious complaint. Now their morale collapsed even though the food situation had improved. It had become patently obvious that the official reports could no longer be trusted and that the enemy had regained the territory it had lost during the great offensives.

The disquiet at home was greatly intensified by the letters received from the troops at the front and the comments made by troops on leave. The soldiers constantly referred to the war as a "swindle." As one Bavarian officer noted in his postwar memoirs:

[72] ZMG Reports, March-June 1918. [73] *Ibid.*, Aug. 15, 1918.

> In opposition to the stab-in-the-back legend . . . I want to establish on the basis of my own experience that the mood of dissatisfaction was carried into the homeland by the troops on leave . . . at a time when the homeland did not think of opposing the war and its leaders. Many an open-hearted member of the *Landwehr* told me how he found things out there, how badly they were fed, how everything meant for the front was left in the occupied areas [*Etappe*], how senseless and purposeless the whole story was, how the men were mistreated in this or that unit, etc. If there was much exaggeration and if the individual soldier used individual instances to judge the entire situation, there were still many people smart enough and clearminded enough to recognize that everything was not in order. And this conviction was carried from the front to the homeland and not vice versa.[74]

Ultimately, the OHL ruined everyone's morale. Both the soldiers and the workers had given their best, and they now had nothing to show for it.

It is indicative of the exhaustion of the workers during the summer and fall of 1918 that their chief demand was for the reduction of hours. The labor leaders had warned the government that the big danger was not strikes but rather an unwillingness on the part of the workers to exert themselves in the old way. They were so overworked and undernourished that they no longer had sufficient energy. At the same time it must be recognized that the eight-hour day was an important union goal and that a reduction of hours necessarily had implications for the future. As in the wage question, so in the hours question, immediate wartime problems were intermeshed with the struggle between labor and management over the social policy of the future.[75]

Although demands for a reduction of hours antedated the

[74] BHStA, Abt. IV, MK, Handakt 429, Nachlass Karl Aschenbrenner, p. 76.

[75] See *AGSOD*, III, p. 1306 and *Arbeitgeberzeitung*, July 7, 1918.

summer of 1918, they became widespread in July of that year. Throughout the Ruhr the metalworkers demanded a reduction of the work week from sixty to fifty-six hours. General von Gayl insisted that the question be handled on a factory by factory basis. He promised not to oppose a reduction of hours where it would not prove detrimental to production, but he warned that he would not tolerate any strikes over this question. The unions themselves were anxious to avoid strikes, and although some short wild strikes did break out and although many workers willfully stopped working four hours early on Saturday afternoons, the unions did succeed in persuading the workers to use the conciliation agencies and arbitration committees. In the hearings that followed during the next three months, the majority of the agencies refused to reduce hours because of the danger to production. The agencies in Düsseldorf and Mühlheim asked the War Office to send commissars to advise them concerning the effect a reduction of hours would have on production. Finally, the agency in Duisburg decided to try a reduction of hours on an experimental basis. In September the War Office was still pondering the question. The unions had thus performed a major service for the government by compelling the workers to use the conciliation agencies. Similarly, they cooperated with General von Gayl in preventing serious wage strikes in the Ruhr coal mines, where once again a wage increase was traded for a price increase.[76]

In Upper Silesia the union leaders were unable to create even such an uneasy truce. Although General von Heinemann had been replaced by a new Deputy Commanding General, General von Egloffstein, nothing had really changed. The notorious Captain Nebelung continued to serve as economic adviser to the Deputy Commanding General. The restrictions

[76] See General von Gayl's note of Aug. 22, 1918, StAMü, Oberbergamt Dortmund B, Nr. 119, Bd. 227; *Metallarbeiter-Zeitung*, Aug. 10, 1918; *Correspondenzblatt*, Sept. 21, 1918; *Arbeitgeberzeitung*, July 1, Sept. 1-15, 1918; War Office discussion, July 11, 1918, BHStA, Abt. IV, MK, K Mob 11a, Bd. IV, Bl. 84.

on union meetings severely hampered union activities, and Privy Councilor Hilger was as stubborn as ever. In May the editor of the Polish language newspaper put out by the Free Trade Unions was drafted into the army. The most important means of communication between the unions and the Polish workers was thus removed. This was obviously Nebelung's intention because the editor was tubercular and certainly of no value to the army. At the same time the unions, responding to the dissatisfaction of the workers, raised demands for a general wage increase and an eight and a half hour day. The workers did agree to have these questions brought before the conciliation agency in Breslau. The hearings, much to the irritation of the workers, were delayed because the chairman was sick. When the hearings were finally held, the agency granted a wage increase which Privy Councilor Hilger promptly labeled a "premium for laziness." He refused to accept the agency's award. That the demands of the workers were not excessive is demonstrated by the fact that the Catholic Worker Association, which was a yellow union, supported a reduction of hours, as did General von Egloffstein and some of the employers. In a letter to Colonel Bauer of July 11, the Catholic Union leader, Dr. Fleischer, was extremely critical of Hilger's stand and pointed out that when an employer acted the way he did, then the workers felt entitled to take matters into their own hands also.[77]

This the workers did, and the strikes in Silesia in June and July were so serious that troops had to be brought in and the mines had to be militarized. In the course of quelling these strikes, the military authorities made the unpleasant discovery that the militarization of the mines had made "little impression" on the workers. As Egloffstein reported, "This is the first case that I know of where a part of the population has not

[77] On the Silesian situation, see Fleischer to Bauer, July 11, 1918, and Legien to Scheüch, Aug. 19, 1918, in BA, Nachlass Bauer, Nr. 13; Reichstag Debates, July 4, 1918, 312, pp. 5166ff.; VdESI meeting, Sept. 2, 1918, BA, R 13I/155; *Bergarbeiter-Zeitung*, July 20, 1918.

accepted military instructions and has scorned military measures."[78] In a report of July 19 Egloffstein blamed the strike on union agitation, although he confessed that the use of union meetings to persuade the strikers to return to work had proved most effective. The sources of information for Egloffstein's report are most illustrative of the way things were being managed in Upper Silesia. When an investigation was made by the War Office, it was discovered that Egloffstein had secured his information from Captain Nebelung, who in turn had received his information from the industrialists. When the War Office asked the Deputy Commanding General to check his facts, the latter promptly sent a questionnaire to the industrialists asking whether or not his report was accurate!

The chairman of the General Commission, Legien, presented these facts to General Scheüch and Colonel Bauer and warned that a continuation of the policies of the Deputy Commanding Generals was bound to incite new strikes and that the unions could not be made responsible for the production losses that would occur. In a reply of September 23 Bauer indicated that he was "very interested" in Legien's report. He agreed "that nothing is more damaging than a policy of pinpricks and irritations." In his conclusion, however, he made the usual claim that the OHL had no "official influence" over the Deputy Commanding Generals, although he did promise to exercise unofficial influence through General Scheüch.[79]

Given the disastrous situation in September, Bauer was undoubtedly most anxious to pacify Legien. Nevertheless, he was underplaying the OHL's real influence. The OHL had done much to promote harsh measures. On July 20 Carl Duisberg held a meeting of the Düsseldorf Industry Club to discuss ways and means of fighting the demand for shorter hours. At this meeting Bauer asked the industrialists to show "firmness and decisiveness" and warned that "every sign of

[78] *AGSOD*, III, pp. 1460-1465.

[79] Legien to Scheüch, Aug. 19, 1918; Legien to Bauer, Sept. 14, 1918; and Bauer to Legien, Sept. 23, 1918, BA, Nachlass Bauer, Nr. 13.

vacillation makes itself felt."[80] Similarly, on August 4 Ludendorff informed the government that "when the workers try to shorten the working hours by strikes, they work directly against the patriotic interest." This attitude was understandable, but he then went on to criticize General Egloffstein and the Mayor of Düsseldorf for giving support to the idea of reducing hours.[81] At a conference with the Emperor and Chancellor on August 14, Ludendorff demanded "severer internal discipline," and the Emperor, as a consequence, commanded that the War Ministry and Deputy Commanding Generals insure "a stricter enforcement of the authority of the state."[82]

Thus, even in August Ludendorff was unwilling to promote a more liberal internal policy. Similarly, he continued to block the government's efforts to make a clear statement of its intention to restore Belgium's independence. This unwillingness to face reality was most evident in Ludendorff's conduct of military operations. He still refused to retreat to strong defensive positions. On August 9 he told Colonel von Mertz that "we cannot win the war anymore, but we must not lose it either." A strange statement from a man who had always preached "Victory or defeat, there is no third possibility!" At the meeting with the Emperor and Chancellor on August 14, an attempt was made to define the "third possibility": "The Chief of the General Staff . . . has so far defined the military situation as to say that we can no longer hope to break down the fighting spirit of our enemies by military action, and that we must set as the object of our campaign that of gradually wearing down the enemy's fighting spirit by a strategic defensive."[83] The Emperor then declared that it was necessary to seek neutral mediation at the "opportune moment." Hertling

[80] See Bauer's notes, *ibid.*

[81] Count Limburg-Stirum to Hertling, Aug. 4, 1918, DZA Potsdam, Kriegsakten 1, Bd. 13, Bl. 12.

[82] Ludendorff, *Urkunden*, pp. 499-502.

[83] *Ibid.* For the previous quotations, see Wolfgang Foerster, *Der Feldherr Ludendorff im Unglück. Eine Studie über seine seelische Haltung in der Endphase des ersten Weltkrieges*, Wiesbaden, 1952, p. 133n, and Tschuppik, *Ludendorff*, p. 352.

defined such a moment as being "after the next successes in the West." Hindenburg concluded by arguing that he "hopes that it would yet be possible to remain fixed on French territory, and thereby in the end enforce our will upon the enemy." Ludendorff changed the wording of this statement in the protocol to read that "it would be possible to remain fixed on French territory." This was absurd, however, for successful defensive engagements could only be conducted from satisfactory defensive positions, and Ludendorff would not engage in an organized retreat.

By September the conflict between illusion and reality had become too great for Ludendorff. Burdened with the sinking fortunes of his country, army, and reputation, studying maps until the early hours of the morning, unwilling to abstain from interfering in the minute details of his subordinates' work, Ludendorff was being worn out. His physical and mental deterioration alarmed his staff. They begged him to replace the Chief of the Operations Section, Colonel Wetzell, with an older and more experienced officer like General von Lossberg or General von Seeckt. In this way the detail work could be taken from Ludendorff's hands. Ludendorff continually refused to take this suggestion, undoubtedly because he feared that the way was being paved for a successor. Finally, General von Stein intervened and forced Ludendorff to replace Wetzell with Colonel von Heye. This solution was not very satisfactory because Heye was not the type of man to stand up to Ludendorff. Toward the latter part of September, Ludendorff's depression deepened, and a nerve specialist, Dr. Hochheimer, had to be called in. Hochheimer forced Ludendorff to get some rest and the depression began to abate. In private conversation with Hochheimer, however, Ludendorff admitted that he felt "introverted, mistrustful, and misanthropic." Hochheimer noted that "the man is completely alone."[84]

What Ludendorff feared, as he told Colonel Nicolai, was

[84] Report of Kraft von Delmensingen, Sept. 9, 1918, BHStA, Abt. II, MA 1, Nr. 975, Bl. 346, and Foerster, *Ludendorff im Unglück*, pp. 71-81.

revolution. Indeed, at times he feared it more than the military situation and felt as if he were fighting "a two-front war against the inner and the outer enemy." The OHL had always fought for the establishment of a propaganda ministry to conduct a unified propaganda program, and the government, for very bureaucratic reasons, it must be said, had always refused. The OHL still clung to this idea during August-September 1918, but it had a very strange conception of enlightenment. Thus on September 24, with the German armies in full retreat, General von Wrisberg was telling the Reichstag Budget Committee that "the High Command . . . looks forward full of confidence to future events." The committee greeted this report with "disdainful, mocking laughter." This growing loss of faith in the OHL was accompanied by a new government crisis. The debate over suffrage reform in the Prussian House of Lords was not going favorably for the government. The handling of the Law of Siege was the subject of mounting attack. Finally, and most important, the conviction was growing that the enemy would only deal with a parliamentary regime, and that the ailing Hertling was not a suitable leader in such a dire hour.[85]

On September 26 the Allies launched a great offensive in the West. On the same day Bulgaria requested an armistice. With Bulgaria out of the war and her railroads in Allied hands, German communications with Constantinople and German use of the Danube would be seriously threatened. Most immediate was the danger to Germany's position in Rumania, whose reentry into the war was now likely. Rumanian oil was vital to the German war effort. Without it, Germany's oil supplies would disappear within six months. Finally, Austria-

[85] On Ludendorff's fear of revolution, see Foerster, *Ludendorff im Unglück*, pp. 62-63; on the propaganda question, see Walter Vogel, *Die Organisation der amtlichen Presse und Propagandapolitik des Deutschen Reiches von den Anfangen bis zum Beginn des Jahres 1933*, Berlin, 1941, pp. 22-68; for the Budget Committee hearing, see Hans Peter Nanssen, *Diary of a Dying Empire*, O. O. Winther, trans., Bloomington, Indiana, 1955, p. 296; on the crisis, see Lerchenfeld to Dandl, Sept. 11-29, 1918, BHStA, Abt. II, MA 1, Nr. 923.

Hungary would certainly withdraw from the war the moment Rumania reentered it. Thus, Bulgaria's collapse would inevitably lead to Germany's isolation.[86]

Ludendorff's complete inability to tell the government the truth forced the officers on his staff to take the initiative. On September 26 Heye, Mertz, and Bartenwerffer informed the Foreign Office that the immediate introduction of peace negotiations was a necessity. When informed of this move, Ludendorff not only gave his approval, but also came to the astonishing conclusion that what was needed was something more than the introduction of peace negotiations. On the evening of September 28 he persuaded Hindenburg to call for the immediate conclusion of an armistice. Hertling and Foreign Secretary Hintze were informed of this very fateful decision the next day. Hintze had been planning to make an appeal to Wilson for a peace based on the Fourteen Points at an "opportune moment." Before doing so he wanted to have a new, "broad national" government set up so as to appeal to Wilson's democratic instincts. Ludendorff had approved of this plan before September 29, but he had given no indication that it would have to be implemented in such a way as to indicate that Germany was on the verge of collapse and that she was submitting to the indignity of internal reform in order to placate the enemy. Now, a "revolution from above" was, in Hintze's view, a vital necessity. Ludendorff accepted this without objection and insisted that the important thing was speed.[87]

In taking this step Ludendorff was motivated by illusion, fear, and sinister calculation. Both Ludendorff and his officers wanted to give the troops a chance to catch their breath, but where the latter were willing to accept a further retreat of the German armies and a temporary continuation of the fighting until an armistice could be arranged, Ludendorff hoped that he would be able to keep his armies stationed at the Siegfried Line by securing an immediate armistice. Ludendorff thus

[86] Rosenberg, *Birth of the German Republic*, pp. 240-241.

[87] See Wolfgang Sauer's *Bündnis Ebert-Groener* for the details.

hoped to hide his weakness by taking a step which could only have the consequence of exposing it in the clearest possible manner, and he expected Foch to behave like an eighteenth century general and grant an armistice permitting both sides to remain on the existing battle lines. Although willing to admit that, were he Foch, he certainly would not grant such terms, he nevertheless felt impelled to take this action because it was his "last straw." In any case he was certain that "if the enemy is too impudent in his demands, or otherwise the possibility of bettering our situation shows only through a war to the knife, then, believe me, we will fight to the last."[88]

This optimism sounds rather bizarre in the light of Ludendorff's very dismal evaluation of the reliability of his troops. Indeed, it is ironic that Ludendorff, who always claimed that it was the homeland that destroyed the morale of the army, seemed most worried about the effect that the army might have on the homeland. As he explained to his staff on October 1:

> Our own army is, unfortunately, heavily infected with the poison of Spartacist-Socialist ideas. There is no relying on the troops anymore. . . . He [Ludendorff] cannot operate with divisions that cannot be relied upon any longer. So it is to be expected that the enemy will succeed soon, with the help of the battle-thirsty Americans, in winning a great victory, a breakthrough in the grand style. Then our western army will lose its last self-control and, in complete chaos, flee back across the Rhine and bring revolution to Germany. This catastrophe must be avoided.[89]

At the same time Ludendorff did recognize that his sudden request for an armistice might serve as a "signal for revolution" at home.

Ultimately, however, Ludendorff did hold one trump in his hand which made all the risks bearable. It would be the new,

[88] Thaer, *Generalstabsdienst*, p. 236.
[89] *Ibid.*

"broad national" government that would have to make the armistice and the peace. Ludendorff was conscious of this fact from the very beginning. The stab-in-the-back legend was not born on November 9, when the Revolution took place. As has been demonstrated, it existed much earlier. Most important, it was very much on Ludendorff's mind when he insisted on an armistice and agreed to a "revolution from above." In contrast to the preceding weeks, Ludendorff was very calm on this occasion as well as afterward. This was undoubtedly due, in part, to the fact that he had finally come to a decision. It seems likely, however, that there was a deeper psychological reason. Ludendorff knew that he had at last found a means of placing the blame for the disaster elsewhere. On the morning of October 1 he told the officers of his staff:

> At present we have no Chancellor. Who it will be is as yet unknown. But I have asked His Majesty to now bring into the government those circles for whom we have chiefly to thank that things have come so far. We will therefore see these people brought into the ministries. They shall conclude the peace that now must be concluded. They shall drink the soup they have cooked up for us.[90]

This idea took hold with incredible speed. Thus on October 7 the Bavarian representative to the OHL reported:

> One frequently hears the view concerning the internal political situation that it is very good that the left wing parties will have to take the odium for the peace upon themselves. The storm of popular anger will then direct itself against them.
>
> Later one hopes to swing into the saddle again and rule on according to the old prescription.[91]

Indeed, as in 1848, the Prussian officer corps expected military counterrevolution to both defeat revolution from below and

[90] *Ibid.*

[91] Report of Oct. 7, 1918, BHStA, Abt. IV, MK, III a XV 39.

act as a substitute for bureaucratic reform from above. The Bavarian liaison officer at Crown Prince Rupprecht's headquarters reported on October 7 that

> Almost all of them [the Prussian officers] consider democratization the greatest possible misfortune there could be. A democratic Prussia is, for them, no Prussia at all. Many seem to hope that the possibility may arise of restoring the previous system through an act of force. In their view it was only the refusal of the military demands by the leftist parties in the Reichstag . . . during the war that has plunged us into misfortune. They cannot or do not want to attain full clarity concerning the military situation.[92]

The new government of Prince Max von Baden, which included two Socialists, thus made a fatal error when it gave way to Ludendorff's pressure for an armistice and agreed to take responsibility for this step. It did not have Richard Merton's wisdom and did not compel the OHL to "dish out its own soup."

Ludendorff's illusions were quickly shattered. When Foch did not present the armistice terms he expected, he demanded a continuation of the war. His armistice request, however, had broken the back of whatever powers of resistance remained to the German people. The words that most condemn him were those uttered by the archconservative Heydebrand, who upon hearing of Ludendorff's armistice request, cried out, "We have been lied to and deceived, and that is what we based our policy on!" On October 26, after Ludendorff had sought to sabotage the government's continued negotiations with Wilson, Ludendorff was compelled to resign. Colonel Bauer, who had been plotting against him since July, ostentatiously submitted his resignation also.[93]

92 Report of Kraft von Delmensingen, *ibid.*, Nr. 945, Bl. 223-224.

93 On Heydebrand's reaction, see Nanssen, *Diary*, p. 319. In early October Bauer begged the OHL liaison officer at the Foreign Office, Colonel von Haeften, to put aside all "sentimentalities" and advise

It is perhaps a fitting climax to this description of Ludendorff's wartime career to note that, just before leaving office, he had embarked upon a new production program, the Scheer U-boat program. The Chief of the Admiralty Staff, Admiral Scheer, was convinced that a gigantic U-boat program was necessary because the war might have to be continued against the maritime powers alone and because the submarines might compel England to seek a more moderate peace with Germany. On September 19, 1918, almost exactly two years after the meeting in the War Ministry which had launched the Hindenburg Program, the industrialists assembled for a discussion of the program. Once again they were certain that the program could be fulfilled; once again they demanded that thousands of skilled workers be released from the front; once again they demanded a high profit. On October 21 Ludendorff gave his approval to the program and ordered that skilled workers requested in connection with it be released from the front. It may thus be safely said that Ludendorff had learned nothing in two years.[94]

Prince Max to dismiss Ludendorff. He also sought to influence Stresemann and Koeth in this sense. See BA, Nachlass Haeften, HO8-35/4.

[94] For the protocol of the meeting, see MF, Marine Archiv, Nr. 2047, and for Ludendorff's order, see *ibid.*, Nr. 6447. The author is grateful to Dr. Werner Deist for bringing the Scheer Program to his attention.

Epilogue

THE conduct of the German war effort during the First World War was marked by a complete breakdown of "substantial rationality," of "intelligent insight into the inter-relations of events in a given situation."[1] Germany's war aims were an unattainable conglomeration of the aspirations of industrialist and agrarian interest groups, bureaucratic *Machtpolitiker*, militarists, and Pan-German dreamers. It was hoped that the realization of these imperialist goals would strengthen the old authoritarian system and the special interests it served. Instead, the prolonged war led to the final disintegration of the Bismarckian state. The Emperor virtually went into seclusion; the bureaucracy surrendered to the army; the army led the nation to disaster and then abdicated power itself. Neither the bureaucracy nor the army was capable of giving the nation the direction it needed, and the Reichstag failed to fill the gap. At the same time the class basis of the Bismarckian state, and its destructive tendencies, were revealed in the crassest manner. The Junkers continuously sabotaged the government's food supply and ruthlessly undermined the regime's prestige in their attack on its foreign and domestic policies. The industrialists joined in this assault and engaged in an underhanded feud with the War Ministry and the War Office. Only when the army was willing to grant high profits and suppress labor did it receive the full support of the industrialists.

[1] Karl Mannheim, *Man and Society in an Age of Reconstruction*, New York, 1954, pp. 53ff. Substantial rationality is to be distinguished from functional rationality, i.e., "(a) Functional organization with reference to a definite goal; and (b) a consequent calculability when viewed from the standpoint of an observer or a third person seeking to adjust himself to it." The relations between the War Ministry and the industrialists during the first part of the war are a good example of two functionally rational groups acting in a manner that is functionally irrational from the standpoint of one another. In a manner quite relevant to this study, Mannheim suggests that the development of a functionally rationalized society may lead to a loss of the capacity for substantial rationality and a growing tendency to "appeal to the leader" to solve the problems thereby created.

No less depressing was the manner in which organized labor had been absorbed into this system of political and economic opportunism. Because the war effort could not succeed without the help of organized labor, the bureaucracy and the army sought to come to terms with it at the cheapest possible price. The labor leaders found themselves living in two worlds. As semiofficial agents of the government, they encouraged their followers to support a war whose success would have strengthened the hand of their opponents. As representatives of the workers, they took advantage of their newly won power to extract concessions from the government. Pressed from below and bribed from above, they were compelled to disappoint everyone. They denounced strike agitators to the army and then defended and even joined the strikes they officially deplored. Their greatest success, the Auxiliary Service Law, was attainable only through the abrogation of the worker's fundamental right to change his job, and this intensified the dissatisfaction of the workers. At the same time their insistence upon Paragraph 9 led to conflict with the authorities. Such was the price which the labor leaders paid for their attempt to come to terms with a bankrupt system. Here, too, functional rationality had triumphed.

If the competing groups within German society pursued their special interests to the disregard of the fundamental problems of their society, however, they were also compelled to recognize that their survival was endangered by the mismanagement of Germany's affairs and the growing threat of revolution. Thus the interest groups and the army continuously demanded the creation of new and more efficient forms of executive authority in the form of an economic dictator, a War Office, or a political dictator. At the same time they insisted on the right to regulate their own affairs and to play a decisive role in the policies of executive agencies through advisory councils. What they wanted, in short, was a dictator or a powerful agency which scrupulously adhered to their policies. The effort to find a man or an agency that would be "above politics" was always determined by special political purposes. This pattern of political behavior, the two chief components of which were the tendency to reduce politics to a series of tactical alliances among competing interest groups and the tendency to search for some new authority to correct the disorder created by the system, is of exceptional importance. It lies at the very heart of the agreements between industry and labor and between the army and labor which did so much to prevent the thoroughgoing political and social reconstruction required by the failure of the old regime.

After the conclusion of their "social partnership" in November 1918, the industrialists and the union leaders tried to propagate the myth that the industrialists' acceptance of the social partnership was not the product of the Revolution but rather the outcome of a long series of negotiations which had begun in 1917. This interpretation totally neglected the fact that until October 1918 the leaders of heavy industry were, with few exceptions, adamant in their refusal to accept collective bargaining. Although willing to collaborate with the unions in the demobilization, they were unwilling to offer the unions the kind of concessions that would have made such collaboration possible. Even in July 1918, when Ludendorff's great offensives had failed and a farsighted official of the electrotechnical industry, Hans von Raumer, sought to resume negotiations to establish "an organic collaboration with the unions . . . before the flood of events overcame us all," the leaders of heavy industry continued to remain aloof.[2]

There was, however, an important grain of truth in the claim that industrialist resistance to cooperation with the unions was weakened in the course of the war. On the one

[2] Hans von Raumer, "Unternehmer und Gewerkschaften in der Weimarer Zeit," *Deutsche Rundschau*, 80, April 1954, pp. 428-429. For Legien's claim that the industrialists' acceptance of the social partnership preceded the revolution, see his speech in the "Niederschrift der konstituierenden Sitzung des Zentralausschusses der Zentralarbeitsgemeinschaft der industriellen und gewerblichen Arbeitgeber und Arbeitnehmer Deutschlands (12. Dezember 1919)," DZA Merseburg, Rep. 120BB, VII, Fach 1, Nr. 3[a], Bd. I.

hand, heavy industry's old allies, the Junkers, the bureaucracy, and the army, had failed to withstand the rising power of organized labor. Indeed, the bureaucracy and the army had compelled heavy industry to accept the onerous Auxiliary Service Law, had given de facto recognition to the unions, and had treated wage movements and strikes with unpardonable lassitude. On the other hand, industry was irritated by the severe restrictions of the war economy and the continuous interference of the bureaucrats and the Reichstag in its affairs. The attempt to use the War Office for its special purposes had also failed. If industry was to attain the self-government it desired, it needed freedom from bureaucratic and parliamentary restrictions. Yet how could industry free itself from such hindrances without the help of organized labor? The attempt to fight the government and labor at once would only have served to unite these forces. The unions, like the industrialists, were irritated by the clumsy bureaucratic machinery of the old regime. The union leaders shared the industrialists' fear of the growing revolutionary sentiment among the workers. Finally, both groups shared the tendency to think in purely bread and butter terms and to dislike the combination of doctrinaire verbiage and thoughtless logrolling which typified the Reichstag. The significance of the secret negotiations between industrialist and union leaders during the war was not that the former were ready to accept collective bargaining, but rather that the employers were already toying with the idea of using the unions against the bureaucracy, against the Reichstag, and against the workers, and that the unions were predisposed to cooperate with the employers. These negotiations anticipated the character of the final arrangements made in the fall of 1918.

Until October the employers expected to get the best of all possible worlds. A German military victory would, they hoped, strengthen the authoritarian regime and, as a consequence, their position vis-à-vis the unions. Union cooperation could thus have been bought at a minimal price. Ludendorff's failure terminated their dilatory tactics. They knew that the days of the old order were numbered, and they were among the first to abandon it. On October 9 the leading iron industrialists met at Düsseldorf to discuss ways and means of warding off revolution and socialization. They correctly surmised that the Max von Baden regime would last no more than four or five weeks, and they considered the German middle class too weak to act as a satisfactory ally for the protection of industry's interests. One possibility remained open to them: "Only the organized workers seemed to have an overwhelming influence. From this fact one drew the conclusion that, in the midst of the failing power of the state and the government, industry can only find strong allies in the camp of the workers, and they are the unions."[3] Hugo Stinnes was empowered to negotiate with the trade union leaders. The general significance of this step cannot be underestimated. Faced with economic chaos and a potential threat to their property, the industrialists were, in effect, abandoning their long-standing alliance with the Junkers and the authoritarian state for an alliance with organized labor. It was completely in keeping with this attitude that the bankers and leading industrialists were among the first to demand the abdication of Emperor William II.[4]

Following the meeting of October 9, labor-management negotiations were held in Düsseldorf, Berlin, and elsewhere. The employers agreed to recognize the unions as the representatives of labor, establish factory workers committees, and organize labor exchanges and mediation agencies on the basis of parity between labor and management. They refused, however, to terminate their support of yellow unions, to establish collective wage agreements throughout industry, or to introduce the eight hour day in all industries. Despite the defeat of

[3] Speech by Dr. Reichert of the VdESI, quoted in Richter, *Gewerkschaften*, p. 203. See *ibid.*, pp. 203ff. for a description of the negotiations.

[4] See Wolfgang Sauer's interpretation in his forthcoming *Bündnis Ebert-Groener*.

such major portions of their program, the unions agreed to industry's terms.

Having made as few unpleasant concessions as possible, Stinnes and his colleagues turned to the immediate problem of securing union support against the bureaucracy and the Reichstag in the demobilization. On November 2 the two interest groups decided to demand that the government establish a demobilization office with "extensive executive powers." At its head was to be a state secretary, "a Ludendorff for the tasks of the demobilization,"[5] who would be advised by representatives from the employer and union organizations. The new agency was to have complete control over the employment of the returning troops, the distribution of contracts, the supply of raw materials to the factories, and the general transformation from a wartime to a peacetime economy. Thus the interest-group program was composed of the same combination of authoritarian and corporatist strands which had typified the efforts to organize the war economy. It was of dubious constitutionality in that it excluded the federal states from participation in the decision-making process. At the same time it pushed aside the legally constituted agency that had been established for the demobilization, the Imperial Economic Office. In short, the interest groups wanted an economic dictator who would implement their program without the interference of either the duly constituted legislative or executive bodies.

The government of Prince Max von Baden, feeble as it was, turned a "cold shoulder" toward this plan to exclude it from the determination of economic policy. On November 5, however, the representatives of labor and management informed Prince Max that, in the words of Legien, "if the government does not create the institutions which we consider necessary, . . . then it will have to carry out the demobilization without

[5] Erich Matthias and Rudolf Morsey, *Die Regierung des Prinzen Max von Baden*, Düsseldorf, 1962, p. 569.

the help of the labor and employer organizations."[6] This blackmail worked, and on November 7 Colonel Koeth was appointed State Secretary of the new Demobilization Office. Koeth had the confidence of both labor and heavy industry. He had ruthlessly cut off the coal supply of nonessential plants and had protected the profits of heavy industry. He was an ardent advocate of centralization and could be counted on to distribute coal and food in the manner desired by the interest groups. At the same time he had always been diplomatic in his dealings with the trade unions. Koeth's first demand was that the unions and the employer organizations create a central organization, a "social partnership," in order to work with the new Demobilization Office more effectively. This need had already been anticipated and work had been begun.

The outbreak of the Revolution on November 9, 1918, caused the trade union leaders to express reservations concerning the advisability of entering into a permanent social partnership with the employers. It is possible that some of them felt that this would commit them to oppose socialization. It is more likely that they wished to avoid creating this impression. Whatever the case, they were extremely anxious to reach an agreement with the employers and finally accepted the employer request for a permanent social partnership. Legien told Stinnes that he was of the view that Socialism was "to be sure, the final goal, but that it would be many decades before it was carried out."[7] Legien's greatest fear was chaos, which would destroy the economy and ruin his organizations. He needed the employers because he was convinced that only they had the skills necessary to keep the economy going. He also feared the radicals in his own camp, particularly the soldiers and workers councils. When the latter began interfering with union functions, they were warned that the unions would simply

[6] See Legien's speech and description in the "Niederschrift," DZA Merseburg, Rep. 120BB, VII, Fach 1, Nr. 3[a], Bd. I.

[7] Unless otherwise indicated, the discussion and quotations below are based upon the protocol of the VdESI Executive meeting of Nov. 14, 1918, BA, R 13I/152.

cease their activity and then there would be an "employer strike with all its terrible consequences. Finally, Legien had little faith in compulsory measures undertaken by the revolutionary government. As Stinnes reported: "The unions correctly say that that which is now introduced by compulsion by the government and which actually has no real legitimation cannot have the same significance as a voluntary agreement between the unions and the industries. The latter will remain; the former is something that can be abrogated again." It is difficult to fathom the logic behind this remark. If the uncertainty of the times made a voluntary agreement between labor and management desirable, the very novelty of the situation militated against the expectation that it would last. Most important, the "significance" of labor's triumph would ultimately depend upon the success of the Revolution. For the trade unions to question the legitimacy of the revolutionary regime's actions at this point was not merely inappropriate, it was also destructive. Their task, if anything, was to legitimize the Revolution by giving it their full support. Unhappily, they were so opportunistic, so habituated to the struggle for the attainment of immediate goals within the existing sociopolitical framework, and so fearful of disorder, that they were willing to settle for an immediate and illusionary success.

Thus the unions concluded an agreement whose terms were prejudicial to the further development of the Revolution. It was drawn up on November 12, the very same day on which the Council of People's Commissars abrogated the Auxiliary Service Law, with the exception of its provisions for the mediation and arbitration of labor disputes, and committed itself to the realization of a Socialist program. The industrialists naturally were forced to make some new concessions, but Stinnes skillfully gave them an ambiguous character. The employers agreed to discontinue all financial support of the yellow unions. The latter were to continue to exist if they could survive without employer support. Furthermore, Legien secretly promised to permit them to take part in labor-management negotiations when things calmed down. Legien undoubtedly did not think this concession particularly significant since the survival of the yellow unions without employer support was very doubtful, but it is quite astonishing that Legien could bring himself to make such a concession. The eight hour day was to apply to all industries, but overtime work was permissible. Even more important, a secret protocol was drawn up making this part of the agreement valid only if the other countries would agree to introduce the eight hour day. Germany's perilous economic situation unquestionably made rigid schematization undesirable, but the secret protocol did commit the unions to vitiate their support of the eight hour day at the very moment when the revolutionary regime declared it in force as of January 1, 1919. With their usual care for the wording of the agreement, the employers also accepted the general introduction of collective wage agreements, but "in accordance with the conditions of the affected industry." Stinnes succeeded in warding off all attempts to give the workers the right to interfere in the operation of the plants or oversee business affairs. The functions of the workers committees were strictly limited to matters pertaining to the projected collective wage agreements. Finally, the agreement provided for the establishment of a permanent Central Committee for all of industry and suborganizations for the various industries to implement the agreement and to act for the interests of both parties in the demobilization and the "maintenance of economic life." Thus the effort to make the interest-group alliance the center of the socioeconomic decision-making process continued despite the fact that the regime had changed and despite the demands for socialization or greater worker control over the factories.

The industrialists were fully conscious of the advantages which their alliance with labor had brought them, and they knew that they had gotten off cheaply. In a discussion of the agreement at the executive committee of the Association of German Iron and Steel Industrialists on November 14, 1918,

Privy Councilor Hilger led his colleagues along the road to Damascus:

> Gentlemen, I stand before you today a Saul transformed into a Paul. Today we cannot get on without negotiations with the unions. Yes, gentlemen, we should be happy that the unions still find themselves ready to deal with us in the manner in which they have, for only through negotiations with the unions, through our agreement with the unions, can we prevent—call it what you will—anarchy, Bolshevism, rule of the Spartacists, or chaos.

He considered the agreement a "colossal achievement," which was "far more favorable" than he had ever expected. In a similar vein Stinnes warned his colleagues not to take the talk of nationalizing key industries seriously: "I would advise you to pay as little attention as possible to these things, but rather to settle the matter here, for if it is settled here, then the other alternative will disappear of itself."

It would be a mistake, however, to confuse a change of tactics with a spiritual conversion. When it came to assessing the reasons for Germany's failure, Hilger was as much of a Saul as ever:

> This is neither the time nor the place to discuss the question of guilt, but we want to establish that those who from the very beginning did not oppose the revolutionary movements in the interior of the Fatherland with the necessary energy and vigor are guilty of complicity in the entire collapse. . . . I have warned many times and stood alone in doing so. I remind you of the negotiations concerning the Auxiliary Service Law, where I fought alone with Stinnes.

If industrialists like Rathenau, Borsig, Sorge, and Rieppel were inclined to take a more positive view of collaboration with the unions and regard such collaboration as desirable in itself, the leadership of heavy industry persisted in taking a purely instrumental approach to the entire matter. Less than a month after the conclusion of the Stinnes-Legien Agreement on November 15, 1918, Stinnes was beginning to pay a different kind of "social insurance premium against insurrections" by giving financial support to the demagogue Eduard Stadtler, who was calling for the establishment of a "national socialist" dictatorship.[8] The lesson is perfectly clear. German heavy industry would accept help from wherever it came, be it from Legien and Stadtler or, twelve years later, from Hitler.

The question of whether union support of the workers councils and union encouragement of powerful and effective factory councils would have provided more viable alternatives to the alliance with industry lies beyond the scope of this study. What can be established here is that the trade union leadership did not really try to find viable alternatives to their policy. Instead they stuck fast to the unpolitical craft union orientation of the prewar period. The war, however, had done much to accelerate the growth of industrial unionism. The wartime and immediate postwar growth of the Free Trade Unions was based, by and large, upon the influx of women, youths, and unskilled workers from the large urban factories into the movement. These workers had little sympathy for the old traditions of the craft unions and were hostile to traditional authorities. Embittered by the war and politicized by the Revolution, they were prone to join hands with the old vanguard of industrial unionism, the metalworkers, in an attack on the rule of both the factory owner and the union secretary. In rejecting the demands of these workers for a major transformation of authority relationships within the factory, the trade union leaders were expressing not only their feeling of dependence upon the employers but also their anxiety concerning the threat to their leadership of the working class.[9]

[8] G. W. F. Hallgarten, *Hitler, Reichswehr und Industrie*, Frankfurt a.M., 1955, p. 92.

[9] On this problem, see Eberhard Kolb, *Die Arbeiterräte in der deutschen Innenpolitik 1918-1919*, Düsseldorf, 1962, and Peter von Oertzen, *Betriebsräte in der Novemberrevolution*, pp. 271ff.

The evidence does suggest, however, that the unions could have done more to restrict the authority of management. Hilger's satisfaction with the Stinnes-Legien Agreement and his surprise over its "favorable" nature clearly demonstrate that the industrialists expected and might have accepted worse. Most important was the extent to which the union leaders were willing to commit themselves to a standing alliance with the industrialists. It was one thing to enter into a temporary agreement for the purpose of securing an orderly demobilization, another to enter into a "social partnership" which indicated a commitment to maintain capitalistic institutions and authority relationships without serious modification.

The entire spirit of the "social partnership" was expressed by an industrialist in December 1919: "Gentlemen, we Germans have never had any talent for politics. Now, therefore, after the bankruptcy of our political order, it behooves us to harness our economic forces for maximum production."[10] Maximum production for what and for whose benefit? After four years of economic and human waste, this problem deserved consideration. The union leaders always used the dangerous condition of the German economy and the need to revive production as an excuse for their cautious policy. Yet it was precisely the fact that Germany's economic rate of growth had been seriously set back by the war and the fact that her economic revival would require extensive industrial rationalization that made it necessary to insure that labor would not bear all the sacrifices of the reconstruction. The problem was a political one, and it could never be solved by right wing Socialist efforts to implement the corporatist schemes of Wichard von Moellendorff, a man so caught up in his technocratic mode of thought that he had expected to use the Hindenburg Program to realize his brave new world.[11]

If General Groener's hope that an alliance of army, industry,

[10] "Niederschrift," DZA Merseburg, Rep. 120BB, VII, Fach 1, Nr. 3[a], Bd. I.

[11] Bowen, *Corporative State*, pp. 195ff.

and labor would save the monarchy was disappointed, his expectation that it would save what could be saved of the old order was not. Groener was, indeed, the ideal man to replace Ludendorff on October 27, 1918. As Ebert told him, the labor leaders "would always remember our collaboration with you during the war with pleasure."[12] He had the confidence of the labor leaders and the intellectual competence and willingness to accept reality to save the officer corps. As might be expected, he fought harder than the industrialists to save the monarchy, but when the monarchy could no longer be saved, he, like the industrialists, gave preference to the interest he represented and saved the officer corps.

As the Stinnes-Legien Agreement bound the industrialists to recognize the unions in return for union protection of employer interests, so the Ebert-Groener alliance bound the army to support the Republic in return for the Republic's support of order. The initial purpose of the latter alliance, like the former, was to secure an orderly demobilization. Here again, however, the labor leaders drifted into a more permanent alliance because they feared the workers and because they were unable or unwilling to use their imaginations and find another alternative.[13]

This failure of leadership not only destroyed the Revolution's chances of success, but also seriously damaged the capacity of the Social Democratic Party and the trade unions to preserve and defend the Weimar Republic. As during the war, so after its conclusion, their alliance with the forces of the old regime and failure to find a new and imaginative policy produced discord and rebellion within the ranks of the labor movement. If their timidity prevented them from getting the upper hand over the army and industry, their failure to do so subjected them to such pressure from below that they were compelled to antagonize their erstwhile allies. The army drifted into

[12] Matthias and Morsey, *Regierung des Prinzen Max von Baden*, p. 561.

[13] Sauer, *Bündnis Ebert-Groener*.

isolation as a "state within the state," anachronistic in its social composition and psychologically disoriented because of its inability to find a focus of loyalty and because of its constant conspiratorial activity. As the state, because of the dissatisfaction of the workers, took an increasingly active and, from the standpoint of the industrialists, excessively expensive role in social and economic affairs, the social partnership decayed, and the union leaders and industrialists retreated into their old slogans and attitudes. It was, however, on the basis of the truce between labor and management that the Weimar Republic had been founded, and the Republic could not survive long without it. The final blow came in March 1930 when labor-management disagreement brought down the Great Coalition and began the disintegration of the Republic.

It was then that the groups hardest hit by the war and the inflation, the groups which had been permitted to drift in a limbo of resentment against both capital and labor had their day and joined the ranks of National Socialism. Through their wartime and revolutionary experience, the army and industry had learned that the workers could not be controlled unless they were organized and that their goals could not be attained without the aid of mass movements. It is interesting to note that after Hitler's seizure of power the industrialists gave serious consideration to the resurrection of the "social partnership" of 1918.[14] Hitler, however, gave the industrialists more than they had bargained for in the form of an organized and disciplined Labor Front which would not demand even Legien's price. Similarly, the army finally accepted a "drummer," who would rally the nation behind rearmament and aggression. Groener's policy, to be sure, had breathed a last gasp when his protégé, General von Schleicher, vainly had sought to revive the old wartime collaboration between the army and the trade unions in 1932. The army's incompetence as an agency for the organization and control of the masses,

[14] Karl Dietrich Bracher, Wolfgang Sauer, and Gerhard Schulz, *Die nationalsozialistische Machtergreifung*, Köln and Opladen, 1962, p. 232.

however, had been revealed fourteen years earlier. Ludendorff's dream came true, and the army had a "strong man" in Berlin who was prepared to realize the frustrated militaristic dream of total mobilization in a new and even more insane Hindenburg Program, the Four Year Plan. The tactical alliances the army and industry concluded with Hitler, however, produced unanticipated results. This time the effort to combine authoritarianism with corporate independence failed, not because, as in the First World War, the interest groups made effective executive action impossible, but rather because, unlike Ebert and Legien, Hitler understood that his revolution could not succeed unless he destroyed the independent power of the army and industry.

Appendix: The Auxiliary Service Law of December 5, 1916[1]

I. Every male German between the ages of seventeen and sixty who is not serving in the armed forces is obligated to perform Patriotic Auxiliary Service during the war.

II. All persons will be considered to be rendering Patriotic Auxiliary Service who are employed in government agencies, in official institutions, in war industry, in agriculture and forestry, in caring for the sick, in war economic organizations of any kind, or in other occupations or trades which directly or indirectly are important for war administration of national supplies, so far as the number of these persons does not exceed the need.

Those who before August 1, 1916, were engaged in agriculture or forestry need not be taken from this occupation to be transferred to another form of Patriotic Auxiliary Service.

III. The administration of the Patriotic Auxiliary Service will be carried on by the War Office established in the Royal Prussian War Ministry.

IV. The question whether and to what extent the number of persons employed by a government agency exceeds the need will be determined by the Imperial or state authorities in collaboration with the War Office. The question of what is to be regarded as an official institution as well as whether and to what extent the number of persons employed by such exceeds the need will be decided by the War Office in collaboration with the Imperial or state authorities.

For the rest, the question of whether an occupation or trade is important in the sense of Section II, as well as to whether

[1] This translation relies heavily upon "The Civilian Service Bill of December 5, 1916," in R. H. Lutz, ed., *Fall of the German Empire*, 2 vols., Stanford, Stanford University Press, 1932, II, pp. 99-103. In certain cases, however, terminology and wording have been changed for purposes of consistency with the terminology used in this study. I am grateful to the Stanford University Press for their permission to use this material.

and to what extent the number of persons engaged in an occupation, organization, or trade exceeds the need, will be decided by committees that will be formed for the district of every Deputy Commanding General or for parts of the district.

V. Every committee (Section IV, Clause 2) shall consist of an officer as chairman, two high state officials, one of whom must belong to the Factory Inspectorate, and two representatives each from the employers and the employees. The officer and the representatives of capital and labor shall be appointed by the War Office, or in Bavaria, Saxony, and Württemberg by the War Ministry, which in these states is responsible for executing the law in agreement with the War Office. The higher state officials are appointed by the state authorities or by an authority appointed by them. If the district of a Deputy Commanding General extends over the territory of several federal states, the officials shall be appointed by the authorities of these states; in the decisions of the committee the officials of the state in whose territory the business concerned lies will take part.

VI. Complaint against the decisions of the committee (Section IV, Clause 2) shall be made to the central agency established by the War Office, consisting of two officers of the War Office, one of whom shall be chairman, two officials nominated by the central authority of that state to which the business, organization, or person following the occupation belongs, and one representative each from the employers and the employees. These representatives will be appointed as in Section V, Clause 2. If maritime interests are affected, one of the officers shall be appointed from the Imperial Naval Office. In complaints against decisions of Bavarian, Saxon, or Württemberg committees, one of the officers is to be appointed by the War Ministry of the state concerned.

VII. Men liable to Auxiliary Service who are not employed in the sense of Section II may at any time be compelled to serve in some form of Patriotic Auxiliary Service.

The calling up will be as a rule through an announcement

issued by the War Office or an authority to be appointed by the state central authorities calling on men to report themselves voluntarily. If there is not sufficient response to this appeal, then an individual summons shall be sent out in writing by a committee to be formed, as a rule, for each district of a Recruiting Commission, which shall consist of an officer as chairman, a high official, and two representatives each from the employers and the employees. When the voting is equal the chairman shall have the casting vote. The officer and the representatives of the employers and the employees shall be appointed as in Section V, Clause 2. The official shall be appointed by the state central authorities, or an authority appointed by them.

Everyone who receives the special written summons must seek employment in one of the branches mentioned in Section II. If employment on the terms of the summons is not obtained in two weeks, the committee will assign the man to an occupation.

Appeals against the committee's decision will be decided by the committee formed by the Deputy Commanding General (Section IV, Clause 2). Appeals will not postpone the obligation to serve.

VIII. In making assignments due regard will be given as far as possible to age, family conditions, place of residence, and health, as well as to previous occupation. Also the question whether the prospective pay will be sufficient to support the employed and to provide for his dependents shall be investigated.

IX. No one may take into his employ a man liable to Patriotic Auxiliary Service who is employed in a position denoted in Section II or who has been employed during the previous two weeks unless the applicant produces a certificate from his late employer that he has agreed to the man's leaving his service.

Should the employer refuse to give a certificate, complaint may be made to a committee to be appointed, as a rule, for every district of a Recruiting Commission and to consist of a representative of the War Office as chairman and three representatives each from the employers and the employees. Two each of these representatives are permanent; the others are to be taken from the same occupation as the man concerned. If the committee acknowledges, after investigating the case, that there are good reasons for leaving the employment, then it shall issue a certificate which will serve instead of the employer's certificate.

A suitable improvement of working conditions in the Auxiliary Service shall be considered a particularly good reason.

X. The War Office shall issue instructions for the procedure of the committees mentioned in Section IV, Clause 2; Section VII, Clause 2; and Section IX, Clause 2.

Nomination lists from the economic organizations of the employers and the employees are to be gathered in connection with the appointment of representatives of the employers and the workers to the committees (Sections V, VI, VII, Clause 2, Section IX, Clause 2) by the War Office.

Insofar as there already exist committees (war boards, etc.) similar to those charged with carrying out the duties of the committees specified in Section IX, Clause 2, they can, with the permission of the War Office, act in place of the latter committees.

XI. In all businesses engaged in Patriotic Auxiliary Service which fall under Section VII of the Industrial Ordinance and in which as a rule at least fifty workers are employed, there shall be standing workers committees.

If standing workers committees according to Paragraph 134 h of the Industrial Ordinance, or according to the Mine Laws, do not exist for such businesses, they are to be established. The members of these workers committees shall be chosen by workers of full age employed in the business, or in a branch of the business, from among themselves, by direct and secret voting on the principle of proportionate representation. Details shall be fixed by the central authorities of the states.

In businesses employing more than fifty white-collar workers there shall be formed white-collar workers committees having the same powers as the workers committees and formed in the same manner as the standing workers committees in Clause 1 above.

XII. It is the duty of the workers committees to promote a good understanding among the workers and between the workers and their employers. It must bring to the employer's notice all suggestions, wishes, and complaints of the workers referring to the organization of the business, the wages, and the other matters concerning the workers and their welfare, and must give its opinion on them.

If at least one fourth of the members of the workers committee desire it, a meeting must be held, and the subject to be discussed must be placed upon the order of the day.

XIII. If in a business of the nature denoted in Section XI disputes arise over wages or other conditions of labor, and no agreement can be arrived at between the employer and the workers committee, then, unless both parties appeal to an Industrial Court or a Miners Court or a Mercantile Court as a court of arbitration, the committee referred to in Section IX, Clause 2, shall be called upon by each party to mediate. In this case Sections 66 and 68-73 of the Industrial Courts Law shall be made use of with the regulation that an award is to be given if one of the two parties does not appeal or does not plead, also that persons concerned in any particular dispute, whether as employer or as member of the workers committee, shall have no voice in making the award.

If in any business engaged in Patriotic Auxiliary Service to which Regulation 7 of the Industrial Ordinance is applicable there is no standing workers committee according to the Industrial Ordinance or the Mining Law, or according to Section XI, Clause 2 or Clause 3, of this law, then in disputes between workers and employers over wages or other labor conditions, the committee of Section IX, Clause 2, shall be called in as mediator. The same applies to agricultural enterprises. The provisions of Clause 1, Sentence 2, are also applicable.

If the employer does not submit to the award, then the workers shall receive, if they desire, the certificate (Section IX) entitling them to leave their employment. If the workers do not submit to the award, then the certificate will not be given to them for the cause on which the award has been made.

XIV. The use of their present legal right to unite and meet shall not be restricted for persons engaged in Patriotic Auxiliary Service.

XV. For industrial concerns of the army and navy administrations, regulations shall be made by the proper superior authorities in the meaning of Sections XI and XIII.

XVI. Industrial workers appointed under this law to agricultural labor are not subject to regulations of the legislation concerning agricultural laborers.

XVII. Information concerning questions of employment and labor, as well as concerning wages and business conditions, when demanded by public notice or by direct questioning of the War Office, must be imparted. The War Office is empowered to inspect the business through its representative.

XVIII. Imprisonment not exceeding one year and a fine not exceeding 10,000 marks, or either of these penalties, or detention, shall be the penalty for (1) anyone refusing employment assigned to him on the basis of Section VII, Clause 3, or without urgent reasons delaying the performance of such work; (2) anyone employing a worker contrary to the regulation in Section IX, Clause 1; (3) anyone not imparting within the appointed time the information provided for in Section XV or willfully making false or incomplete statements in giving his information.

XIX. The Bundesrat issues the necessary instructions for carrying out this law. General regulations need the consent of

a committee of fifteen members appointed by the Reichstag out of its own members.

The War Office is bound to keep the committee well informed on all important events, to give it any desired information, to accept its resolutions, and to obtain its opinion befor issuing important orders of a general nature.

The committee is empowered to meet during the proroga tion of the Reichstag.

The Bundesrat can punish neglect to carry out its instru tions with imprisonment not exceeding one year and a fi not exceeding 10,000 marks, or with either of these penalti or with detention.

XX. The law comes into operation on the day of publicati The Bundesrat will fix the time when it shall be abroga If the Bundesrat makes no use of this power within one mo after the conclusion of peace with the European Powers, the law is annulled.

Bibliographical Note[1]

THE Western student of German history is blessed by past wars and burdened by contemporary politics. Thanks to the capture of many of the German archives at the close of the last war and the third change of government since the fall of the Second Empire, there has been little effort made to preserve the intimate secrets of that regime. As a result, the author encountered no restrictions when using the Federal Republic's archives. Unfortunately, however, I was not permitted to make a personal visit to the branches of the *Deutsches Zentralarchiv* at Potsdam and Merseburg, which contain many of the most important documents of the Imperial and Prussian Governments. Nevertheless, these archives were kind enough to provide me with valuable information concerning special problems arising out of my research and to send me microfilm copies of certain exceptionally important documents unavailable elsewhere. Happily, the vast majority of the documentary materials needed for this study were available in the West and, indeed, in unexpected plenitude. In the light of this fact, I hope that the comments below will be of interest, not only to the general reader, but also to scholars confronting the problems of research in this period of German history.

The most important source of Imperial and Prussian Government documents, of personal papers, and of industrialist papers was the *Bundesarchiv* in Koblenz. The papers of the Prussian Ministry of Justice were of particular significance because they contained many Prussian Cabinet protocols, e.g., all of those pertaining to the Auxiliary Service Law. The collection of *Nachlässe* at the *Bundesarchiv* is particularly out-

[1] Scholars wishing to pursue these matters further are invited to examine the very detailed bibliography in my dissertation, *Army, Industry and Labor in Germany 1914-1918*, Cambridge, Mass., 1963, in the archives of the Widener Memorial Library at Harvard University. For reasons of space, a listing of the published sources used has been omitted. The full title of all such sources, however, may be located by looking up the author's name in the index for guidance to the appropriate footnote.

standing, and the papers of Colonel Max Bauer, General Wild von Hohenborn, and Wichard von Moellendorff were of exceptional significance for this study. An extremely important collection held by this archive is the papers of the Association of German Iron and Steel Industrialists. This is unquestionably the finest documentary source now available on the attitudes and policies of German heavy industry.

One of the chief problems for the study of the military history of the Second Empire has been the destruction of the old *Heeresarchiv* in Potsdam by Allied bombing in 1945. It is at this point that the federal structure of the old Empire comes to the rescue of the scholar. The *Bayerisches Hauptstaatsarchiv, Abteilung IV* in Munich was the major source of the military documents used in this study. The mammoth collection of War Office documents contains detailed reports on the events which took place in Berlin, as well as copies of the most important directives emanating from the Prussian War Office and War Ministry. The reports of the Bavarian military representatives to the OHL were particularly valuable for tracing changes in mood and attitude at Supreme Headquarters.

The ambassadorial reports and letters of Bavaria's representatives in Berlin contained in the *Bayerisches Hauptstaatsarchiv, Abteilung II* in Munich provided significant details on the activities of the Bundesrat and the policies of Germany's civilian leadership in Berlin.

The *Hauptstaatsarchiv Stuttgart* holds the documents of both the civilian and the military authorities of Württemberg. In contrast to the Bavarian archives, however, the papers of the former tended to be of greater significance than the latter. The ambassadorial reports from Berlin and Munich were particularly useful. The protocols of the meetings of the Reichstag Budget Committee, the only other copy of which is located at Merseburg, was of major importance for this study.

The military documents mentioned so far have been those pertaining to the German army. The large collection of German naval documents located in the *Militärgeschichtliches*

Forschungsamt in Freiburg, however, also provided vital material because of the navy's involvement in the labor question and because of the Imperial Naval Office's frequent communication with the OHL.

For all the wartime efforts to achieve greater centralization, the principle of decentralization, as represented by the Deputy Commanding Generals, remained important throughout the war. The documents of the *Regierung Bromberg* in the *Hauptarchiv* in Berlin-Dahlem provide an excellent picture of conditions in one of the chief agricultural areas of Prussia and shed much light on the unenlightened rule of General von Vietinghoff. The papers of the *Regierung Münster* in the *Staatsarchiv Münster* are of exceptional importance for an understanding of conditions in the Ruhr and are indispensable for the policies of General von Gayl. This archive also contains the very valuable records of the Royal Mines Office at Dortmund, which are important not only with regard to the aforementioned problems, but also with regard to the coal mine strikes during the war. Finally, the collection of *Regierung Düsseldorf* papers in the *Staatsarchiv Düsseldorf*, although badly damaged in the last war, contain important materials on the labor and food problems.

There seem to be very few surviving unpublished Social Democratic and trade union documents on social policy during the war. The International Institute for Social History in Amsterdam contains some personal papers with scattered information and the important protocols of the meetings of the Socialist Reichstag *Fraktion.* The *SPD Bibliothek und Archiv* in Bonn also had very few important unpublished documents for my purposes. The one exception was the collection of protocols of the joint wartime meetings of the Party Committee and the Reichstag *Fraktion.* Both of these institutions, however, possess very significant collections of newspapers, yearbooks, and party and trade union congress reports, as do the *IG Metall Bibliothek* in Frankfurt and the *Stadtbibliothek* in Monchen-Gladbach.

A final group of unpublished sources of great value for this study were the captured personal papers and documents filmed by the United States National Archives. Foremost among these were the papers of General Wilhelm Groener, a microfilm copy of which is located in the Widener Memorial Library of Harvard University. Much important material was also gleaned from the papers of Dr. Gustav Stresemann. The filmed copy used is to be found in the Nicholas Murray Butler Library of Columbia University. Finally, the National Archives has filmed a series of important studies of the mobilization and economic problems of the First World War made by personnel of the *Wehrmacht* during the 1930's. These studies are useful because they are based upon documents from the old *Heeresarchiv*. They are catalogued in the *Guides to German Records Microfilmed at Alexandria, Virginia. No. 7, Part 1, Records of Headquarters, German Armed Forces High Command. Microcopy T-77*, Washington, 1959. The original copies of the personal papers and studies mentioned in this paragraph are to be found in the *Bundesarchiv* in Koblenz.

INDEX

Index (*Authors' names appear in italics*)